Blank Canvas
My So=Called Artist's Journey

3

STORY &
ART

**Akiko
Higashimura**

Blank Canvas

My So-Called Artist's Journey

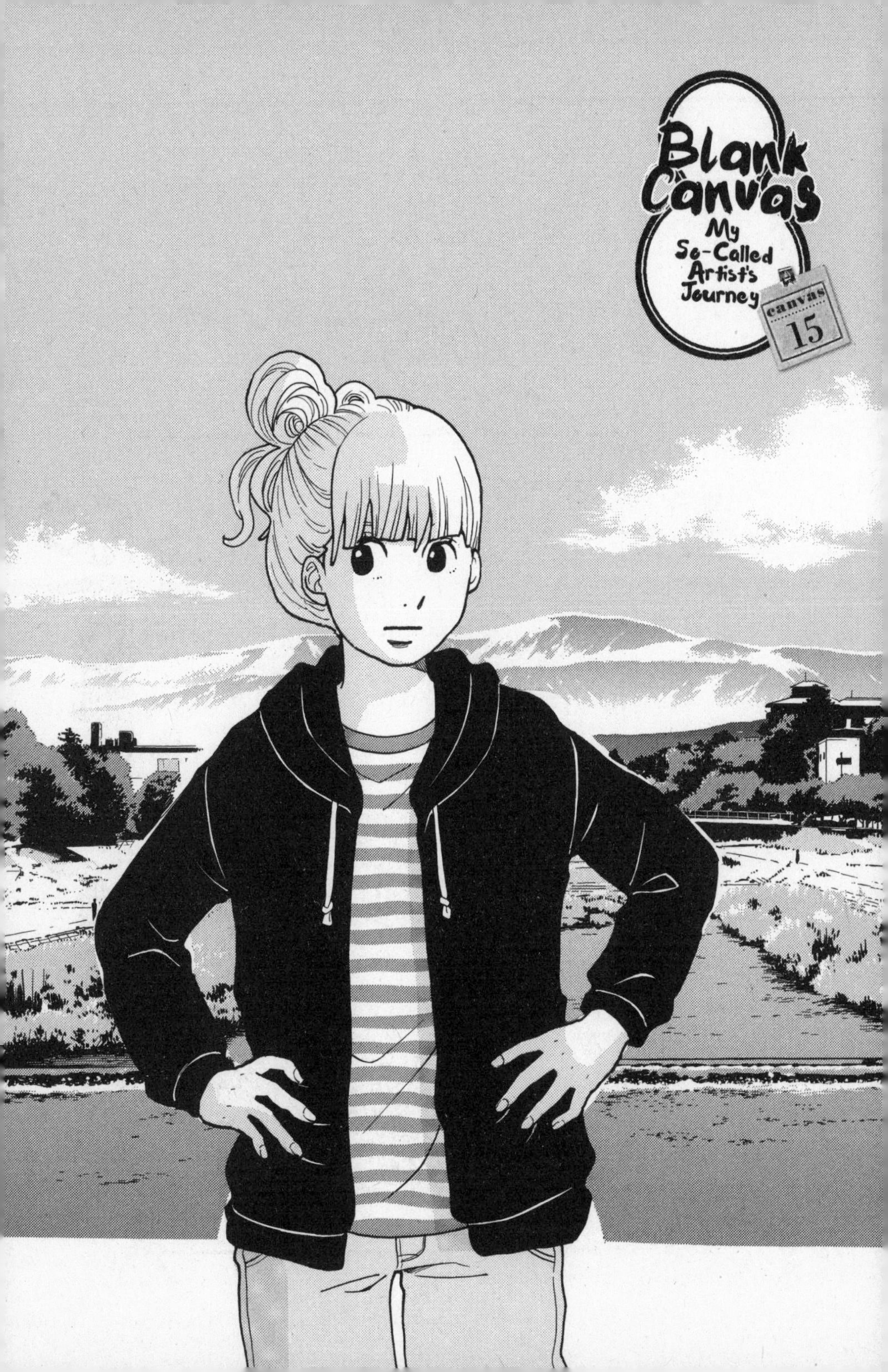
Blank Canvas
My So-Called Artist's Journey
canvas
15

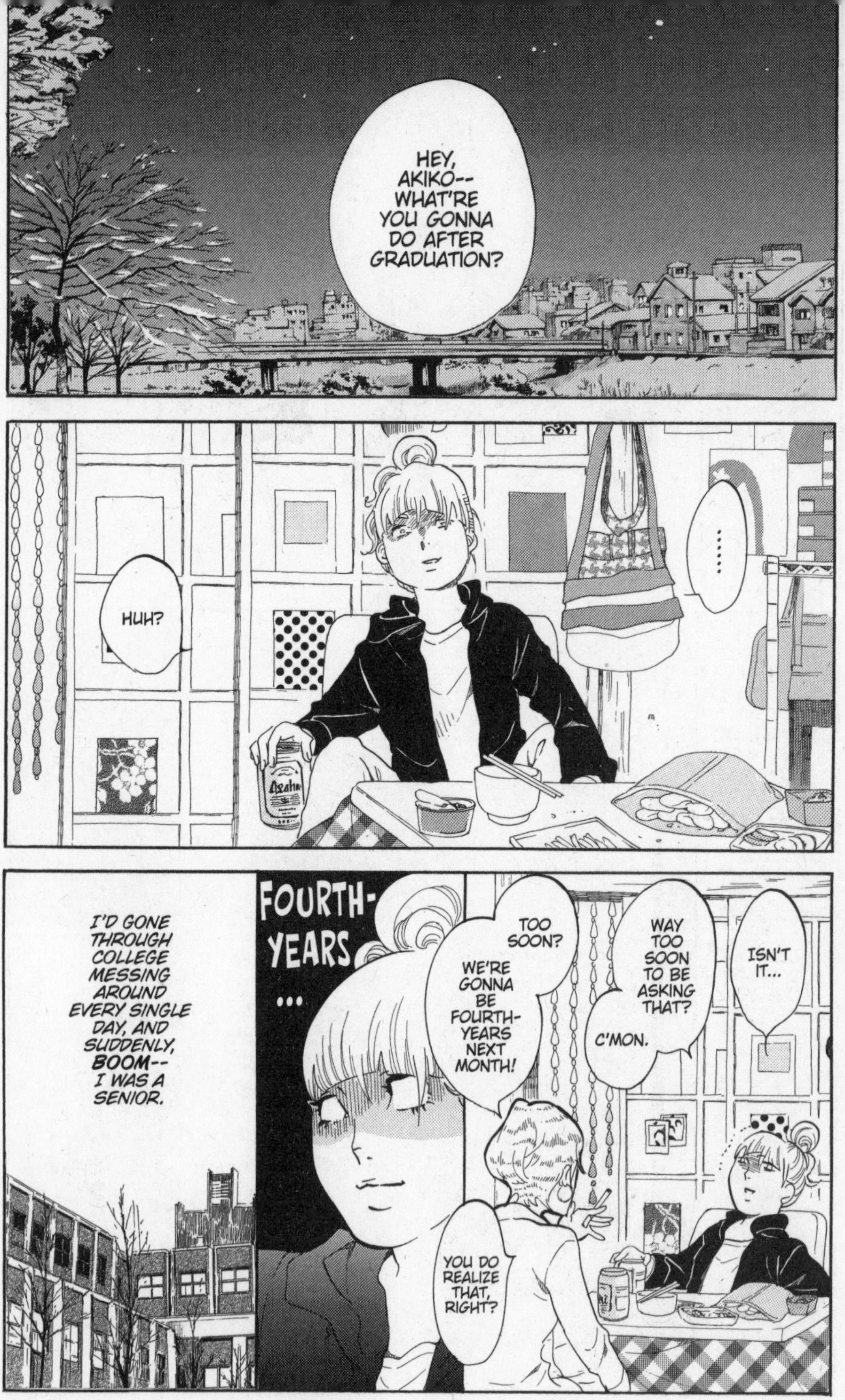
HEY, AKIKO-- WHAT'RE YOU GONNA DO AFTER GRADUATION?
......
HUH?
ISN'T IT...
WAY TOO SOON TO BE ASKING THAT?
C'MON.
TOO SOON?
WE'RE GONNA BE FOURTH-YEARS NEXT MONTH!
YOU DO REALIZE THAT, RIGHT?
FOURTH-YEARS ...
I'D GONE THROUGH COLLEGE MESSING AROUND EVERY SINGLE DAY, AND SUDDENLY, BOOM-- I WAS A SENIOR.

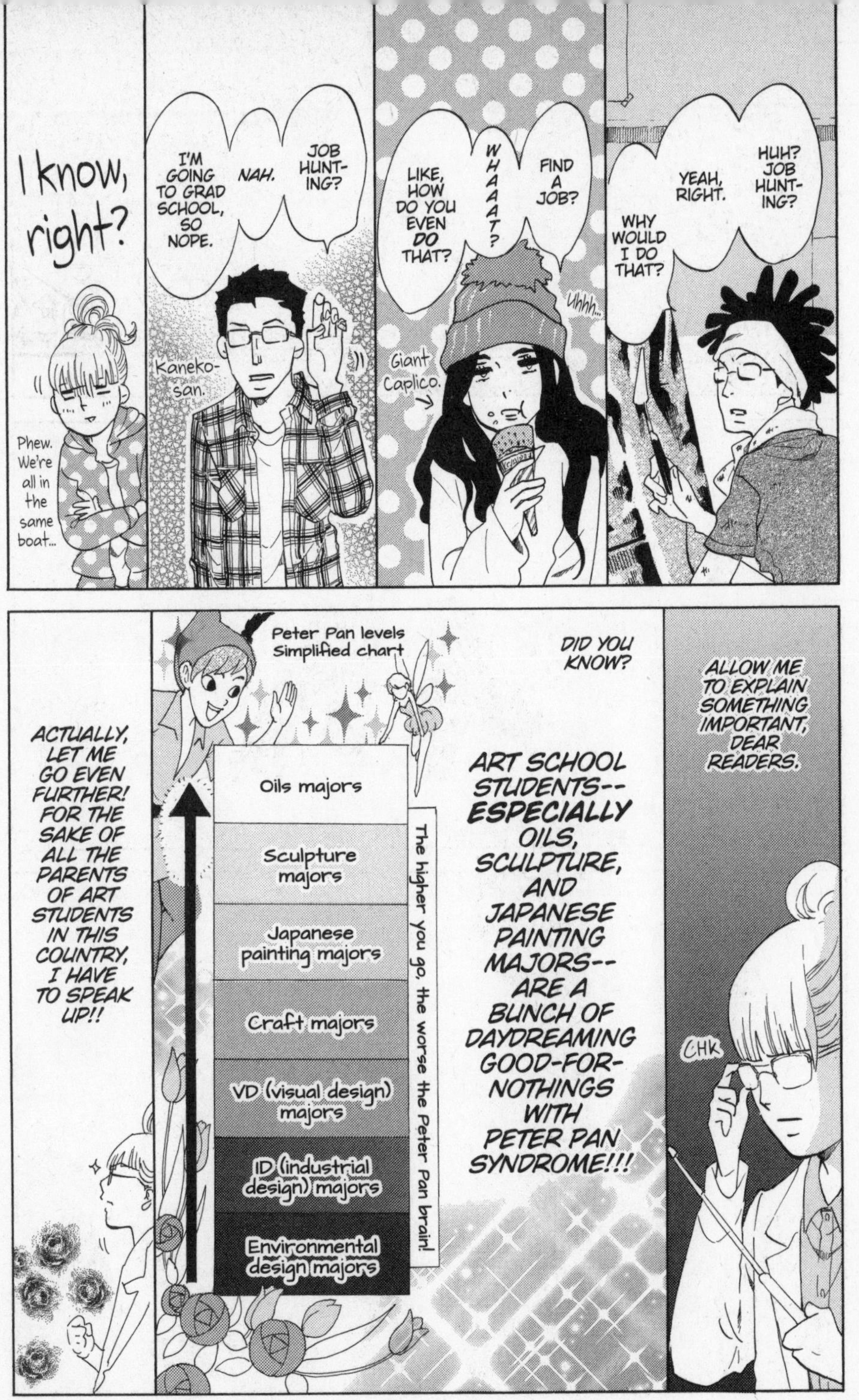
HUH? JOB HUNT-ING?
YEAH, RIGHT.
WHY WOULD I DO THAT?
FIND A JOB?
WHAAAAT?
LIKE, HOW DO YOU EVEN DO THAT?
Uhhh...
Giant Caplico.
JOB HUNT-ING?
NAH.
I'M GOING TO GRAD SCHOOL, SO NOPE.
Kaneko-san.
I know, right?
Phew. We're all in the same boat...
ALLOW ME TO EXPLAIN SOMETHING IMPORTANT, DEAR READERS.
CHK
DID YOU KNOW?
ART SCHOOL STUDENTS-- ESPECIALLY OILS, SCULPTURE, AND JAPANESE PAINTING MAJORS-- ARE A BUNCH OF DAYDREAMING GOOD-FOR-NOTHINGS WITH PETER PAN SYNDROME!!!
Peter Pan levels Simplified chart
Oils majors
Sculpture majors
Japanese painting majors
Craft majors
VD (visual design) majors
ID (industrial design) majors
Environmental design majors
The higher you go, the worse the Peter Pan brain!
ACTUALLY, LET ME GO EVEN FURTHER! FOR THE SAKE OF ALL THE PARENTS OF ART STUDENTS IN THIS COUNTRY, I HAVE TO SPEAK UP!!

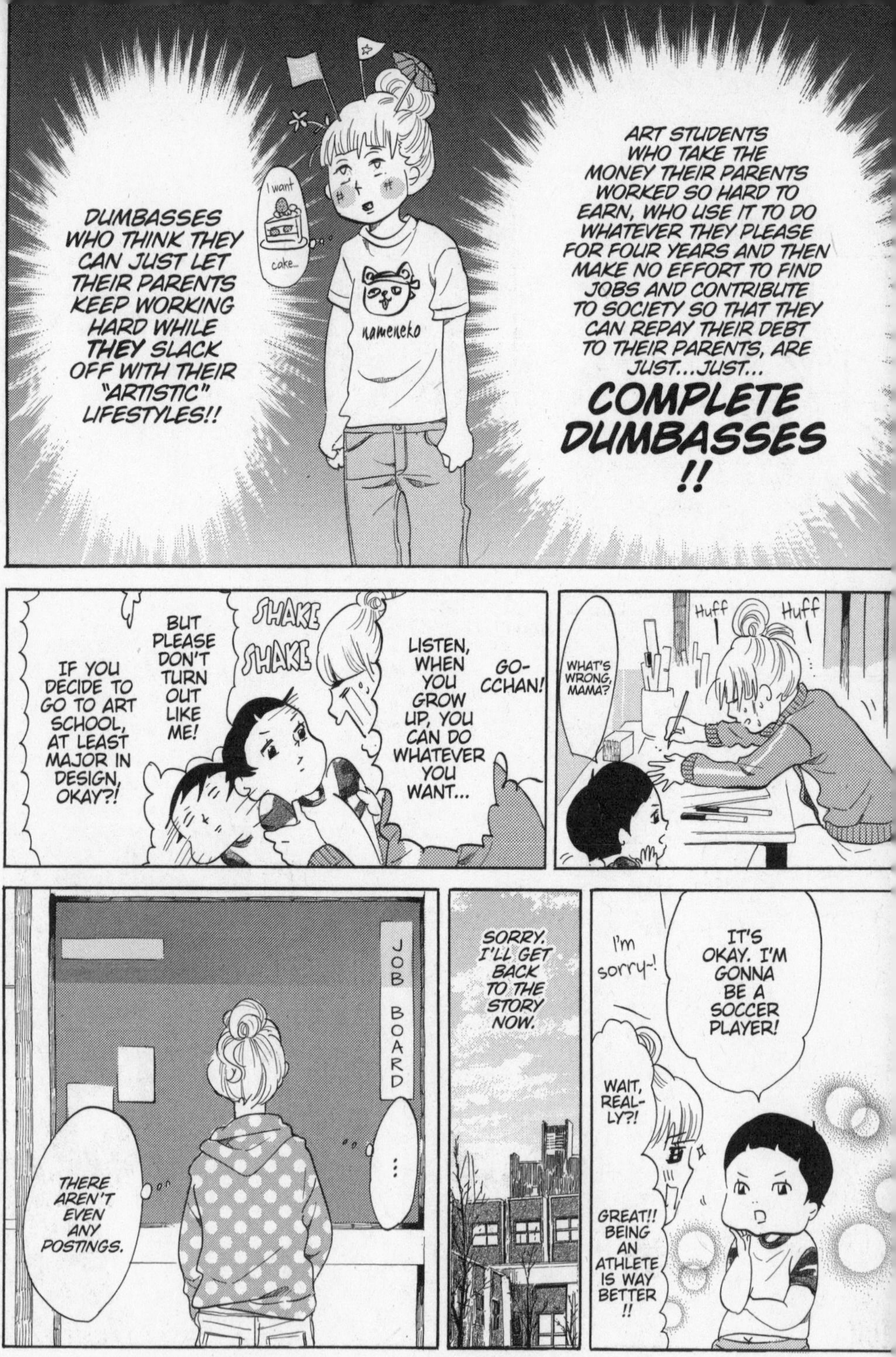
ART STUDENTS WHO TAKE THE MONEY THEIR PARENTS WORKED SO HARD TO EARN, WHO USE IT TO DO WHATEVER THEY PLEASE FOR FOUR YEARS AND THEN MAKE NO EFFORT TO FIND JOBS AND CONTRIBUTE TO SOCIETY SO THAT THEY CAN REPAY THEIR DEBT TO THEIR PARENTS, ARE JUST...JUST...
COMPLETE DUMBASSES!!
I want cake...
DUMBASSES WHO THINK THEY CAN JUST LET THEIR PARENTS KEEP WORKING HARD WHILE THEY SLACK OFF WITH THEIR "ARTISTIC" LIFESTYLES!!
nameneko
Huff Huff
WHAT'S WRONG, MAMA?
GO-CCHAN!
LISTEN, WHEN YOU GROW UP, YOU CAN DO WHATEVER YOU WANT...
SHAKE SHAKE
BUT PLEASE DON'T TURN OUT LIKE ME!
IF YOU DECIDE TO GO TO ART SCHOOL, AT LEAST MAJOR IN DESIGN, OKAY?!
IT'S OKAY. I'M GONNA BE A SOCCER PLAYER!
I'm sorry~!
WAIT, REALLY?!
GREAT!! BEING AN ATHLETE IS WAY BETTER!!
SORRY. I'LL GET BACK TO THE STORY NOW.
JOB BOARD
...
THERE AREN'T EVEN ANY POSTINGS.

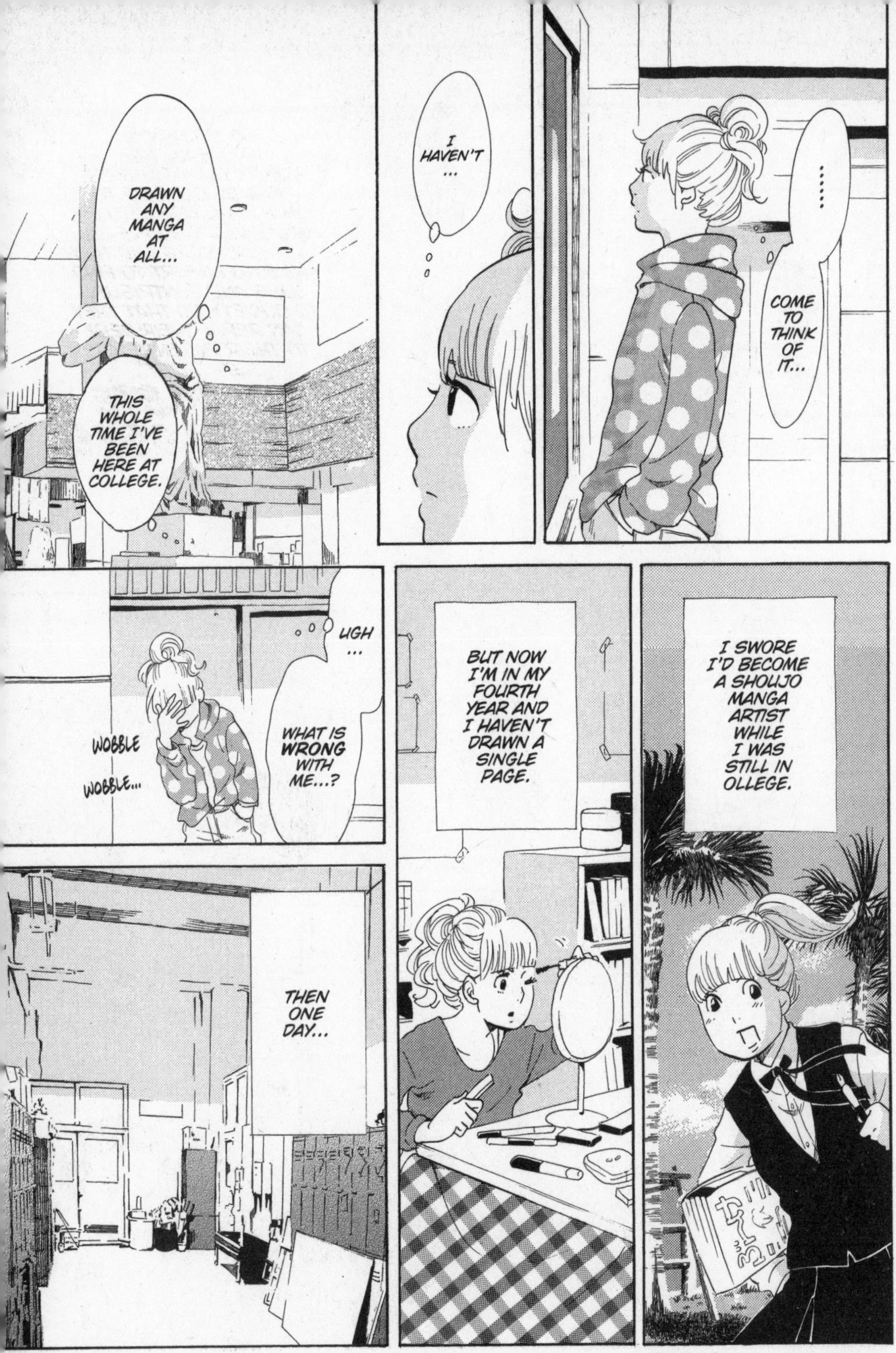
......
COME TO THINK OF IT...
I HAVEN'T ...
DRAWN ANY MANGA AT ALL...
THIS WHOLE TIME I'VE BEEN HERE AT COLLEGE.
I SWORE I'D BECOME A SHOUJO MANGA ARTIST WHILE I WAS STILL IN OLLEGE.
BUT NOW I'M IN MY FOURTH YEAR AND I HAVEN'T DRAWN A SINGLE PAGE.
UGH ...
WHAT IS WRONG WITH ME...?
WOBBLE
WOBBLE...
THEN ONE DAY...
Magazine: Bouquet.

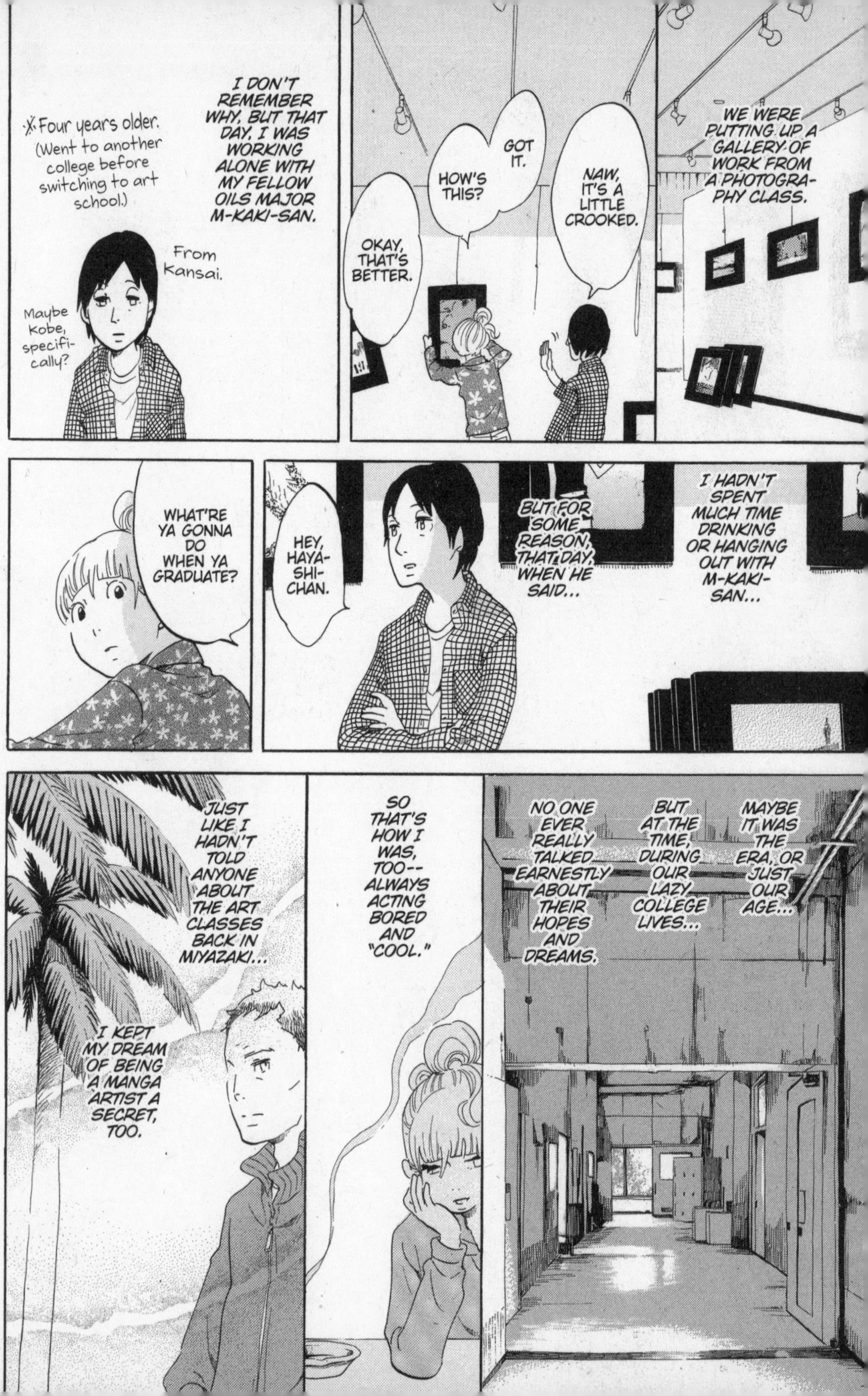
WE WERE PUTTING UP A GALLERY OF WORK FROM A PHOTOGRAPHY CLASS.
NAW, IT'S A LITTLE CROOKED.
GOT IT.
HOW'S THIS?
OKAY, THAT'S BETTER.
I DON'T REMEMBER WHY, BUT THAT DAY, I WAS WORKING ALONE WITH MY FELLOW OILS MAJOR M-KAKI-SAN.
※ Four years older. (Went to another college before switching to art school.)
From Kansai.
Maybe Kobe, specifically?
I HADN'T SPENT MUCH TIME DRINKING OR HANGING OUT WITH M-KAKI-SAN...
BUT FOR SOME REASON, THAT DAY, WHEN HE SAID...
HEY, HAYASHI-CHAN.
WHAT'RE YA GONNA DO WHEN YA GRADUATE?
MAYBE IT WAS THE ERA, OR JUST OUR AGE...
BUT AT THE TIME, DURING OUR LAZY COLLEGE LIVES...
NO ONE EVER REALLY TALKED EARNESTLY ABOUT THEIR HOPES AND DREAMS.
SO THAT'S HOW I WAS, TOO-- ALWAYS ACTING BORED AND "COOL."
JUST LIKE I HADN'T TOLD ANYONE ABOUT THE ART CLASSES BACK IN MIYAZAKI...
I KEPT MY DREAM OF BEING A MANGA ARTIST A SECRET, TOO.

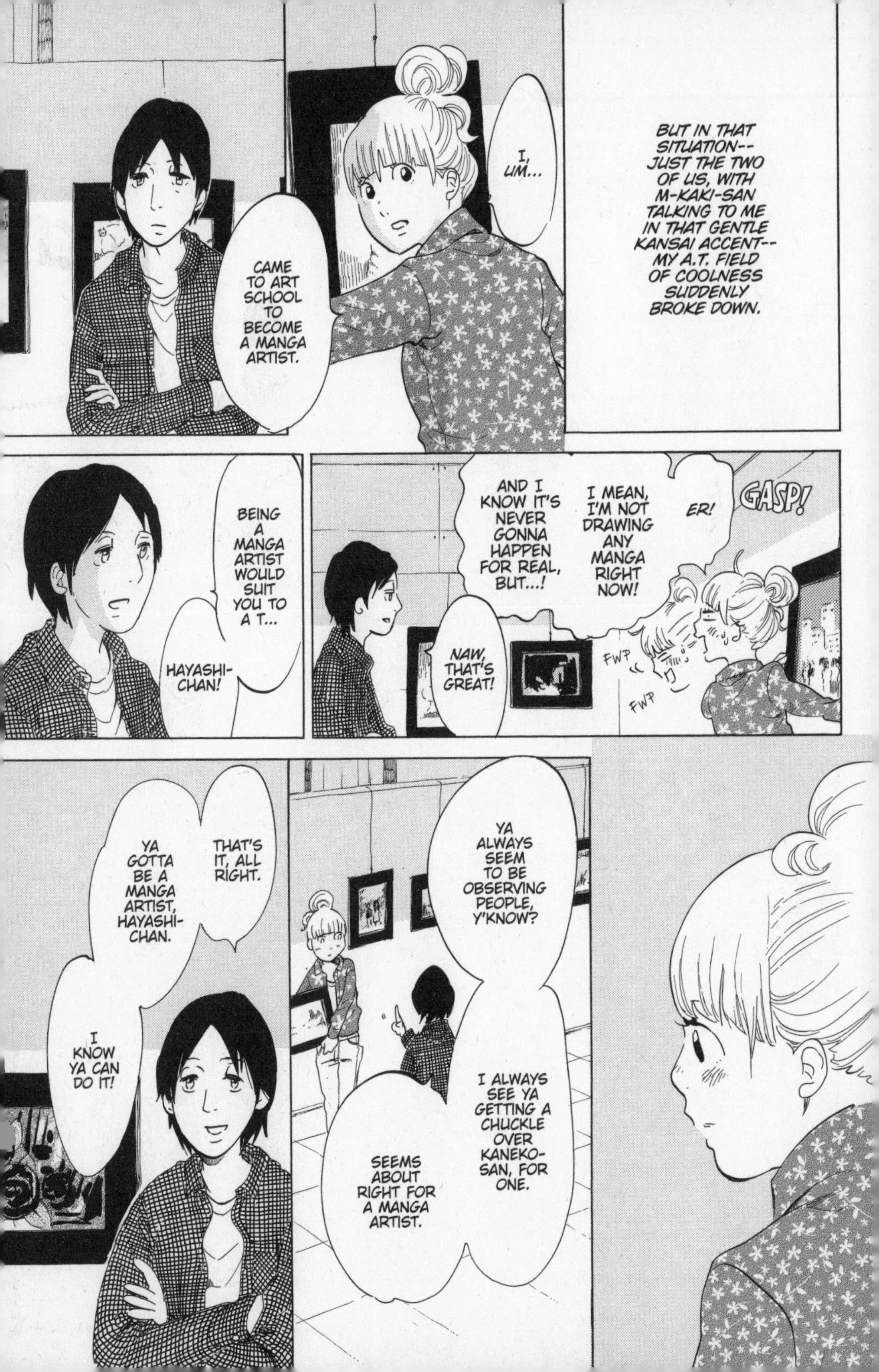
BUT IN THAT SITUATION-- JUST THE TWO OF US, WITH M-KAKI-SAN TALKING TO ME IN THAT GENTLE KANSAI ACCENT-- MY A.T. FIELD OF COOLNESS SUDDENLY BROKE DOWN.
I, UM...
CAME TO ART SCHOOL TO BECOME A MANGA ARTIST.
GASP!
ER!
I MEAN, I'M NOT DRAWING ANY MANGA RIGHT NOW!
AND I KNOW IT'S NEVER GONNA HAPPEN FOR REAL, BUT...!
FWP
FWP
NAW, THAT'S GREAT!
BEING A MANGA ARTIST WOULD SUIT YOU TO A T...
HAYASHI-CHAN!
YA ALWAYS SEEM TO BE OBSERVING PEOPLE, Y'KNOW?
I ALWAYS SEE YA GETTING A CHUCKLE OVER KANEKO-SAN, FOR ONE.
SEEMS ABOUT RIGHT FOR A MANGA ARTIST.
THAT'S IT, ALL RIGHT.
YA GOTTA BE A MANGA ARTIST, HAYASHI-CHAN.
I KNOW YA CAN DO IT!

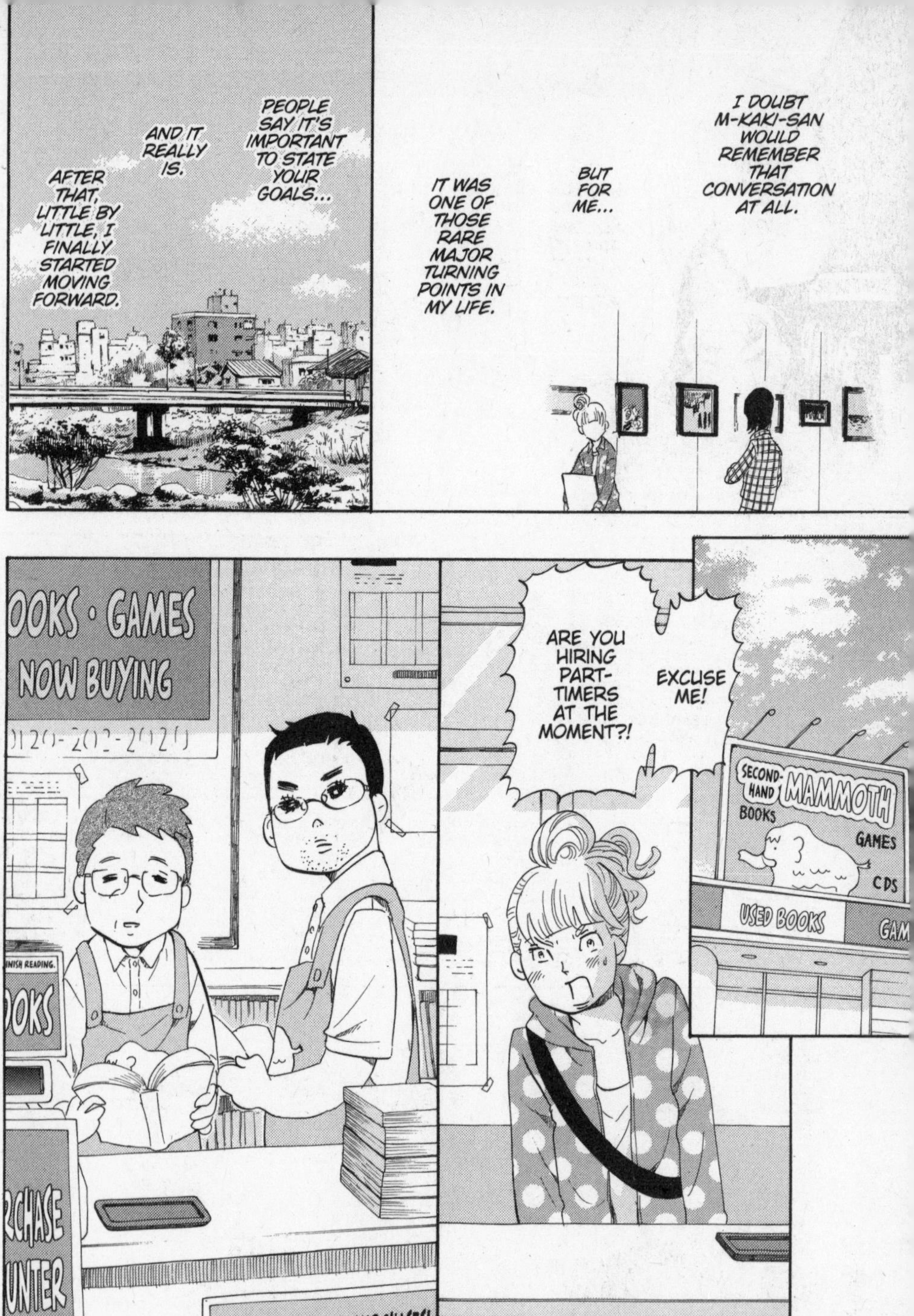
I DOUBT M-KAKI-SAN WOULD REMEMBER THAT CONVERSATION AT ALL.
BUT FOR ME...
IT WAS ONE OF THOSE RARE MAJOR TURNING POINTS IN MY LIFE.
PEOPLE SAY IT'S IMPORTANT TO STATE YOUR GOALS...
AND IT REALLY IS.
AFTER THAT, LITTLE BY LITTLE, I FINALLY STARTED MOVING FORWARD.
SECOND-HAND MAMMOTH
BOOKS
GAMES
CDS
USED BOOKS
EXCUSE ME!
ARE YOU HIRING PART-TIMERS AT THE MOMENT?!
OOKS · GAMES
NOW BUYING
WE DO IN-HOME PURCHASES!

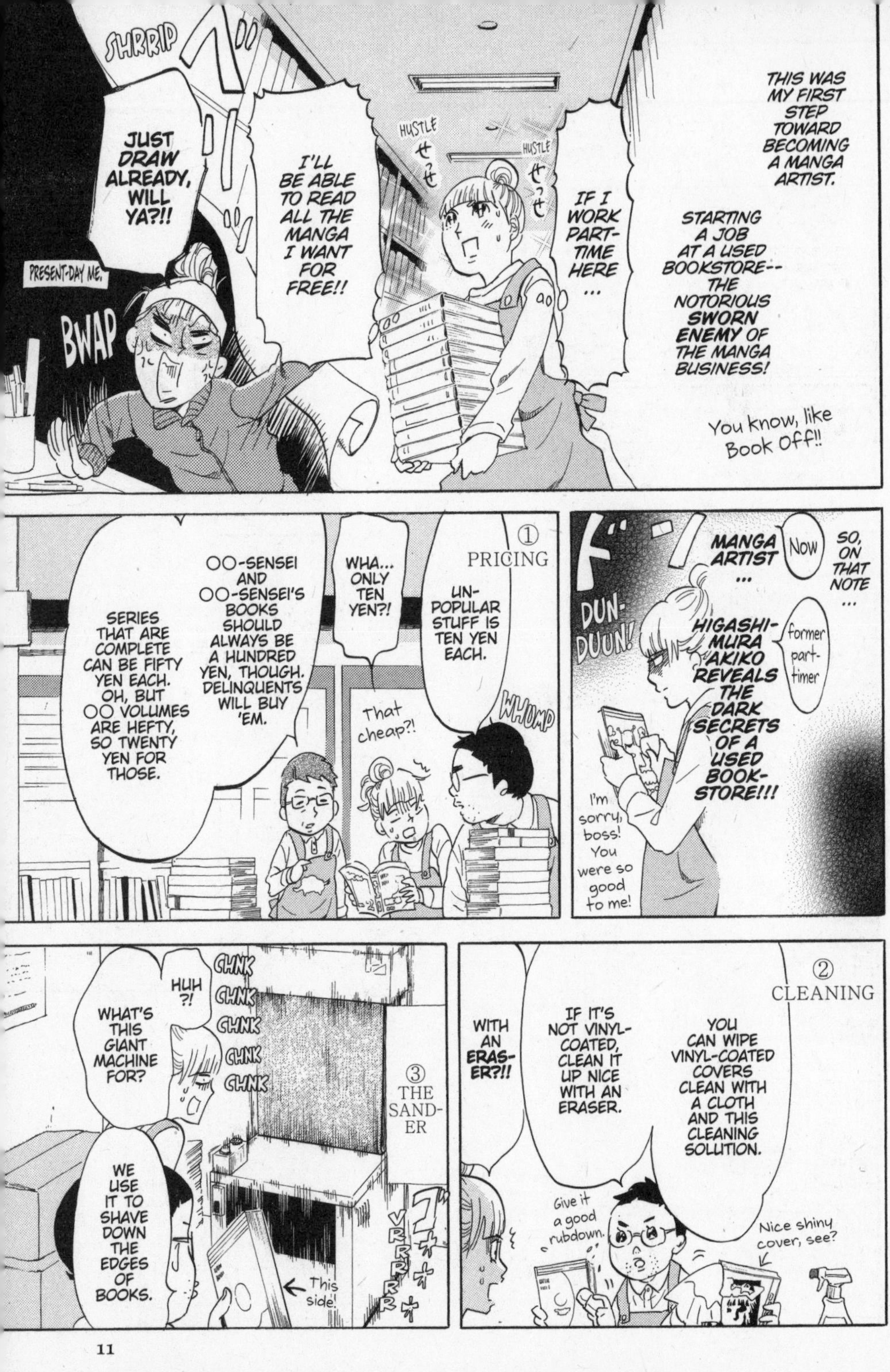
THIS WAS MY FIRST STEP TOWARD BECOMING A MANGA ARTIST.
STARTING A JOB AT A USED BOOKSTORE--THE NOTORIOUS SWORN ENEMY OF THE MANGA BUSINESS!
You know, like Book Off!!
IF I WORK PART-TIME HERE...
HUSTLE
HUSTLE
I'LL BE ABLE TO READ ALL THE MANGA I WANT FOR FREE!!
SHRRIP
JUST DRAW ALREADY, WILL YA?!!
PRESENT-DAY ME.
BWAP
SO, ON THAT NOTE...
Now
MANGA ARTIST...
HIGASHIMURA AKIKO REVEALS THE DARK SECRETS OF A USED BOOKSTORE!!!
former part-timer
DUN-DUUN!
I'm sorry, boss! You were so good to me!
① PRICING
UN-POPULAR STUFF IS TEN YEN EACH.
WHA... ONLY TEN YEN?!
WHUMP
That cheap?!
○○-SENSEI AND ○○-SENSEI'S BOOKS SHOULD ALWAYS BE A HUNDRED YEN, THOUGH. DELINQUENTS WILL BUY 'EM.
SERIES THAT ARE COMPLETE CAN BE FIFTY YEN EACH. OH, BUT ○○ VOLUMES ARE HEFTY, SO TWENTY YEN FOR THOSE.
② CLEANING
YOU CAN WIPE VINYL-COATED COVERS CLEAN WITH A CLOTH AND THIS CLEANING SOLUTION.
IF IT'S NOT VINYL-COATED, CLEAN IT UP NICE WITH AN ERASER.
WITH AN ERASER?!!
Nice shiny cover, see?
Give it a good rubdown.
③ THE SANDER
CHNK
CHNK
CHNK
CHNK
CHNK
HUH ?!
WHAT'S THIS GIANT MACHINE FOR?
VRRRRR
This side!
WE USE IT TO SHAVE DOWN THE EDGES OF BOOKS.

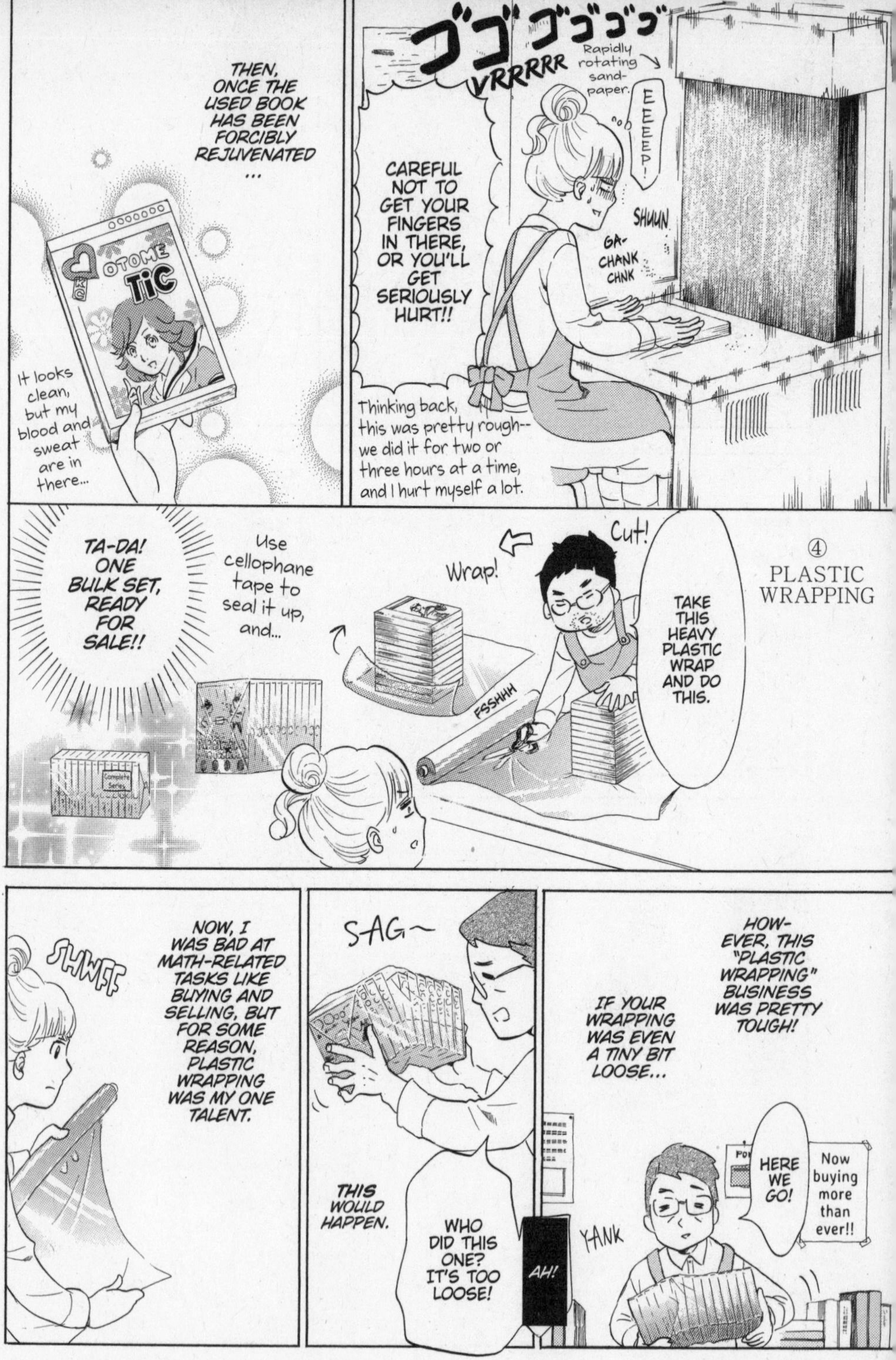
ゴゴゴゴゴ
VRRRRR
Rapidly rotating sand-paper.
EEEEP!
CAREFUL NOT TO GET YOUR FINGERS IN THERE, OR YOU'LL GET SERIOUSLY HURT!!
SHUUN
GA-CHANK CHNK
Thinking back, this was pretty rough--we did it for two or three hours at a time, and I hurt myself a lot.
THEN, ONCE THE USED BOOK HAS BEEN FORCIBLY REJUVENATED...
OTOME TiC
It looks clean, but my blood and sweat are in there...
④ PLASTIC WRAPPING
TAKE THIS HEAVY PLASTIC WRAP AND DO THIS.
Cut!
Wrap!
FSSHHH
Use cellophane tape to seal it up, and...
TA-DA! ONE BULK SET, READY FOR SALE!!
Complete Series
HOW-EVER, THIS "PLASTIC WRAPPING" BUSINESS WAS PRETTY TOUGH!
IF YOUR WRAPPING WAS EVEN A TINY BIT LOOSE...
Now buying more than ever!!
HERE WE GO!
YANK
SAG~
THIS WOULD HAPPEN.
WHO DID THIS ONE? IT'S TOO LOOSE!
AH!
NOW, I WAS BAD AT MATH-RELATED TASKS LIKE BUYING AND SELLING, BUT FOR SOME REASON, PLASTIC WRAPPING WAS MY ONE TALENT.
SHWFF

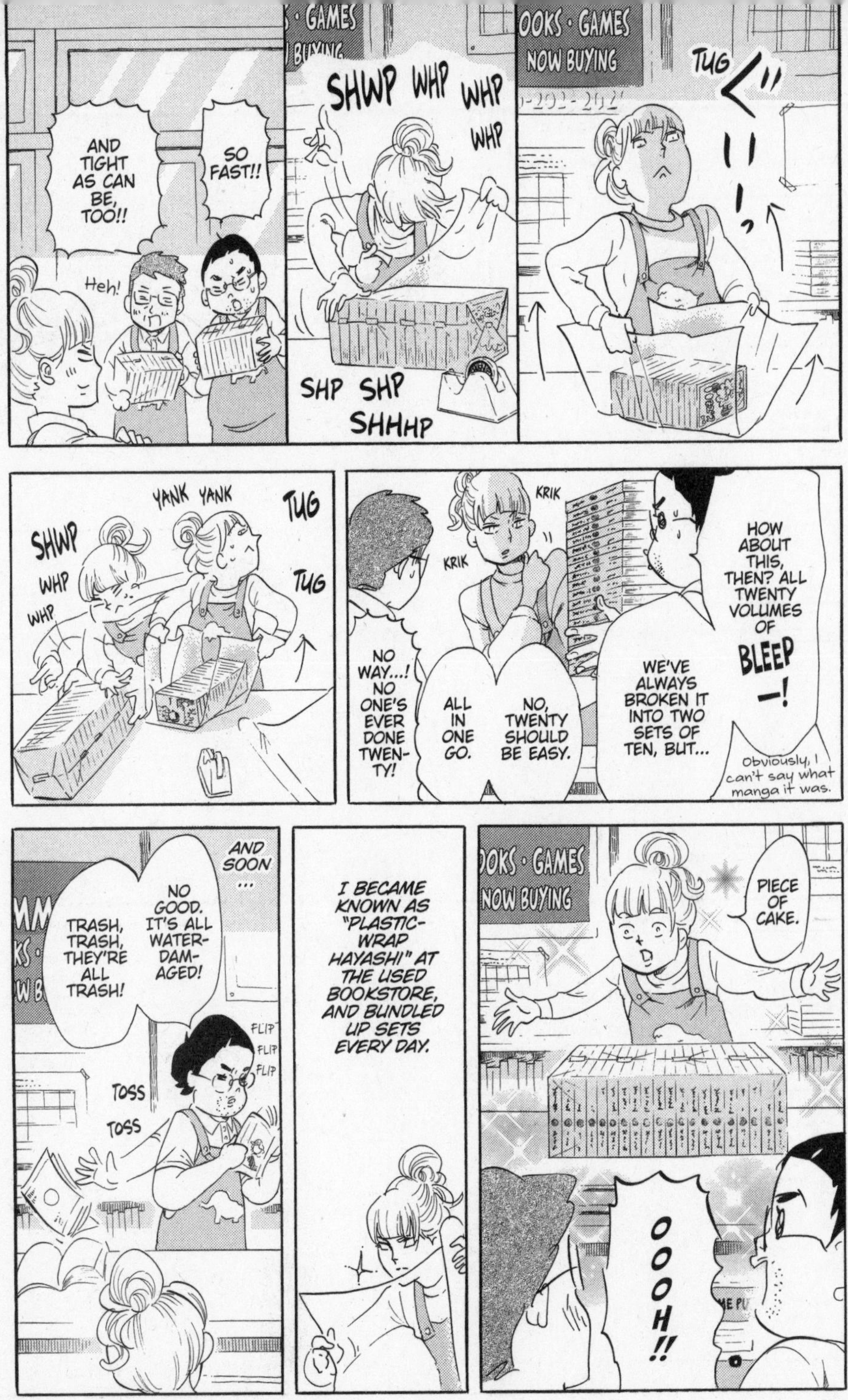
TUG
OOKS · GAMES
NOW BUYING
SHWP WHP WHP WHP
SHP SHP SHHHP
· GAMES
SO FAST!!
AND TIGHT AS CAN BE, TOO!!
Heh!
HOW ABOUT THIS, THEN? ALL TWENTY VOLUMES OF BLEEP—!
WE'VE ALWAYS BROKEN IT INTO TWO SETS OF TEN, BUT...
Obviously, I can't say what manga it was.
KRIK
NO, TWENTY SHOULD BE EASY.
ALL IN ONE GO.
KRIK
NO WAY...! NO ONE'S EVER DONE TWENTY!
TUG
YANK YANK
TUG
SHWP
WHP
WHP
PIECE OF CAKE.
OOKS · GAMES
NOW BUYING
OOOOH!!
I BECAME KNOWN AS "PLASTIC-WRAP HAYASHI" AT THE USED BOOKSTORE, AND BUNDLED UP SETS EVERY DAY.
AND SOON...
NO GOOD. IT'S ALL WATER-DAMAGED!
TRASH, TRASH, THEY'RE ALL TRASH!
FLIP FLIP FLIP
TOSS
TOSS

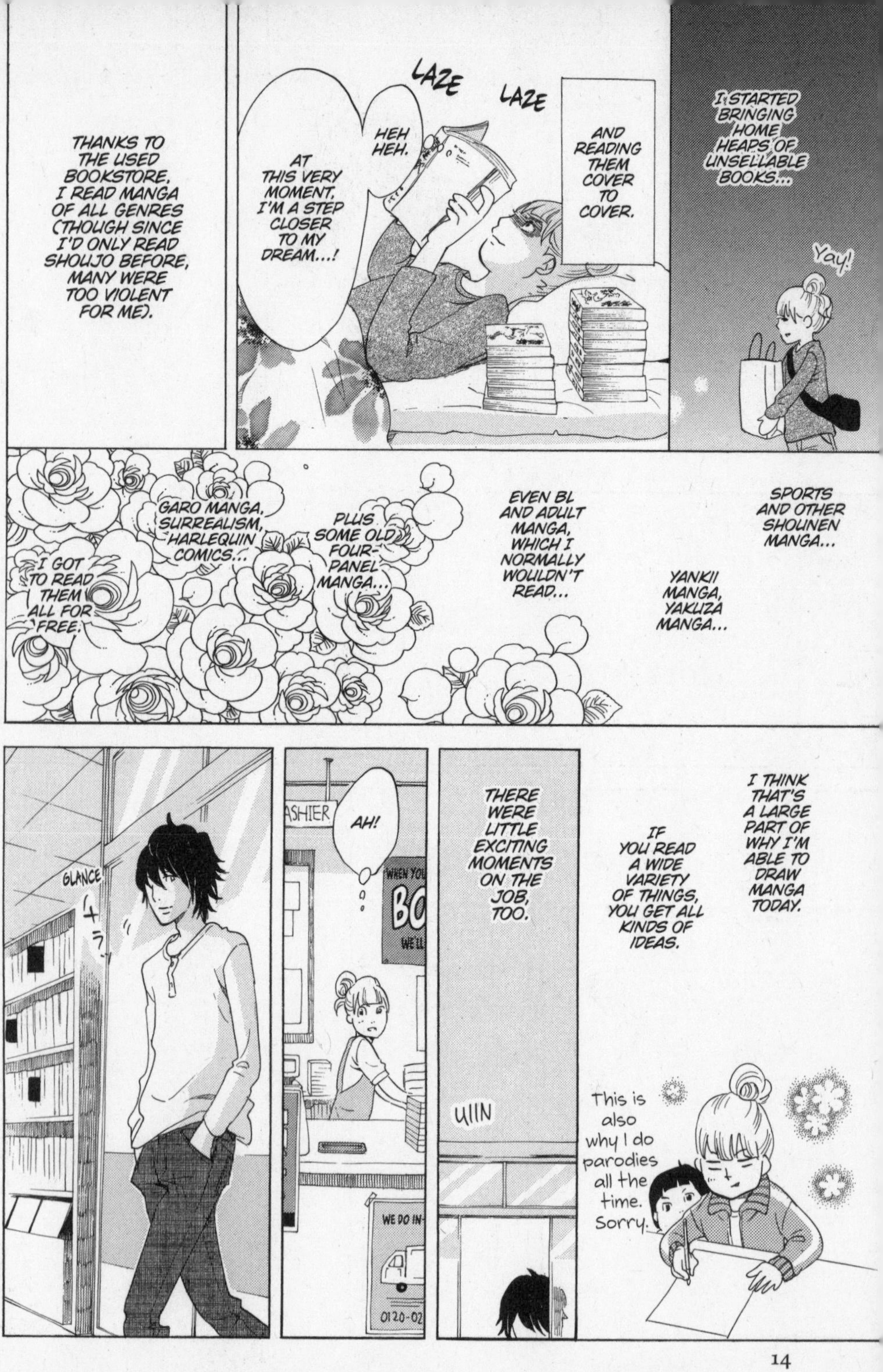
I STARTED BRINGING HOME HEAPS OF UNSELLABLE BOOKS...
Yay!
LAZE
LAZE
AND READING THEM COVER TO COVER.
HEH HEH.
AT THIS VERY MOMENT, I'M A STEP CLOSER TO MY DREAM...!
THANKS TO THE USED BOOKSTORE, I READ MANGA OF ALL GENRES (THOUGH SINCE I'D ONLY READ SHOUJO BEFORE, MANY WERE TOO VIOLENT FOR ME).
SPORTS AND OTHER SHOUNEN MANGA...
YANKII MANGA, YAKUZA MANGA...
EVEN BL AND ADULT MANGA, WHICH I NORMALLY WOULDN'T READ...
PLUS SOME OLD FOUR-PANEL MANGA...
GARO MANGA, SURREALISM, HARLEQUIN COMICS...
I GOT TO READ THEM ALL FOR FREE.
I THINK THAT'S A LARGE PART OF WHY I'M ABLE TO DRAW MANGA TODAY.
IF YOU READ A WIDE VARIETY OF THINGS, YOU GET ALL KINDS OF IDEAS.
This is also why I do parodies all the time. Sorry.
THERE WERE LITTLE EXCITING MOMENTS ON THE JOB, TOO.
UIIN
ASHIER
AH!
WHEN YOU
BO
WE'LL
WE DO IN-
0120-02
GLANCE

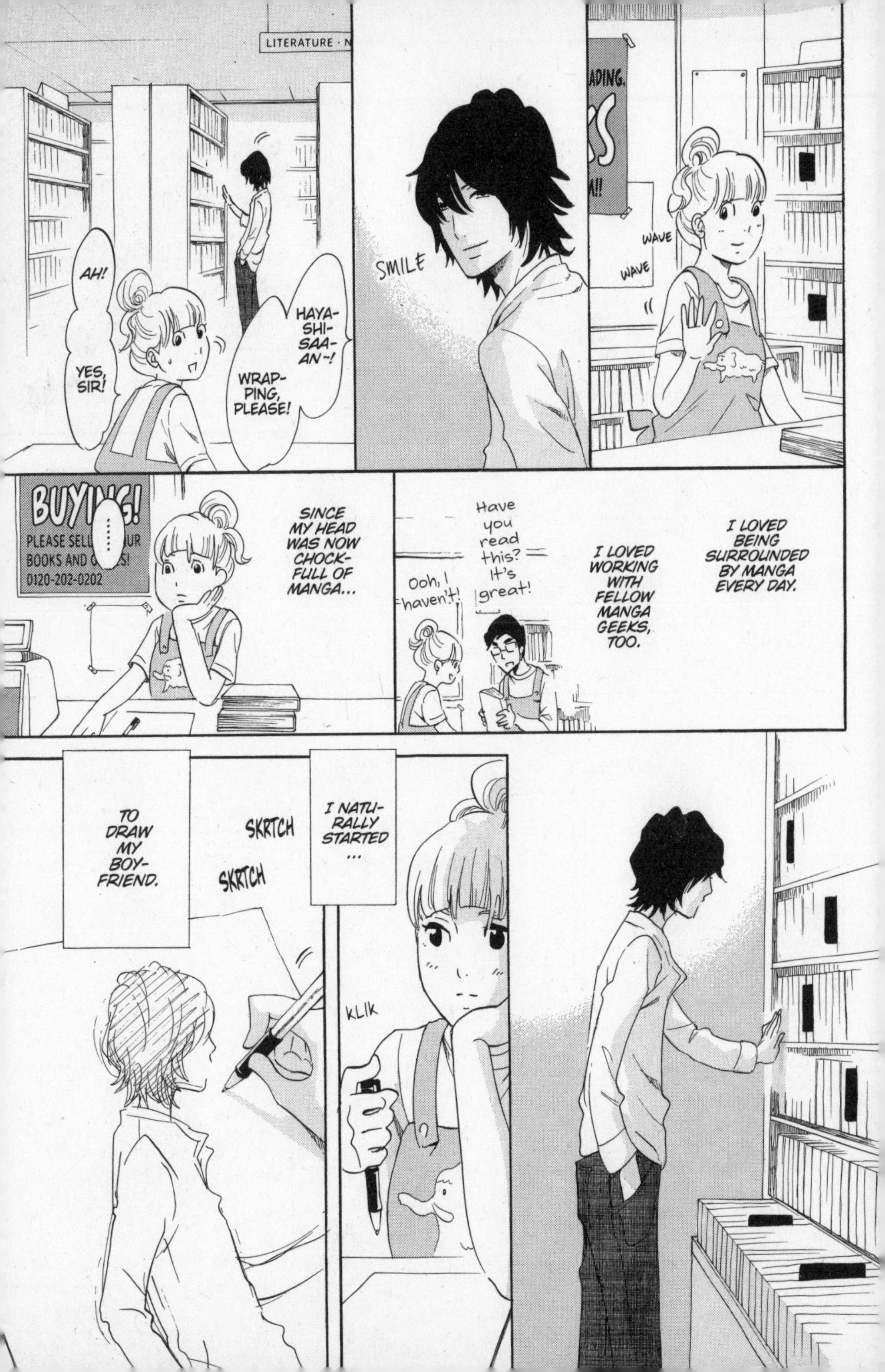
WAVE
WAVE
SMILE
LITERATURE ·
HAYA-SHI-SAAA-AN~!
AH!
WRAP-PING, PLEASE!
YES, SIR!
I LOVED BEING SURROUNDED BY MANGA EVERY DAY.
I LOVED WORKING WITH FELLOW MANGA GEEKS, TOO.
Have you read this? It's great!
Ooh, I haven't!
SINCE MY HEAD WAS NOW CHOCK-FULL OF MANGA...
......
BUYING!
0120-202-0202
I NATU-RALLY STARTED ...
KLIK
TO DRAW MY BOY-FRIEND.
SKRTCH
SKRTCH

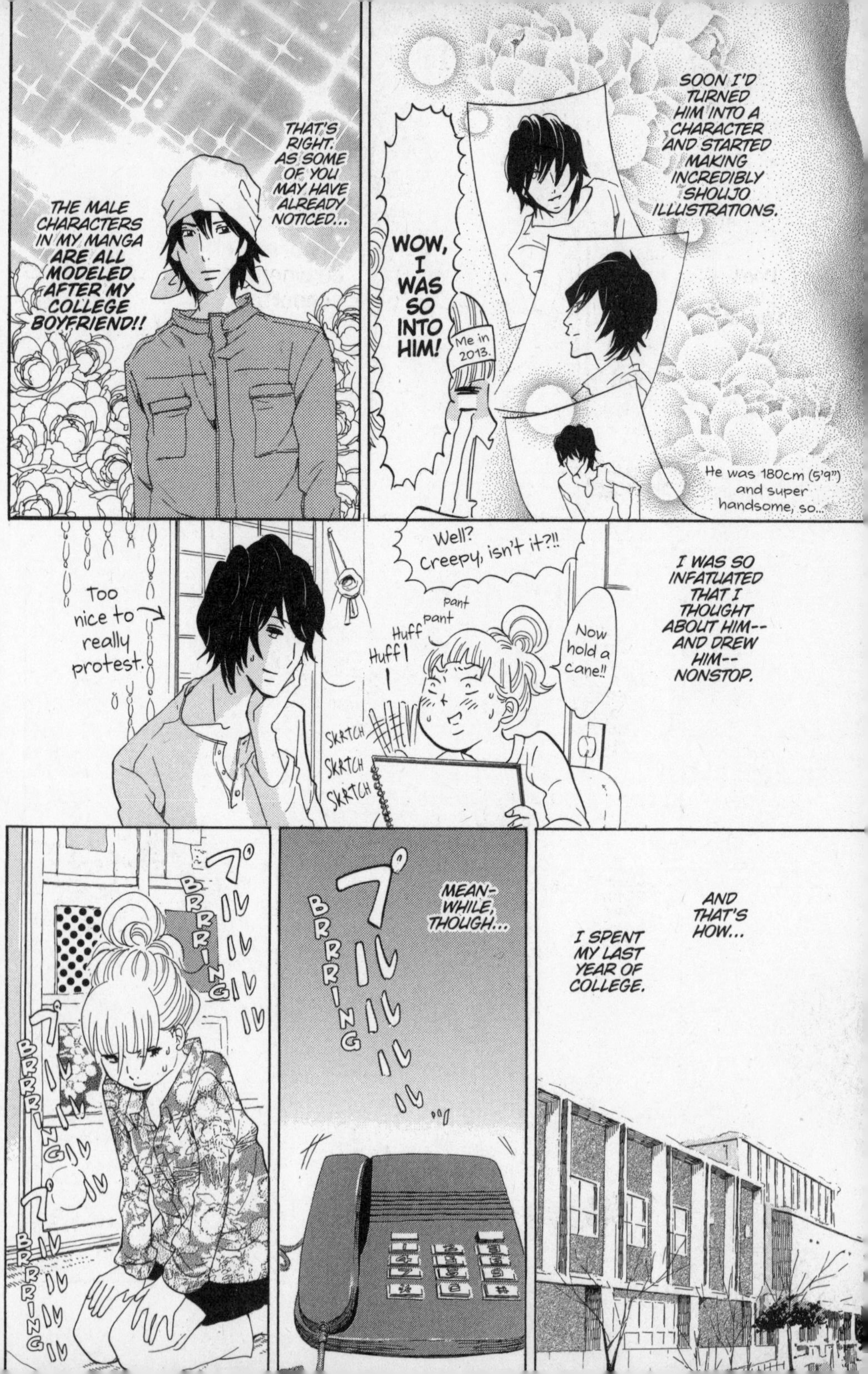
SOON I'D TURNED HIM INTO A CHARACTER AND STARTED MAKING INCREDIBLY SHOUJO ILLUSTRATIONS.
WOW, I WAS SO INTO HIM!
Me in 2013.
He was 180cm (5'9") and super handsome, so...
THAT'S RIGHT. AS SOME OF YOU MAY HAVE ALREADY NOTICED...
THE MALE CHARACTERS IN MY MANGA ARE ALL MODELED AFTER MY COLLEGE BOYFRIEND!!
I WAS SO INFATUATED THAT I THOUGHT ABOUT HIM-- AND DREW HIM-- NONSTOP.
Well? Creepy, isn't it?!!
Now hold a cane!!
pant pant
Huff Huff!
SKRTCH SKRTCH SKRTCH
Too nice to really protest.
AND THAT'S HOW...
I SPENT MY LAST YEAR OF COLLEGE.
MEAN-WHILE, THOUGH...
BRRRING
プルルルル
BRRRING
プルルルル
BRRRING
プルル
BRRRING
プルル

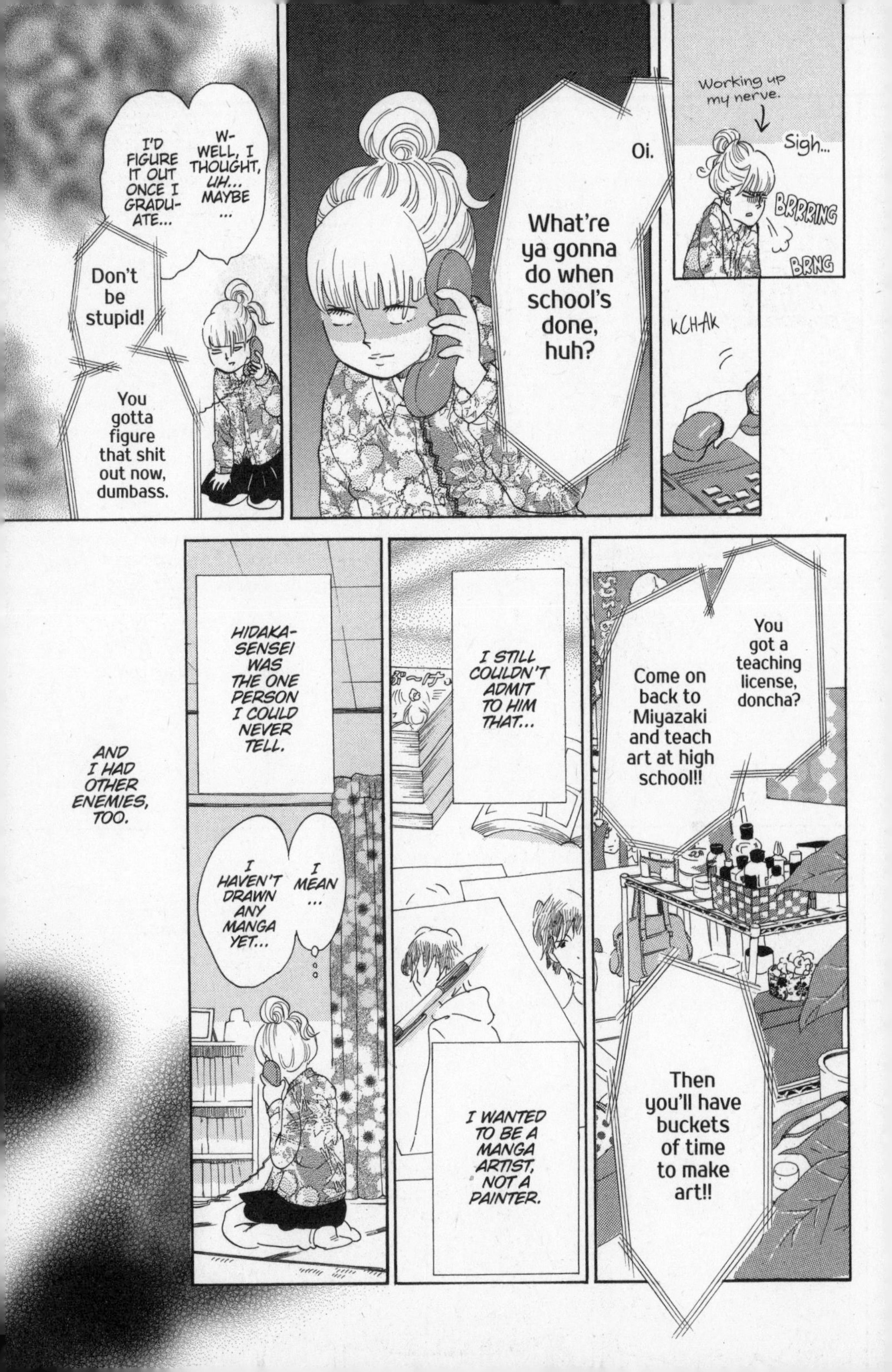
Working up my nerve.
Sigh...
BRRRING
BRNG
KCHAK
Oi.
What're ya gonna do when school's done, huh?
W-WELL, I THOUGHT, UH... MAYBE...
I'D FIGURE IT OUT ONCE I GRADUATE...
Don't be stupid!
You gotta figure that shit out now, dumbass.
You got a teaching license, doncha?
Come on back to Miyazaki and teach art at high school!!
Then you'll have buckets of time to make art!!
I STILL COULDN'T ADMIT TO HIM THAT...
I WANTED TO BE A MANGA ARTIST, NOT A PAINTER.
HIDAKA-SENSEI WAS THE ONE PERSON I COULD NEVER TELL.
I MEAN...
I HAVEN'T DRAWN ANY MANGA YET...
AND I HAD OTHER ENEMIES, TOO.

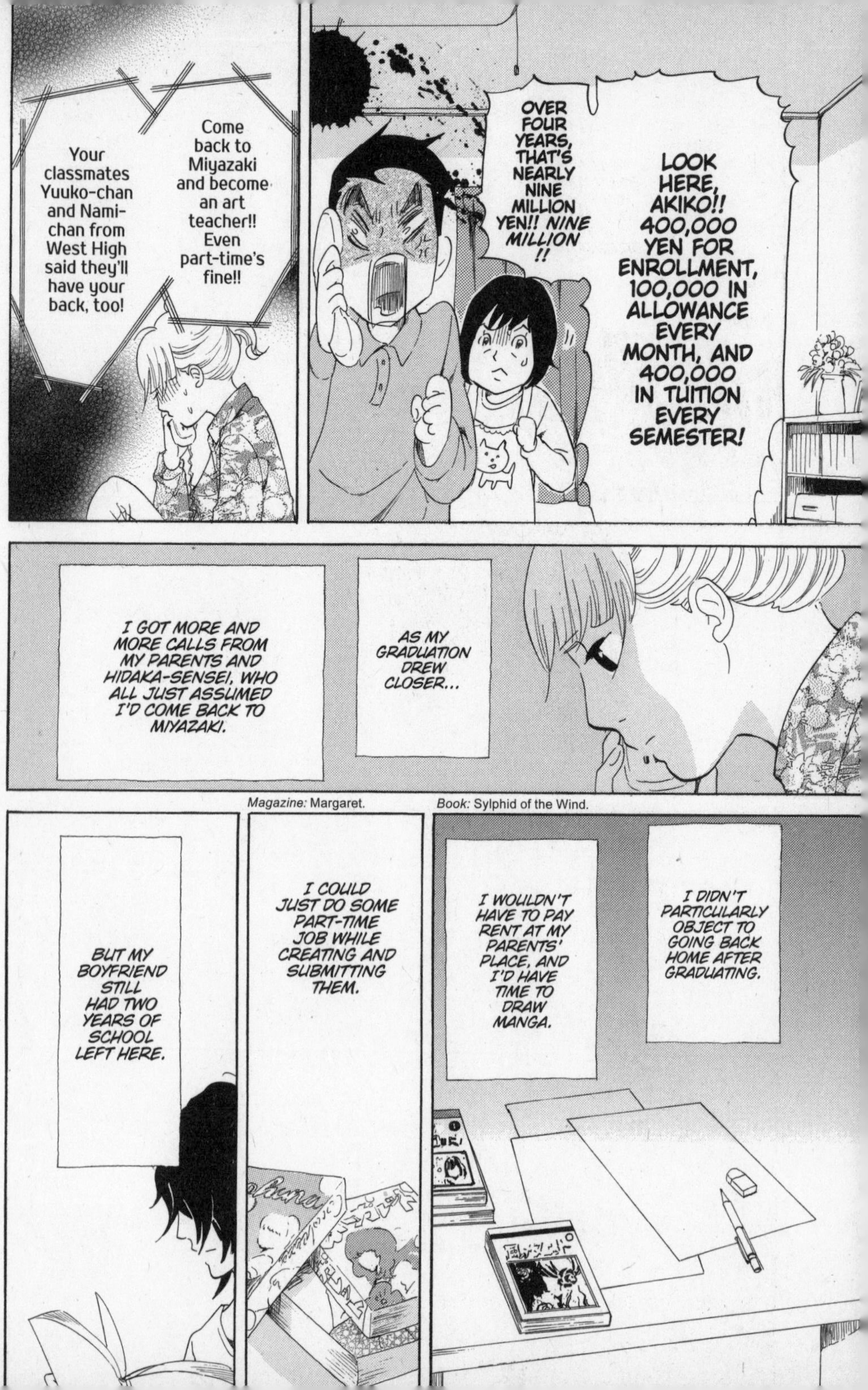
LOOK HERE, AKIKO!! 400,000 YEN FOR ENROLLMENT, 100,000 IN ALLOWANCE EVERY MONTH, AND 400,000 IN TUITION EVERY SEMESTER!
OVER FOUR YEARS, THAT'S NEARLY NINE MILLION YEN!! *NINE MILLION*!!
Come back to Miyazaki and become an art teacher!! Even part-time's fine!!
Your classmates Yuuko-chan and Nami-chan from West High said they'll have your back, too!
AS MY GRADUATION DREW CLOSER...
I GOT MORE AND MORE CALLS FROM MY PARENTS AND HIDAKA-SENSEI, WHO ALL JUST ASSUMED I'D COME BACK TO MIYAZAKI.
I DIDN'T PARTICULARLY OBJECT TO GOING BACK HOME AFTER GRADUATING.
I WOULDN'T HAVE TO PAY RENT AT MY PARENTS' PLACE, AND I'D HAVE TIME TO DRAW MANGA.
I COULD JUST DO SOME PART-TIME JOB WHILE CREATING AND SUBMITTING THEM.
BUT MY BOYFRIEND STILL HAD TWO YEARS OF SCHOOL LEFT HERE.

Book: Sylphid of the Wind.

Magazine: Margaret.

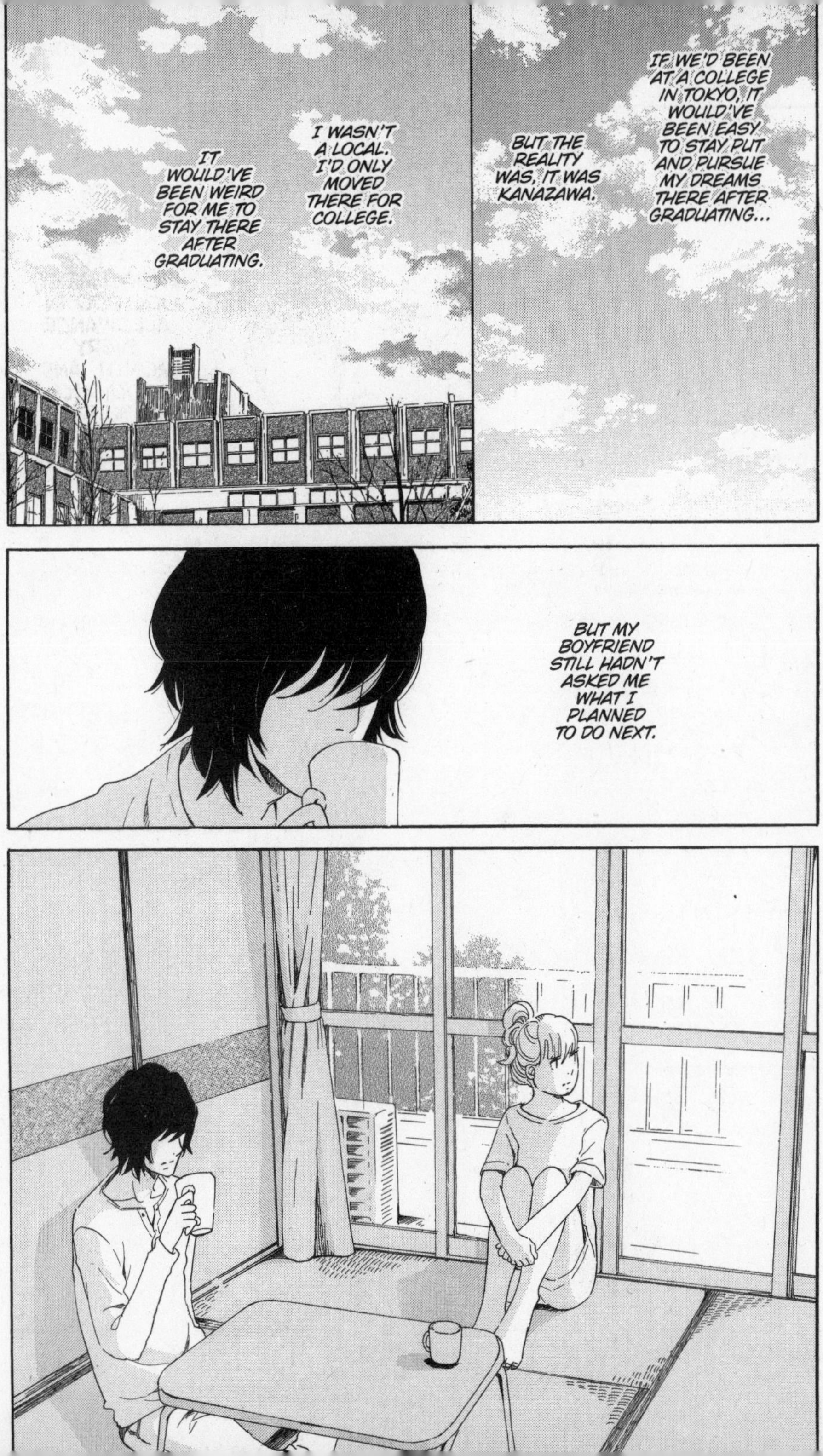
IF WE'D BEEN AT A COLLEGE IN TOKYO, IT WOULD'VE BEEN EASY TO STAY PUT AND PURSUE MY DREAMS THERE AFTER GRADUATING...
BUT THE REALITY WAS, IT WAS KANAZAWA.
I WASN'T A LOCAL. I'D ONLY MOVED THERE FOR COLLEGE.
IT WOULD'VE BEEN WEIRD FOR ME TO STAY THERE AFTER GRADUATING.
BUT MY BOYFRIEND STILL HADN'T ASKED ME WHAT I PLANNED TO DO NEXT.

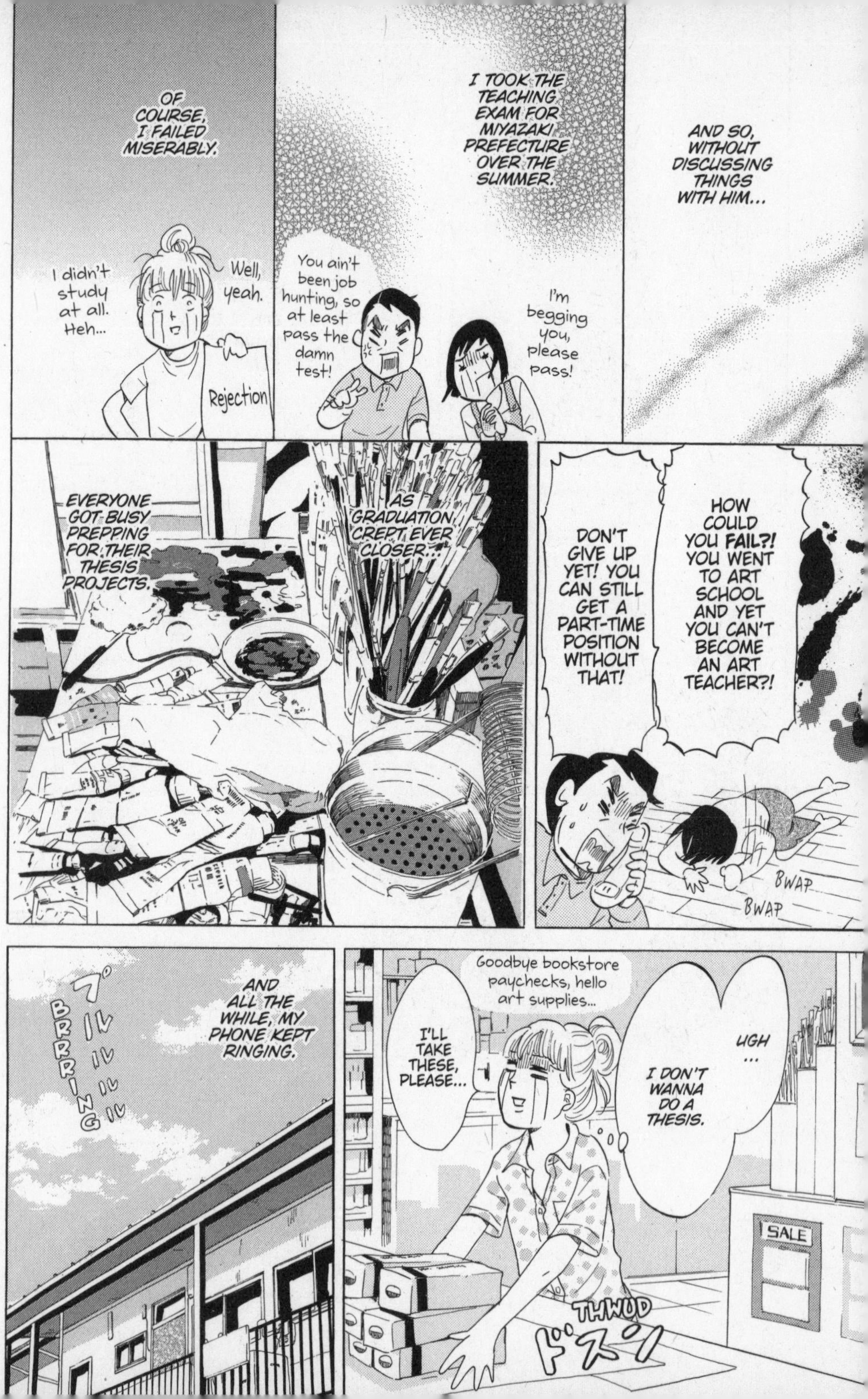
AND SO, WITHOUT DISCUSSING THINGS WITH HIM...
I TOOK THE TEACHING EXAM FOR MIYAZAKI PREFECTURE OVER THE SUMMER.
I'm begging you, please pass!
You ain't been job hunting, so at least pass the damn test!
OF COURSE, I FAILED MISERABLY.
Well, yeah.
I didn't study at all. Heh...
Rejection
HOW COULD YOU FAIL?! YOU WENT TO ART SCHOOL AND YET YOU CAN'T BECOME AN ART TEACHER?!
DON'T GIVE UP YET! YOU CAN STILL GET A PART-TIME POSITION WITHOUT THAT!
BWAP
BWAP
AS GRADUATION CREPT EVER CLOSER...
EVERYONE GOT BUSY PREPPING FOR THEIR THESIS PROJECTS.
UGH ...
I DON'T WANNA DO A THESIS.
Goodbye bookstore paychecks, hello art supplies...
I'LL TAKE THESE, PLEASE...
SALE
THWUD
ドスン
AND ALL THE WHILE, MY PHONE KEPT RINGING.
BRRRING
プルルルル

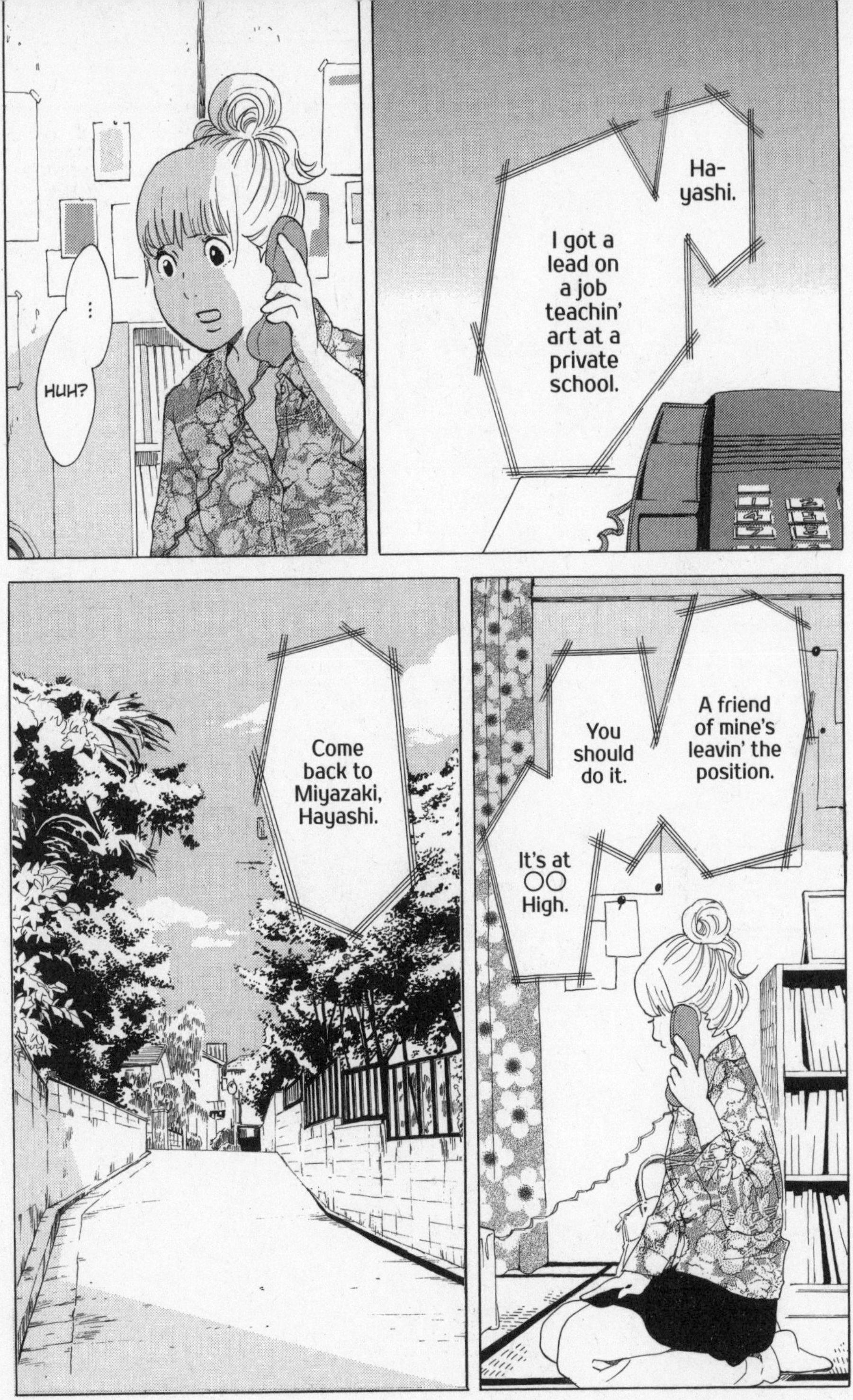
Hayashi. I got a lead on a job teachin' art at a private school.
... HUH?
A friend of mine's leavin' the position.
You should do it.
It's at ○○ High.
Come back to Miyazaki, Hayashi.

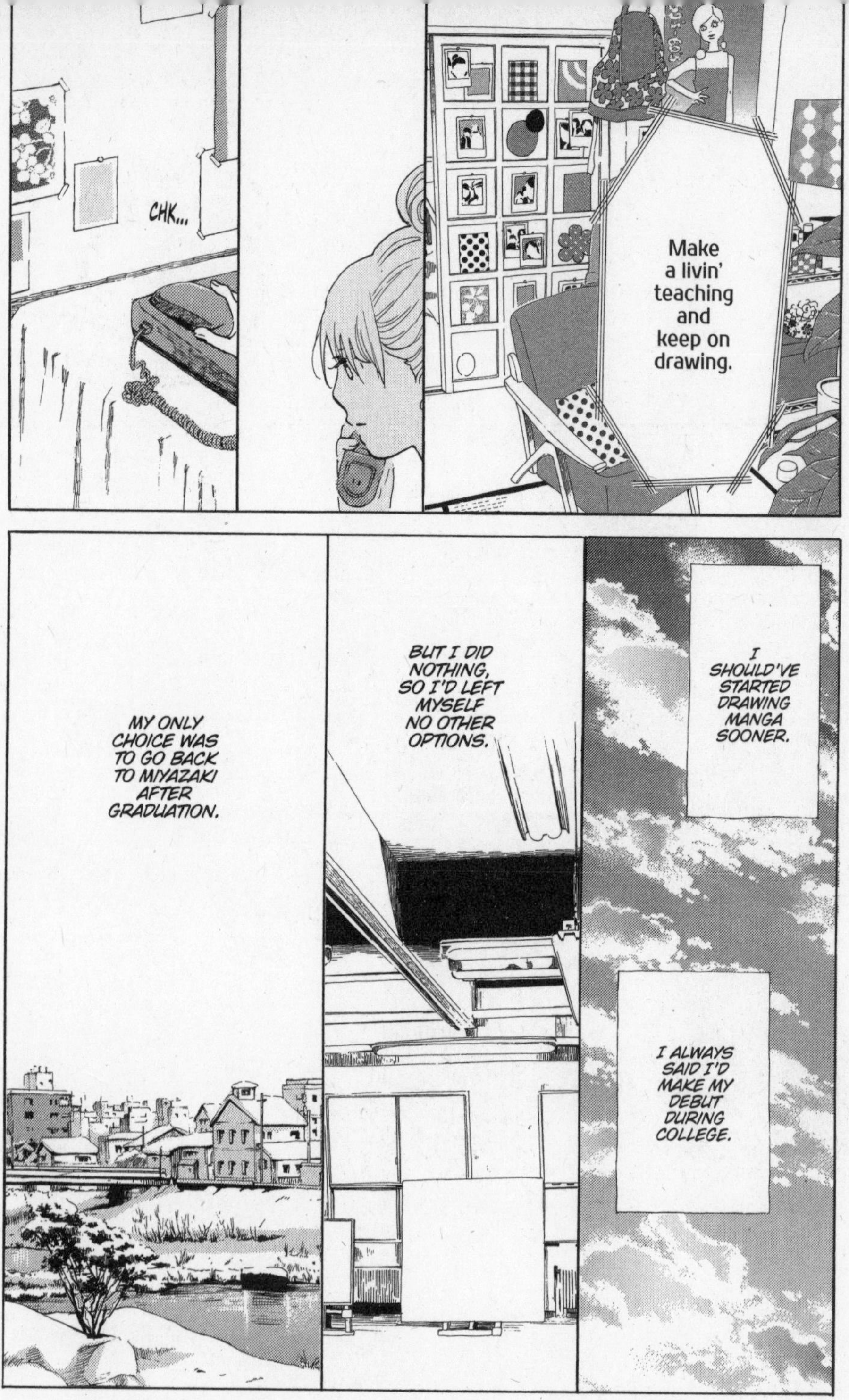
Make a livin' teaching and keep on drawing.
CHK...
I SHOULD'VE STARTED DRAWING MANGA SOONER.
I ALWAYS SAID I'D MAKE MY DEBUT DURING COLLEGE.
BUT I DID NOTHING, SO I'D LEFT MYSELF NO OTHER OPTIONS.
MY ONLY CHOICE WAS TO GO BACK TO MIYAZAKI AFTER GRADUATION.

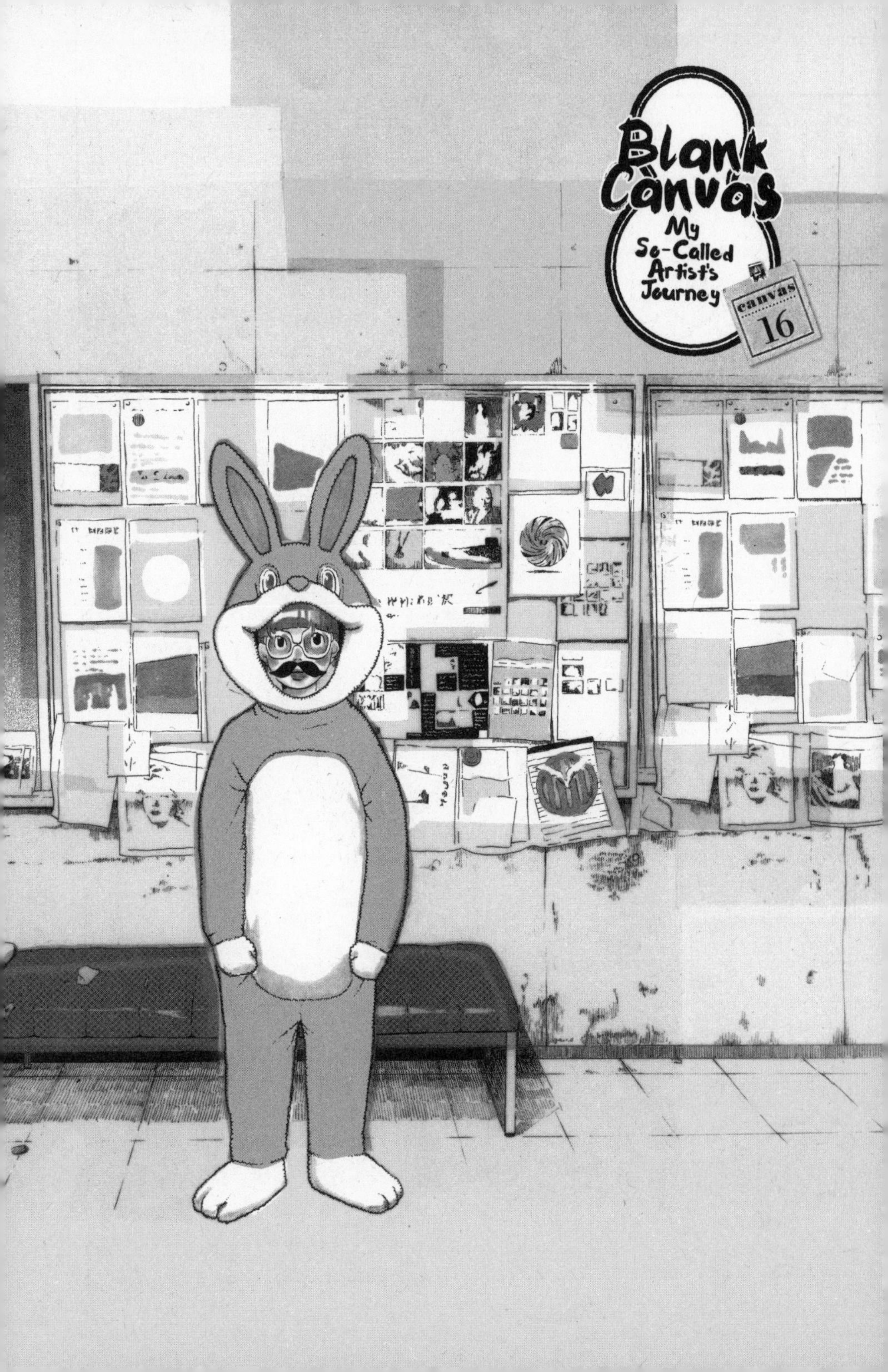
Blank Canvas
My So-Called Artist's Journey
canvas
16

Blank Canvas
My So-Called Artist's Journey

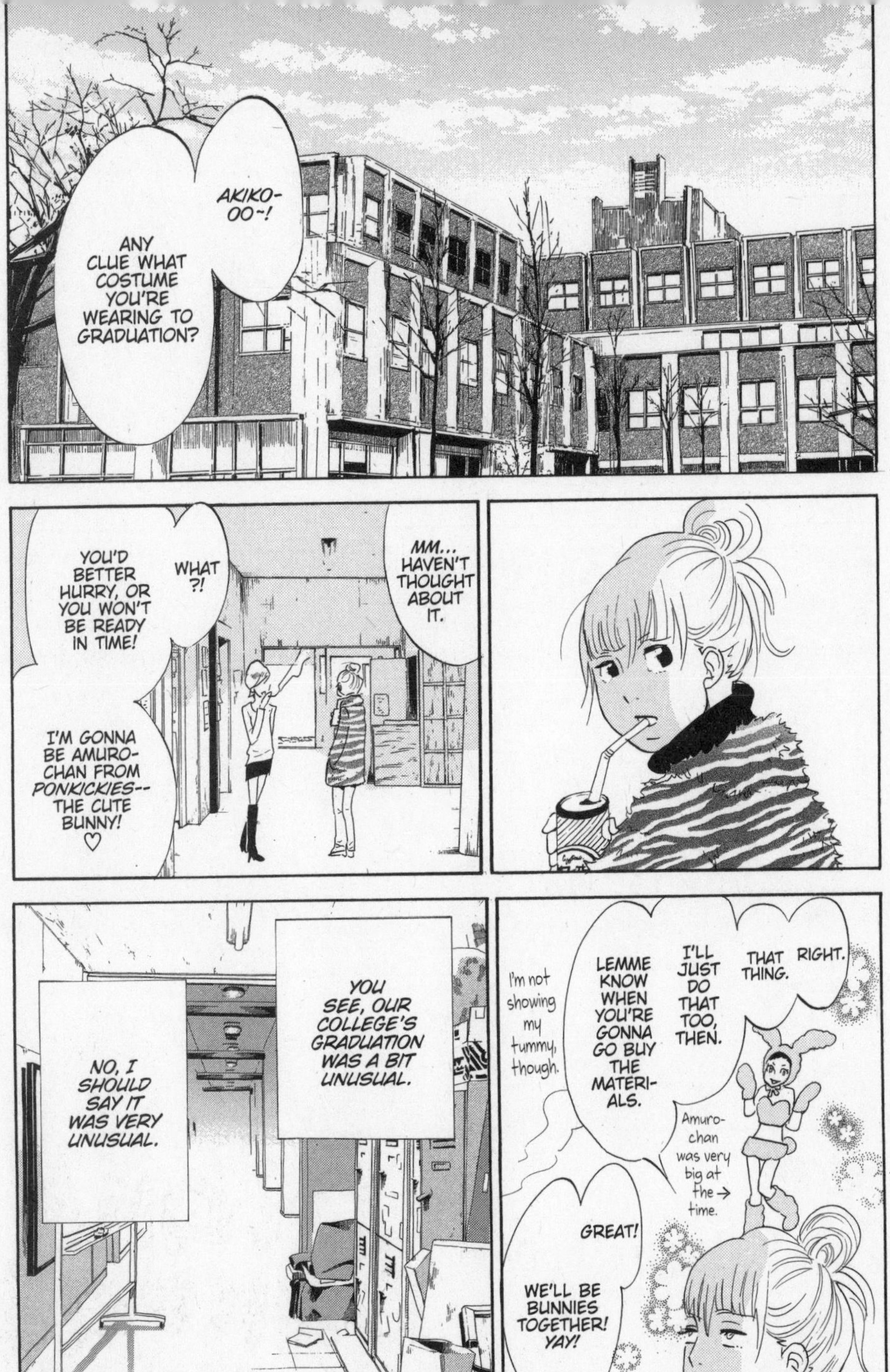
AKIKO-OO~!
ANY CLUE WHAT COSTUME YOU'RE WEARING TO GRADUATION?
MM... HAVEN'T THOUGHT ABOUT IT.
WHAT ?!
YOU'D BETTER HURRY, OR YOU WON'T BE READY IN TIME!
I'M GONNA BE AMURO-CHAN FROM *PONKICKIES*--THE CUTE BUNNY! ♡
RIGHT.
THAT THING.
I'LL JUST DO THAT TOO, THEN.
LEMME KNOW WHEN YOU'RE GONNA GO BUY THE MATERIALS.
I'm not showing my tummy, though.
Amuro-chan was very big at the time. →
GREAT!
WE'LL BE BUNNIES TOGETHER! YAY!
YOU SEE, OUR COLLEGE'S GRADUATION WAS A BIT UNUSUAL.
NO, I SHOULD SAY IT WAS VERY UNUSUAL.

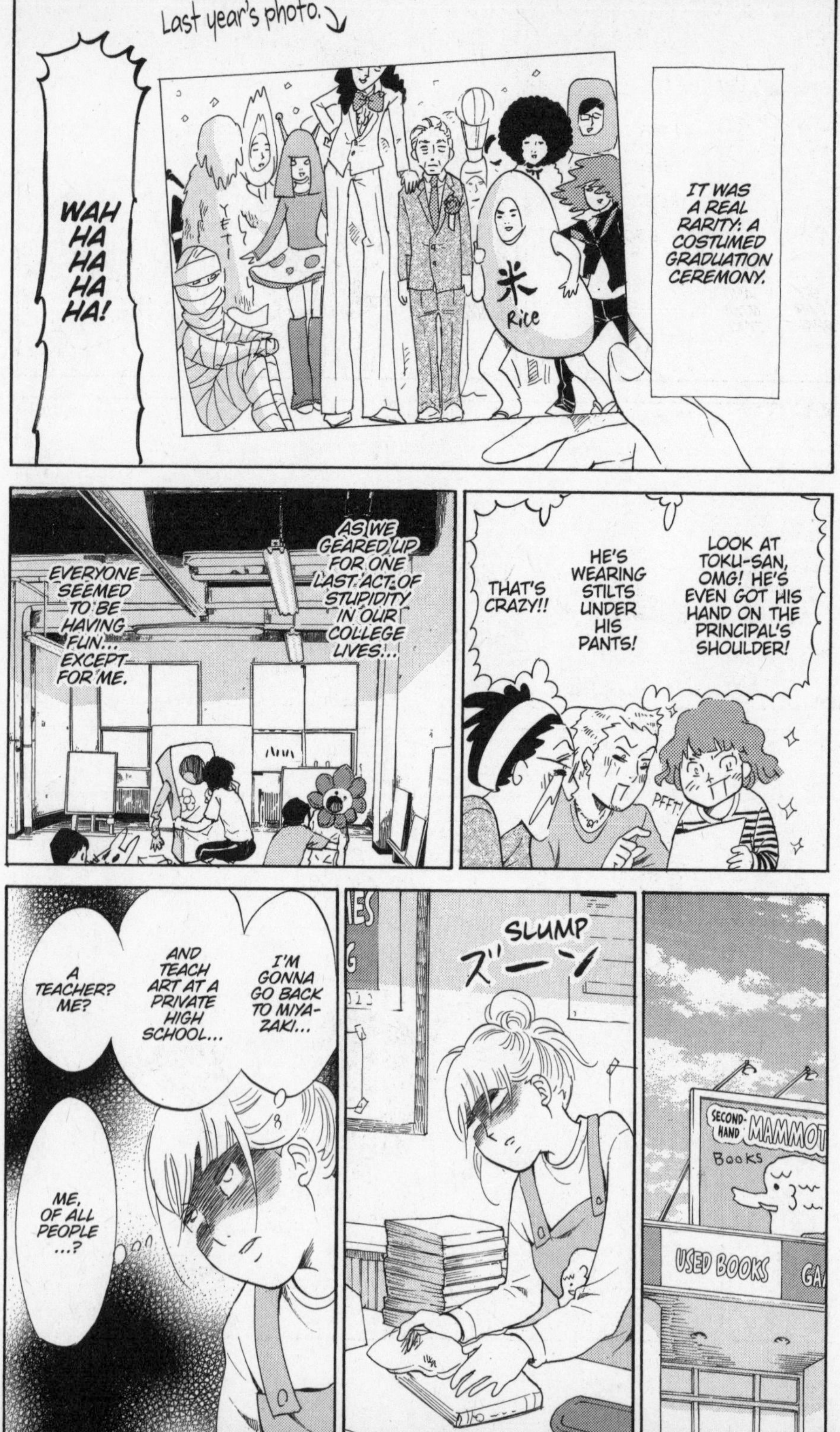
Last year's photo.
IT WAS A REAL RARITY: A COSTUMED GRADUATION CEREMONY.
YETI
米
Rice
WAH HA HA HA HA!
LOOK AT TOKU-SAN, OMG! HE'S EVEN GOT HIS HAND ON THE PRINCIPAL'S SHOULDER!
HE'S WEARING STILTS UNDER HIS PANTS!
THAT'S CRAZY!!
PFFT!
AS WE GEARED UP FOR ONE LAST ACT OF STUPIDITY IN OUR COLLEGE LIVES...
EVERYONE SEEMED TO BE HAVING FUN... EXCEPT FOR ME.
SECOND-HAND
BOOKS
USED BOOKS
SLUMP
ズーン
I'M GONNA GO BACK TO MIYAZAKI...
AND TEACH ART AT A PRIVATE HIGH SCHOOL...
A TEACHER? ME?
ME, OF ALL PEOPLE...?

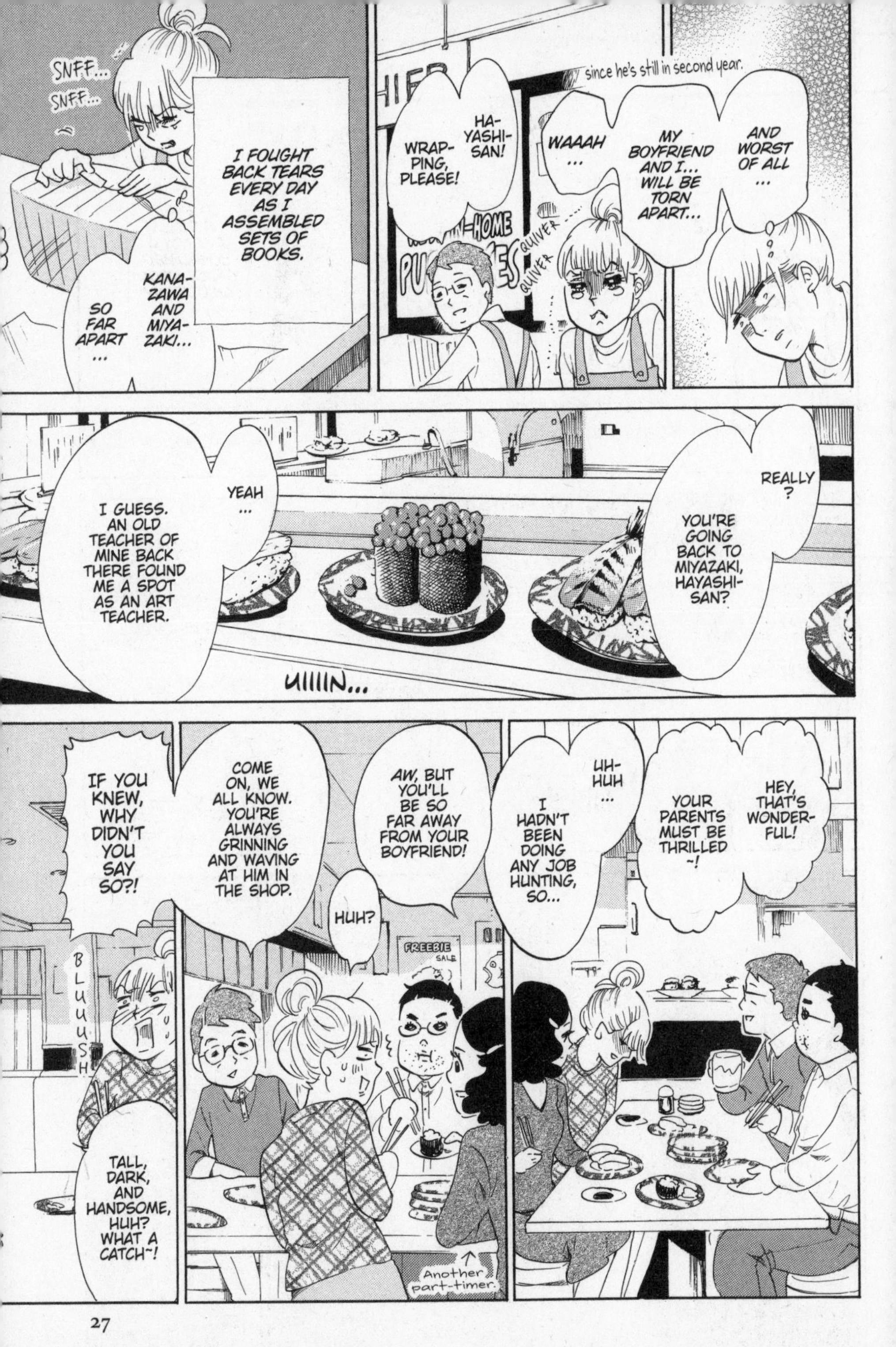
AND WORST OF ALL...
MY BOYFRIEND AND I... WILL BE TORN APART...
since he's still in second year.
WAAAH...
HA-YASHI-SAN!
WRAPPING, PLEASE!
QUIVER QUIVER
I FOUGHT BACK TEARS EVERY DAY AS I ASSEMBLED SETS OF BOOKS.
SNFF... SNFF...
KANA-ZAWA AND MIYA-ZAKI...
SO FAR APART...
REALLY? YOU'RE GOING BACK TO MIYAZAKI, HAYASHI-SAN?
YEAH... I GUESS. AN OLD TEACHER OF MINE BACK THERE FOUND ME A SPOT AS AN ART TEACHER.
UIIIIN...
HEY, THAT'S WONDER-FUL!
YOUR PARENTS MUST BE THRILLED~!
UH-HUH... I HADN'T BEEN DOING ANY JOB HUNTING, SO...
AW, BUT YOU'LL BE SO FAR AWAY FROM YOUR BOYFRIEND!
HUH?
COME ON, WE ALL KNOW. YOU'RE ALWAYS GRINNING AND WAVING AT HIM IN THE SHOP.
FREEBIE SALE
Another part-timer.
IF YOU KNEW, WHY DIDN'T YOU SAY SO?!
BLUUUSH
TALL, DARK, AND HANDSOME, HUH? WHAT A CATCH~!

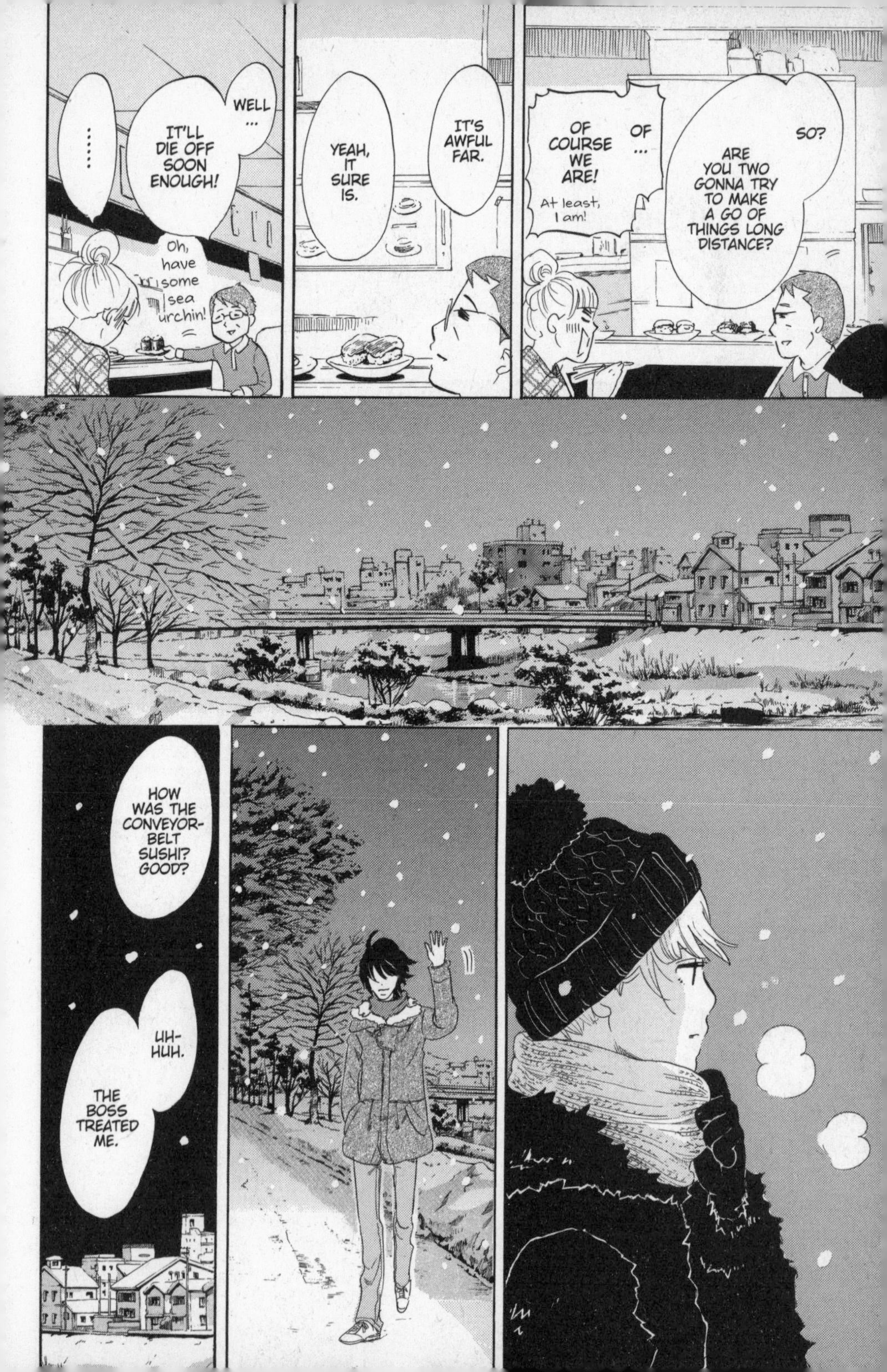
SO?
ARE YOU TWO GONNA TRY TO MAKE A GO OF THINGS LONG DISTANCE?
OF ...
OF COURSE WE ARE!
At least, I am!
IT'S AWFUL FAR.
YEAH, IT SURE IS.
WELL ...
IT'LL DIE OFF SOON ENOUGH!
......
Oh, have some sea urchin!
HOW WAS THE CONVEYOR-BELT SUSHI? GOOD?
UH-HUH.
THE BOSS TREATED ME.

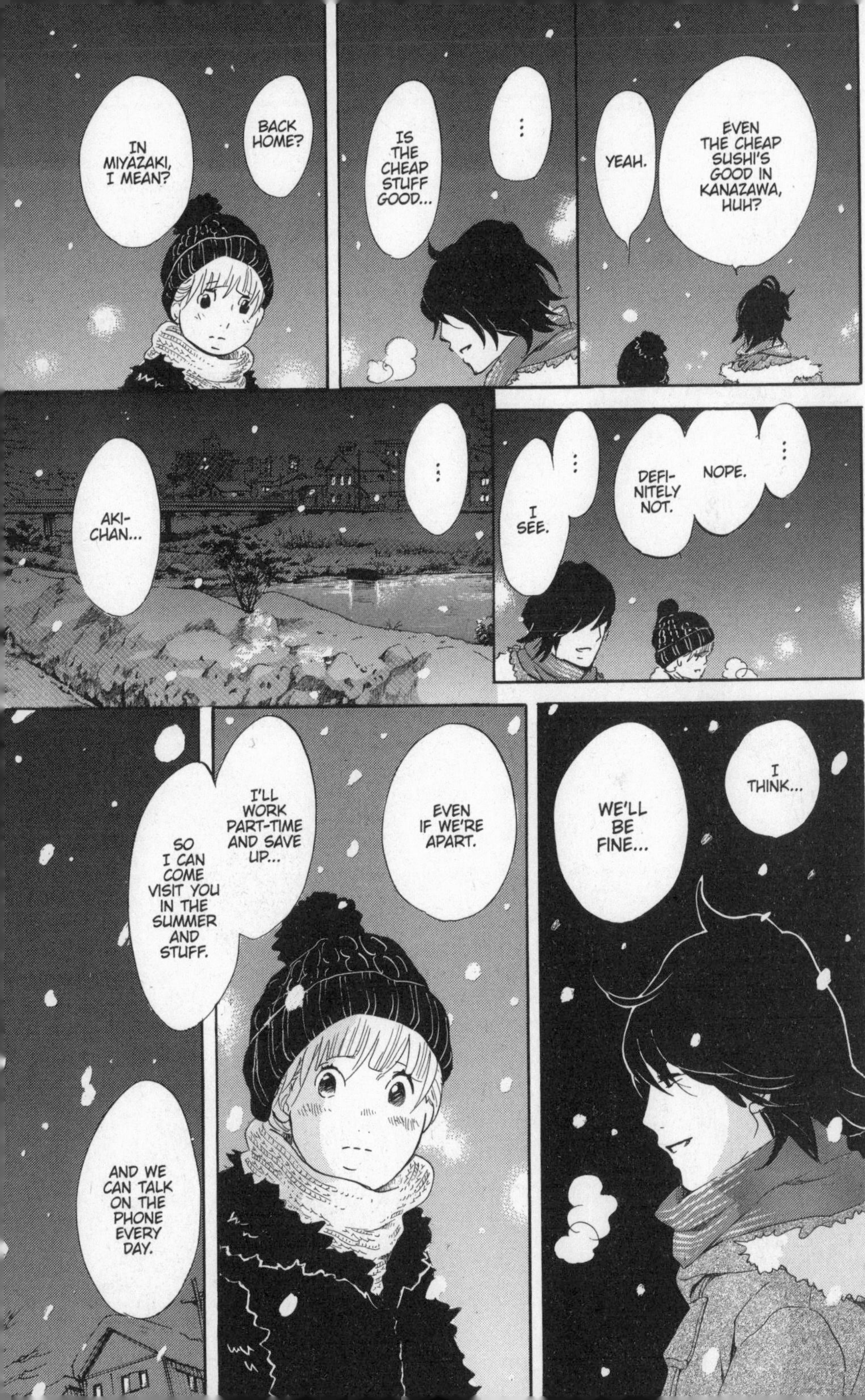
EVEN THE CHEAP SUSHI'S GOOD IN KANAZAWA, HUH?
YEAH.
...
IS THE CHEAP STUFF GOOD...
BACK HOME?
IN MIYAZAKI, I MEAN?
...
NOPE.
DEFI-NITELY NOT.
...
I SEE.
...
AKI-CHAN...
I THINK...
WE'LL BE FINE...
EVEN IF WE'RE APART.
I'LL WORK PART-TIME AND SAVE UP...
SO I CAN COME VISIT YOU IN THE SUMMER AND STUFF.
AND WE CAN TALK ON THE PHONE EVERY DAY.

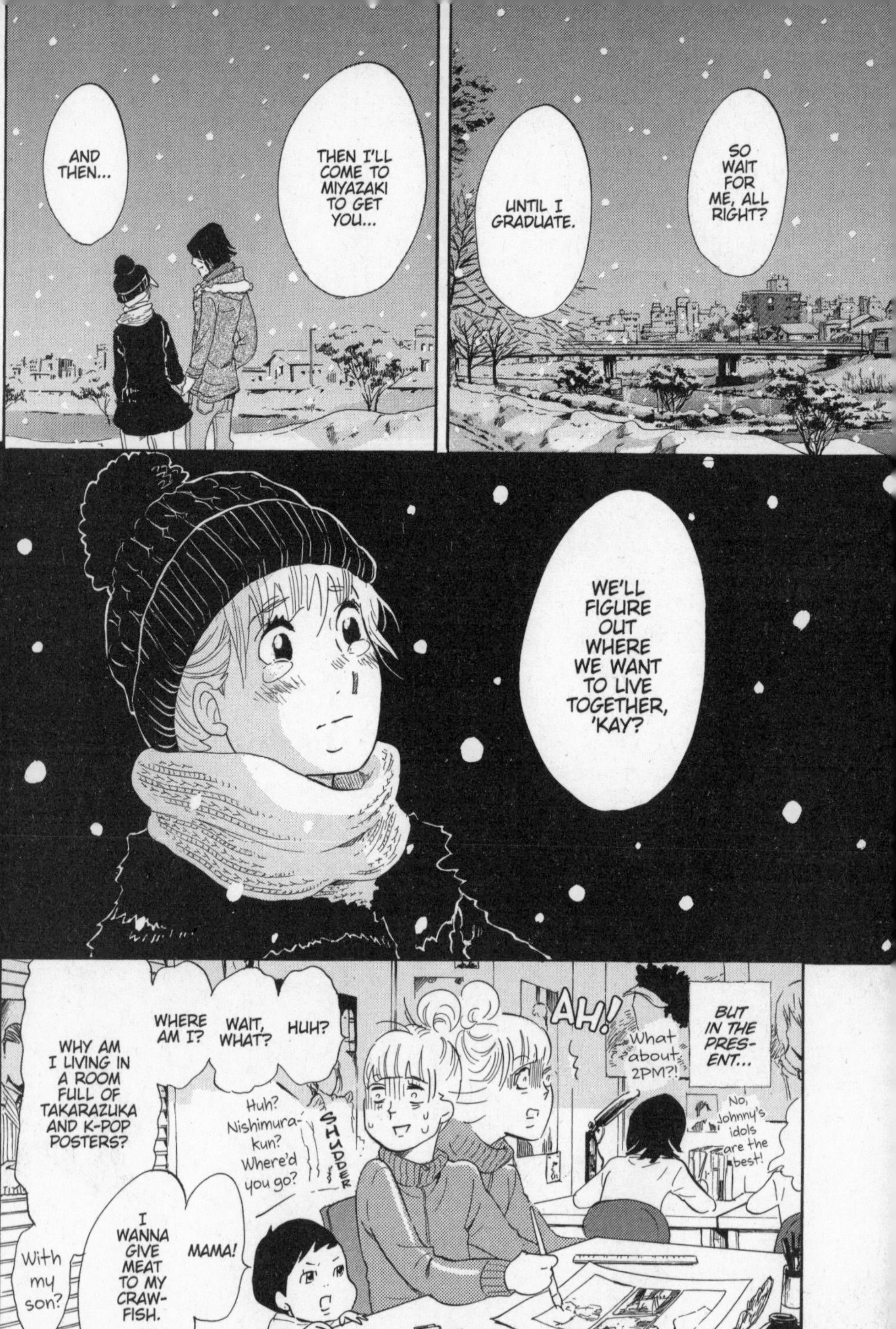

SO WAIT FOR ME, ALL RIGHT?
UNTIL I GRADUATE.
THEN I'LL COME TO MIYAZAKI TO GET YOU...
AND THEN...
WE'LL FIGURE OUT WHERE WE WANT TO LIVE TOGETHER, 'KAY?
BUT IN THE PRESENT...
AH!
What about 2PM?!
No, Johnny's idols are the best!
HUH?
WAIT, WHAT?
WHERE AM I?
WHY AM I LIVING IN A ROOM FULL OF TAKARAZUKA AND K-POP POSTERS?
SHUDDER
Huh? Nishimura-kun? Where'd you go?
MAMA!
I WANNA GIVE MEAT TO MY CRAWFISH.
With my son?

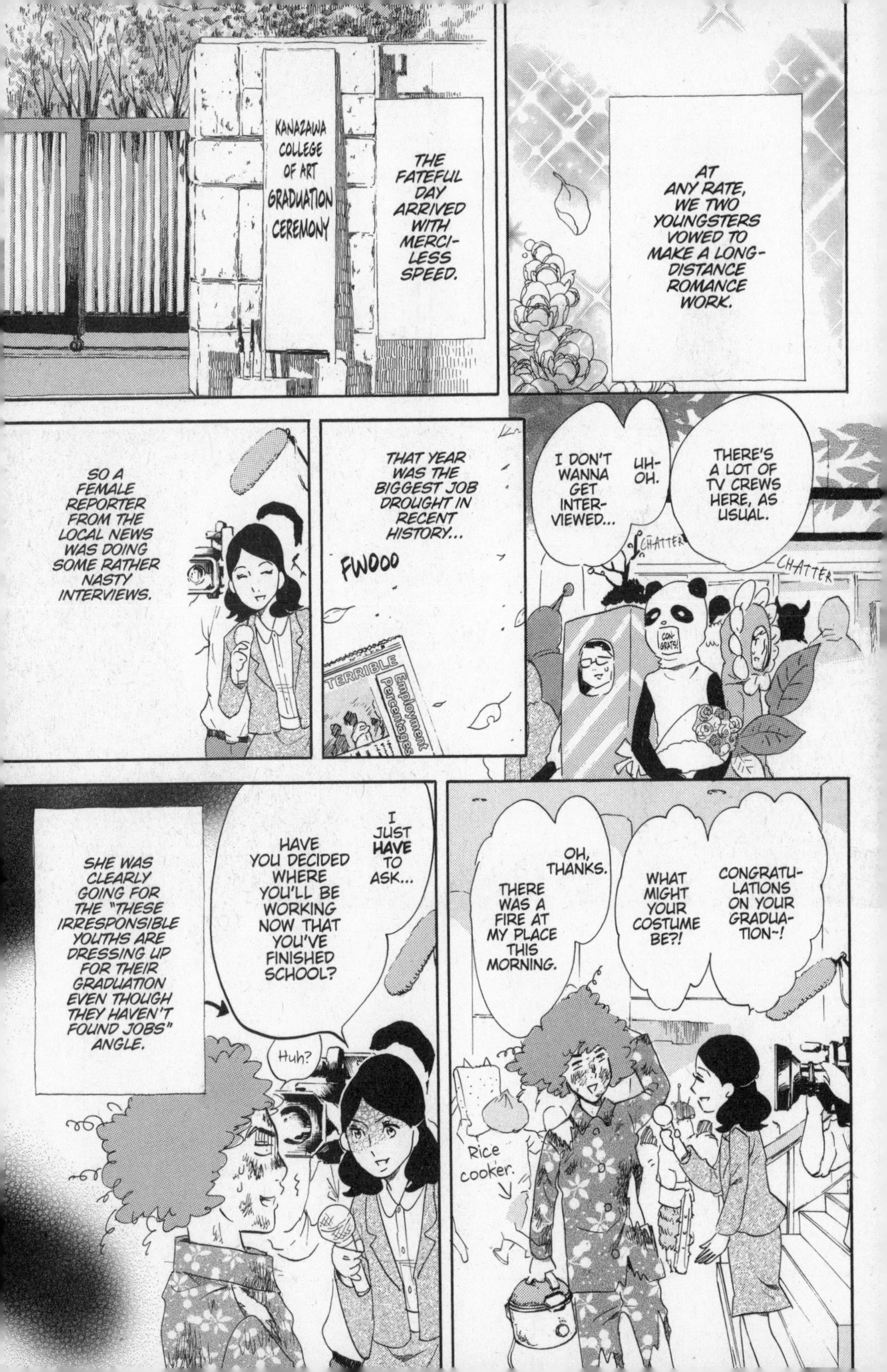
AT ANY RATE, WE TWO YOUNGSTERS VOWED TO MAKE A LONG-DISTANCE ROMANCE WORK.
THE FATEFUL DAY ARRIVED WITH MERCILESS SPEED.
KANAZAWA COLLEGE OF ART GRADUATION CEREMONY
THERE'S A LOT OF TV CREWS HERE, AS USUAL.
UH-OH.
I DON'T WANNA GET INTERVIEWED...
CHATTER
CHATTER
CONGRATS!
THAT YEAR WAS THE BIGGEST JOB DROUGHT IN RECENT HISTORY...
FWOOO
TERRIBLE
Employment Percentages
SO A FEMALE REPORTER FROM THE LOCAL NEWS WAS DOING SOME RATHER NASTY INTERVIEWS.
CONGRATULATIONS ON YOUR GRADUATION~!
WHAT MIGHT YOUR COSTUME BE?!
OH, THANKS.
THERE WAS A FIRE AT MY PLACE THIS MORNING.
Rice cooker.
I JUST **HAVE** TO ASK...
HAVE YOU DECIDED WHERE YOU'LL BE WORKING NOW THAT YOU'VE FINISHED SCHOOL?
Huh?
SHE WAS CLEARLY GOING FOR THE "THESE IRRESPONSIBLE YOUTHS ARE DRESSING UP FOR THEIR GRADUATION EVEN THOUGH THEY HAVEN'T FOUND JOBS" ANGLE.

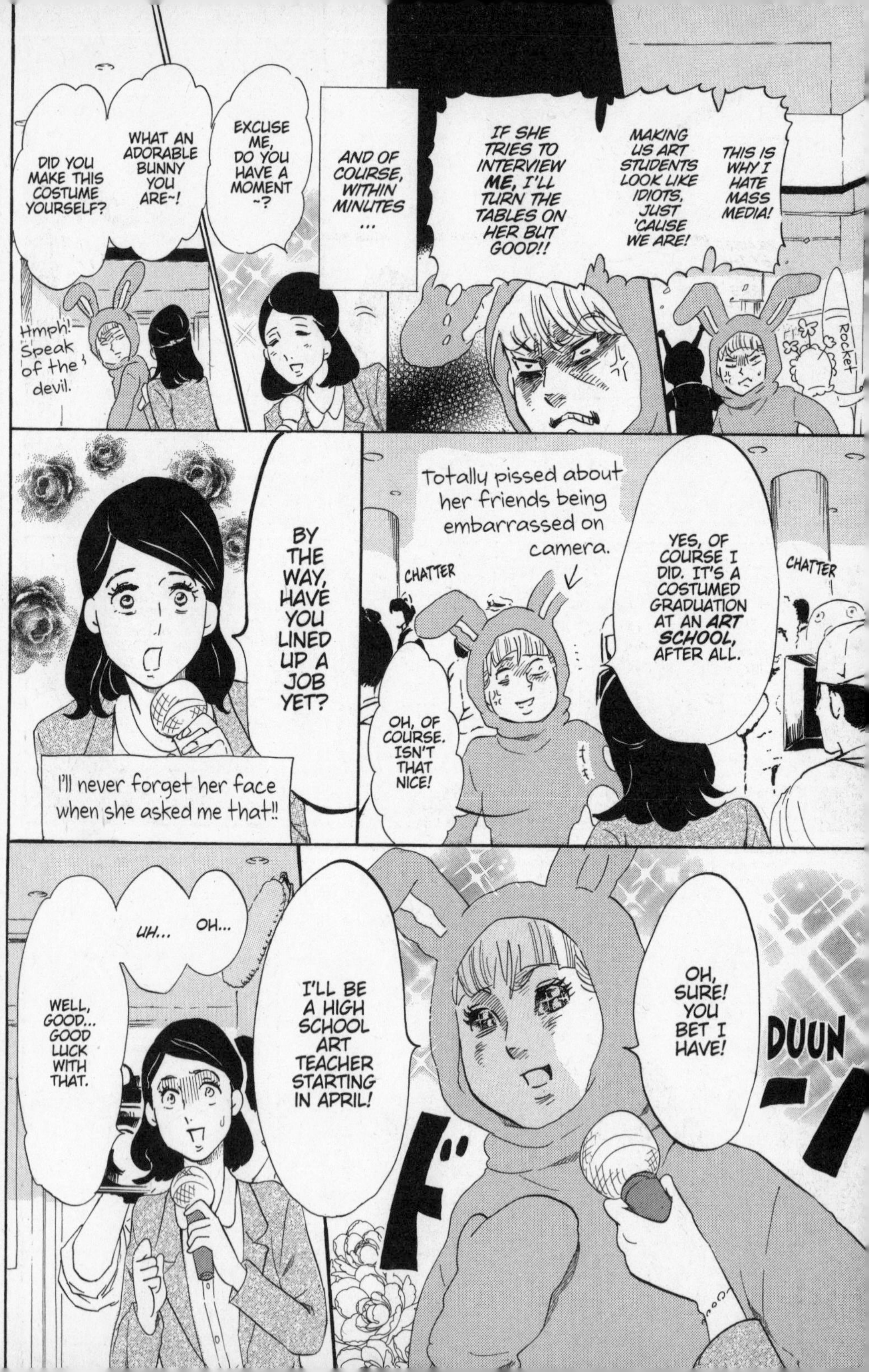

THIS IS WHY I HATE MASS MEDIA!
MAKING US ART STUDENTS LOOK LIKE IDIOTS, JUST 'CAUSE WE ARE!
IF SHE TRIES TO INTERVIEW **ME**, I'LL TURN THE TABLES ON HER BUT GOOD!!
Rocket
AND OF COURSE, WITHIN MINUTES ...
EXCUSE ME, DO YOU HAVE A MOMENT ~?
WHAT AN ADORABLE BUNNY YOU ARE~!
DID YOU MAKE THIS COSTUME YOURSELF?
Hmph! Speak of the devil.
YES, OF COURSE I DID. IT'S A COSTUMED GRADUATION AT AN **ART SCHOOL**, AFTER ALL.
CHATTER
Totally pissed about her friends being embarrassed on camera.
CHATTER
OH, OF COURSE. ISN'T THAT NICE!
BY THE WAY, HAVE YOU LINED UP A JOB YET?
I'll never forget her face when she asked me that!!
OH, SURE! YOU BET I HAVE!
DUUN
I'LL BE A HIGH SCHOOL ART TEACHER STARTING IN APRIL!
UH... OH...
WELL, GOOD... GOOD LUCK WITH THAT.

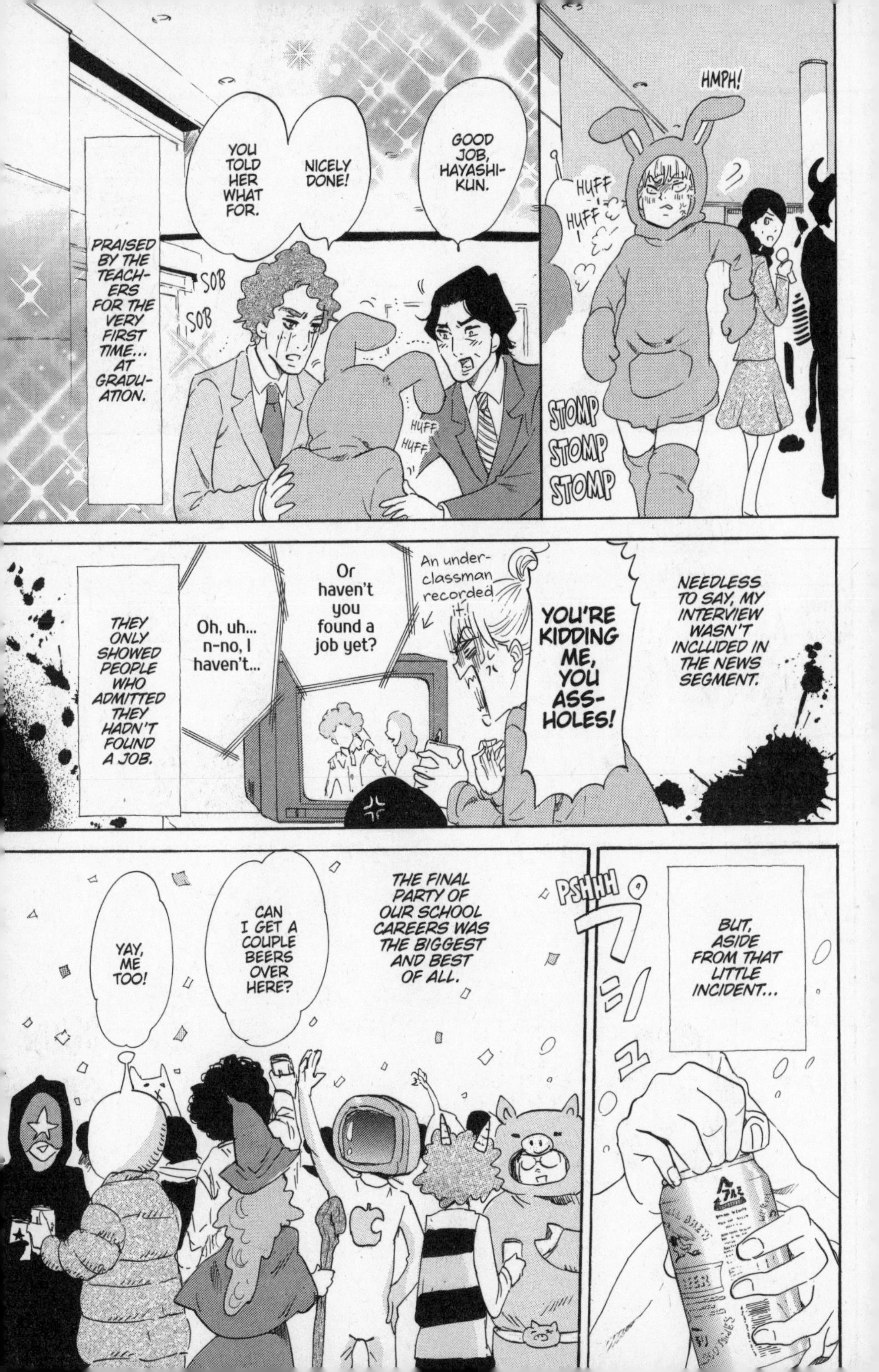
HMPH!
HUFF HUFF
STOMP STOMP STOMP
GOOD JOB, HAYASHI-KUN.
NICELY DONE!
YOU TOLD HER WHAT FOR.
PRAISED BY THE TEACHERS FOR THE VERY FIRST TIME... AT GRADUATION.
SOB SOB
HUFF HUFF
NEEDLESS TO SAY, MY INTERVIEW WASN'T INCLUDED IN THE NEWS SEGMENT.
YOU'RE KIDDING ME, YOU ASSHOLES!
An underclassman recorded it.
Or haven't you found a job yet?
Oh, uh... n-no, I haven't...
THEY ONLY SHOWED PEOPLE WHO ADMITTED THEY HADN'T FOUND A JOB.
PSHHH
BUT, ASIDE FROM THAT LITTLE INCIDENT...
THE FINAL PARTY OF OUR SCHOOL CAREERS WAS THE BIGGEST AND BEST OF ALL.
CAN I GET A COUPLE BEERS OVER HERE?
YAY, ME TOO!

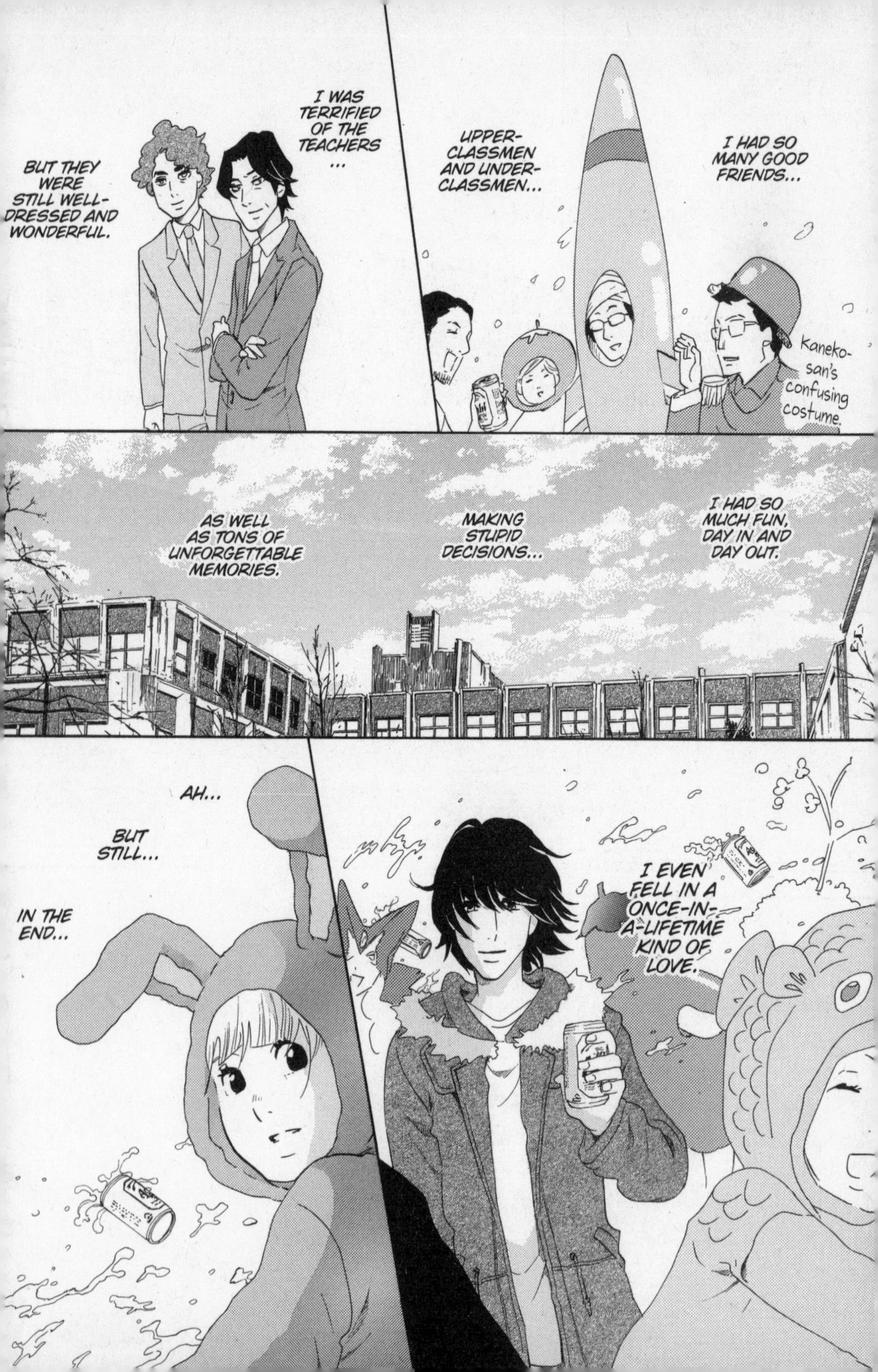
I HAD SO MANY GOOD FRIENDS...
UPPER-CLASSMEN AND UNDER-CLASSMEN...
Kaneko-san's confusing costume.
I WAS TERRIFIED OF THE TEACHERS ...
BUT THEY WERE STILL WELL-DRESSED AND WONDERFUL.
I HAD SO MUCH FUN, DAY IN AND DAY OUT.
MAKING STUPID DECISIONS...
AS WELL AS TONS OF UNFORGETTABLE MEMORIES.
I EVEN FELL IN A ONCE-IN-A-LIFETIME KIND OF LOVE.
AH...
BUT STILL...
IN THE END...

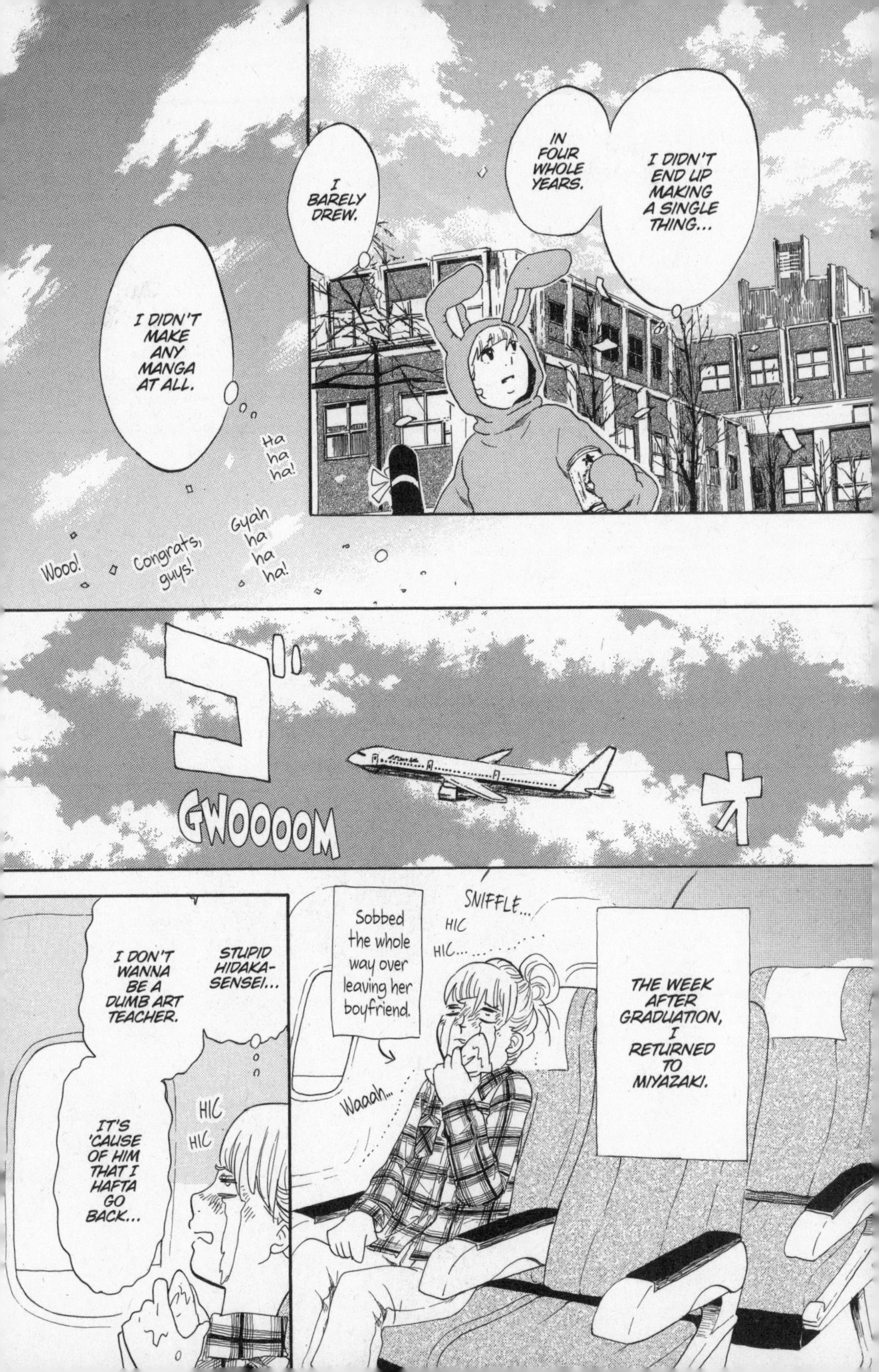

I DIDN'T END UP MAKING A SINGLE THING...
IN FOUR WHOLE YEARS.
I BARELY DREW.
I DIDN'T MAKE ANY MANGA AT ALL.
Ha ha ha!
Gyah ha ha ha!
Congrats, guys!
Wooo!
GWOOOOM
THE WEEK AFTER GRADUATION, I RETURNED TO MIYAZAKI.
SNIFFLE...
HIC
HIC...
Sobbed the whole way over leaving her boyfriend.
Waaah...
STUPID HIDAKA-SENSEI...
I DON'T WANNA BE A DUMB ART TEACHER.
IT'S 'CAUSE OF HIM THAT I HAFTA GO BACK...
HIC
HIC

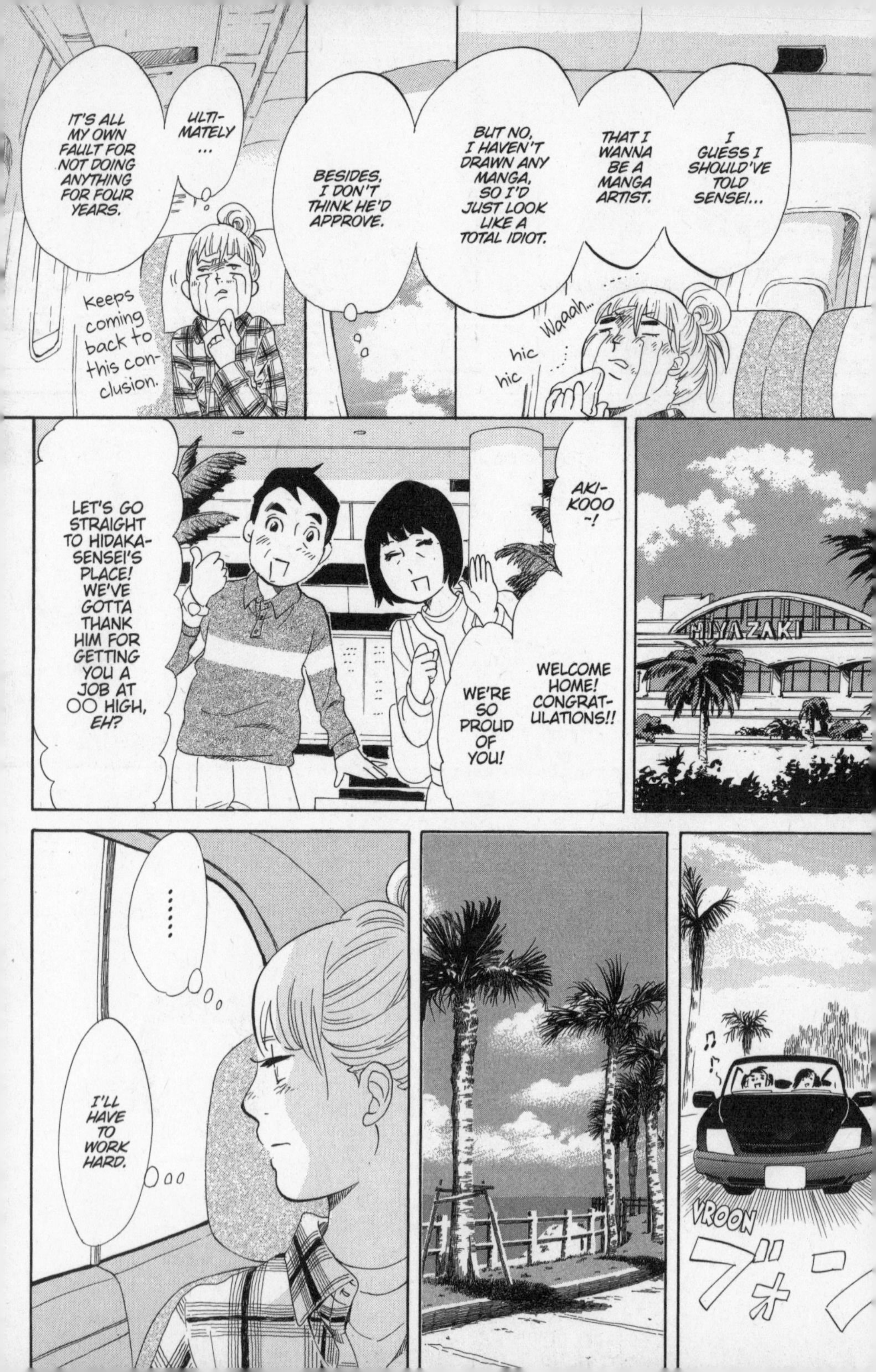
I GUESS I SHOULD'VE TOLD SENSEI...
THAT I WANNA BE A MANGA ARTIST.
BUT NO, I HAVEN'T DRAWN ANY MANGA, SO I'D JUST LOOK LIKE A TOTAL IDIOT.
BESIDES, I DON'T THINK HE'D APPROVE.
Waaah...
hic hic
ULTI-MATELY...
IT'S ALL MY OWN FAULT FOR NOT DOING ANYTHING FOR FOUR YEARS.
Keeps coming back to this con-clusion.
MIYAZAKI
AKI-KOOO~!
WELCOME HOME! CONGRAT-ULATIONS!!
WE'RE SO PROUD OF YOU!
LET'S GO STRAIGHT TO HIDAKA-SENSEI'S PLACE! WE'VE GOTTA THANK HIM FOR GETTING YOU A JOB AT OO HIGH, EH?
VROON
ブォン
......
I'LL HAVE TO WORK HARD.

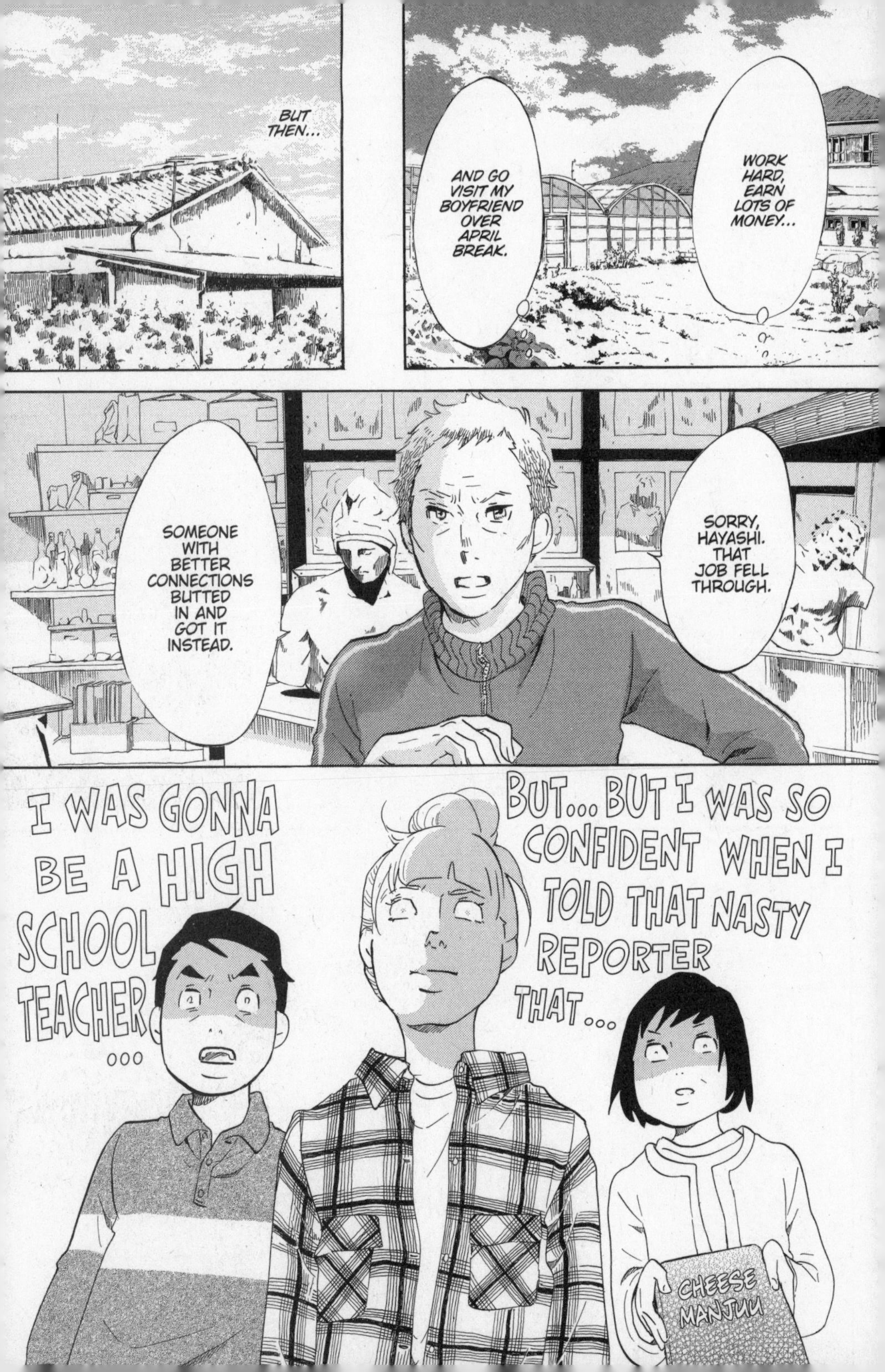
WORK HARD, EARN LOTS OF MONEY...
AND GO VISIT MY BOYFRIEND OVER APRIL BREAK.
BUT THEN...
SORRY, HAYASHI. THAT JOB FELL THROUGH.
SOMEONE WITH BETTER CONNECTIONS BUTTED IN AND GOT IT INSTEAD.
BUT... BUT I WAS SO CONFIDENT WHEN I TOLD THAT NASTY REPORTER THAT...
I WAS GONNA BE A HIGH SCHOOL TEACHER...
CHEESE MANJUU

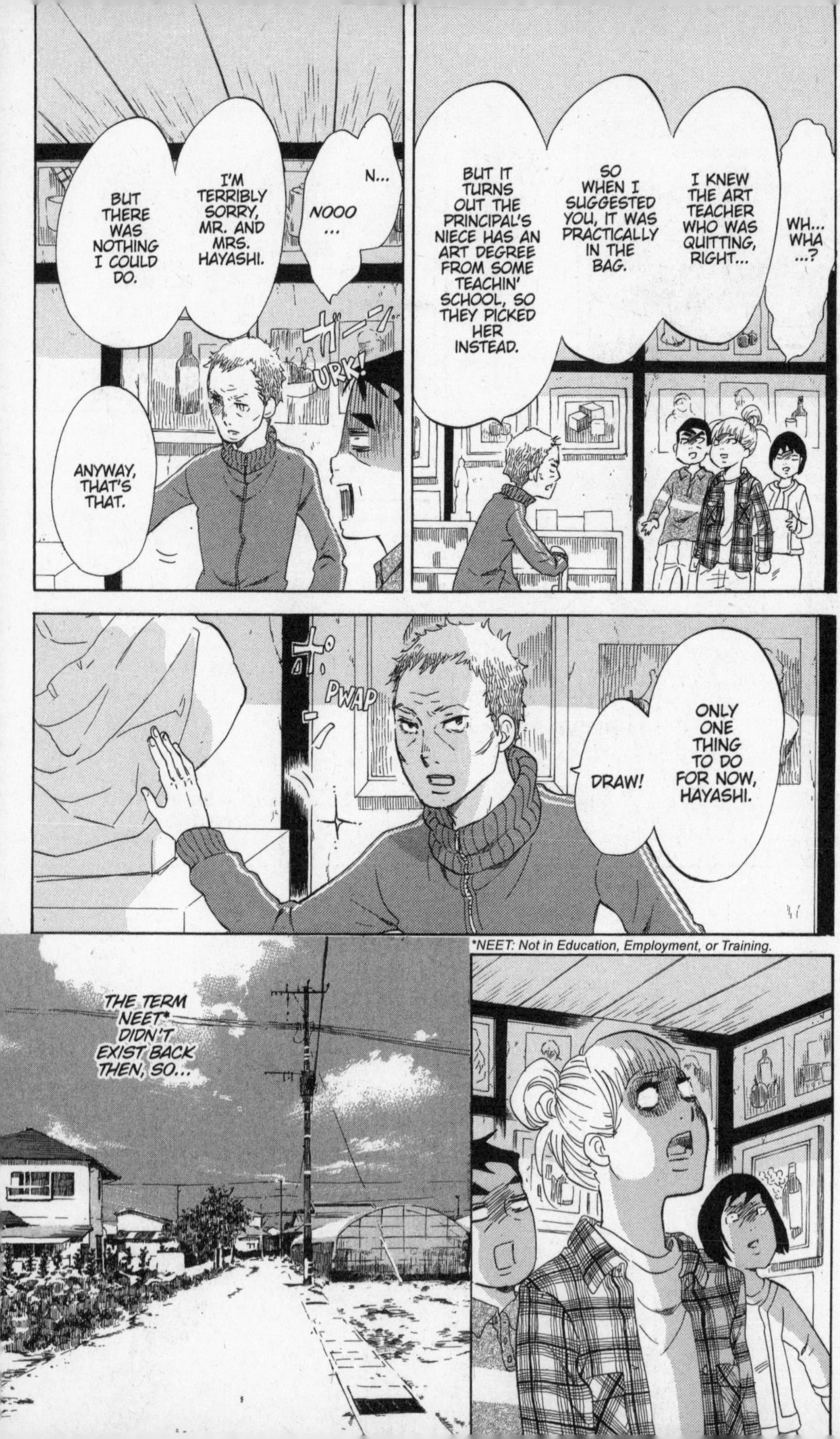
WH... WHA ...?
I KNEW THE ART TEACHER WHO WAS QUITTING, RIGHT...
SO WHEN I SUGGESTED YOU, IT WAS PRACTICALLY IN THE BAG.
BUT IT TURNS OUT THE PRINCIPAL'S NIECE HAS AN ART DEGREE FROM SOME TEACHIN' SCHOOL, SO THEY PICKED HER INSTEAD.
N... NOOO ...
I'M TERRIBLY SORRY, MR. AND MRS. HAYASHI.
BUT THERE WAS NOTHING I COULD DO.
URK!
ANYWAY, THAT'S THAT.
ONLY ONE THING TO DO FOR NOW, HAYASHI.
DRAW!
PWAP
THE TERM NEET* DIDN'T EXIST BACK THEN, SO...

*NEET: Not in Education, Employment, or Training.

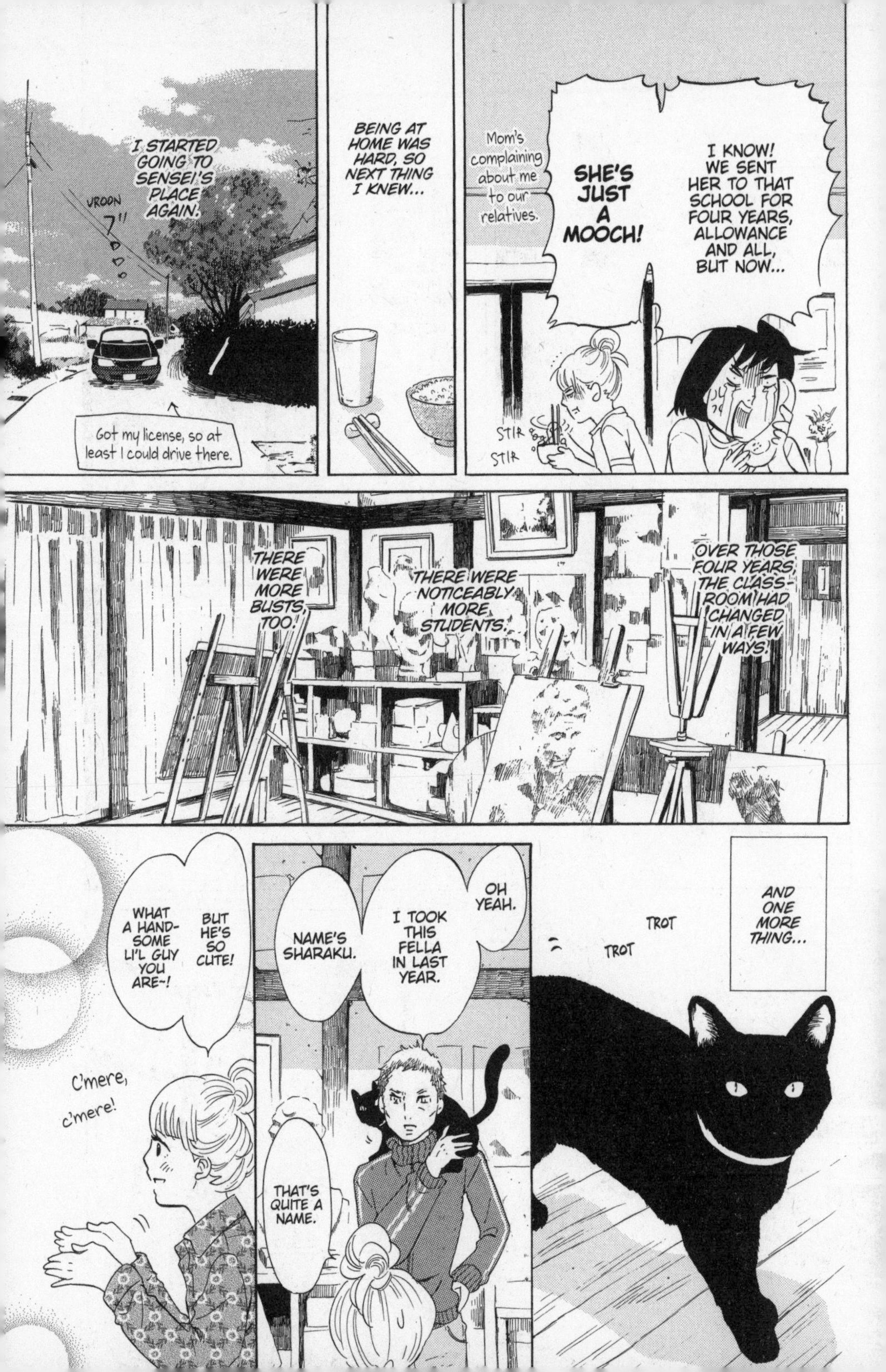
I KNOW! WE SENT HER TO THAT SCHOOL FOR FOUR YEARS, ALLOWANCE AND ALL, BUT NOW...
SHE'S JUST A MOOCH!
Mom's complaining about me to our relatives.
STIR
STIR
BEING AT HOME WAS HARD, SO NEXT THING I KNEW...
I STARTED GOING TO SENSEI'S PLACE AGAIN.
VROON
Got my license, so at least I could drive there.
OVER THOSE FOUR YEARS, THE CLASSROOM HAD CHANGED IN A FEW WAYS.
THERE WERE NOTICEABLY MORE STUDENTS.
THERE WERE MORE BUSTS, TOO.
AND ONE MORE THING...
TROT
TROT
OH YEAH.
I TOOK THIS FELLA IN LAST YEAR.
NAME'S SHARAKU.
THAT'S QUITE A NAME.
BUT HE'S SO CUTE!
WHAT A HANDSOME LI'L GUY YOU ARE~!
C'mere, c'mere!

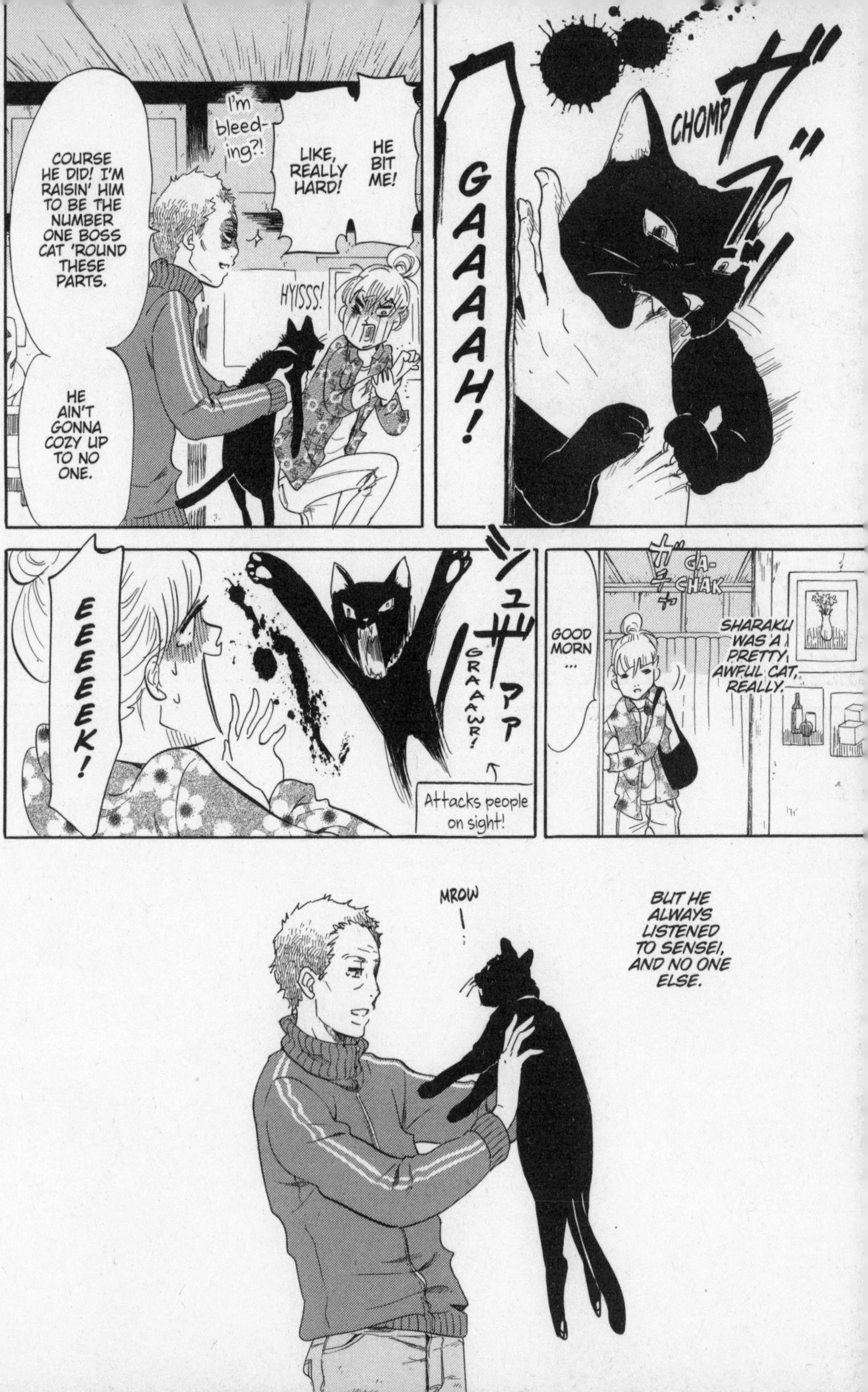
CHOMP
GAAAAAH!
HE BIT ME!
LIKE, REALLY HARD!
I'm bleed-ing?!
HYISSS!
COURSE HE DID! I'M RAISIN' HIM TO BE THE NUMBER ONE BOSS CAT 'ROUND THESE PARTS.
HE AIN'T GONNA COZY UP TO NO ONE.
SHARAKU WAS A PRETTY AWFUL CAT, REALLY.
GA-CHAK
GOOD MORN ...
GRAAAWR!
Attacks people on sight!
EEEEEEK!
BUT HE ALWAYS LISTENED TO SENSEI, AND NO ONE ELSE.
MROW!

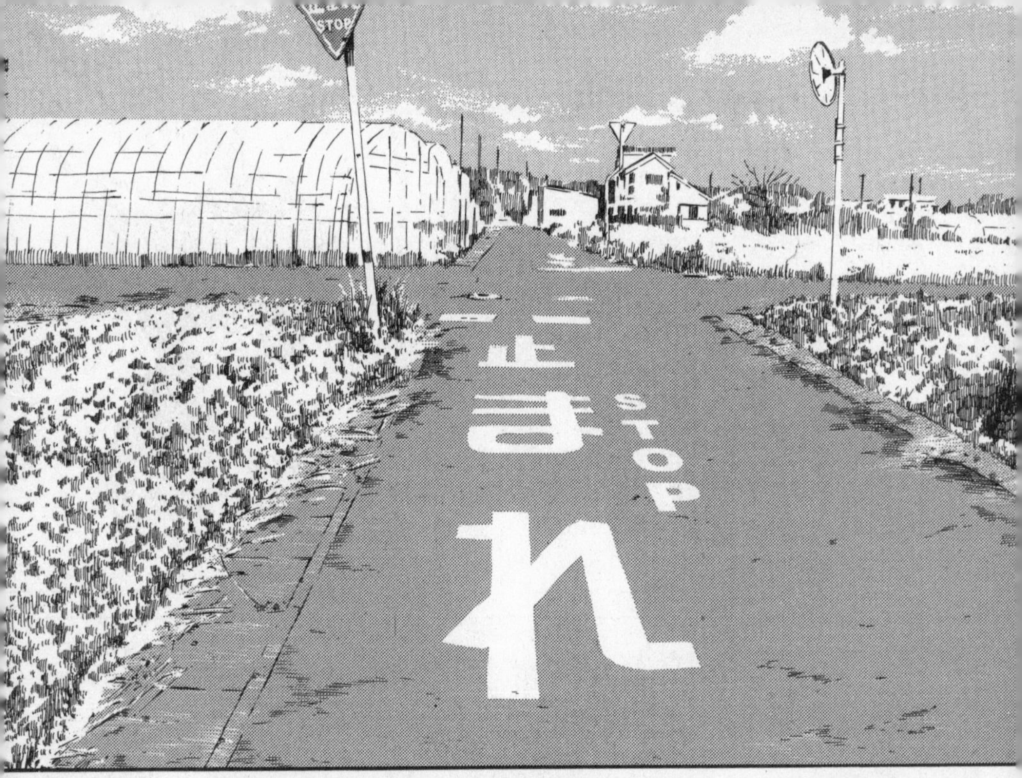
STOP
止まれ
STOP
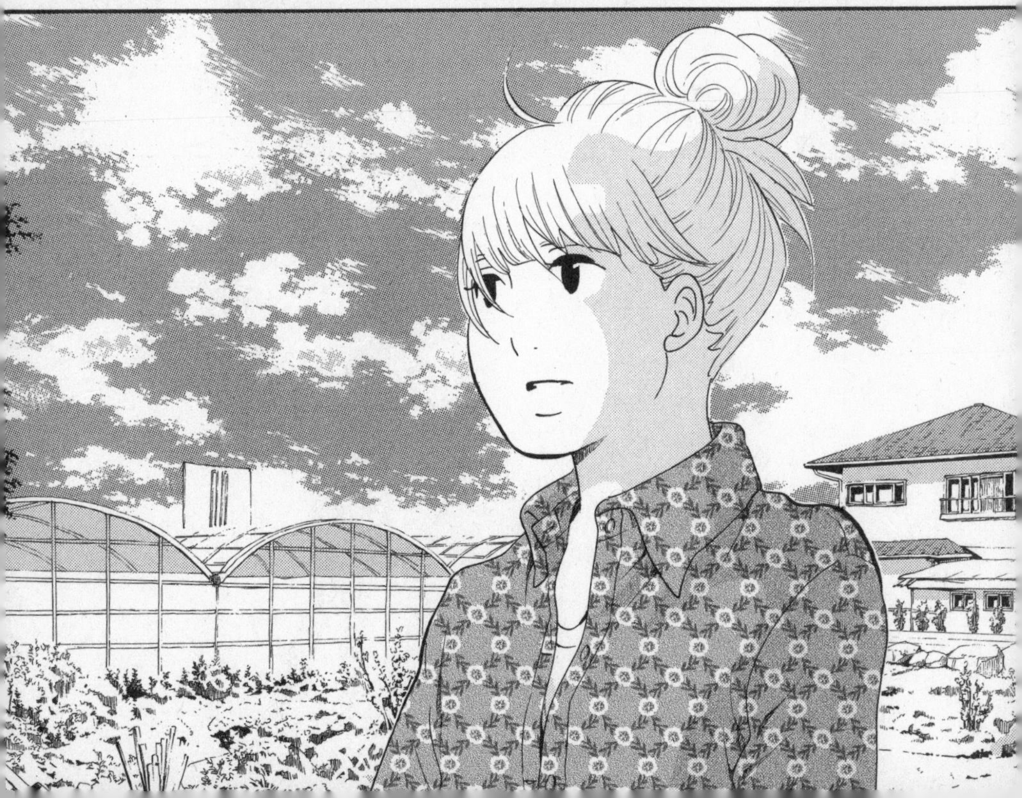

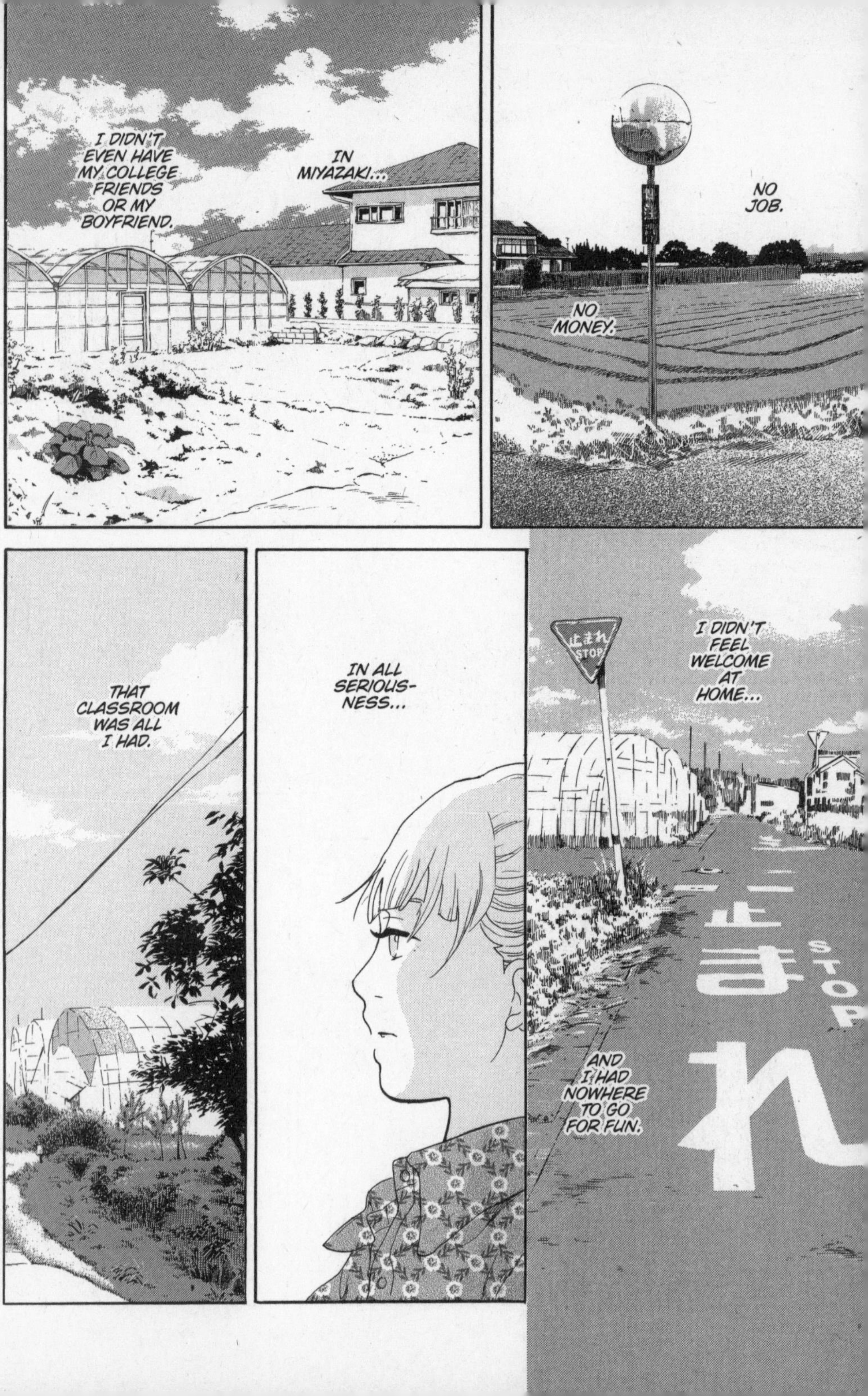
NO JOB.
NO MONEY.
IN MIYAZAKI...
I DIDN'T EVEN HAVE MY COLLEGE FRIENDS OR MY BOYFRIEND.
I DIDN'T FEEL WELCOME AT HOME...
止まれ STOP
STOP
止まれ
AND I HAD NOWHERE TO GO FOR FUN.
IN ALL SERIOUSNESS...
THAT CLASSROOM WAS ALL I HAD.

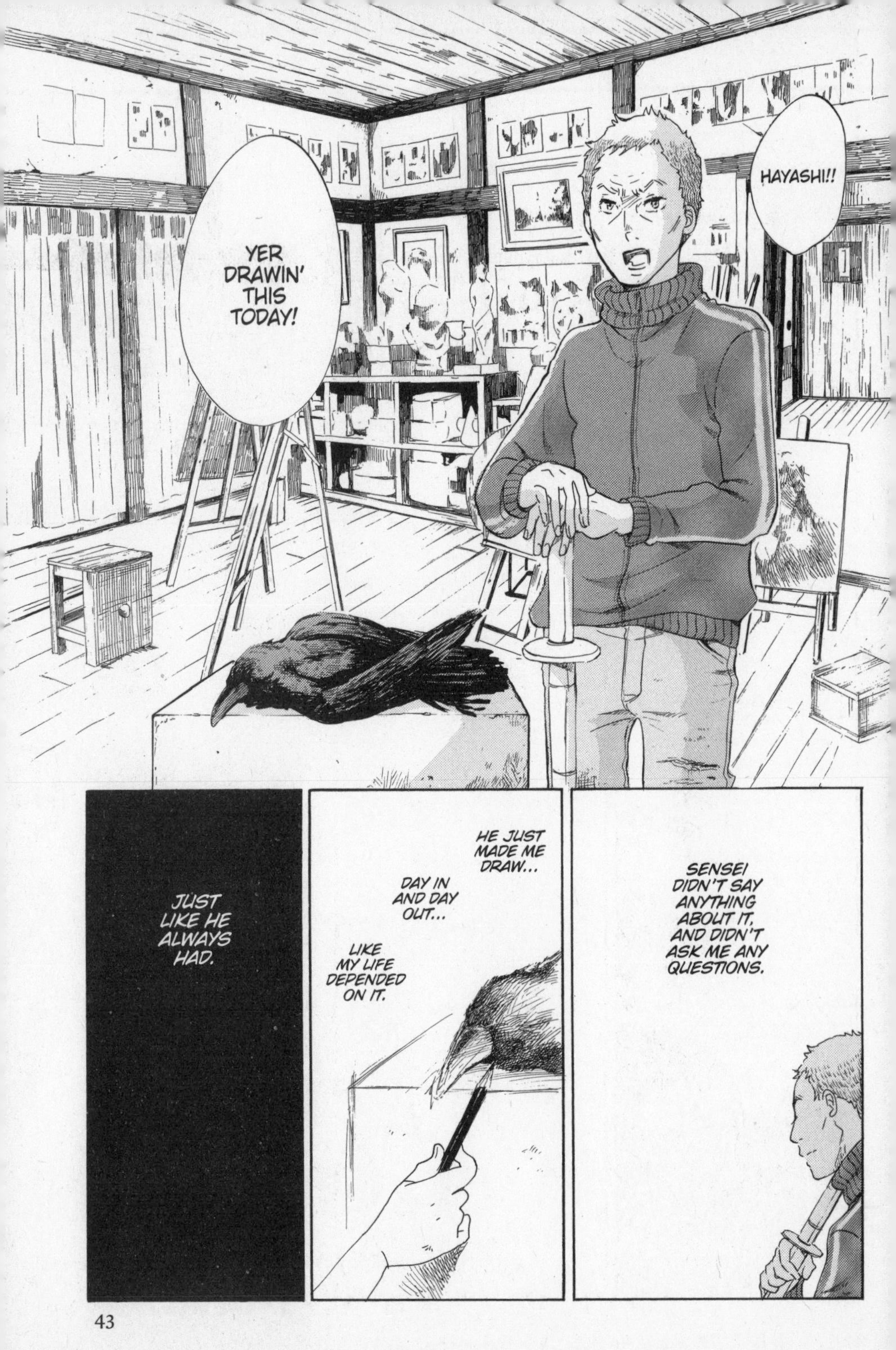
HAYASHI!!
YER DRAWIN' THIS TODAY!
SENSEI DIDN'T SAY ANYTHING ABOUT IT, AND DIDN'T ASK ME ANY QUESTIONS.
HE JUST MADE ME DRAW...
DAY IN AND DAY OUT...
LIKE MY LIFE DEPENDED ON IT.
JUST LIKE HE ALWAYS HAD.

Blank
Canvas
My So-Called
Artist's Journey

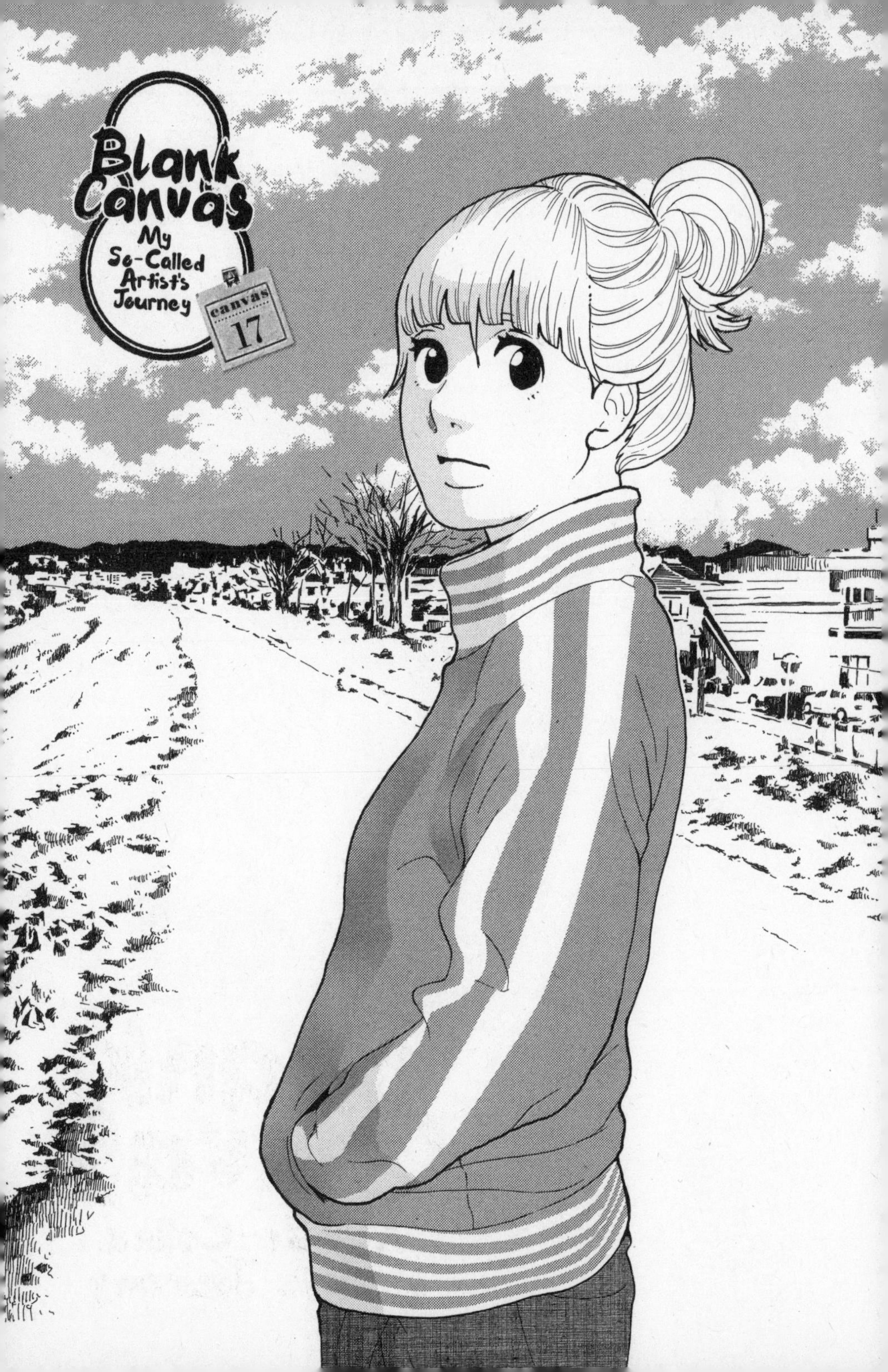
Blank Canvas
My So-Called Artist's Journey
canvas
17

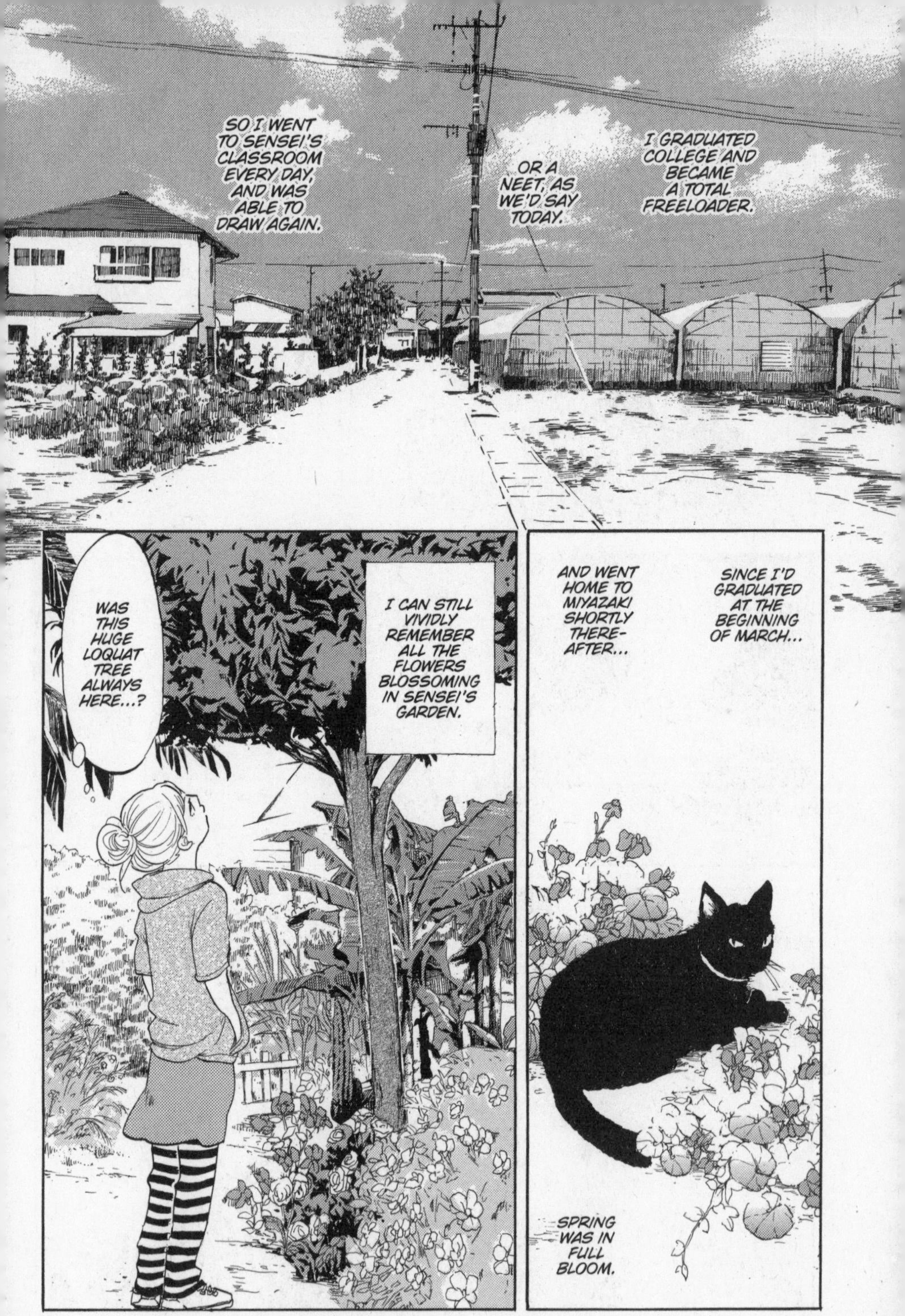
I GRADUATED COLLEGE AND BECAME A TOTAL FREELOADER.
OR A NEET, AS WE'D SAY TODAY.
SO I WENT TO SENSEI'S CLASSROOM EVERY DAY, AND WAS ABLE TO DRAW AGAIN.
SINCE I'D GRADUATED AT THE BEGINNING OF MARCH...
AND WENT HOME TO MIYAZAKI SHORTLY THERE-AFTER...
SPRING WAS IN FULL BLOOM.
I CAN STILL VIVIDLY REMEMBER ALL THE FLOWERS BLOSSOMING IN SENSEI'S GARDEN.
WAS THIS HUGE LOQUAT TREE ALWAYS HERE...?

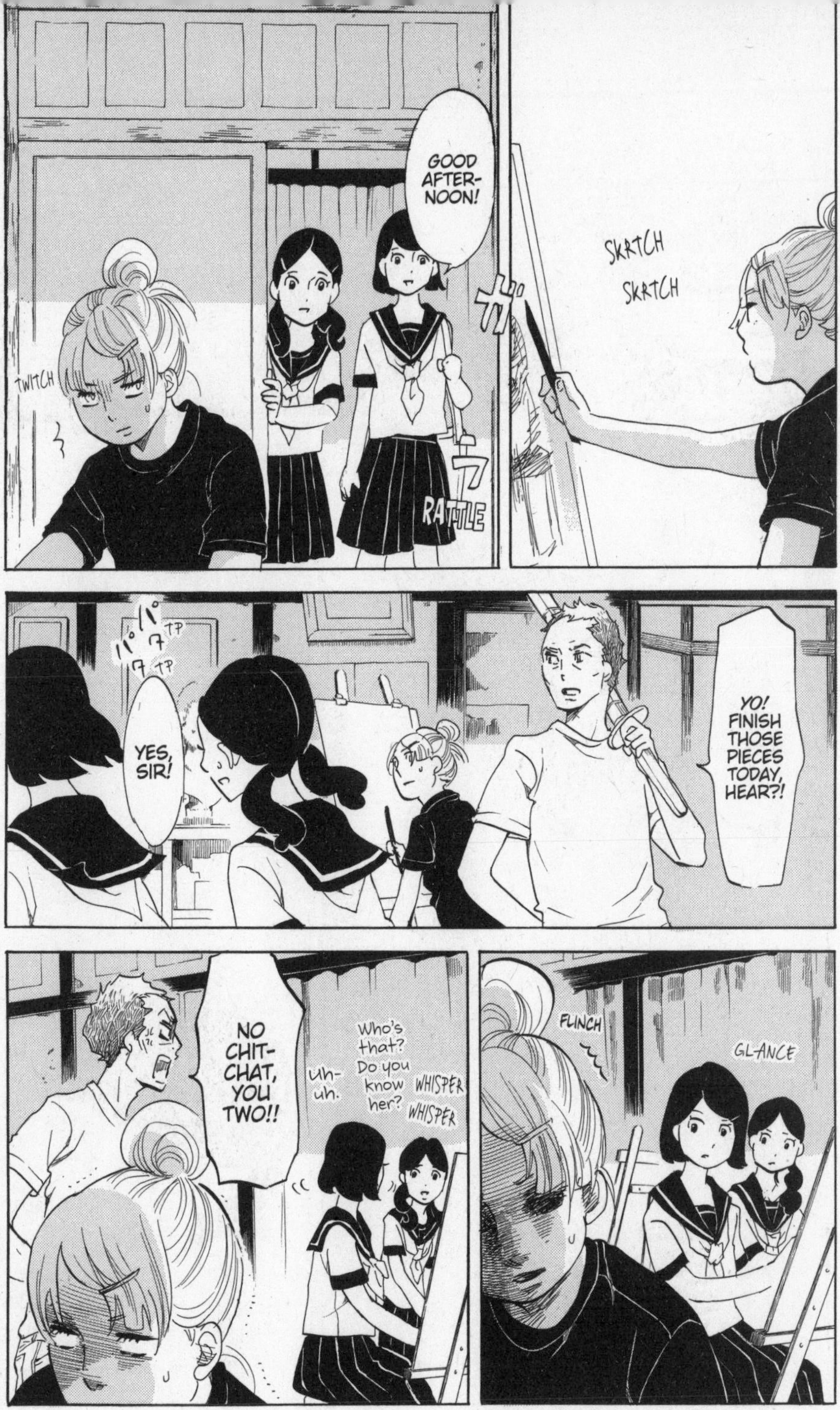
SKRTCH
SKRTCH
GOOD AFTER-NOON!
RATTLE
TWITCH
YO! FINISH THOSE PIECES TODAY, HEAR?!
YES, SIR!
TP
TP
GLANCE
FLINCH
NO CHIT-CHAT, YOU TWO!!
Who's that? Do you know her?
WHISPER
WHISPER
uh-uh.

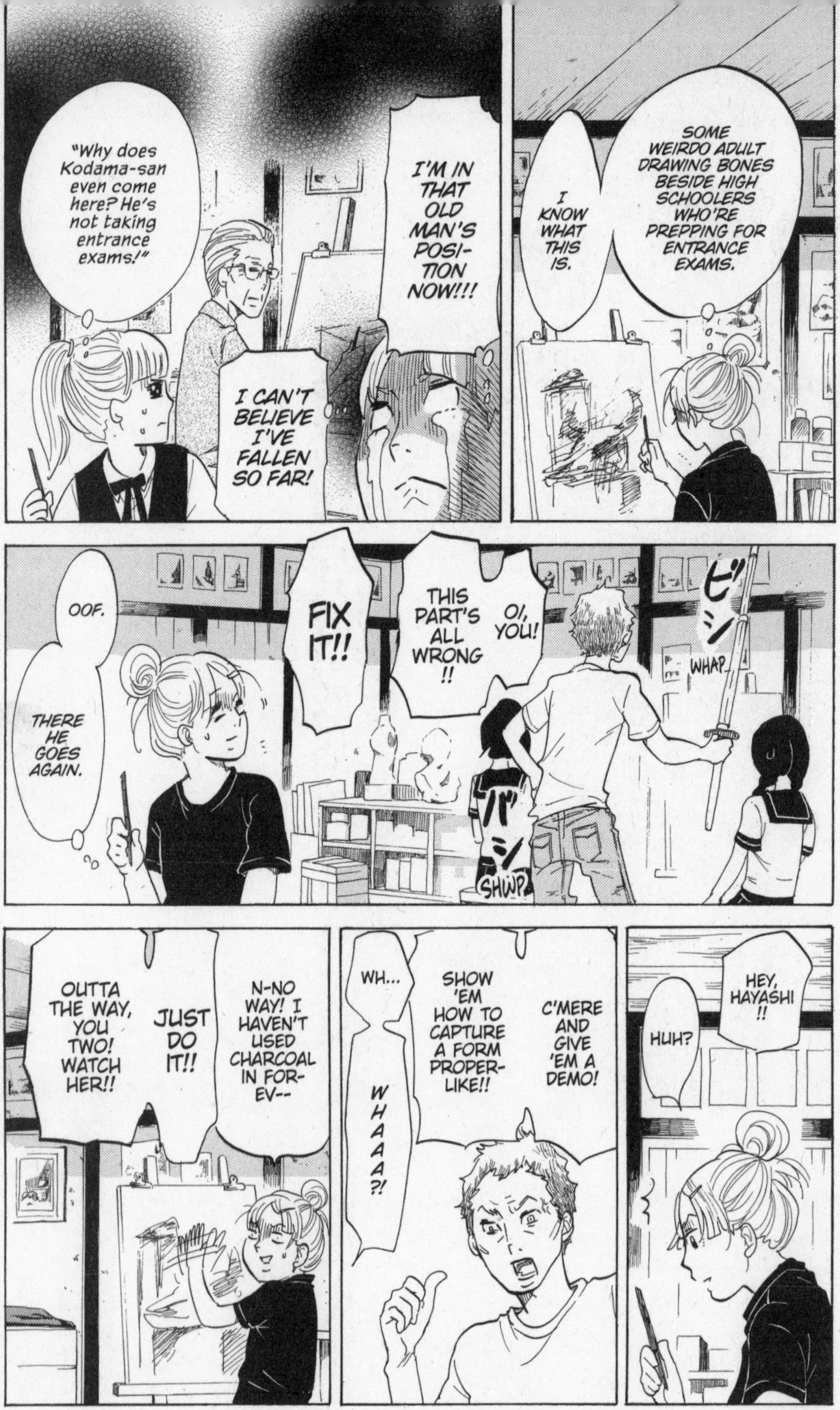
SOME WEIRDO ADULT DRAWING BONES BESIDE HIGH SCHOOLERS WHO'RE PREPPING FOR ENTRANCE EXAMS.
I KNOW WHAT THIS IS.
I'M IN THAT OLD MAN'S POSI-TION NOW!!!
"Why does Kodama-san even come here? He's not taking entrance exams!"
I CAN'T BELIEVE I'VE FALLEN SO FAR!
ビシ
WHAP
OI, YOU!
THIS PART'S ALL WRONG !!
FIX IT!!
OOF.
THERE HE GOES AGAIN.
バシ
SHWP
HEY, HAYASHI !!
HUH?
C'MERE AND GIVE 'EM A DEMO!
SHOW 'EM HOW TO CAPTURE A FORM PROPER-LIKE!!
WH...
WHAAAA?!
N-NO WAY! I HAVEN'T USED CHARCOAL IN FOR-EV--
JUST DO IT!!
OUTTA THE WAY, YOU TWO! WATCH HER!!

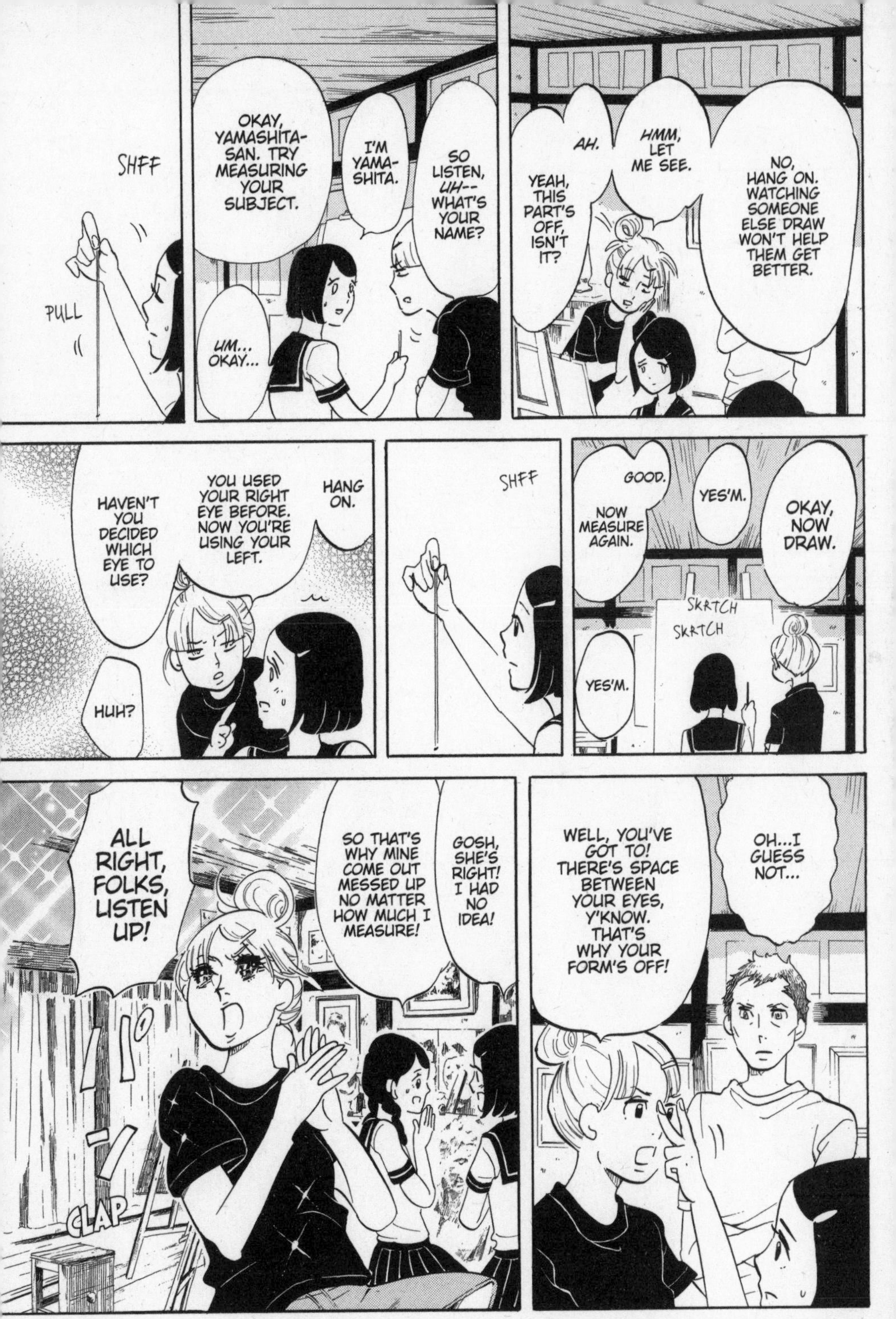
NO, HANG ON. WATCHING SOMEONE ELSE DRAW WON'T HELP THEM GET BETTER.
HMM, LET ME SEE.
AH.
YEAH, THIS PART'S OFF, ISN'T IT?
SO LISTEN, UH-- WHAT'S YOUR NAME?
I'M YAMA-SHITA.
OKAY, YAMASHITA-SAN. TRY MEASURING YOUR SUBJECT.
UM... OKAY...
SHFF
PULL
OKAY, NOW DRAW.
YES'M.
GOOD.
NOW MEASURE AGAIN.
SKRTCH
SKRTCH
YES'M.
SHFF
HANG ON.
YOU USED YOUR RIGHT EYE BEFORE. NOW YOU'RE USING YOUR LEFT.
HAVEN'T YOU DECIDED WHICH EYE TO USE?
HUH?
OH...I GUESS NOT...
WELL, YOU'VE GOT TO! THERE'S SPACE BETWEEN YOUR EYES, Y'KNOW. THAT'S WHY YOUR FORM'S OFF!
GOSH, SHE'S RIGHT! I HAD NO IDEA!
SO THAT'S WHY MINE COME OUT MESSED UP NO MATTER HOW MUCH I MEASURE!
ALL RIGHT, FOLKS, LISTEN UP!
CLAP

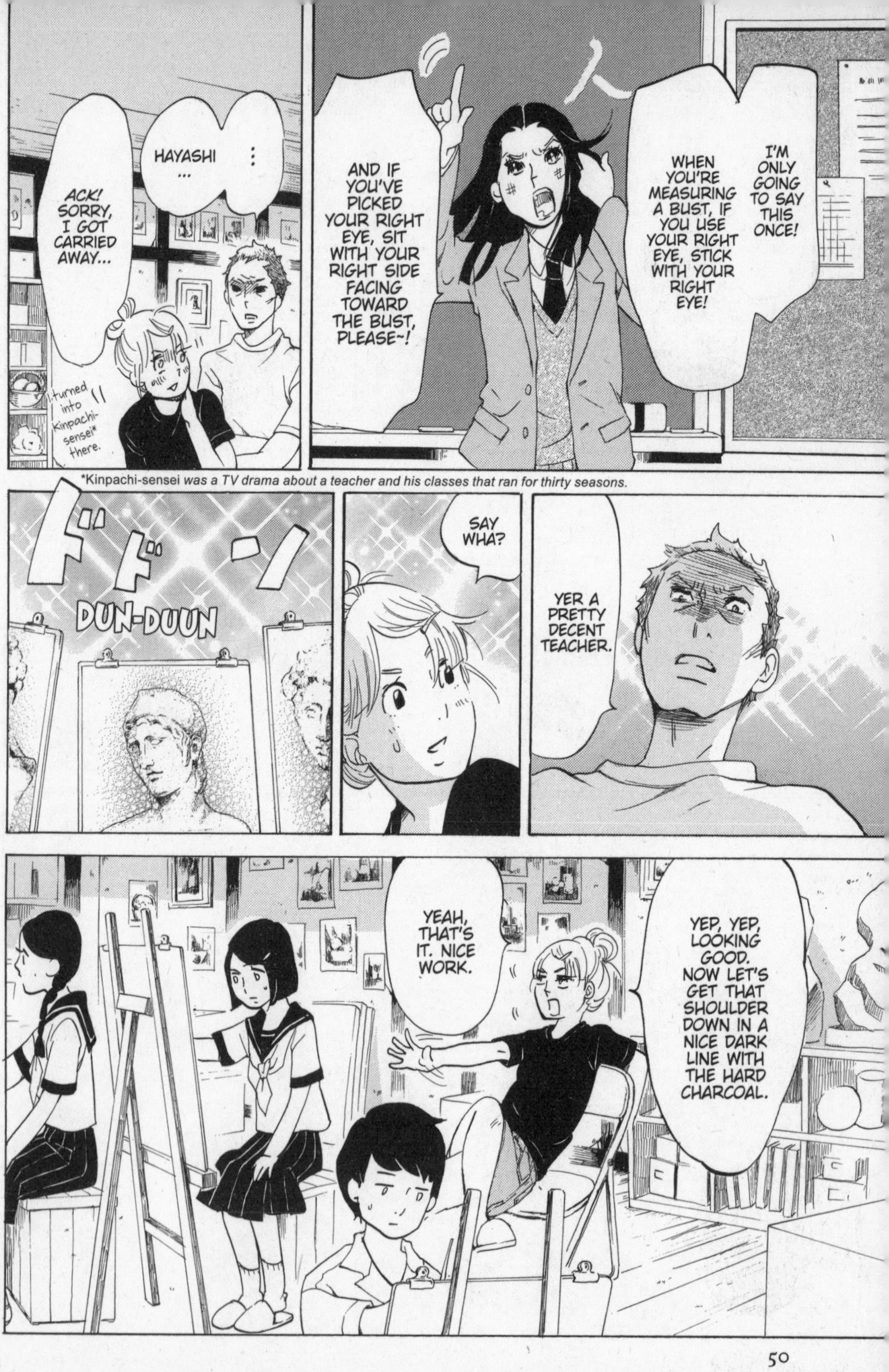
I'M ONLY GOING TO SAY THIS ONCE!
WHEN YOU'RE MEASURING A BUST, IF YOU USE YOUR RIGHT EYE, STICK WITH YOUR RIGHT EYE!
AND IF YOU'VE PICKED YOUR RIGHT EYE, SIT WITH YOUR RIGHT SIDE FACING TOWARD THE BUST, PLEASE~!
HAYASHI ...
...
ACK! SORRY, I GOT CARRIED AWAY...
I turned into Kinpachi-sensei* there.
*Kinpachi-sensei was a TV drama about a teacher and his classes that ran for thirty seasons.
YER A PRETTY DECENT TEACHER.
SAY WHA?
ドドーン
DUN-DUUN
YEP, YEP, LOOKING GOOD. NOW LET'S GET THAT SHOULDER DOWN IN A NICE DARK LINE WITH THE HARD CHARCOAL.
YEAH, THAT'S IT. NICE WORK.

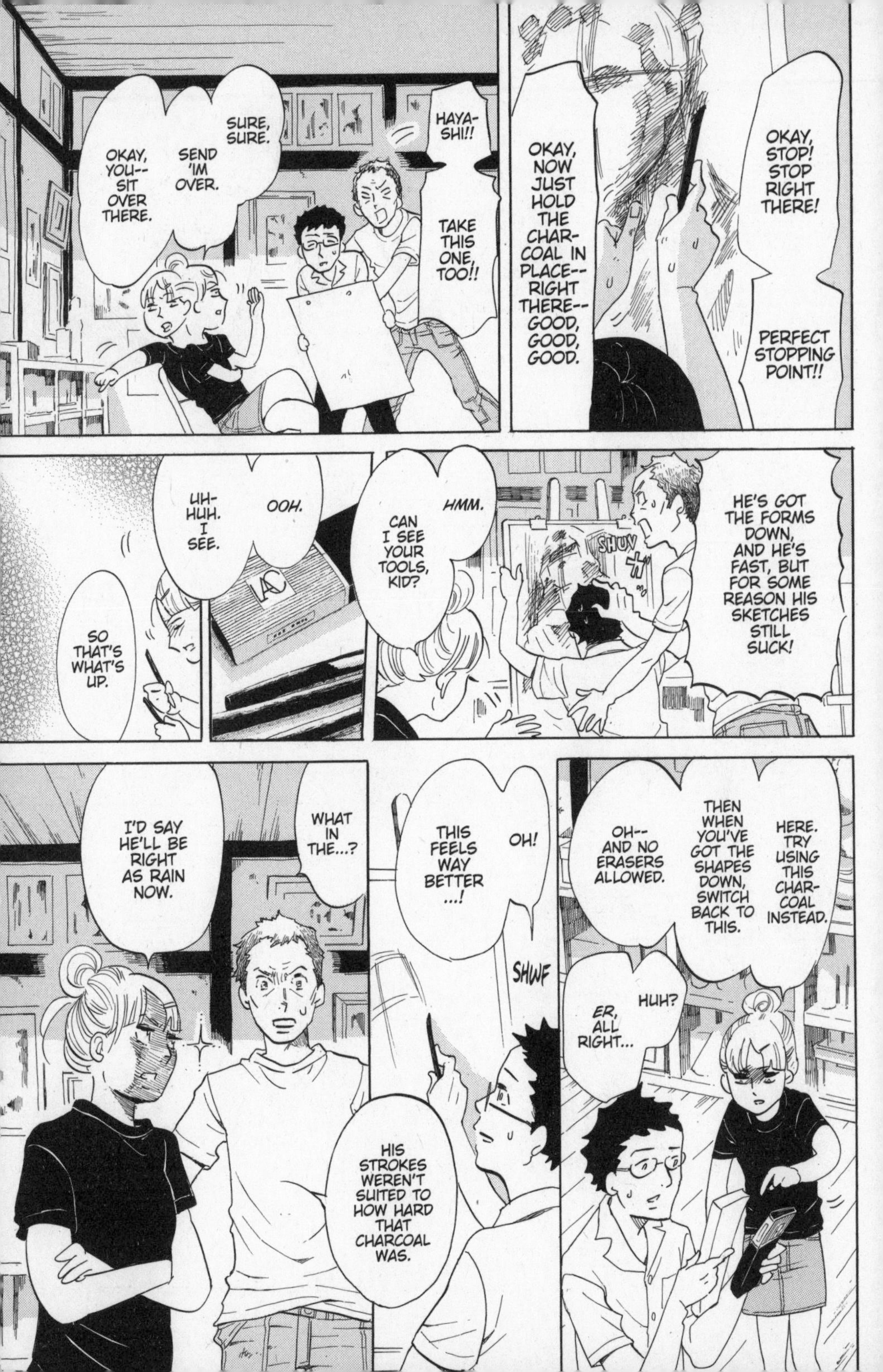
OKAY, NOW JUST HOLD THE CHARCOAL IN PLACE-- RIGHT THERE-- GOOD, GOOD, GOOD.
OKAY, STOP! STOP RIGHT THERE!
PERFECT STOPPING POINT!!
HAYA-SHI!!
TAKE THIS ONE TOO!!
SURE, SURE. SEND 'IM OVER.
OKAY, YOU-- SIT OVER THERE.
HE'S GOT THE FORMS DOWN, AND HE'S FAST, BUT FOR SOME REASON HIS SKETCHES STILL SUCK!
SHUV
HMM.
CAN I SEE YOUR TOOLS, KID?
OOH.
UH-HUH. I SEE.
SO THAT'S WHAT'S UP.
HERE. TRY USING THIS CHARCOAL INSTEAD.
THEN WHEN YOU'VE GOT THE SHAPES DOWN, SWITCH BACK TO THIS.
OH-- AND NO ERASERS ALLOWED.
HUH?
ER, ALL RIGHT...
SHWF
OH!
THIS FEELS WAY BETTER ...!
WHAT IN THE...?
I'D SAY HE'LL BE RIGHT AS RAIN NOW.
HIS STROKES WEREN'T SUITED TO HOW HARD THAT CHARCOAL WAS.

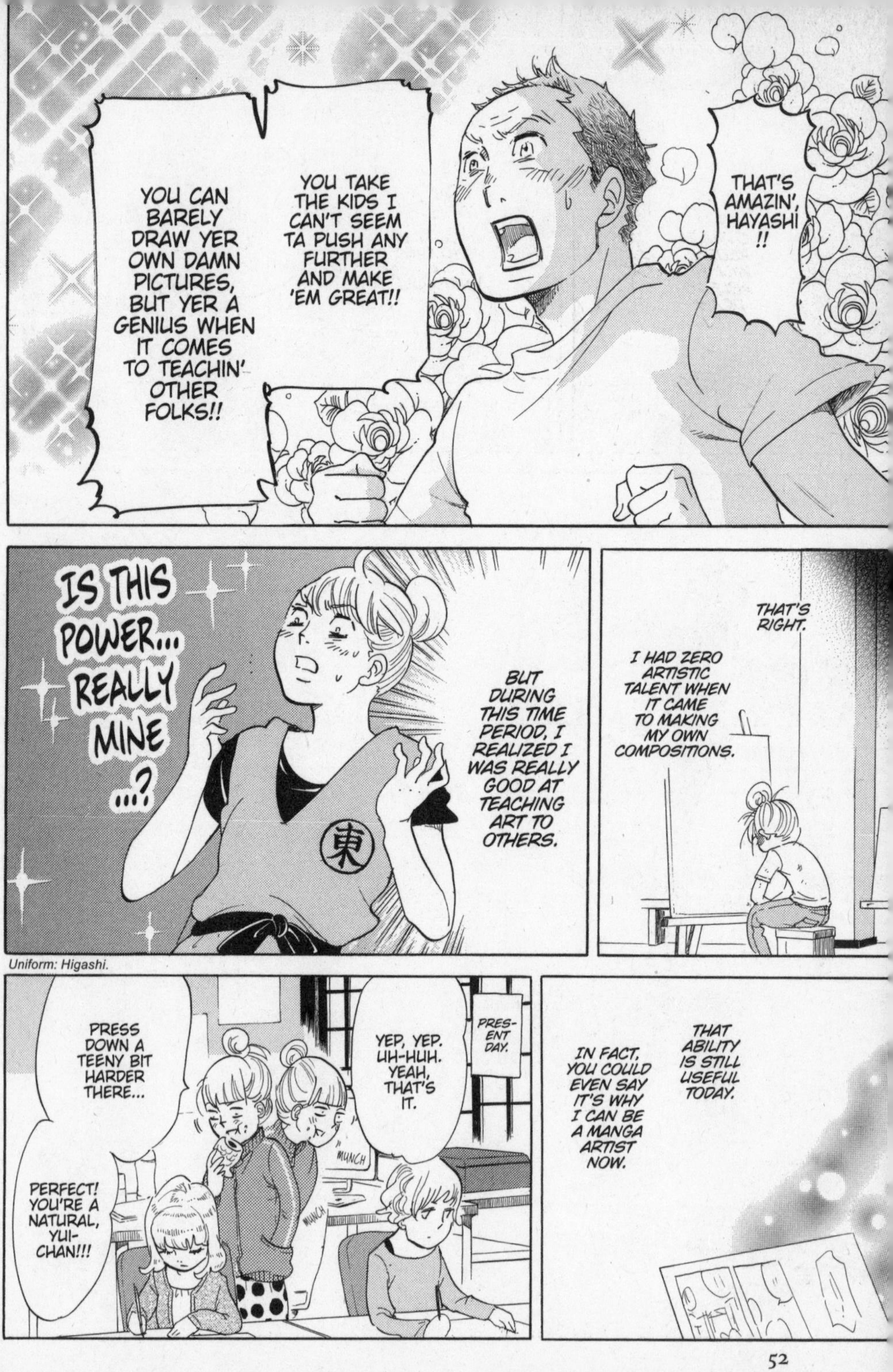
THAT'S AMAZIN', HAYASHI!!
YOU TAKE THE KIDS I CAN'T SEEM TA PUSH ANY FURTHER AND MAKE 'EM GREAT!!
YOU CAN BARELY DRAW YER OWN DAMN PICTURES, BUT YER A GENIUS WHEN IT COMES TO TEACHIN' OTHER FOLKS!!
THAT'S RIGHT.
I HAD ZERO ARTISTIC TALENT WHEN IT CAME TO MAKING MY OWN COMPOSITIONS.
BUT DURING THIS TIME PERIOD, I REALIZED I WAS REALLY GOOD AT TEACHING ART TO OTHERS.
IS THIS POWER... REALLY MINE ...?
THAT ABILITY IS STILL USEFUL TODAY.
IN FACT, YOU COULD EVEN SAY IT'S WHY I CAN BE A MANGA ARTIST NOW.
PRESENT DAY.
YEP, YEP. UH-HUH. YEAH, THAT'S IT.
PRESS DOWN A TEENY BIT HARDER THERE...
MUNCH
MUNCH
PERFECT! YOU'RE A NATURAL, YUI-CHAN!!!
Uniform: Higashi.

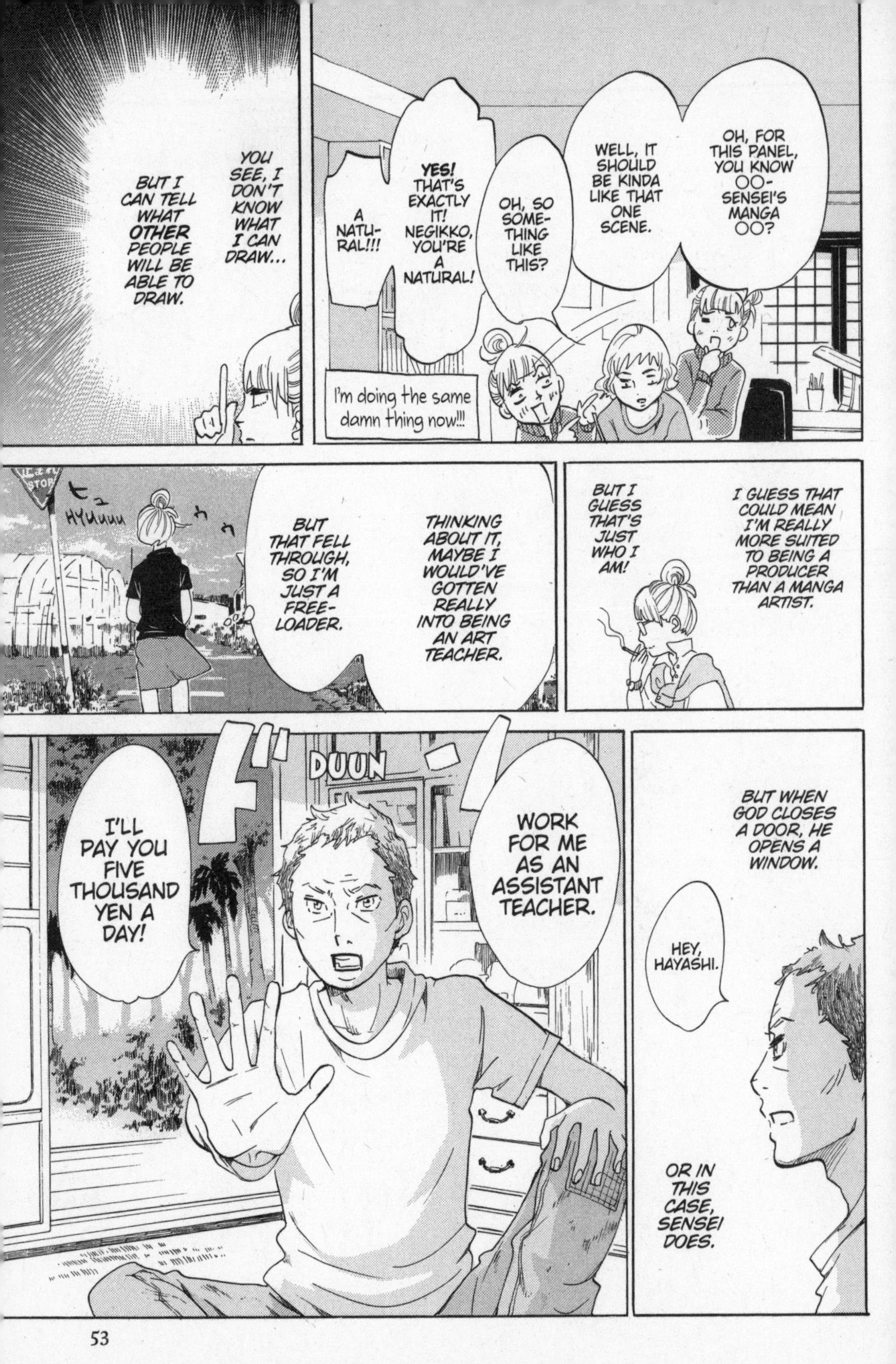
OH, FOR THIS PANEL, YOU KNOW ○○-SENSEI'S MANGA ○○?
WELL, IT SHOULD BE KINDA LIKE THAT ONE SCENE.
OH, SO SOMETHING LIKE THIS?
YES! THAT'S EXACTLY IT! NEGIKKO, YOU'RE A NATURAL!
A NATURAL!!!
I'm doing the same damn thing now!!!
YOU SEE, I DON'T KNOW WHAT I CAN DRAW...
BUT I CAN TELL WHAT OTHER PEOPLE WILL BE ABLE TO DRAW.
I GUESS THAT COULD MEAN I'M REALLY MORE SUITED TO BEING A PRODUCER THAN A MANGA ARTIST.
BUT I GUESS THAT'S JUST WHO I AM!
THINKING ABOUT IT, MAYBE I WOULD'VE GOTTEN REALLY INTO BEING AN ART TEACHER.
BUT THAT FELL THROUGH, SO I'M JUST A FREELOADER.
HYuuuu
STOP
BUT WHEN GOD CLOSES A DOOR, HE OPENS A WINDOW.
HEY, HAYASHI.
OR IN THIS CASE, SENSEI DOES.
DUUN
WORK FOR ME AS AN ASSISTANT TEACHER.
I'LL PAY YOU FIVE THOUSAND YEN A DAY!

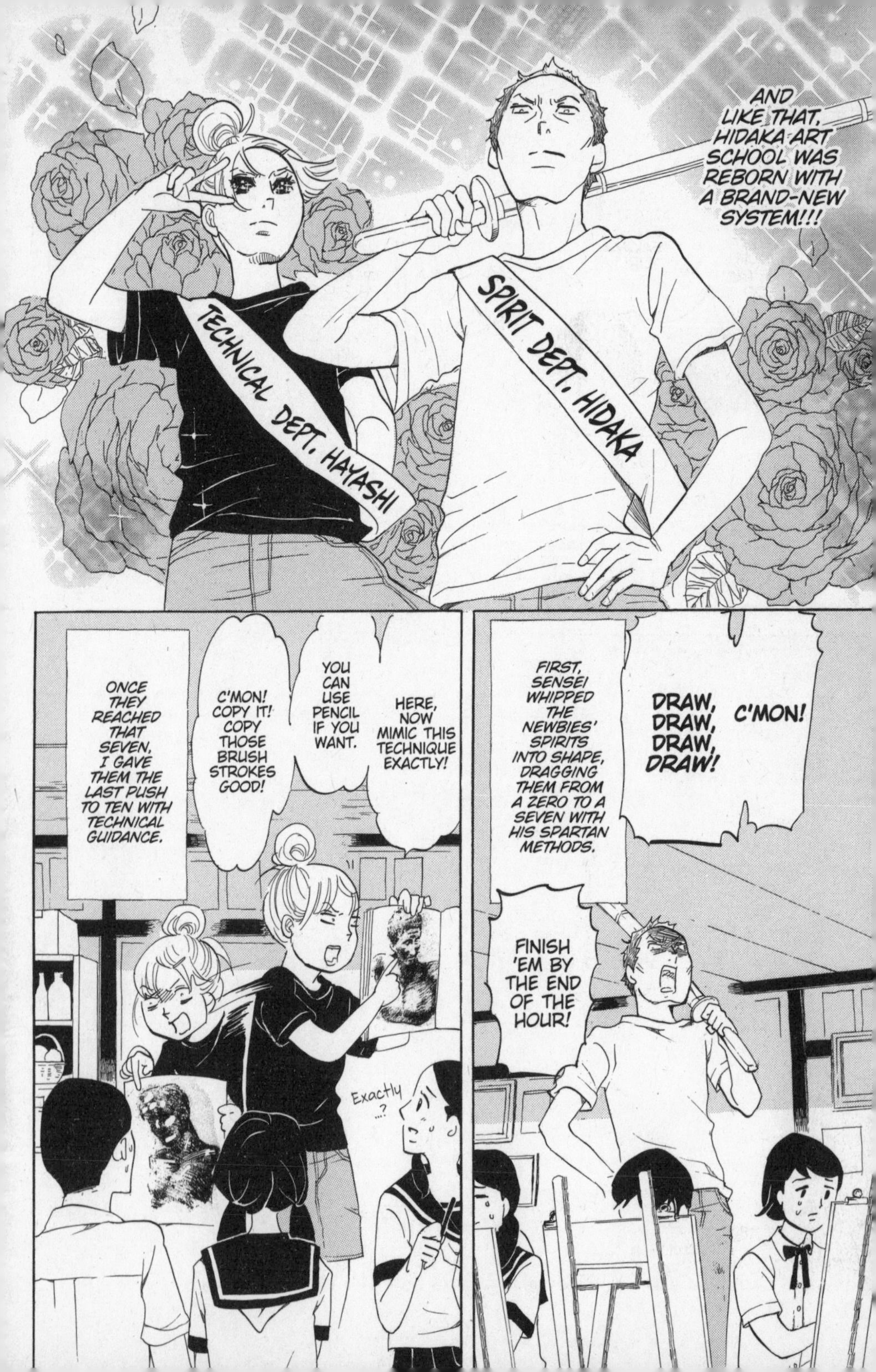
AND LIKE THAT, HIDAKA ART SCHOOL WAS REBORN WITH A BRAND-NEW SYSTEM!!!
SPIRIT DEPT. HIDAKA
TECHNICAL DEPT. HAYASHI
C'MON!
DRAW, DRAW, DRAW, DRAW!
FIRST, SENSEI WHIPPED THE NEWBIES' SPIRITS INTO SHAPE, DRAGGING THEM FROM A ZERO TO A SEVEN WITH HIS SPARTAN METHODS.
FINISH 'EM BY THE END OF THE HOUR!
HERE, NOW MIMIC THIS TECHNIQUE EXACTLY!
YOU CAN USE PENCIL IF YOU WANT.
C'MON! COPY IT! COPY THOSE BRUSH STROKES GOOD!
ONCE THEY REACHED THAT SEVEN, I GAVE THEM THE LAST PUSH TO TEN WITH TECHNICAL GUIDANCE.
Exactly ...?

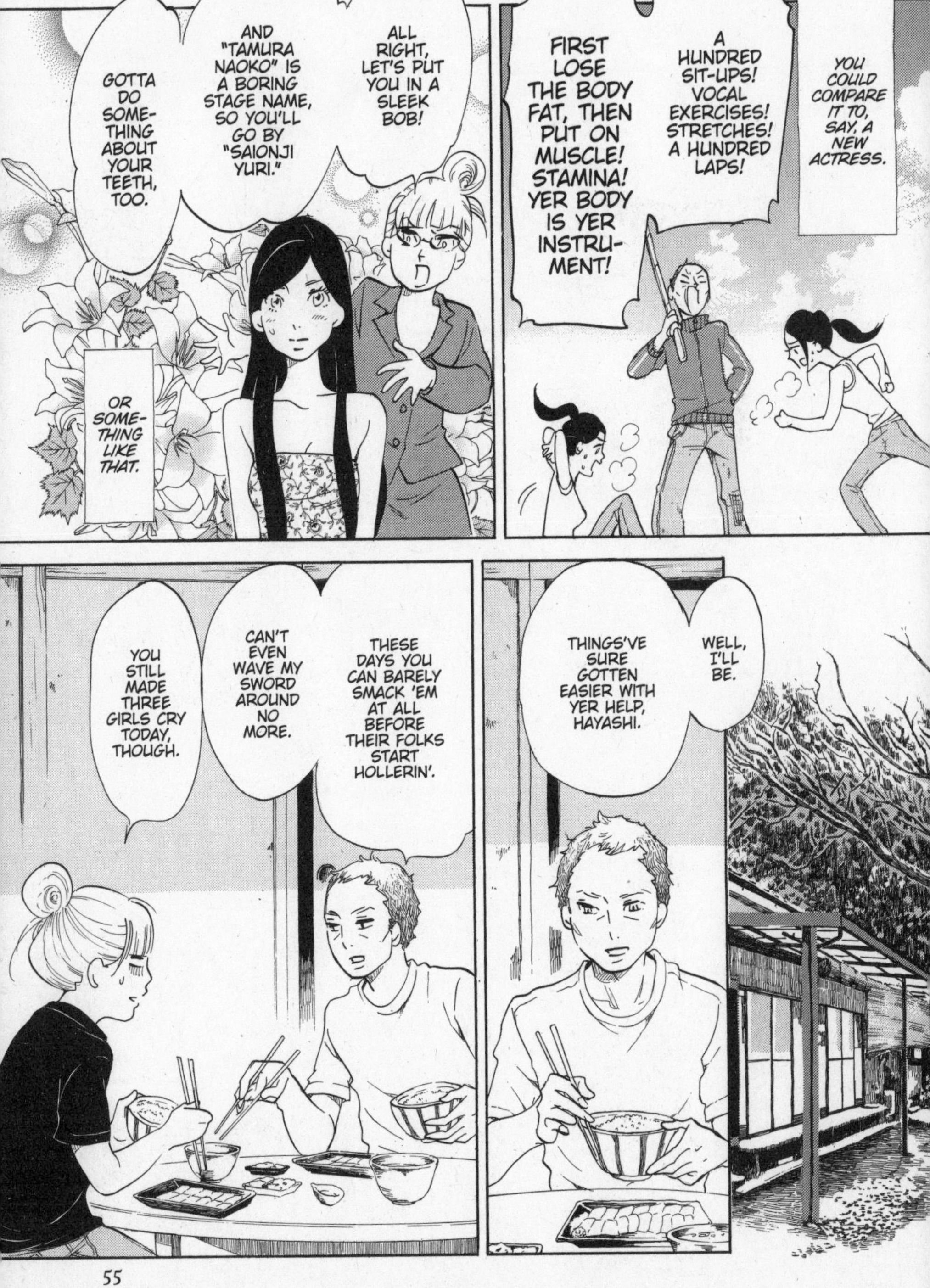
YOU COULD COMPARE IT TO, SAY, A NEW ACTRESS.
A HUNDRED SIT-UPS! VOCAL EXERCISES! STRETCHES! A HUNDRED LAPS!
FIRST LOSE THE BODY FAT, THEN PUT ON MUSCLE! STAMINA! YER BODY IS YER INSTRUMENT!
ALL RIGHT, LET'S PUT YOU IN A SLEEK BOB!
AND "TAMURA NAOKO" IS A BORING STAGE NAME, SO YOU'LL GO BY "SAIONJI YURI."
GOTTA DO SOMETHING ABOUT YOUR TEETH, TOO.
OR SOMETHING LIKE THAT.
WELL, I'LL BE.
THINGS'VE SURE GOTTEN EASIER WITH YER HELP, HAYASHI.
THESE DAYS YOU CAN BARELY SMACK 'EM AT ALL BEFORE THEIR FOLKS START HOLLERIN'.
CAN'T EVEN WAVE MY SWORD AROUND NO MORE.
YOU STILL MADE THREE GIRLS CRY TODAY, THOUGH.

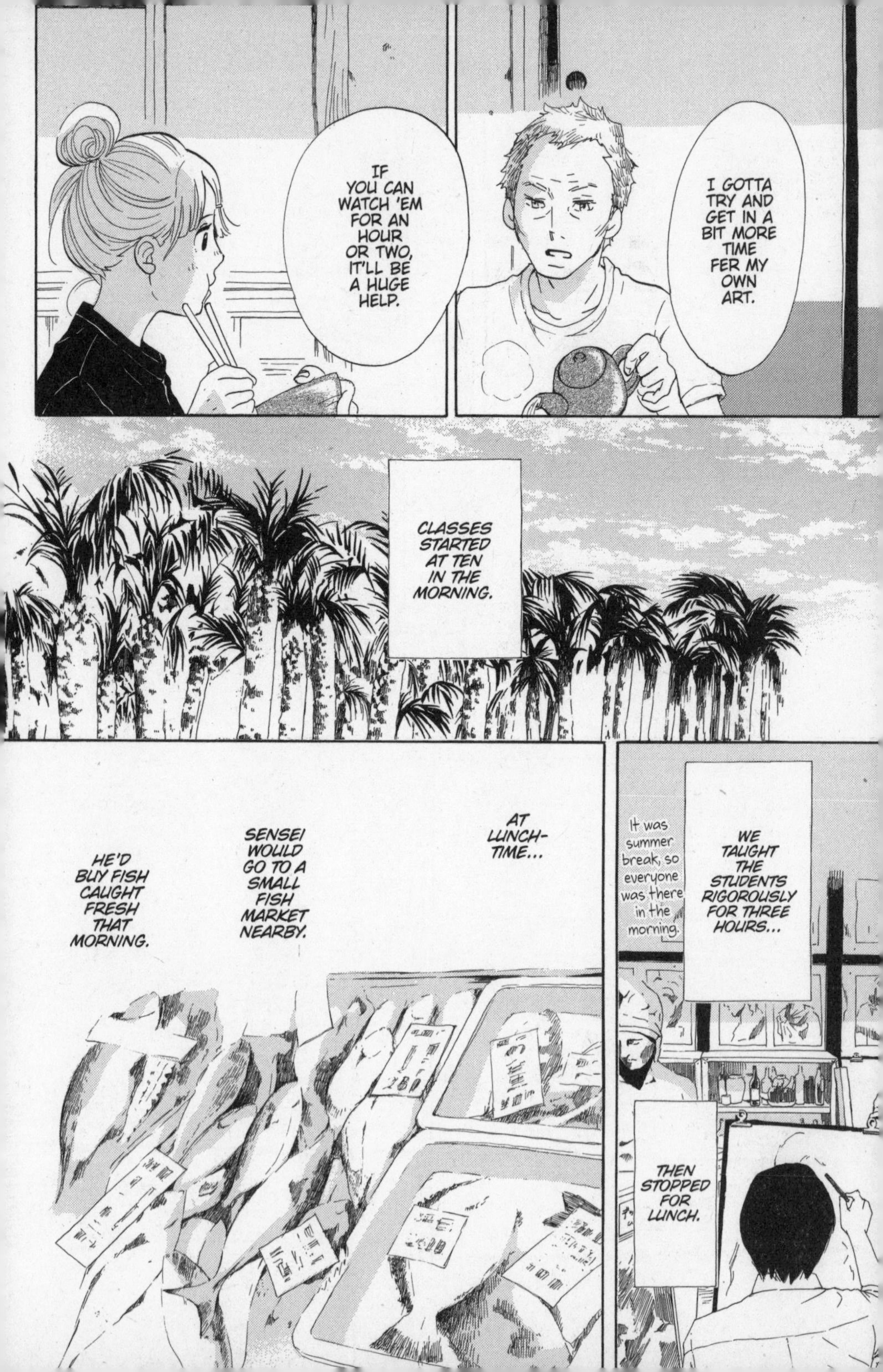
I GOTTA TRY AND GET IN A BIT MORE TIME FER MY OWN ART.
IF YOU CAN WATCH 'EM FOR AN HOUR OR TWO, IT'LL BE A HUGE HELP.
CLASSES STARTED AT TEN IN THE MORNING.
WE TAUGHT THE STUDENTS RIGOROUSLY FOR THREE HOURS...
It was summer break, so everyone was there in the morning.
THEN STOPPED FOR LUNCH.
AT LUNCH-TIME...
SENSEI WOULD GO TO A SMALL FISH MARKET NEARBY.
HE'D BUY FISH CAUGHT FRESH THAT MORNING.

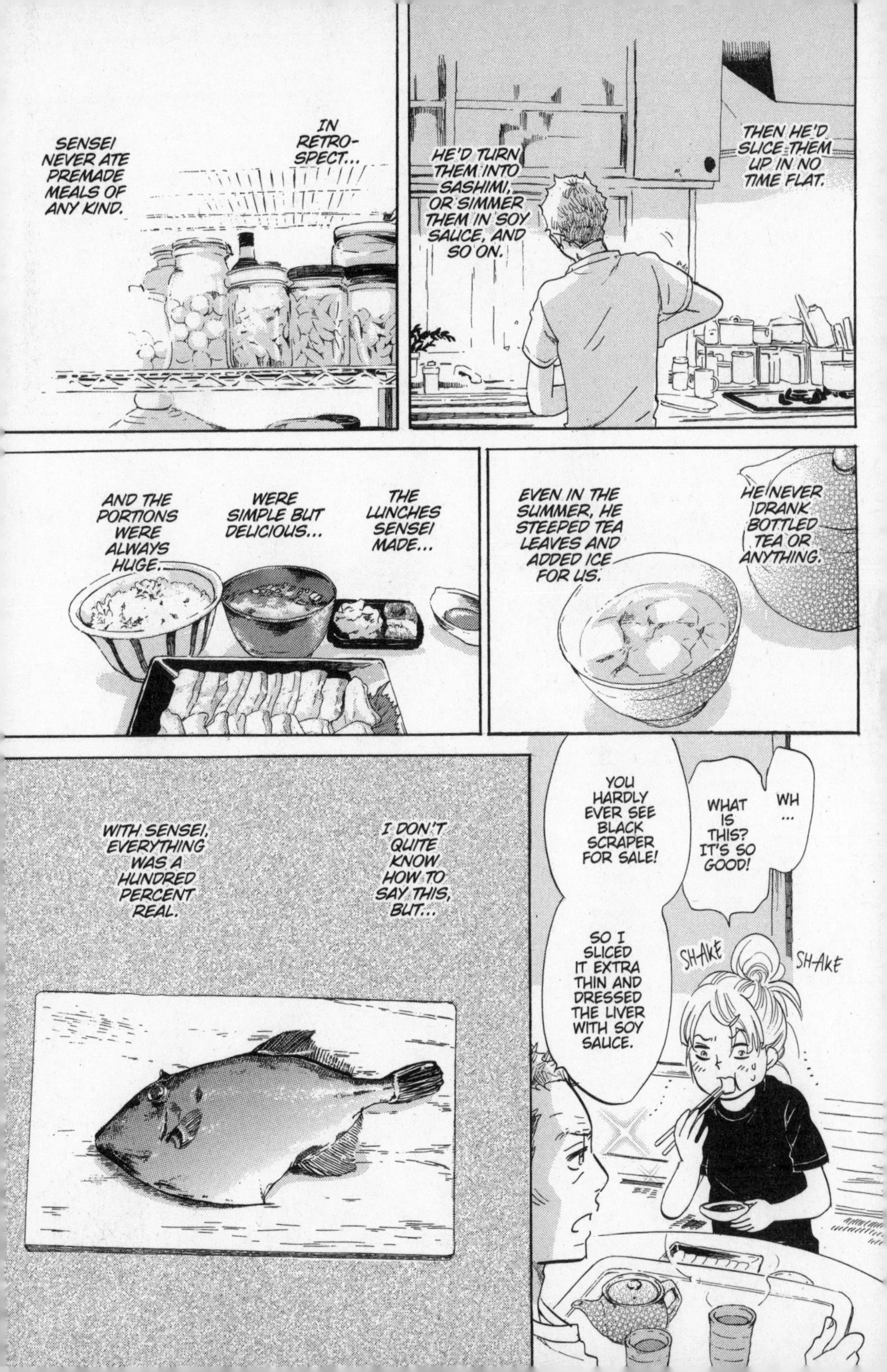
THEN HE'D SLICE THEM UP IN NO TIME FLAT.
HE'D TURN THEM INTO SASHIMI, OR SIMMER THEM IN SOY SAUCE, AND SO ON.
IN RETROSPECT...
SENSEI NEVER ATE PREMADE MEALS OF ANY KIND.
HE NEVER DRANK BOTTLED TEA OR ANYTHING.
EVEN IN THE SUMMER, HE STEEPED TEA LEAVES AND ADDED ICE FOR US.
THE LUNCHES SENSEI MADE...
WERE SIMPLE BUT DELICIOUS...
AND THE PORTIONS WERE ALWAYS HUGE.
WH...
WHAT IS THIS? IT'S SO GOOD!
YOU HARDLY EVER SEE BLACK SCRAPER FOR SALE!
SH-AKE
SH-AKE
SO I SLICED IT EXTRA THIN AND DRESSED THE LIVER WITH SOY SAUCE.
I DON'T QUITE KNOW HOW TO SAY THIS, BUT...
WITH SENSEI, EVERYTHING WAS A HUNDRED PERCENT REAL.

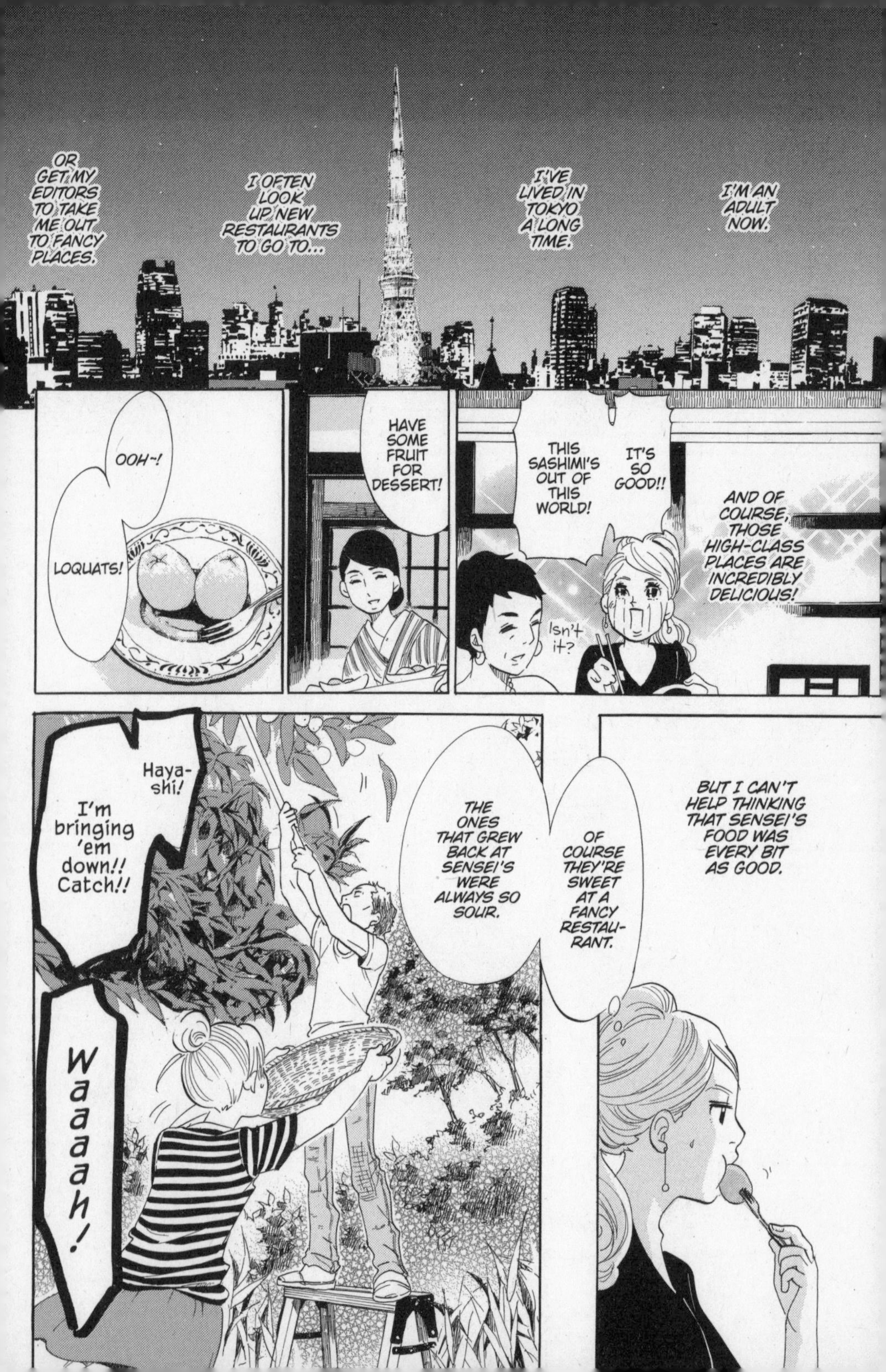
I'M AN ADULT NOW.
I'VE LIVED IN TOKYO A LONG TIME.
I OFTEN LOOK UP NEW RESTAURANTS TO GO TO...
OR GET MY EDITORS TO TAKE ME OUT TO FANCY PLACES.
AND OF COURSE, THOSE HIGH-CLASS PLACES ARE INCREDIBLY DELICIOUS!
IT'S SO GOOD!!
THIS SASHIMI'S OUT OF THIS WORLD!
Isn't it?
HAVE SOME FRUIT FOR DESSERT!
OOH~!
LOQUATS!
BUT I CAN'T HELP THINKING THAT SENSEI'S FOOD WAS EVERY BIT AS GOOD.
OF COURSE THEY'RE SWEET AT A FANCY RESTAURANT.
THE ONES THAT GREW BACK AT SENSEI'S WERE ALWAYS SO SOUR.
Haya-shi!
I'm bringing 'em down!! Catch!!
Waaaah!

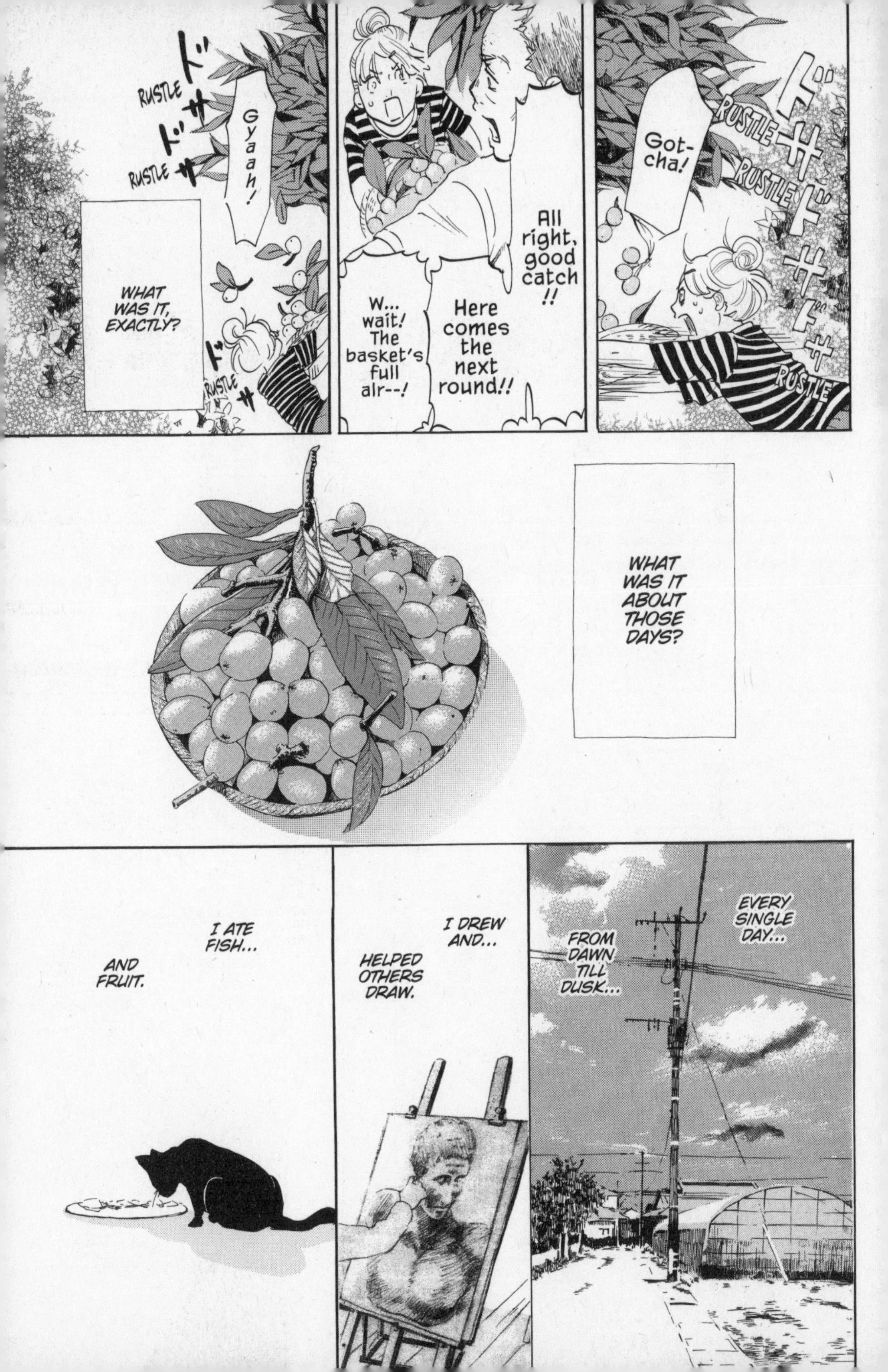
Gotcha!
ド RUSTLE サ
ド RUSTLE サ
ド サ RUSTLE
All right, good catch!!
Here comes the next round!!
W... wait! The basket's full alr--!
Gyaaah!
ド RUSTLE
ド RUSTLE サ
WHAT WAS IT, EXACTLY?
ド RUSTLE サ
WHAT WAS IT ABOUT THOSE DAYS?
EVERY SINGLE DAY...
FROM DAWN TILL DUSK...
I DREW AND...
HELPED OTHERS DRAW.
I ATE FISH...
AND FRUIT.

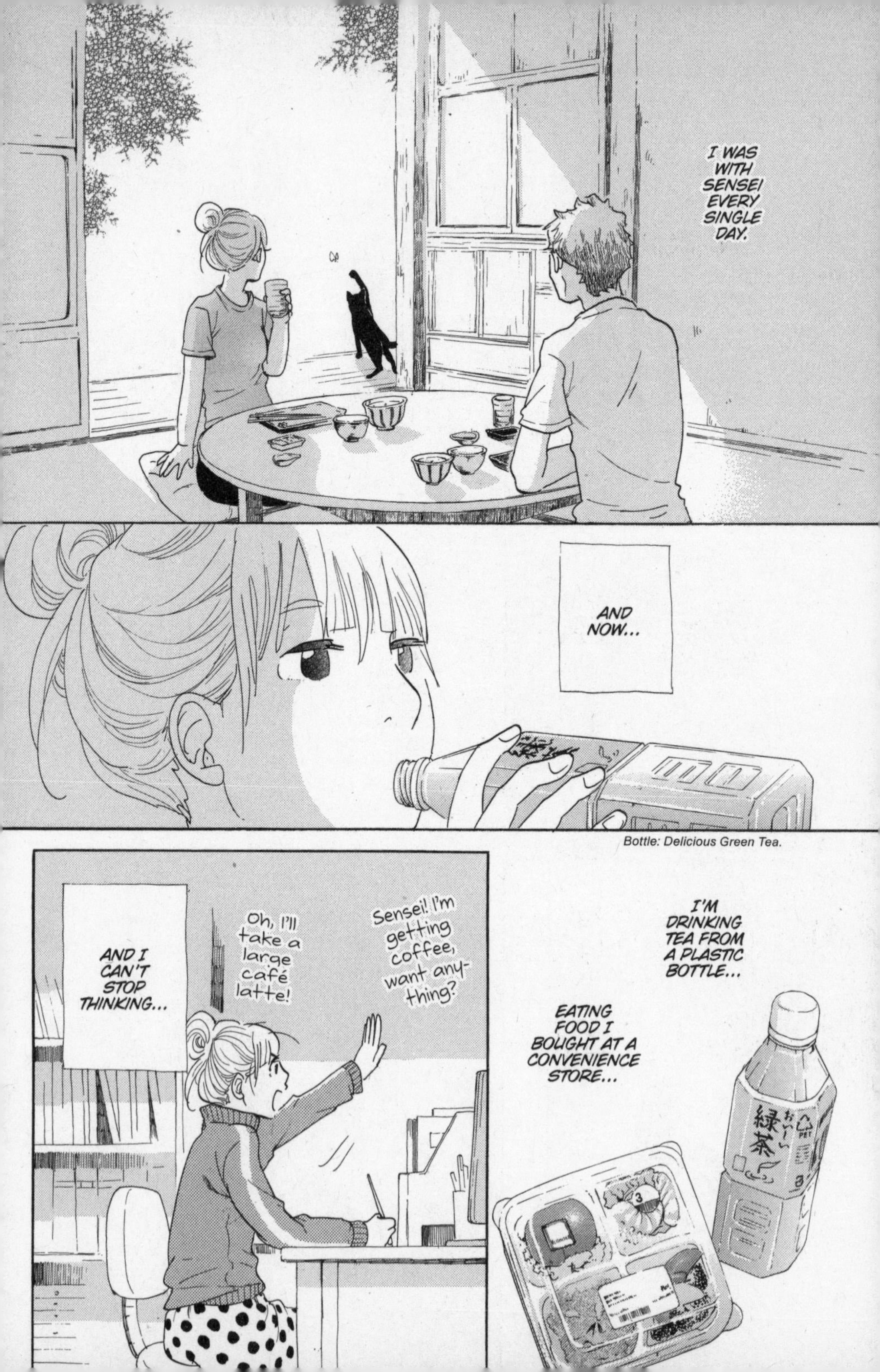
I WAS WITH SENSEI EVERY SINGLE DAY.
AND NOW...
Bottle: Delicious Green Tea.
I'M DRINKING TEA FROM A PLASTIC BOTTLE...
EATING FOOD I BOUGHT AT A CONVENIENCE STORE...
緑茶
Sensei! I'm getting coffee, want anything?
Oh, I'll take a large café latte!
AND I CAN'T STOP THINKING...

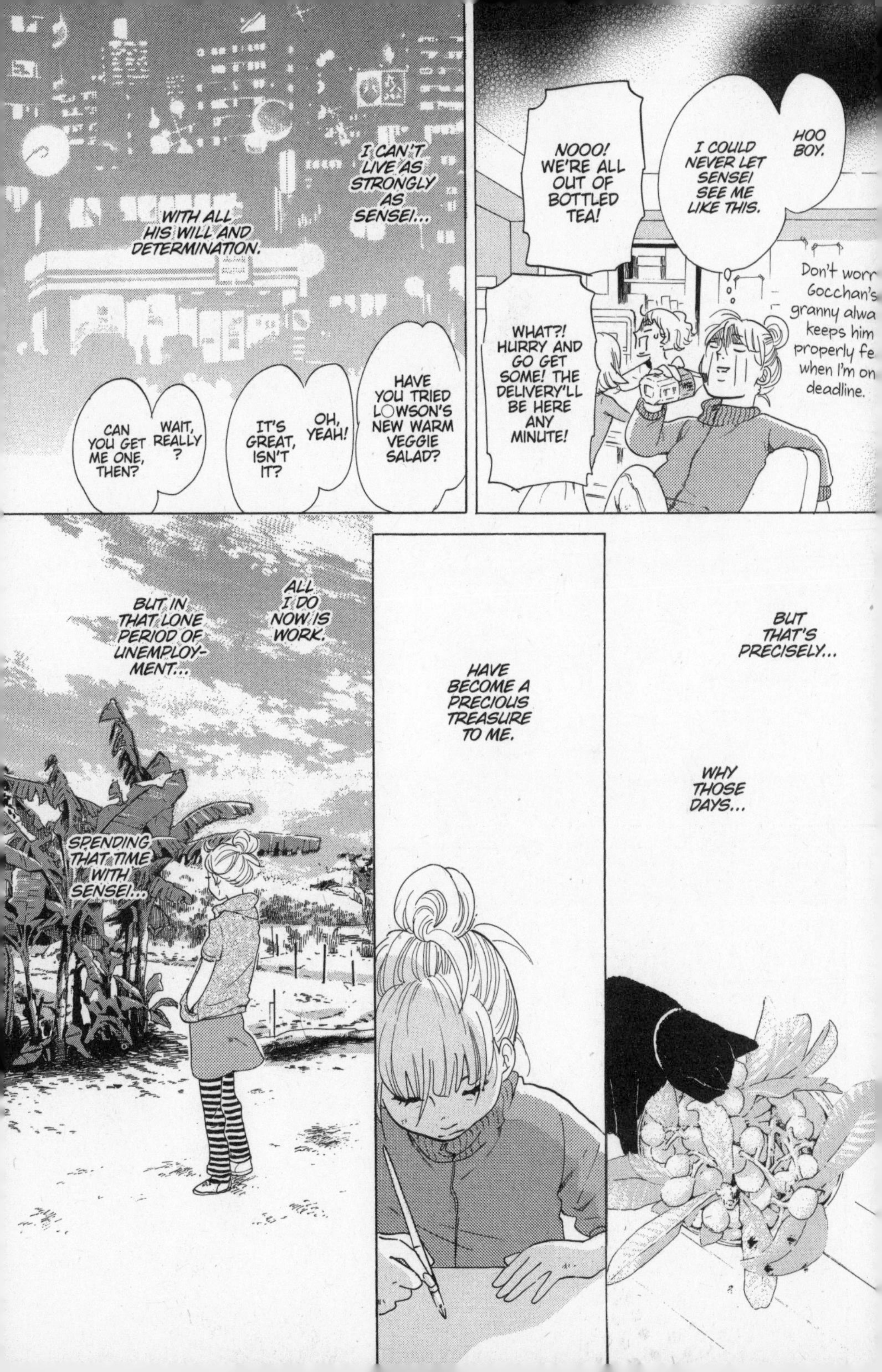
HOO BOY.
I COULD NEVER LET SENSEI SEE ME LIKE THIS.
NOOO! WE'RE ALL OUT OF BOTTLED TEA!
Don't worr Gocchan's granny alwa keeps him properly fe when I'm on deadline.
WHAT?! HURRY AND GO GET SOME! THE DELIVERY'LL BE HERE ANY MINUTE!
I CAN'T LIVE AS STRONGLY AS SENSEI...
WITH ALL HIS WILL AND DETERMINATION.
HAVE YOU TRIED LOWSON'S NEW WARM VEGGIE SALAD?
OH, YEAH!
IT'S GREAT, ISN'T IT?
WAIT, REALLY?
CAN YOU GET ME ONE, THEN?
BUT THAT'S PRECISELY...
WHY THOSE DAYS...
HAVE BECOME A PRECIOUS TREASURE TO ME.
ALL I DO NOW IS WORK.
BUT IN THAT LONE PERIOD OF UNEMPLOYMENT...
SPENDING THAT TIME WITH SENSEI...

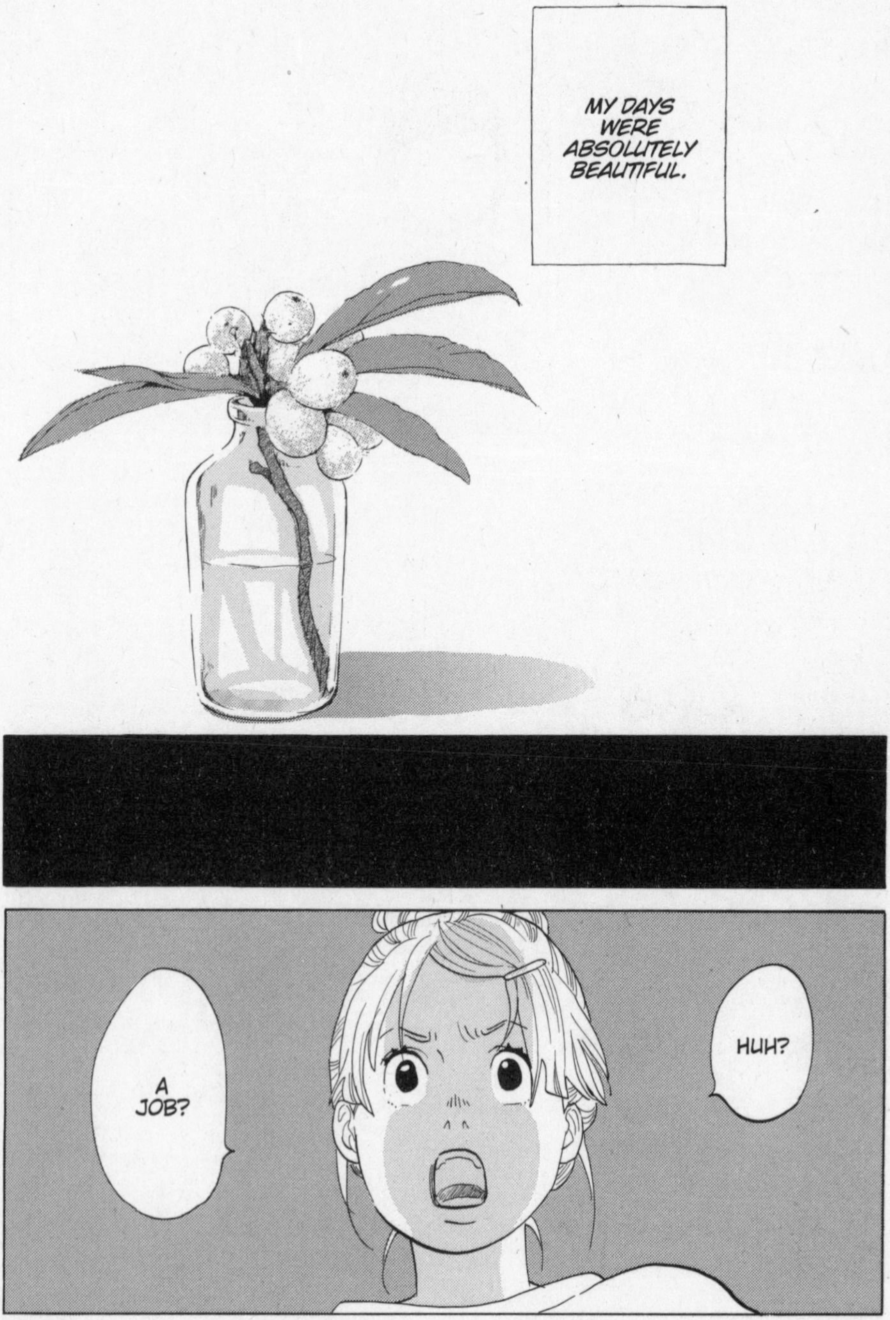
MY DAYS WERE ABSOLUTELY BEAUTIFUL.
HUH?
A JOB?

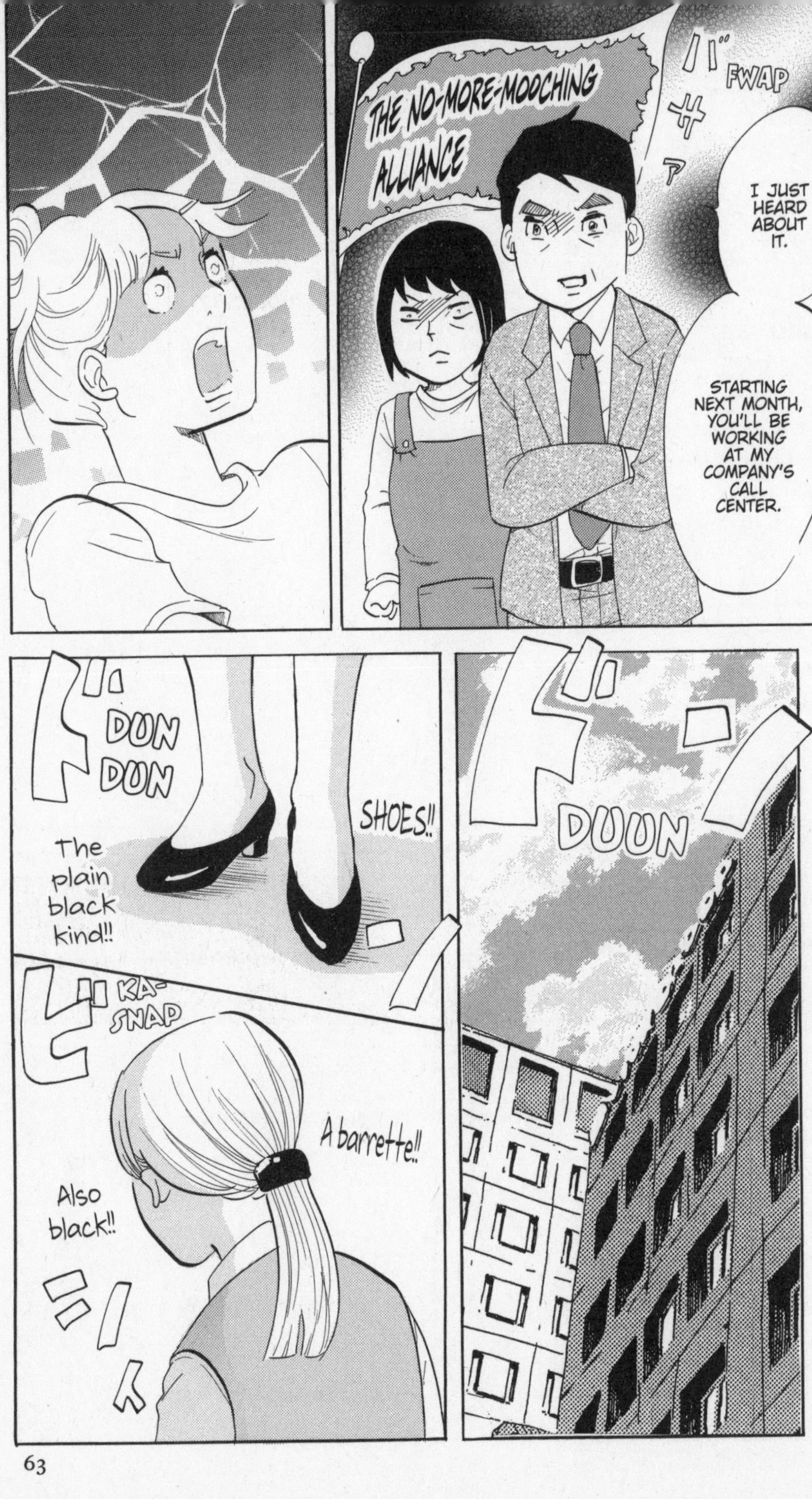
THE NO-MORE-MOOCHING ALLIANCE
FWAP
I JUST HEARD ABOUT IT.
STARTING NEXT MONTH, YOU'LL BE WORKING AT MY COMPANY'S CALL CENTER.
DUUN
DUN DUN
SHOES!!
The plain black kind!!
KA-SNAP
A barrette!!
Also black!!

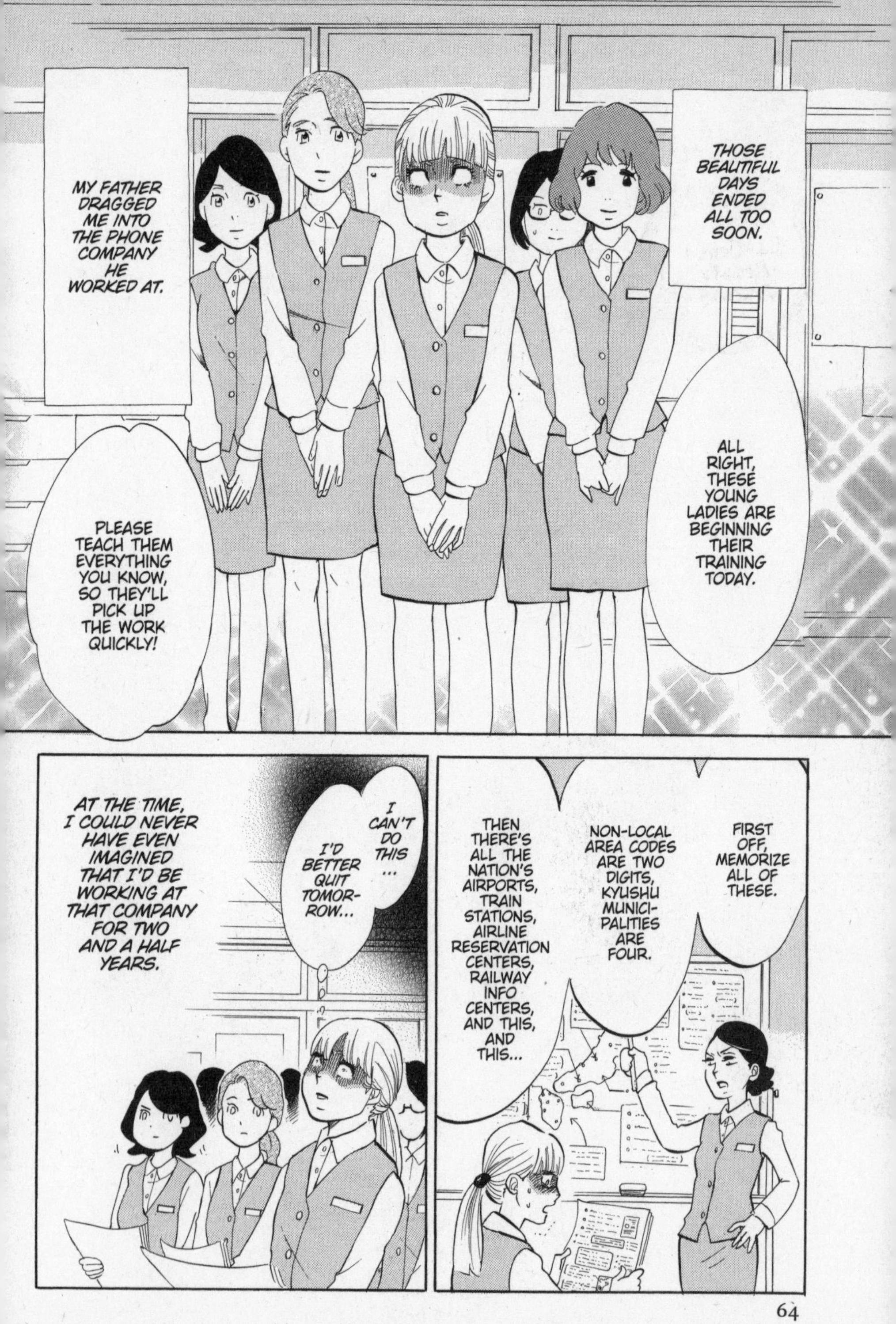
THOSE BEAUTIFUL DAYS ENDED ALL TOO SOON.
MY FATHER DRAGGED ME INTO THE PHONE COMPANY HE WORKED AT.
ALL RIGHT, THESE YOUNG LADIES ARE BEGINNING THEIR TRAINING TODAY.
PLEASE TEACH THEM EVERYTHING YOU KNOW, SO THEY'LL PICK UP THE WORK QUICKLY!
FIRST OFF, MEMORIZE ALL OF THESE.
NON-LOCAL AREA CODES ARE TWO DIGITS, KYUSHU MUNICI-PALITIES ARE FOUR.
THEN THERE'S ALL THE NATION'S AIRPORTS, TRAIN STATIONS, AIRLINE RESERVATION CENTERS, RAILWAY INFO CENTERS, AND THIS, AND THIS...
I CAN'T DO THIS...
I'D BETTER QUIT TOMOR-ROW...
AT THE TIME, I COULD NEVER HAVE EVEN IMAGINED THAT I'D BE WORKING AT THAT COMPANY FOR TWO AND A HALF YEARS.

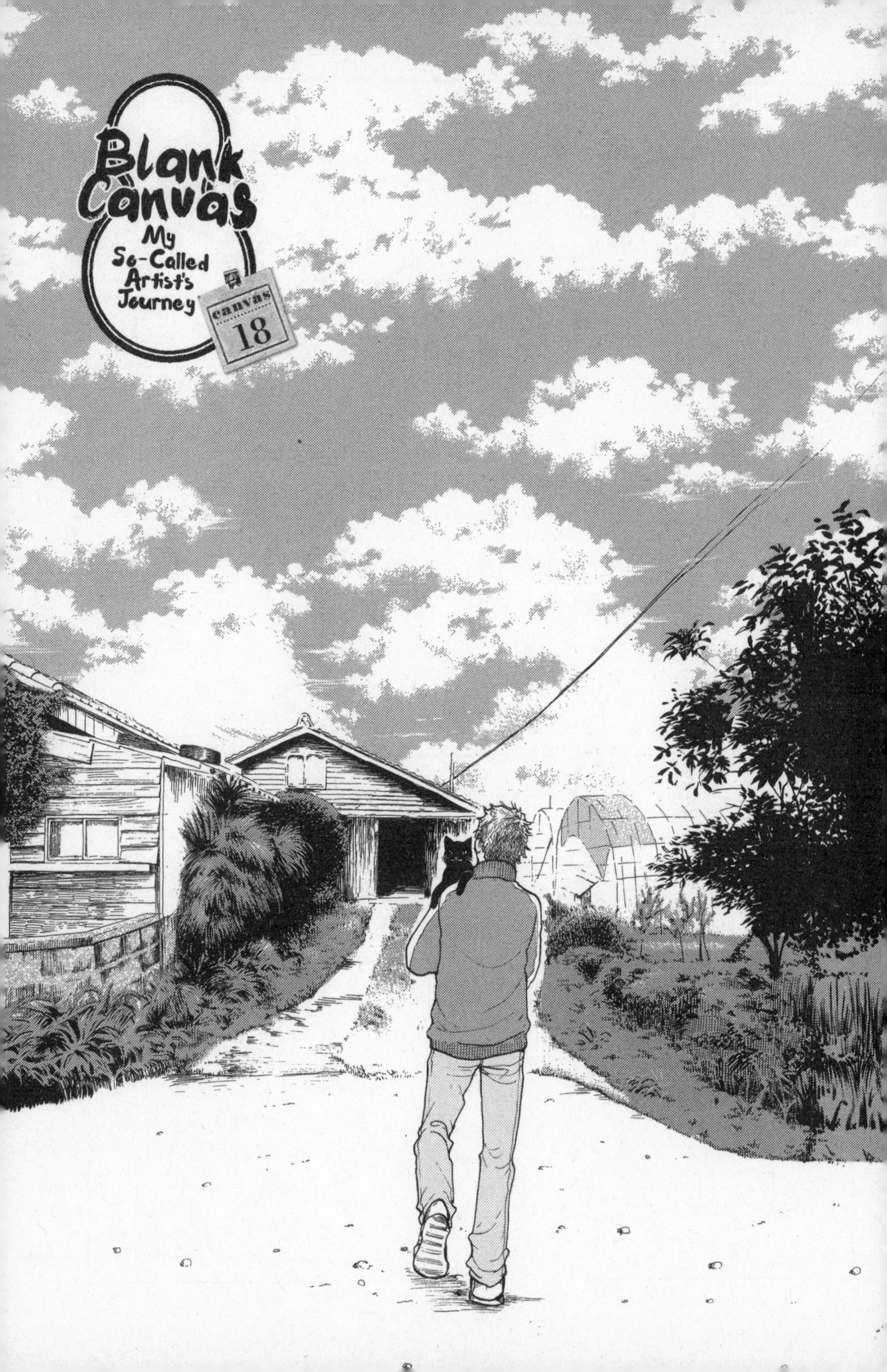
Blank Canvas
My So-Called Artist's Journey
canvas
18

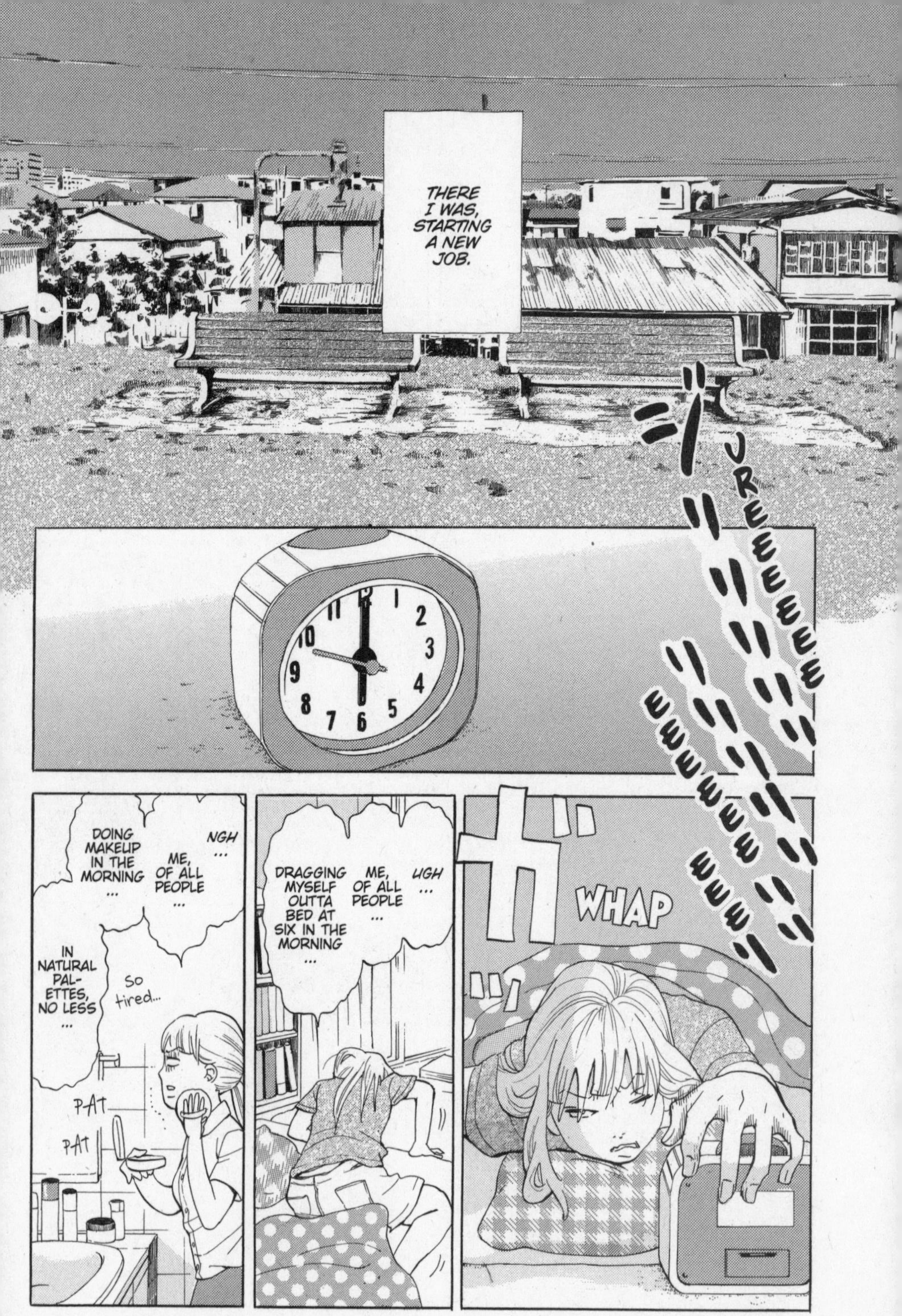
THERE I WAS, STARTING A NEW JOB.
JREEEEEEE
EEEEEEEEE
WHAP
NGH...
ME, OF ALL PEOPLE...
DOING MAKEUP IN THE MORNING...
UGH...
ME, OF ALL PEOPLE...
DRAGGING MYSELF OUTTA BED AT SIX IN THE MORNING...
NGH...
ME, OF ALL PEOPLE...
DOING MAKEUP IN THE MORNING...
IN NATURAL PAL-ETTES, NO LESS...
So tired...
PAT
PAT

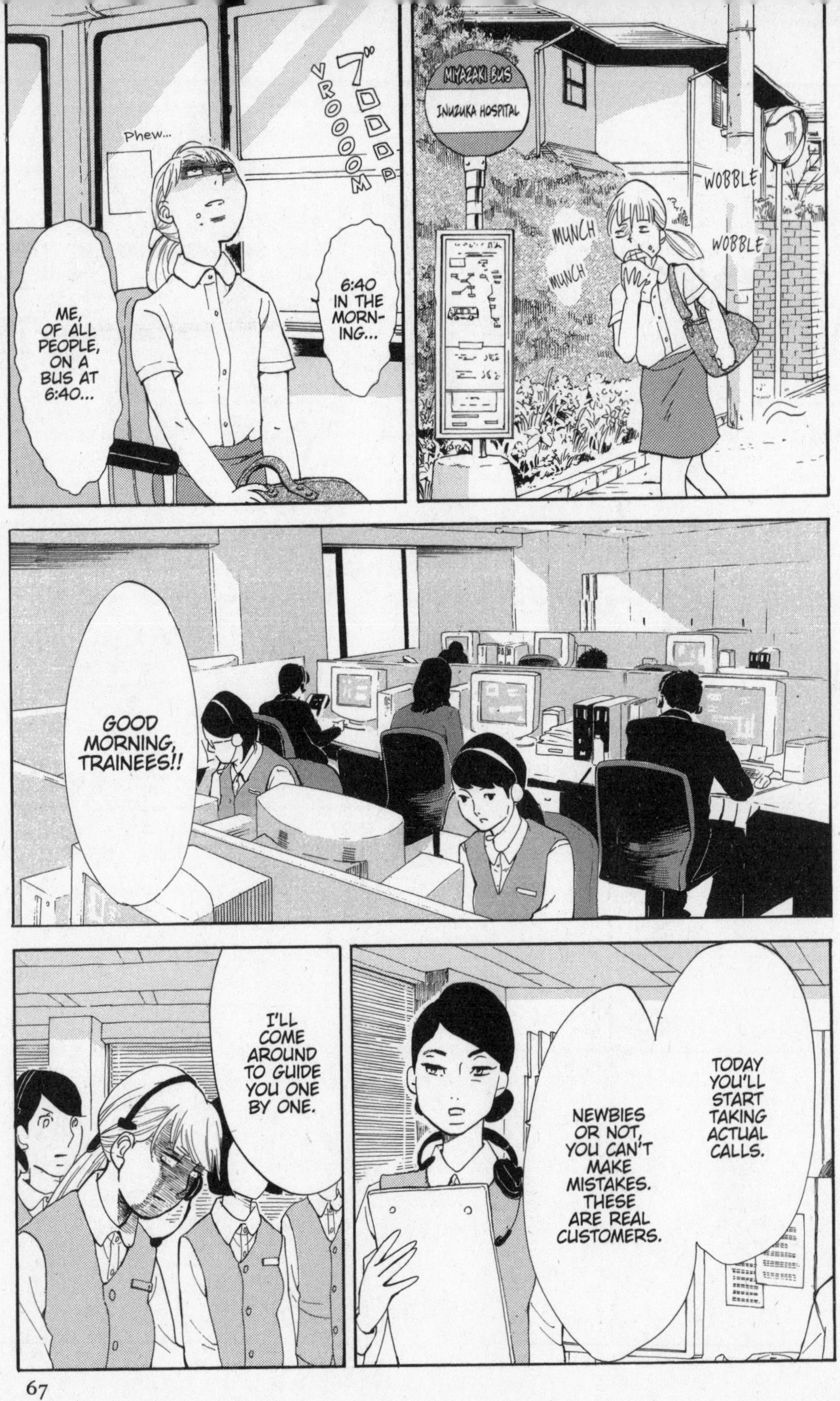
MIYAZAKI BUS
INUZUKA HOSPITAL
MUNCH
MUNCH
WOBBLE
WOBBLE
VROOOOOM
Phew...
6:40 IN THE MORNING...
ME, OF ALL PEOPLE, ON A BUS AT 6:40...
GOOD MORNING, TRAINEES!!
TODAY YOU'LL START TAKING ACTUAL CALLS.
NEWBIES OR NOT, YOU CAN'T MAKE MISTAKES. THESE ARE REAL CUSTOMERS.
I'LL COME AROUND TO GUIDE YOU ONE BY ONE.

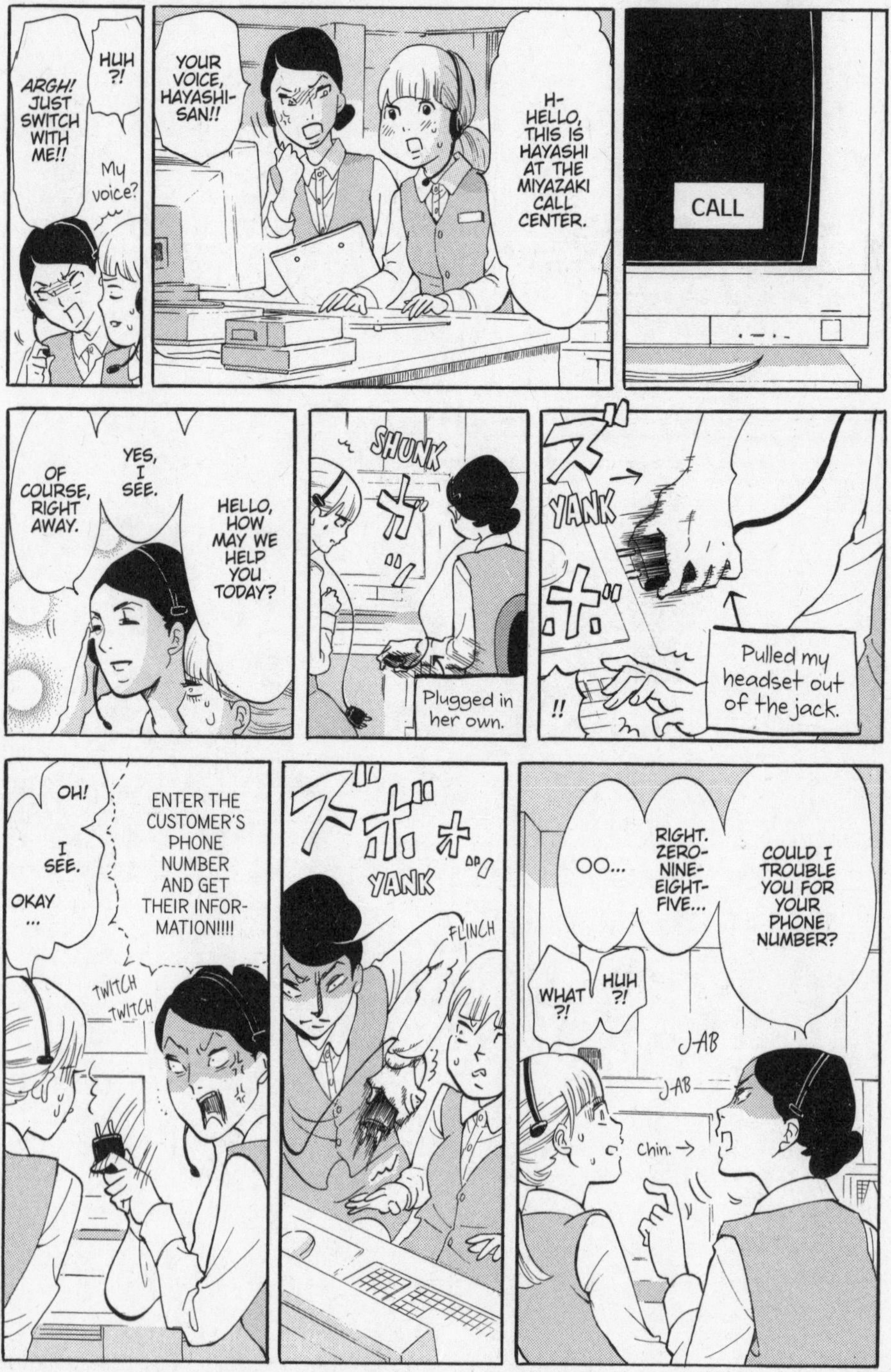
CALL
H-HELLO, THIS IS HAYASHI AT THE MIYAZAKI CALL CENTER.
YOUR VOICE, HAYASHI-SAN!!
HUH ?!
ARGH! JUST SWITCH WITH ME!!
My voice?
YANK
Pulled my headset out of the jack.
!!
SHUNK
Plugged in her own.
HELLO, HOW MAY WE HELP YOU TODAY?
YES, I SEE.
OF COURSE, RIGHT AWAY.
COULD I TROUBLE YOU FOR YOUR PHONE NUMBER?
RIGHT. ZERO-NINE-EIGHT-FIVE...
OO...
HUH ?!
WHAT ?!
JAB
JAB
Chin. →
YANK
FLINCH
ENTER THE CUSTOMER'S PHONE NUMBER AND GET THEIR INFORMATION!!!!
OH!
I SEE.
OKAY ...
TWITCH
TWITCH

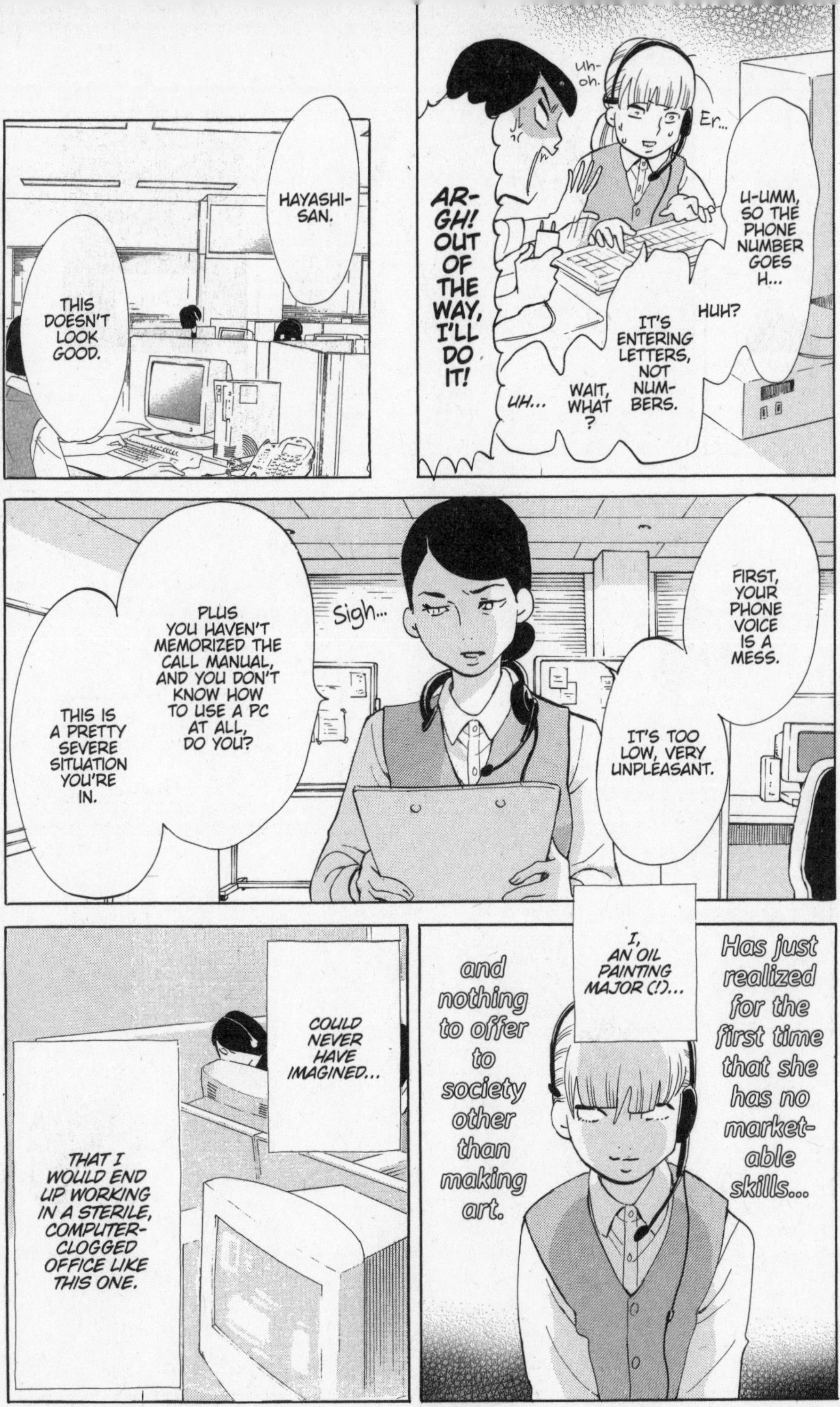
Uh-oh.
Er...
U-UMM, SO THE PHONE NUMBER GOES H...
HUH?
IT'S ENTERING LETTERS, NOT NUMBERS.
WAIT, WHAT?
UH...
ARGH! OUT OF THE WAY, I'LL DO IT!
HAYASHI-SAN.
THIS DOESN'T LOOK GOOD.
FIRST, YOUR PHONE VOICE IS A MESS.
IT'S TOO LOW, VERY UNPLEASANT.
Sigh...
PLUS YOU HAVEN'T MEMORIZED THE CALL MANUAL, AND YOU DON'T KNOW HOW TO USE A PC AT ALL, DO YOU?
THIS IS A PRETTY SEVERE SITUATION YOU'RE IN.
I, AN OIL PAINTING MAJOR (!)...
Has just realized for the first time that she has no market-able skills...
and nothing to offer to society other than making art.
COULD NEVER HAVE IMAGINED...
THAT I WOULD END UP WORKING IN A STERILE, COMPUTER-CLOGGED OFFICE LIKE THIS ONE.

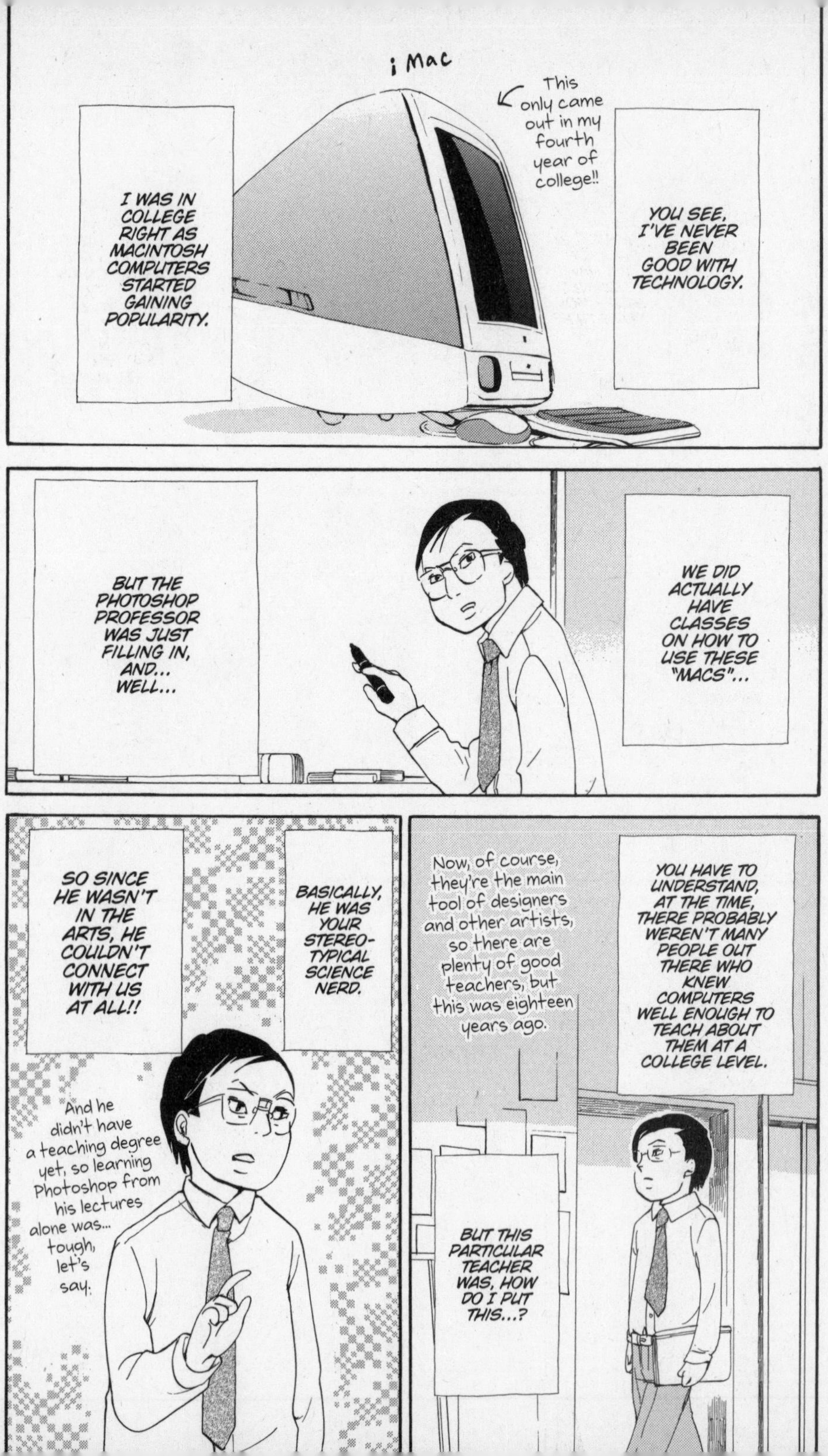
YOU SEE, I'VE NEVER BEEN GOOD WITH TECHNOLOGY.
This only came out in my fourth year of college!!
i Mac
I WAS IN COLLEGE RIGHT AS MACINTOSH COMPUTERS STARTED GAINING POPULARITY.
WE DID ACTUALLY HAVE CLASSES ON HOW TO USE THESE "MACS"...
BUT THE PHOTOSHOP PROFESSOR WAS JUST FILLING IN, AND... WELL...
YOU HAVE TO UNDERSTAND, AT THE TIME, THERE PROBABLY WEREN'T MANY PEOPLE OUT THERE WHO KNEW COMPUTERS WELL ENOUGH TO TEACH ABOUT THEM AT A COLLEGE LEVEL.
Now, of course, they're the main tool of designers and other artists, so there are plenty of good teachers, but this was eighteen years ago.
BUT THIS PARTICULAR TEACHER WAS, HOW DO I PUT THIS...?
BASICALLY, HE WAS YOUR STEREO-TYPICAL SCIENCE NERD.
SO SINCE HE WASN'T IN THE ARTS, HE COULDN'T CONNECT WITH US AT ALL!!
And he didn't have a teaching degree yet, so learning Photoshop from his lectures alone was... tough, let's say.

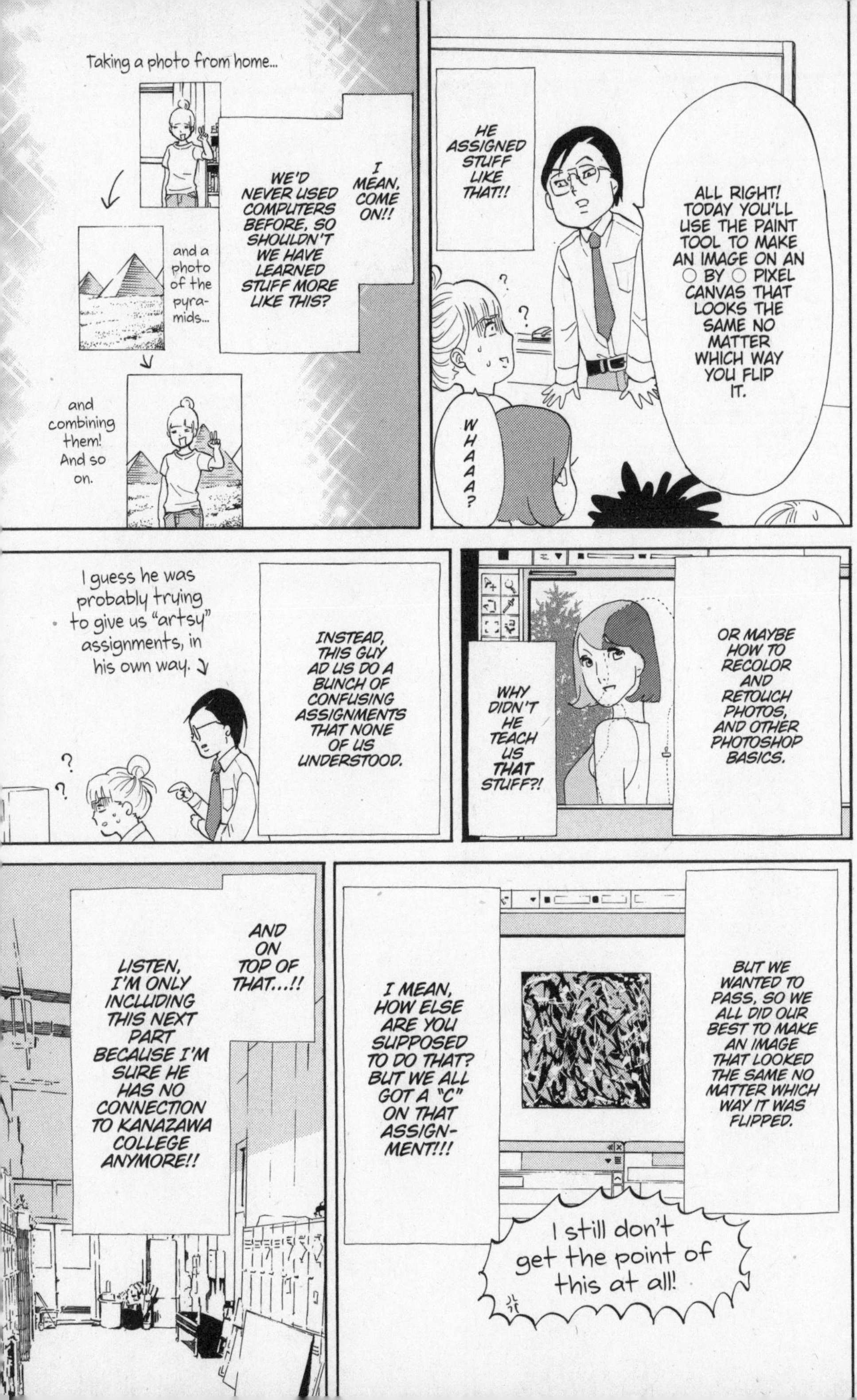
ALL RIGHT! TODAY YOU'LL USE THE PAINT TOOL TO MAKE AN IMAGE ON AN ○ BY ○ PIXEL CANVAS THAT LOOKS THE SAME NO MATTER WHICH WAY YOU FLIP IT.
HE ASSIGNED STUFF LIKE THAT!!
WHAAAA?
I MEAN, COME ON!!
WE'D NEVER USED COMPUTERS BEFORE, SO SHOULDN'T WE HAVE LEARNED STUFF MORE LIKE THIS?
Taking a photo from home...
and a photo of the pyra-mids...
and combining them! And so on.
OR MAYBE HOW TO RECOLOR AND RETOUCH PHOTOS, AND OTHER PHOTOSHOP BASICS.
WHY DIDN'T HE TEACH US THAT STUFF?!
INSTEAD, THIS GUY AD US DO A BUNCH OF CONFUSING ASSIGNMENTS THAT NONE OF US UNDERSTOOD.
I guess he was probably trying to give us "artsy" assignments, in his own way.
BUT WE WANTED TO PASS, SO WE ALL DID OUR BEST TO MAKE AN IMAGE THAT LOOKED THE SAME NO MATTER WHICH WAY IT WAS FLIPPED.
I MEAN, HOW ELSE ARE YOU SUPPOSED TO DO THAT? BUT WE ALL GOT A "C" ON THAT ASSIGN-MENT!!!
I still don't get the point of this at all!
AND ON TOP OF THAT...!!
LISTEN, I'M ONLY INCLUDING THIS NEXT PART BECAUSE I'M SURE HE HAS NO CONNECTION TO KANAZAWA COLLEGE ANYMORE!!

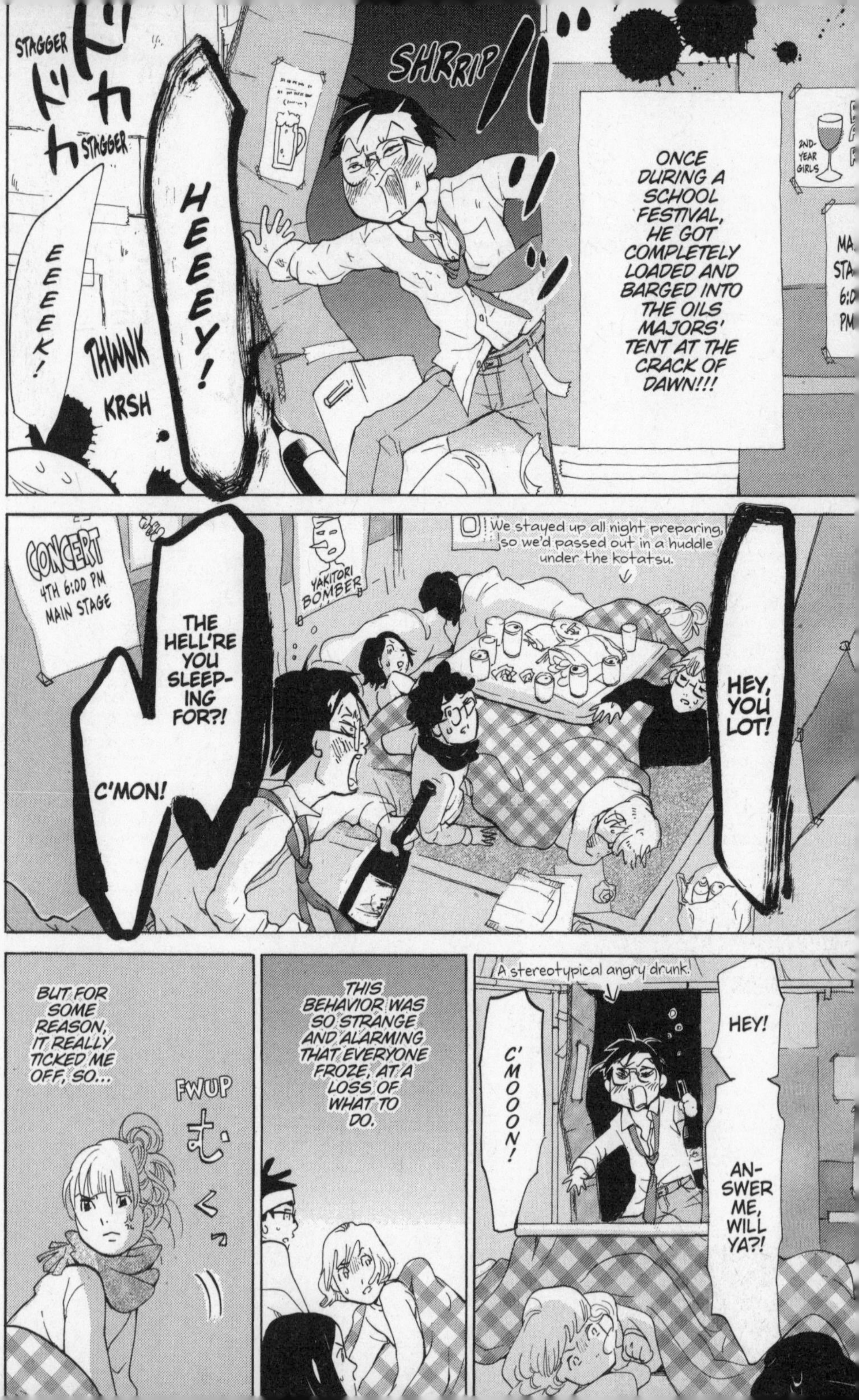
2ND-YEAR GIRLS
ONCE DURING A SCHOOL FESTIVAL, HE GOT COMPLETELY LOADED AND BARGED INTO THE OILS MAJORS' TENT AT THE CRACK OF DAWN!!!
SHRRIP
HEEEEY!
STAGGER
STAGGER
EEEEEK!
THWNK
KRSH
HEY, YOU LOT!
We stayed up all night preparing, so we'd passed out in a huddle under the kotatsu.
YAKITORI BOMBER
THE HELL'RE YOU SLEEPING FOR?!
C'MON!
CONCERT
4TH 6:00 PM MAIN STAGE
A stereotypical angry drunk!
HEY!
ANSWER ME, WILL YA?!
C'MOOOON!
THIS BEHAVIOR WAS SO STRANGE AND ALARMING THAT EVERYONE FROZE, AT A LOSS OF WHAT TO DO.
BUT FOR SOME REASON, IT REALLY TICKED ME OFF, SO...
FWUP
むくっ

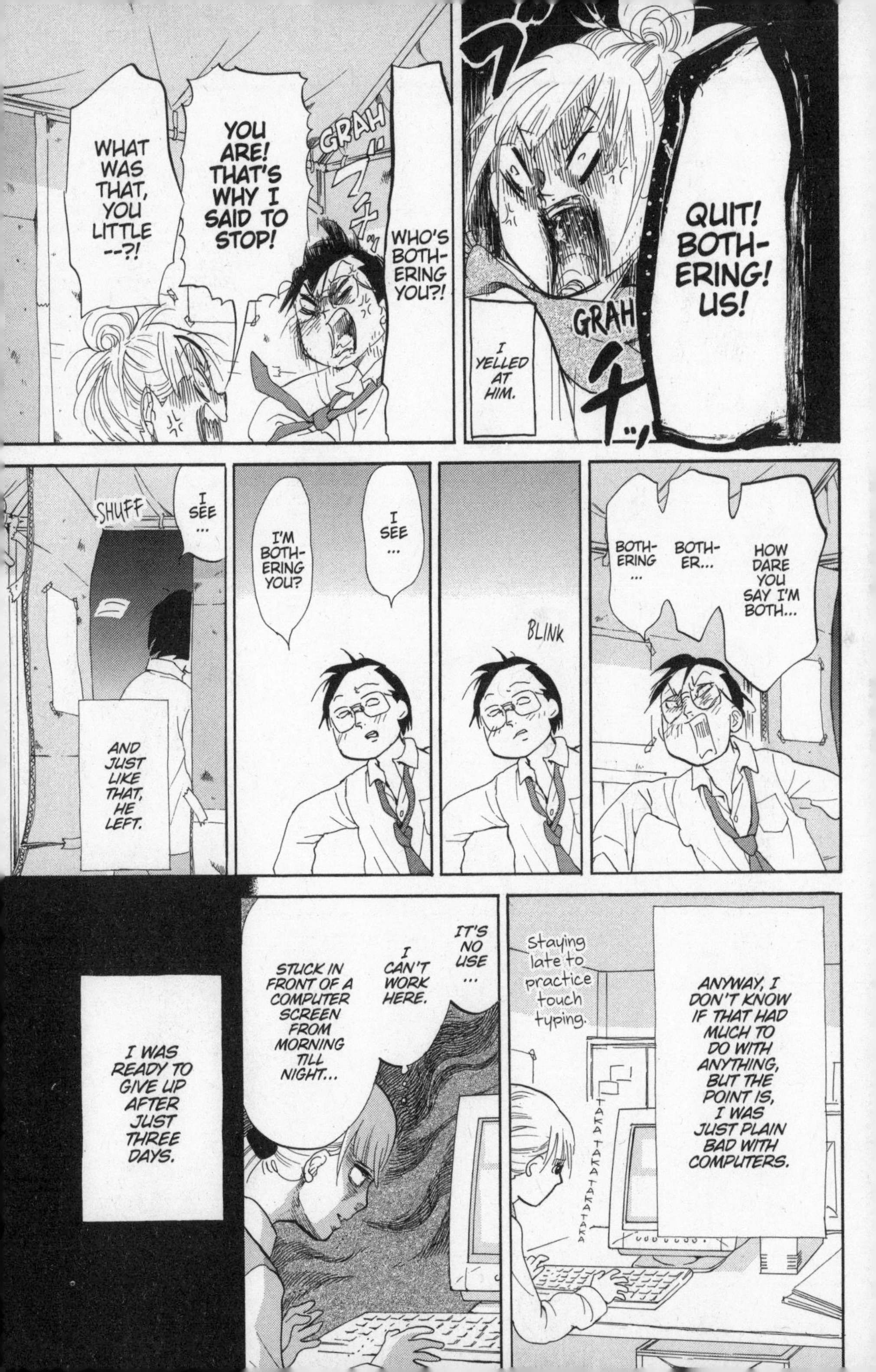
QUIT! BOTHERING! US!
GRAH
I YELLED AT HIM.
WHO'S BOTHERING YOU?!
GRAH
YOU ARE! THAT'S WHY I SAID TO STOP!
WHAT WAS THAT, YOU LITTLE --?!
HOW DARE YOU SAY I'M BOTH...
BOTH-ER...
BOTH-ERING ...
BLINK
I SEE ...
I'M BOTH-ERING YOU?
I SEE ...
SHUFF
AND JUST LIKE THAT, HE LEFT.
ANYWAY, I DON'T KNOW IF THAT HAD MUCH TO DO WITH ANYTHING, BUT THE POINT IS, I WAS JUST PLAIN BAD WITH COMPUTERS.
Staying late to practice touch typing.
TAKA TAKA TAKA TAKA TAKA
IT'S NO USE ...
I CAN'T WORK HERE.
STUCK IN FRONT OF A COMPUTER SCREEN FROM MORNING TILL NIGHT...
I WAS READY TO GIVE UP AFTER JUST THREE DAYS.

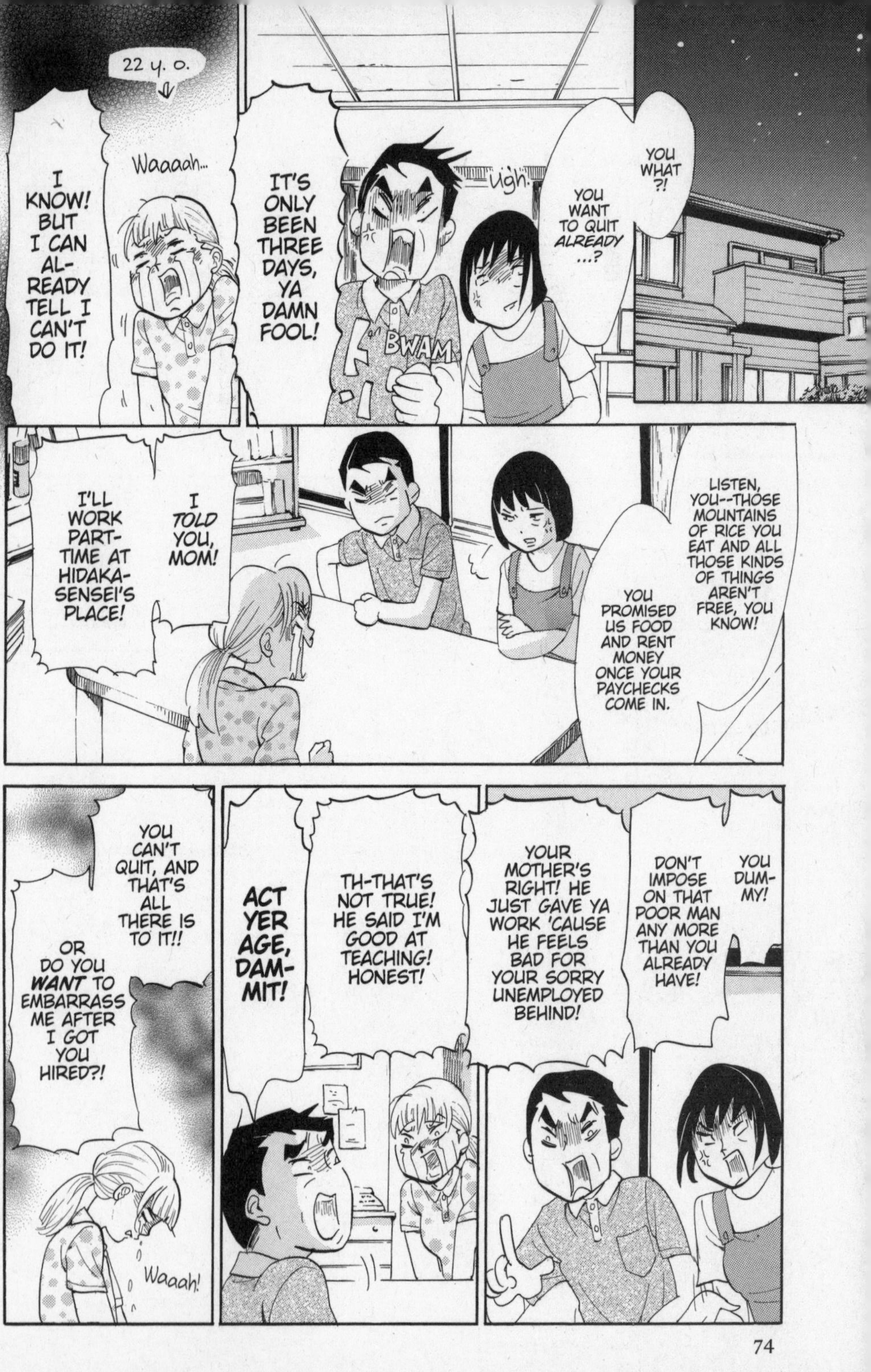
YOU WHAT ?!
YOU WANT TO QUIT *ALREADY* ...?
Ugh.
IT'S ONLY BEEN THREE DAYS, YA DAMN FOOL!
BWAM
22 y. o.
Waaaah...
I KNOW! BUT I CAN ALREADY TELL I CAN'T DO IT!
LISTEN, YOU--THOSE MOUNTAINS OF RICE YOU EAT AND ALL THOSE KINDS OF THINGS AREN'T FREE, YOU KNOW!
YOU PROMISED US FOOD AND RENT MONEY ONCE YOUR PAYCHECKS COME IN.
I *TOLD* YOU, MOM!
I'LL WORK PART-TIME AT HIDAKA-SENSEI'S PLACE!
YOU DUMMY!
DON'T IMPOSE ON THAT POOR MAN ANY MORE THAN YOU ALREADY HAVE!
YOUR MOTHER'S RIGHT! HE JUST GAVE YA WORK 'CAUSE HE FEELS BAD FOR YOUR SORRY UNEMPLOYED BEHIND!
TH-THAT'S NOT TRUE! HE SAID I'M GOOD AT TEACHING! HONEST!
ACT YER AGE, DAMMIT!
YOU CAN'T QUIT, AND THAT'S ALL THERE IS TO IT!!
OR DO YOU *WANT* TO EMBARRASS ME AFTER I GOT YOU HIRED?!
Waaah!

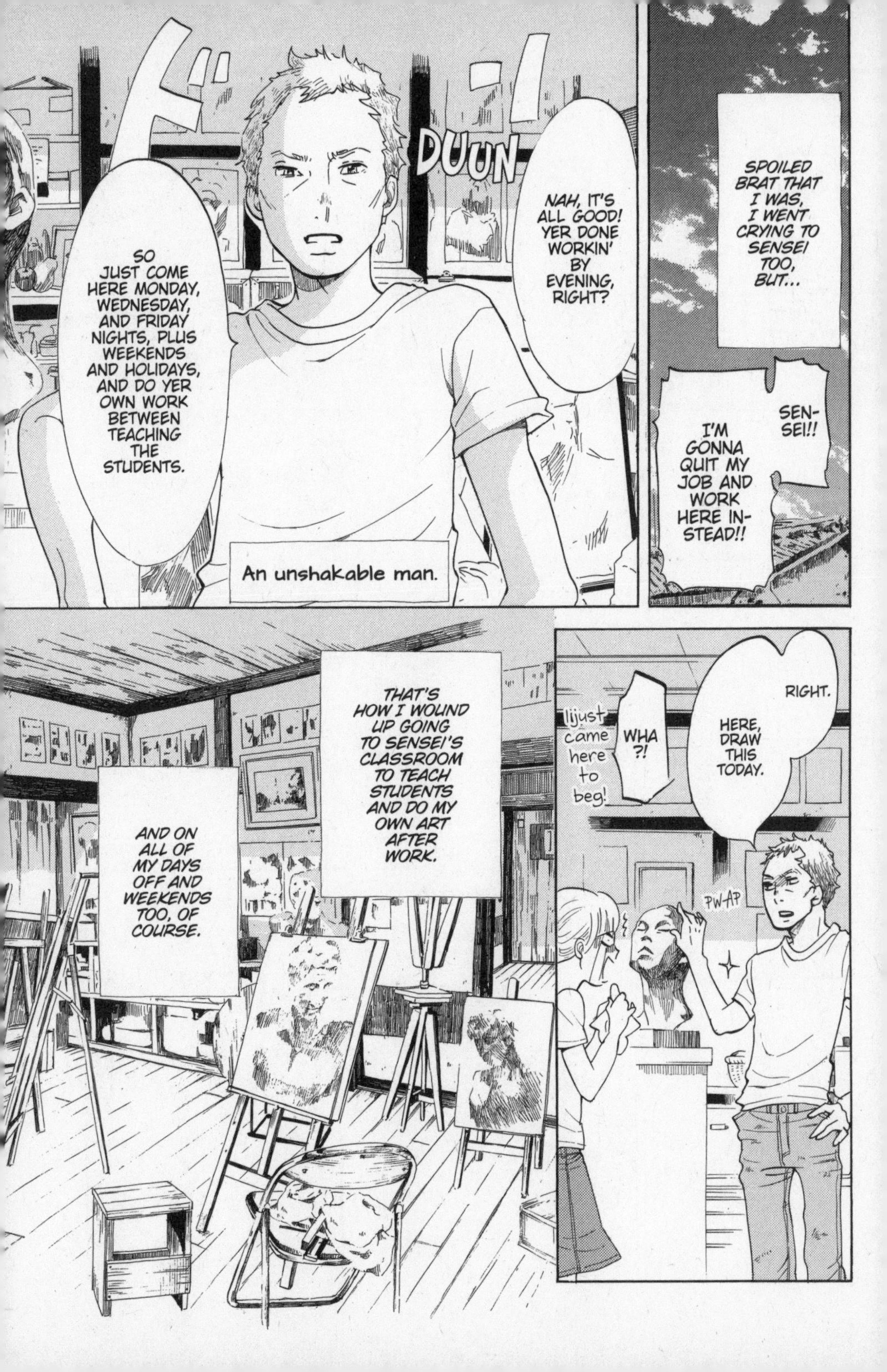

SPOILED BRAT THAT I WAS, I WENT CRYING TO SENSEI TOO, BUT...
SEN-SEI!!
I'M GONNA QUIT MY JOB AND WORK HERE IN-STEAD!!
NAH, IT'S ALL GOOD! YER DONE WORKIN' BY EVENING, RIGHT?
DUUN
SO JUST COME HERE MONDAY, WEDNESDAY, AND FRIDAY NIGHTS, PLUS WEEKENDS AND HOLIDAYS, AND DO YER OWN WORK BETWEEN TEACHING THE STUDENTS.
An unshakable man.
RIGHT.
HERE, DRAW THIS TODAY.
WHA?!
I just came here to beg!
PW-AP
THAT'S HOW I WOUND UP GOING TO SENSEI'S CLASSROOM TO TEACH STUDENTS AND DO MY OWN ART AFTER WORK.
AND ON ALL OF MY DAYS OFF AND WEEKENDS TOO, OF COURSE.

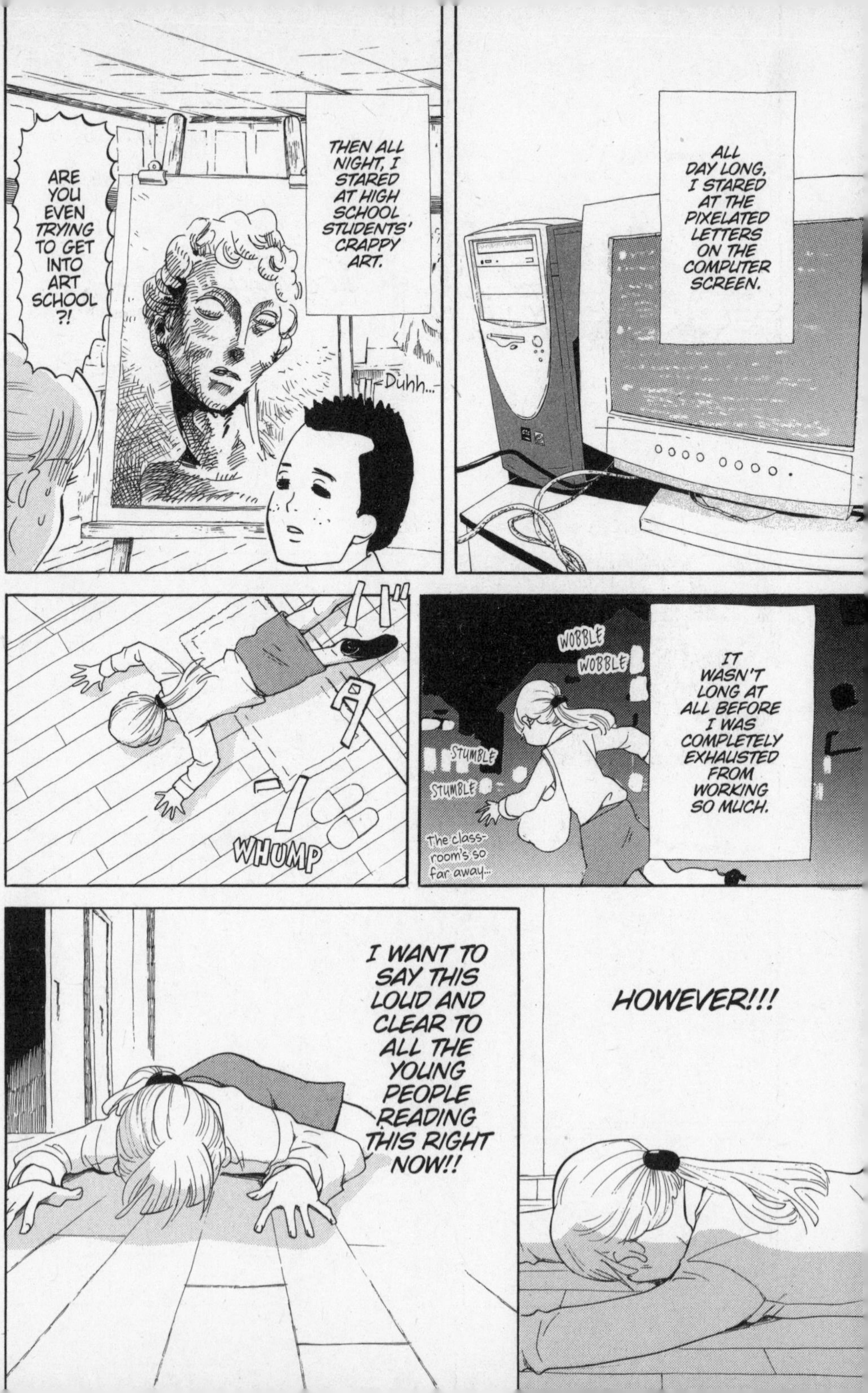
ALL DAY LONG, I STARED AT THE PIXELATED LETTERS ON THE COMPUTER SCREEN.
THEN ALL NIGHT, I STARED AT HIGH SCHOOL STUDENTS' CRAPPY ART.
ARE YOU EVEN TRYING TO GET INTO ART SCHOOL ?!
Duhh...
IT WASN'T LONG AT ALL BEFORE I WAS COMPLETELY EXHAUSTED FROM WORKING SO MUCH.
WOBBLE
WOBBLE
STUMBLE
STUMBLE
The class-room's so far away...
WHUMP
HOWEVER!!!
I WANT TO SAY THIS LOUD AND CLEAR TO ALL THE YOUNG PEOPLE READING THIS RIGHT NOW!!

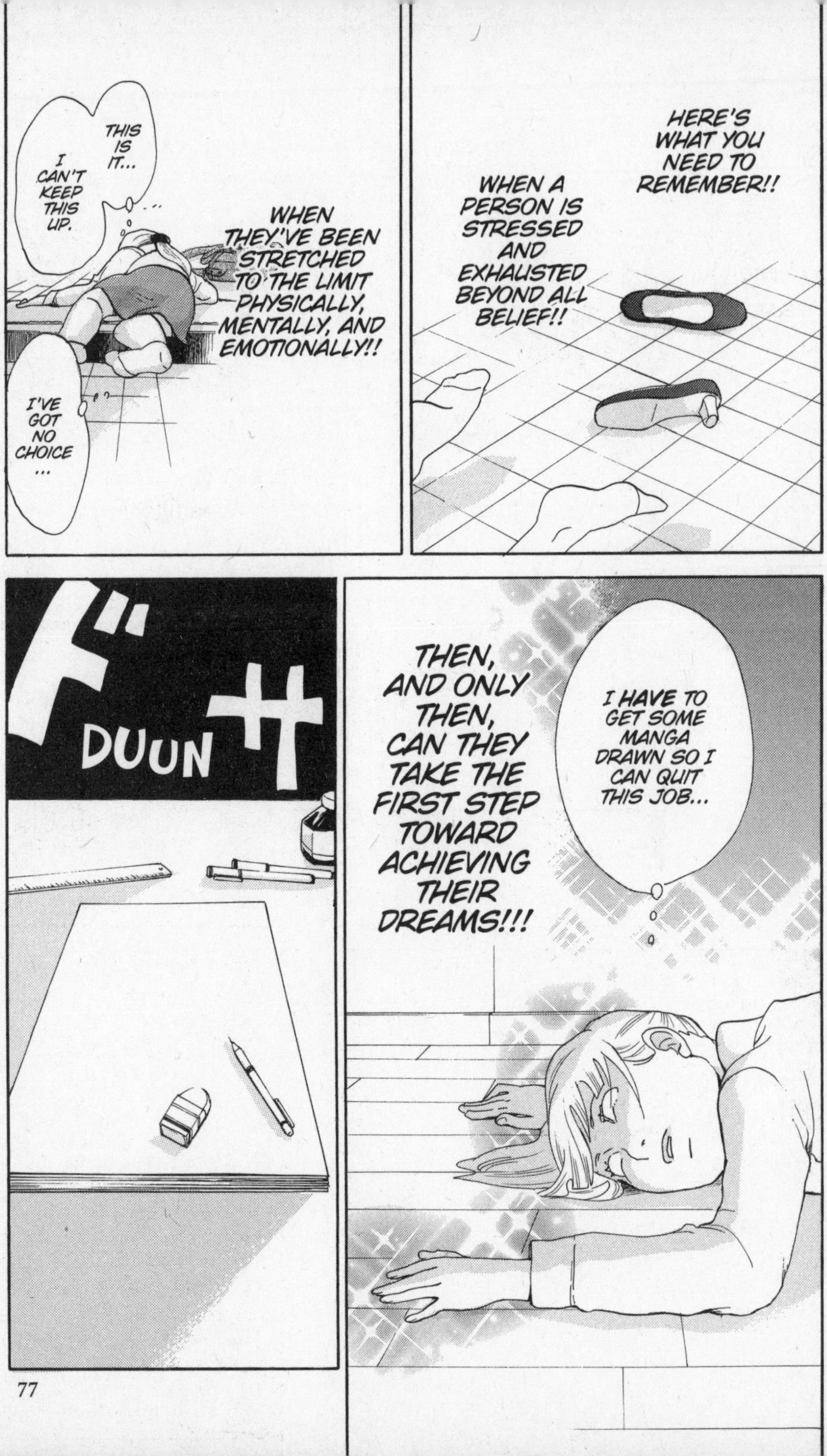
HERE'S WHAT YOU NEED TO REMEMBER!!
WHEN A PERSON IS STRESSED AND EXHAUSTED BEYOND ALL BELIEF!!
WHEN THEY'VE BEEN STRETCHED TO THE LIMIT PHYSICALLY, MENTALLY, AND EMOTIONALLY!!
THIS IS IT...
I CAN'T KEEP THIS UP.
I'VE GOT NO CHOICE ...
I HAVE TO GET SOME MANGA DRAWN SO I CAN QUIT THIS JOB...
THEN, AND ONLY THEN, CAN THEY TAKE THE FIRST STEP TOWARD ACHIEVING THEIR DREAMS!!!
ドーッ
DUUN

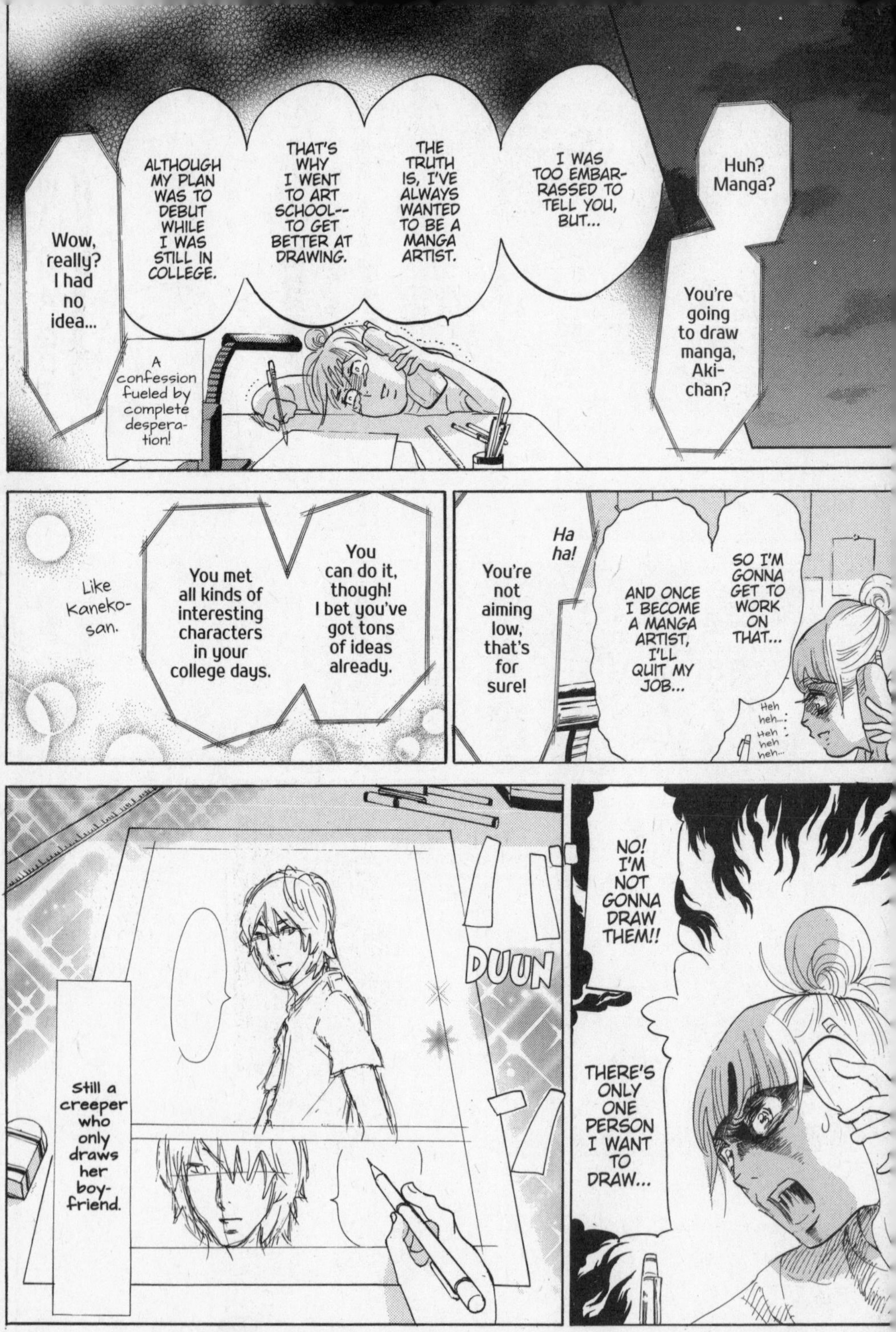

Huh? Manga?
You're going to draw manga, Aki-chan?
I WAS TOO EMBARRASSED TO TELL YOU, BUT...
THE TRUTH IS, I'VE ALWAYS WANTED TO BE A MANGA ARTIST.
THAT'S WHY I WENT TO ART SCHOOL-- TO GET BETTER AT DRAWING.
ALTHOUGH MY PLAN WAS TO DEBUT WHILE I WAS STILL IN COLLEGE.
Wow, really? I had no idea...
A confession fueled by complete desperation!
SO I'M GONNA GET TO WORK ON THAT...
Heh heh... Heh heh heh...
AND ONCE I BECOME A MANGA ARTIST, I'LL QUIT MY JOB...
Ha ha!
You're not aiming low, that's for sure!
You can do it, though! I bet you've got tons of ideas already.
You met all kinds of interesting characters in your college days.
Like Kaneko-san.
NO! I'M NOT GONNA DRAW THEM!!
THERE'S ONLY ONE PERSON I WANT TO DRAW...
DUUN
Still a creeper who only draws her boyfriend.

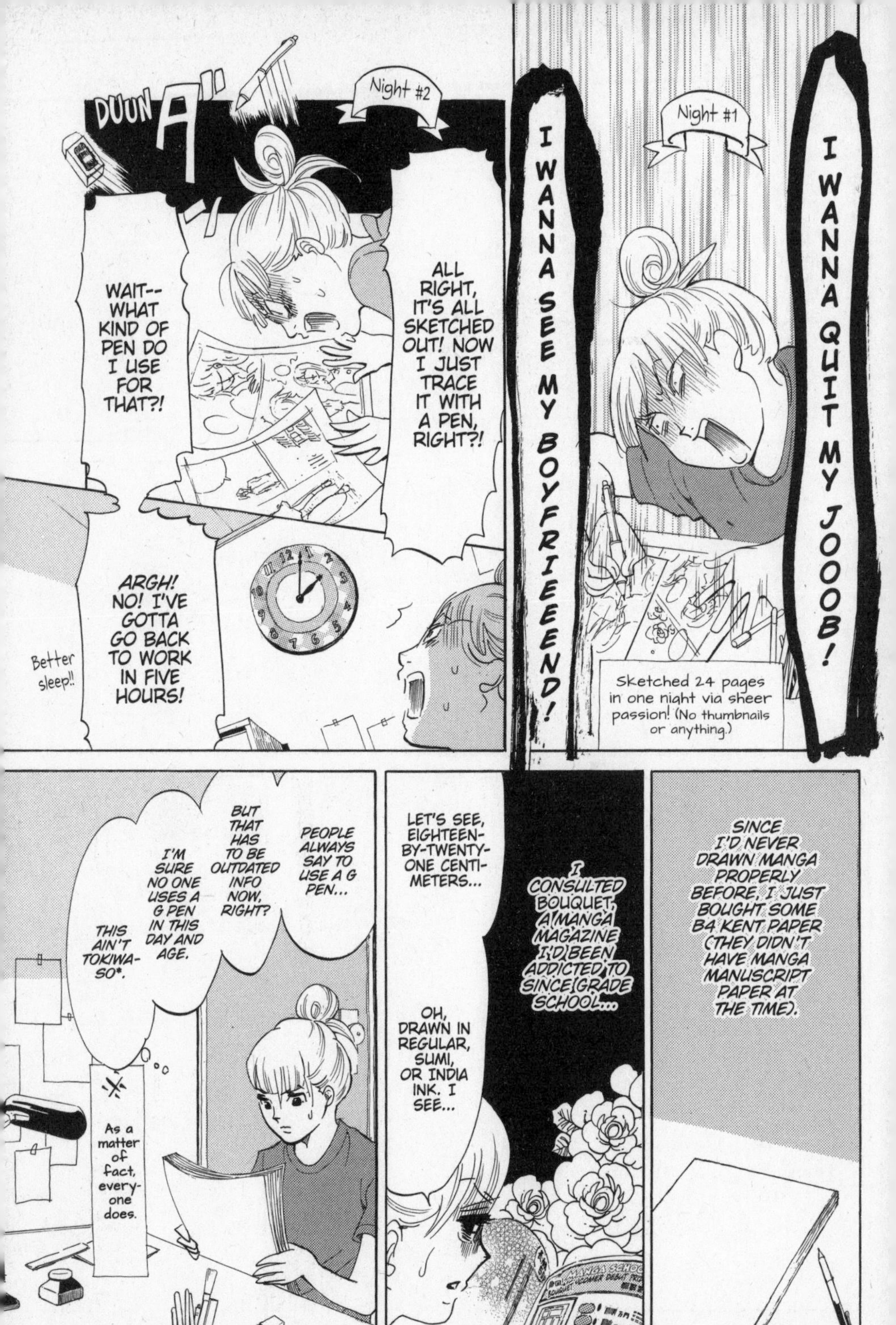
Night #1
I WANNA QUIT MY JOOOOB!
I WANNA SEE MY BOYFRIEEEEND!
Sketched 24 pages in one night via sheer passion! (No thumbnails or anything.)
DUUN
Night #2
ALL RIGHT, IT'S ALL SKETCHED OUT! NOW I JUST TRACE IT WITH A PEN, RIGHT?!
WAIT-- WHAT KIND OF PEN DO I USE FOR THAT?!
ARGH! NO! I'VE GOTTA GO BACK TO WORK IN FIVE HOURS!
Better sleep!!
SINCE I'D NEVER DRAWN MANGA PROPERLY BEFORE, I JUST BOUGHT SOME B4 KENT PAPER (THEY DIDN'T HAVE MANGA MANUSCRIPT PAPER AT THE TIME).
I CONSULTED BOUQUET, A MANGA MAGAZINE I'D BEEN ADDICTED TO SINCE GRADE SCHOOL...
LET'S SEE, EIGHTEEN-BY-TWENTY-ONE CENTIMETERS...
OH, DRAWN IN REGULAR, SUMI, OR INDIA INK. I SEE...
PEOPLE ALWAYS SAY TO USE A G PEN...
BUT THAT HAS TO BE OUTDATED INFO NOW, RIGHT?
I'M SURE NO ONE USES A G PEN IN THIS DAY AND AGE.
THIS AIN'T TOKIWA-SO*.
As a matter of fact, everyone does.

*The Tokyo apartment where Osamu Tezuka and other manga-ka famously lived and worked together.

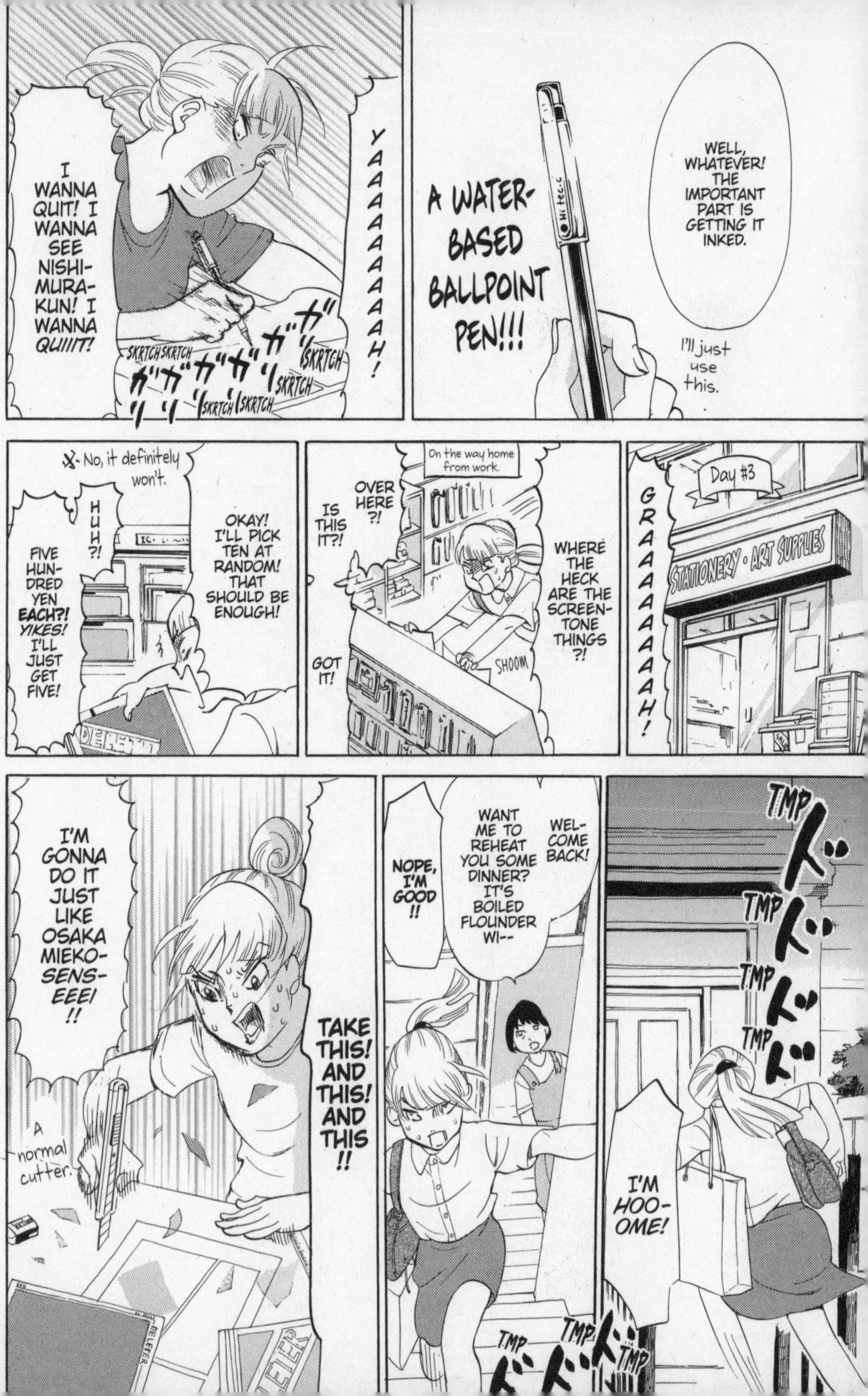

WELL, WHATEVER! THE IMPORTANT PART IS GETTING IT INKED.
I'll just use this.
A WATER-BASED BALLPOINT PEN!!!
YAAAAAAAAAAAH!
I WANNA QUIT! I WANNA SEE NISHIMURA-KUN! I WANNA QUIIIT!
SKRTCH SKRTCH
SKRTCH
SKRTCH
SKRTCH SKRTCH
Day #3
STATIONERY · ART SUPPLIES
GRAAAAAAAAAAH!
On the way home from work.
WHERE THE HECK ARE THE SCREEN-TONE THINGS?!
SHOOM
OVER HERE?!
IS THIS IT?!
GOT IT!
OKAY! I'LL PICK TEN AT RANDOM! THAT SHOULD BE ENOUGH!
HUH?!
FIVE HUNDRED YEN EACH?! YIKES! I'LL JUST GET FIVE!
No, it definitely won't.
TMP
TMP
TMP
TMP
I'M HOO-OME!
WELCOME BACK!
WANT ME TO REHEAT YOU SOME DINNER? IT'S BOILED FLOUNDER WI--
NOPE, I'M GOOD!!
TMP
TMP
TMP
TAKE THIS! AND THIS! AND THIS!!
I'M GONNA DO IT JUST LIKE OSAKA MIEKO-SENSEEEI!!
A normal cutter.

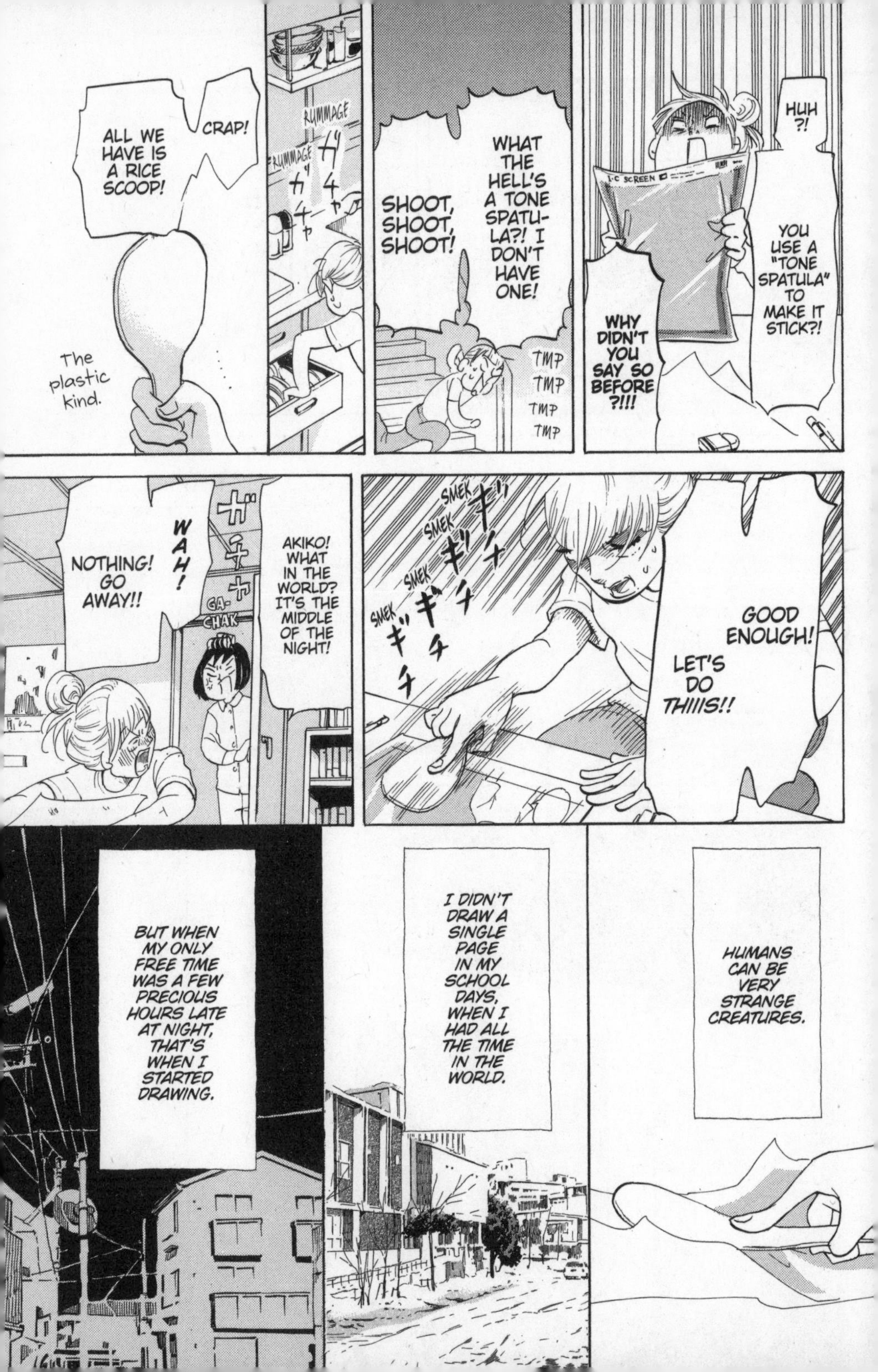
HUH?!
YOU USE A "TONE SPATULA" TO MAKE IT STICK?!
WHY DIDN'T YOU SAY SO BEFORE?!!!
WHAT THE HELL'S A TONE SPATULA?! I DON'T HAVE ONE!
SHOOT, SHOOT, SHOOT!
TMP TMP TMP TMP
RUMMAGE RUMMAGE
CRAP!
ALL WE HAVE IS A RICE SCOOP!
The plastic kind.
GOOD ENOUGH!
LET'S DO THIIIS!!
SMEK SMEK SMEK SMEK
AKIKO! WHAT IN THE WORLD? IT'S THE MIDDLE OF THE NIGHT!
GA-CHAK
WAH!
NOTHING! GO AWAY!!
HUMANS CAN BE VERY STRANGE CREATURES.
I DIDN'T DRAW A SINGLE PAGE IN MY SCHOOL DAYS, WHEN I HAD ALL THE TIME IN THE WORLD.
BUT WHEN MY ONLY FREE TIME WAS A FEW PRECIOUS HOURS LATE AT NIGHT, THAT'S WHEN I STARTED DRAWING.

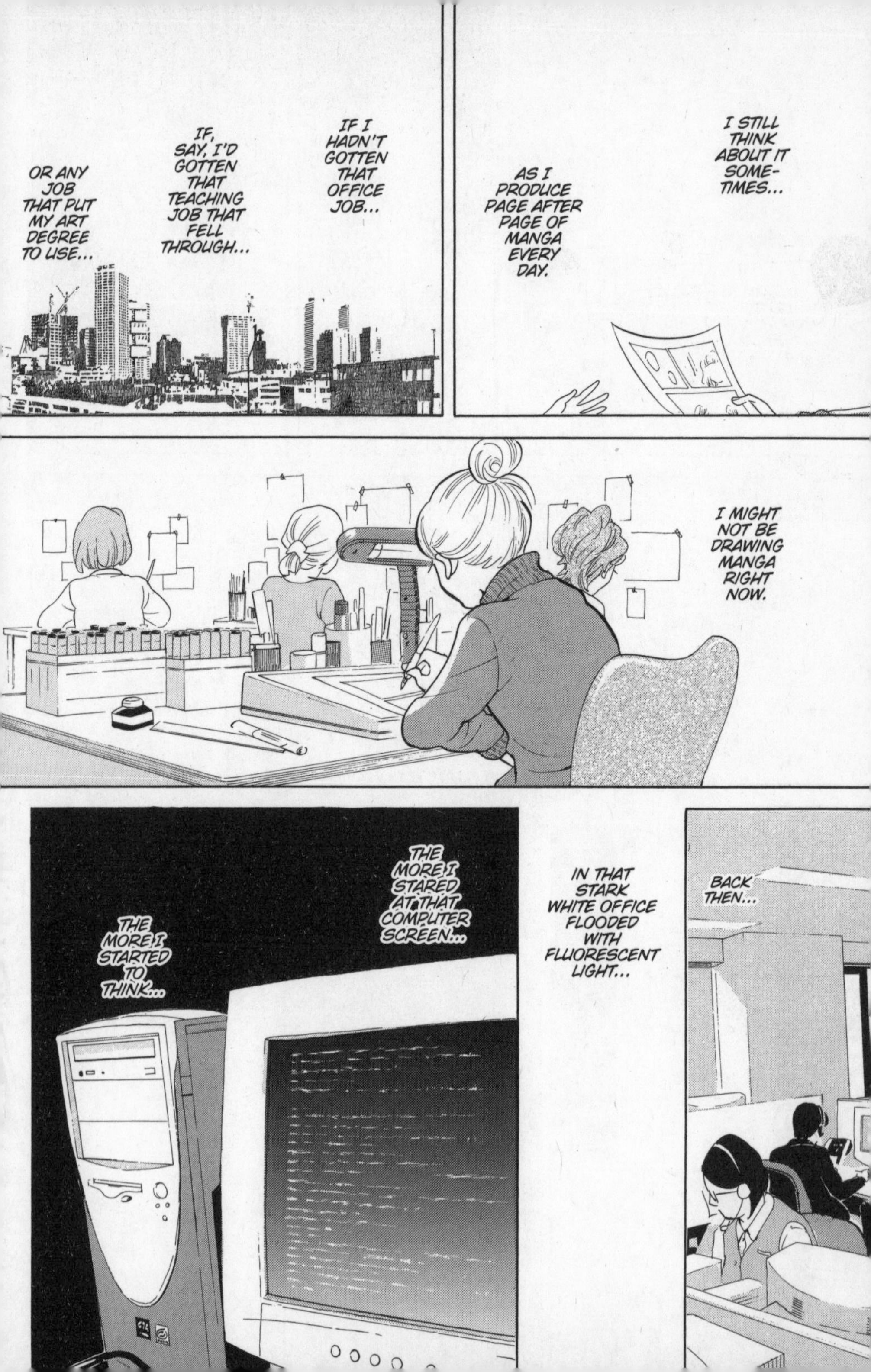
I STILL THINK ABOUT IT SOME-TIMES...
AS I PRODUCE PAGE AFTER PAGE OF MANGA EVERY DAY.
IF I HADN'T GOTTEN THAT OFFICE JOB...
IF, SAY, I'D GOTTEN THAT TEACHING JOB THAT FELL THROUGH...
OR ANY JOB THAT PUT MY ART DEGREE TO USE...
I MIGHT NOT BE DRAWING MANGA RIGHT NOW.
BACK THEN...
IN THAT STARK WHITE OFFICE FLOODED WITH FLUORESCENT LIGHT...
THE MORE I STARED AT THAT COMPUTER SCREEN...
THE MORE I STARTED TO THINK...

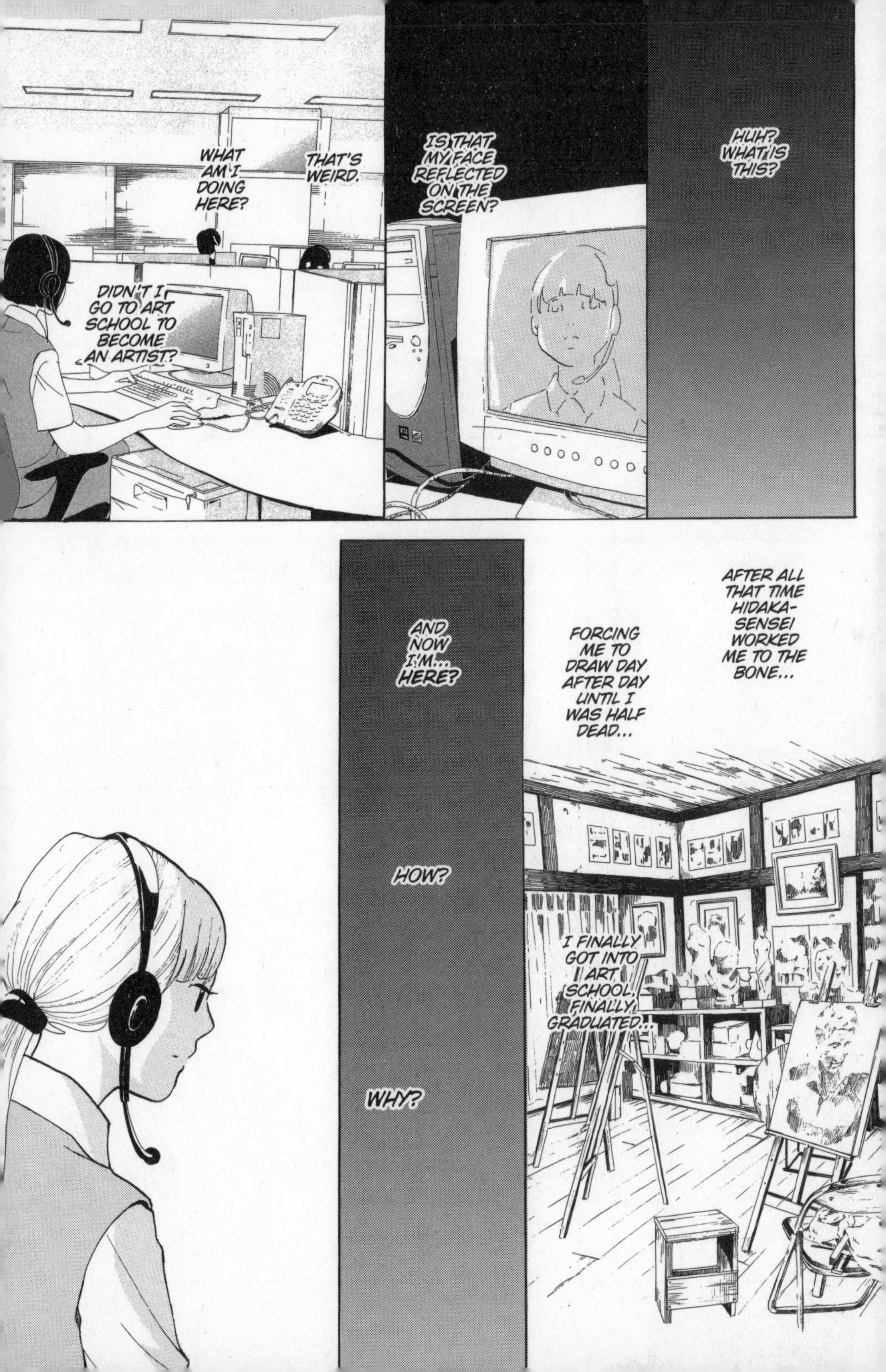
HUH? WHAT IS THIS?
IS THAT MY FACE REFLECTED ON THE SCREEN?
THAT'S WEIRD.
WHAT AM I DOING HERE?
DIDN'T I GO TO ART SCHOOL TO BECOME AN ARTIST?
AFTER ALL THAT TIME HIDAKA-SENSEI WORKED ME TO THE BONE...
FORCING ME TO DRAW DAY AFTER DAY UNTIL I WAS HALF DEAD...
I FINALLY GOT INTO ART SCHOOL, FINALLY GRADUATED...
AND NOW I'M... HERE?
HOW?
WHY?

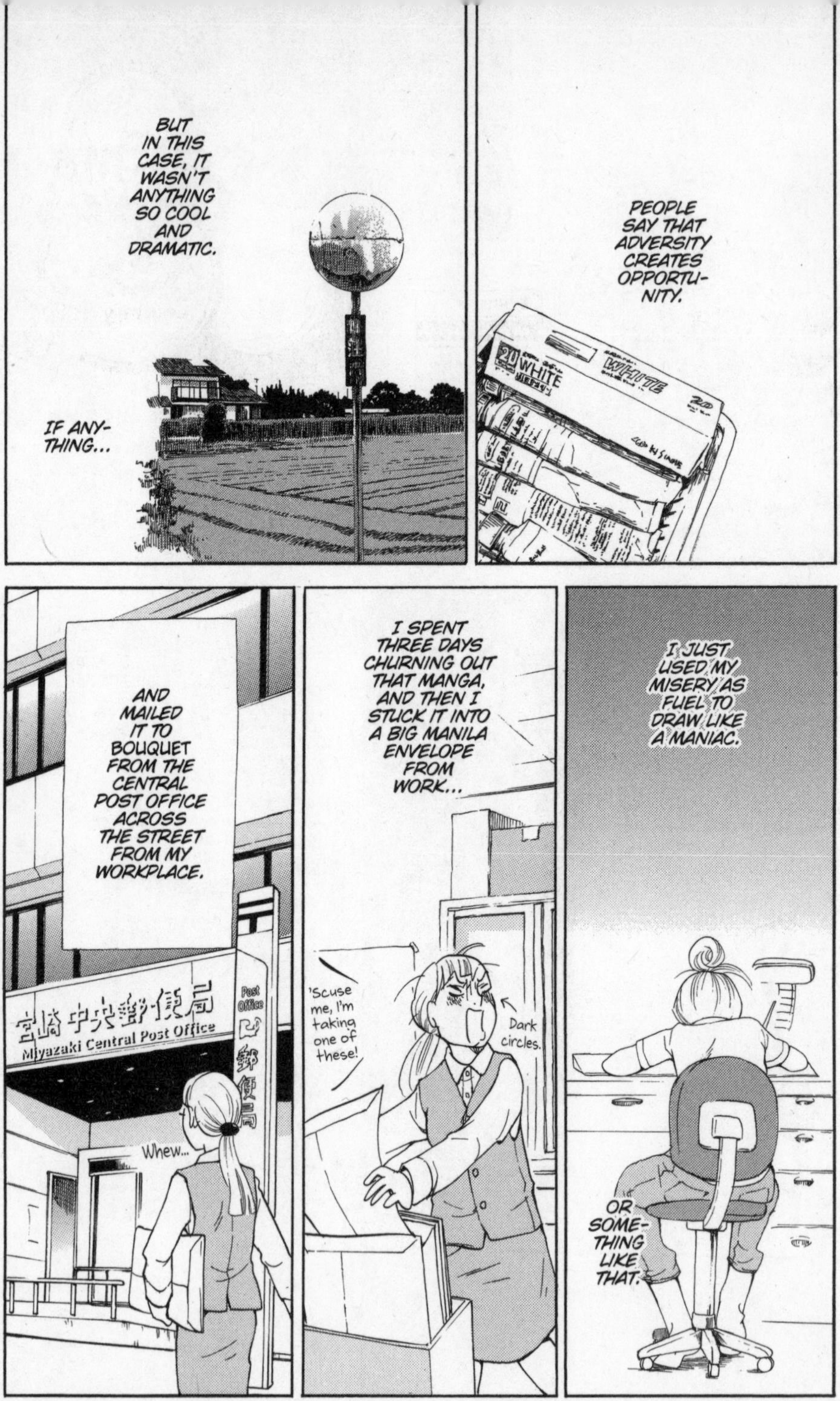
PEOPLE SAY THAT ADVERSITY CREATES OPPORTUNITY.
WHITE
BUT IN THIS CASE, IT WASN'T ANYTHING SO COOL AND DRAMATIC.
IF ANYTHING...
I JUST USED MY MISERY AS FUEL TO DRAW LIKE A MANIAC.
OR SOMETHING LIKE THAT.
I SPENT THREE DAYS CHURNING OUT THAT MANGA, AND THEN I STUCK IT INTO A BIG MANILA ENVELOPE FROM WORK...
'Scuse me, I'm taking one of these!
Dark circles.
AND MAILED IT TO BOUQUET FROM THE CENTRAL POST OFFICE ACROSS THE STREET FROM MY WORKPLACE.
宮崎中央郵便局
Miyazaki Central Post Office
Post Office
〒郵便局
Whew...

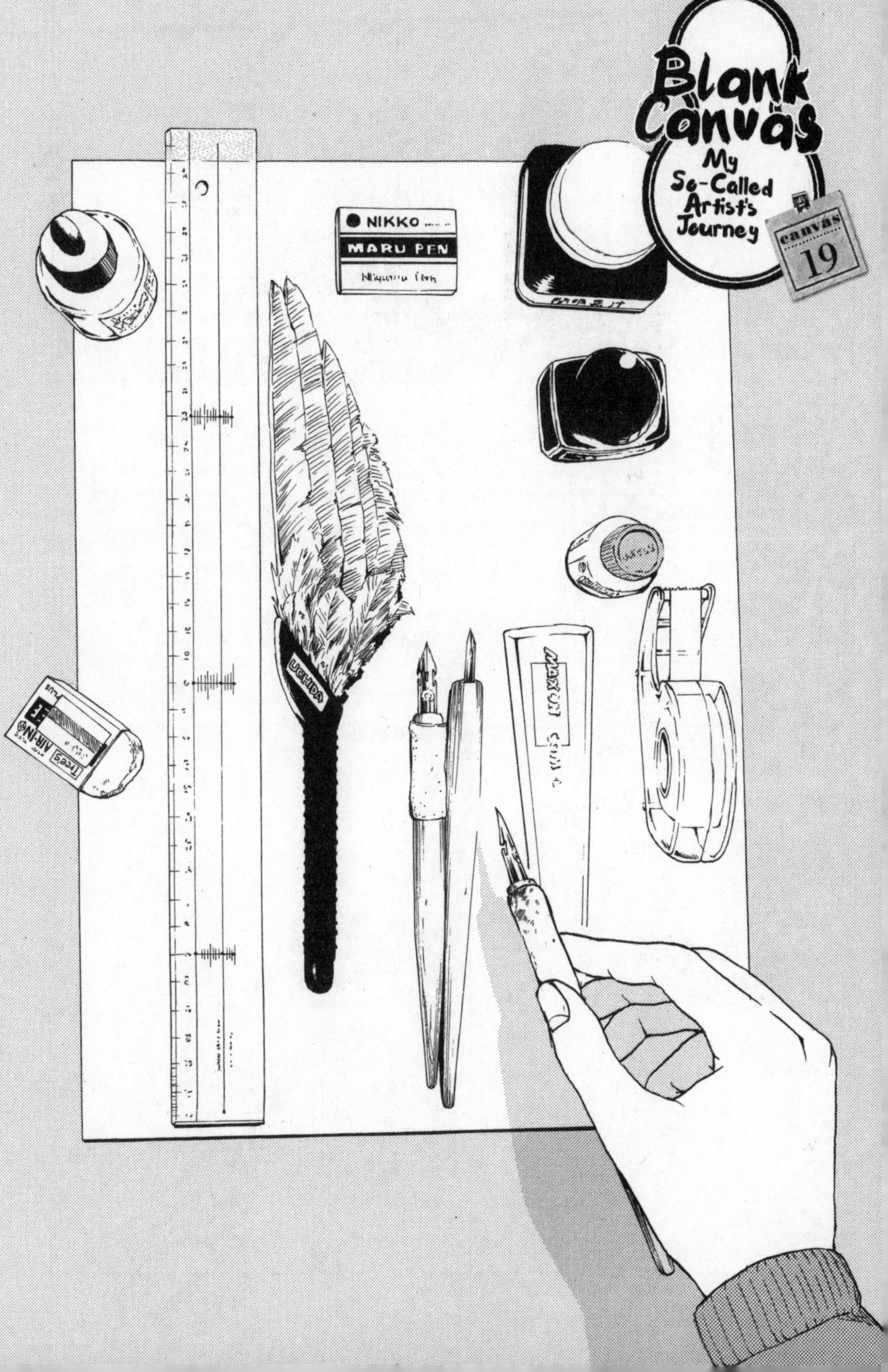
Blank Canvas
My So-Called Artist's Journey
canvas
19
NIKKO
MARU PEN
UCHIDA
MAXON
AIR-IN

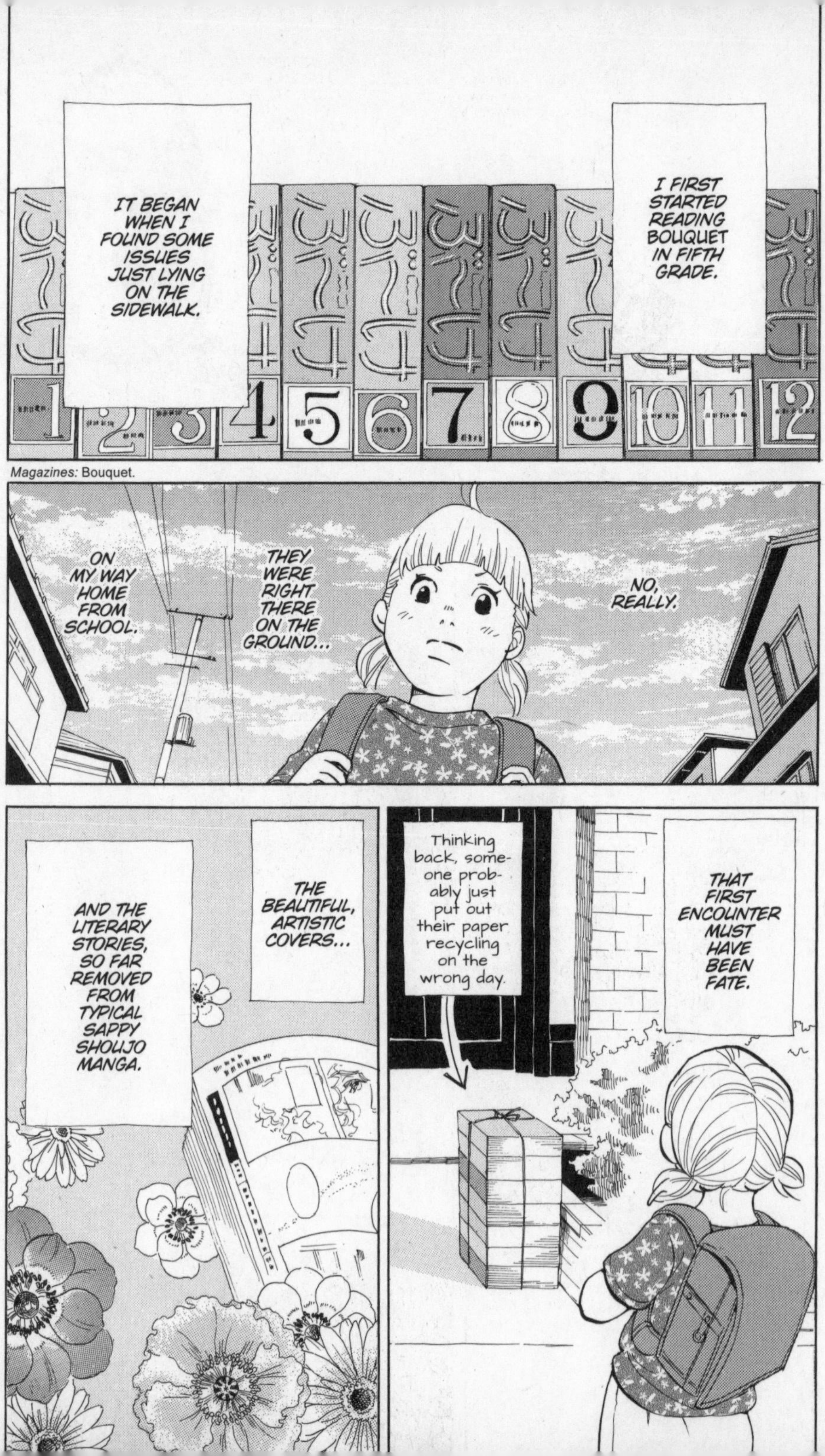
I FIRST STARTED READING BOUQUET IN FIFTH GRADE.
IT BEGAN WHEN I FOUND SOME ISSUES JUST LYING ON THE SIDEWALK.
Magazines: Bouquet.
ON MY WAY HOME FROM SCHOOL.
THEY WERE RIGHT THERE ON THE GROUND...
NO, REALLY.
THAT FIRST ENCOUNTER MUST HAVE BEEN FATE.
Thinking back, someone probably just put out their paper recycling on the wrong day.
THE BEAUTIFUL, ARTISTIC COVERS...
AND THE LITERARY STORIES, SO FAR REMOVED FROM TYPICAL SAPPY SHOUJO MANGA.

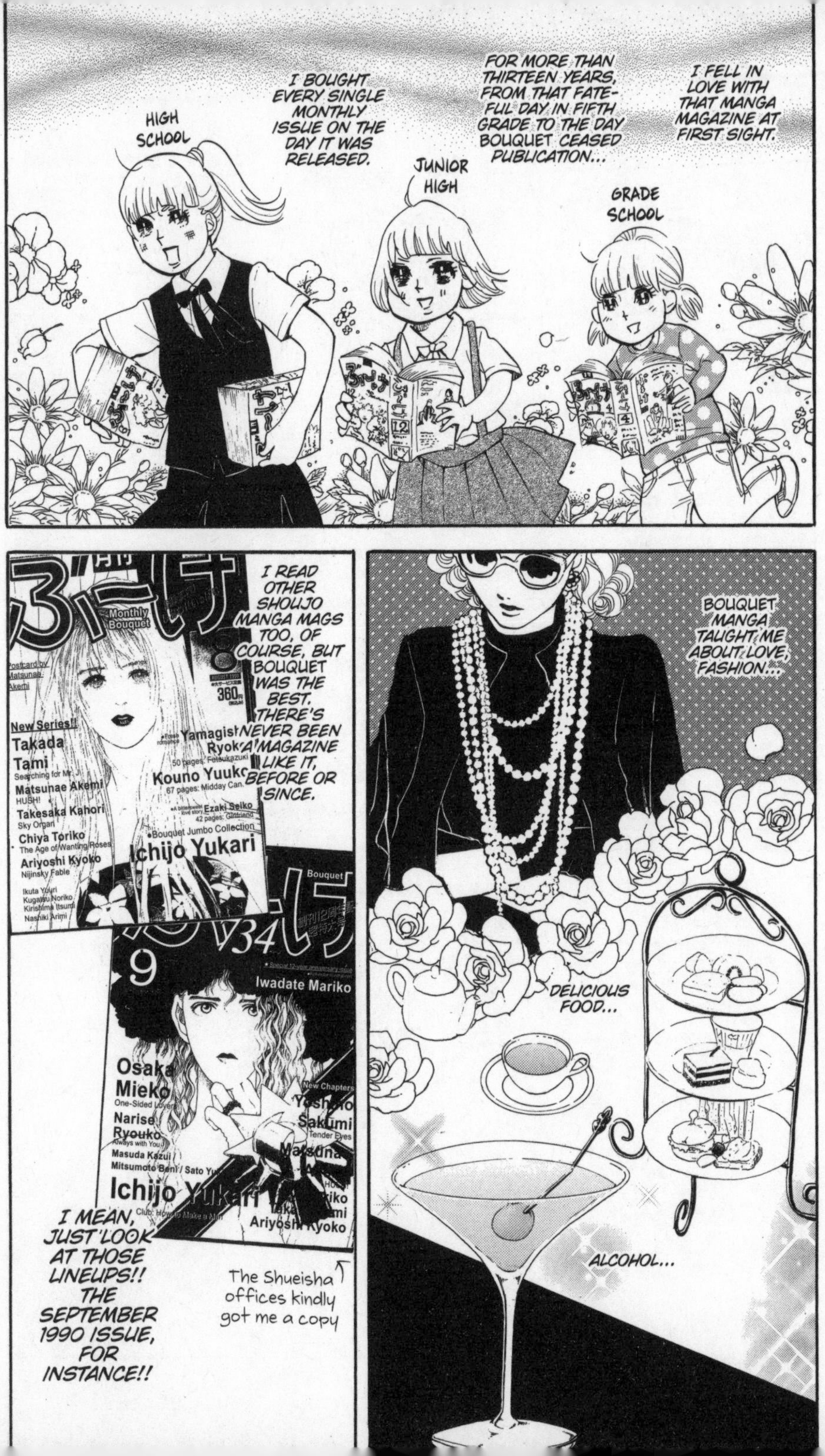
I FELL IN LOVE WITH THAT MANGA MAGAZINE AT FIRST SIGHT.
FOR MORE THAN THIRTEEN YEARS, FROM THAT FATE-FUL DAY IN FIFTH GRADE TO THE DAY BOUQUET CEASED PUBLICATION...
I BOUGHT EVERY SINGLE MONTHLY ISSUE ON THE DAY IT WAS RELEASED.
GRADE SCHOOL
JUNIOR HIGH
HIGH SCHOOL
BOUQUET MANGA TAUGHT ME ABOUT LOVE, FASHION...
DELICIOUS FOOD...
ALCOHOL...
I READ OTHER SHOUJO MANGA MAGS TOO, OF COURSE, BUT BOUQUET WAS THE BEST. THERE'S NEVER BEEN A MAGAZINE LIKE IT, BEFORE OR SINCE.
Monthly Bouquet
Postcard by Matsunae Akemi
360
New Series!!
Takada Tami
Searching for Mr. J
Matsunae Akemi
HUSH!
Takesaka Kahori
Sky Organ
Chiya Toriko
The Age of Wanting Roses
Ariyoshi Kyoko
Nijinsky Fable
Ikuta Youri
Kugatsu Noriko
Kirishima Itsumi
Nashiki Arimi
Kouno Yuuko
67 pages: Midday Can...
Ezaki Seiko
42 pages: Girlfriend
Bouquet Jumbo Collection
Ichijo Yukari
Bouquet
9
Iwadate Mariko
Osaka Mieko
One-Sided Lovers
Narise Ryouko
Always with You
Masuda Kazui
Mitsumoto Beni / Sato Yu...
Ichijo Yukari
New Chapters
Yoshino Sakumi
Tender Eyes
Ariyoshi Kyoko
I MEAN, JUST LOOK AT THOSE LINEUPS!! THE SEPTEMBER 1990 ISSUE, FOR INSTANCE!!
The Shueisha offices kindly got me a copy

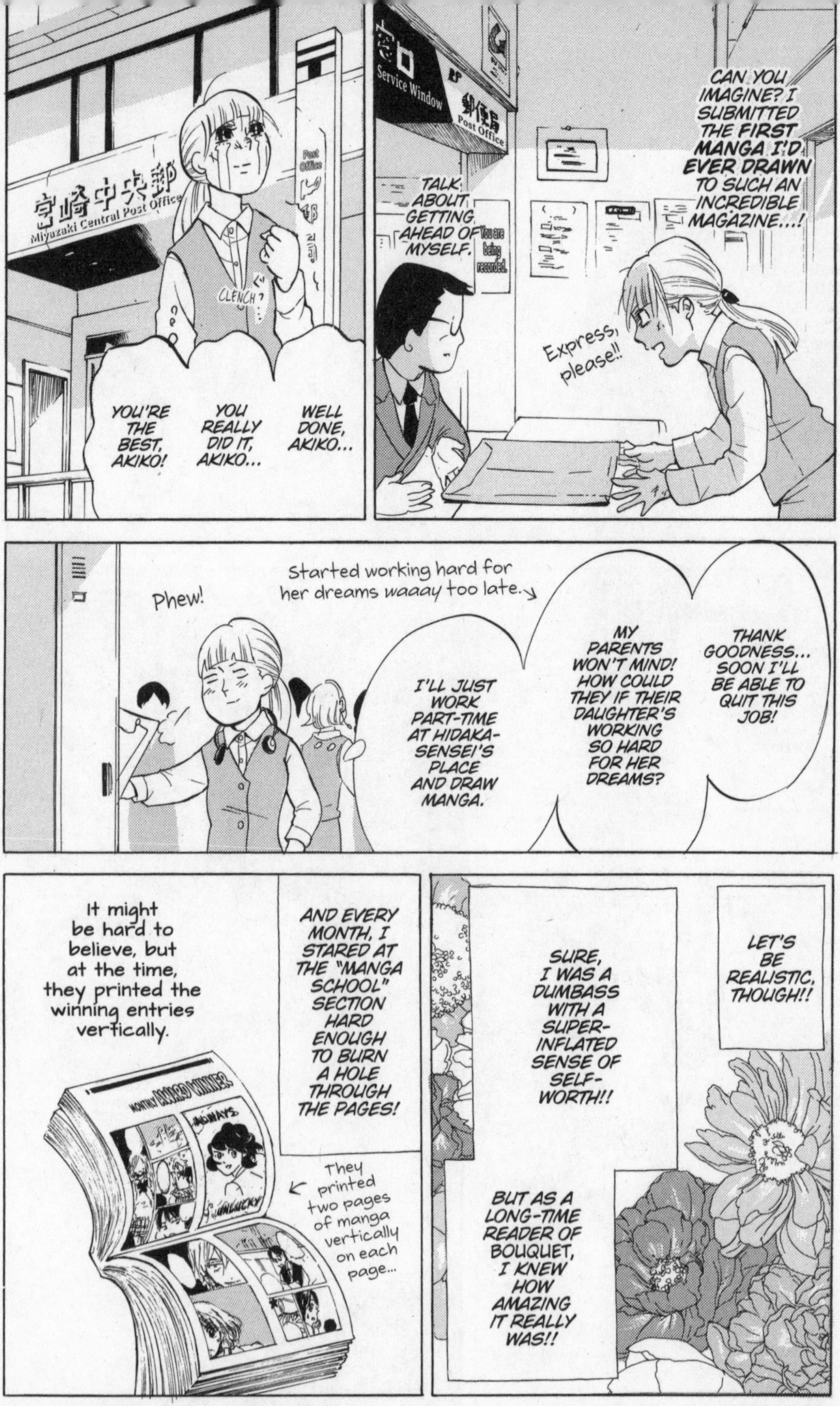
窓口
Service Window
郵便局
Post Office
CAN YOU IMAGINE? I SUBMITTED THE FIRST MANGA I'D EVER DRAWN TO SUCH AN INCREDIBLE MAGAZINE...!
TALK ABOUT GETTING AHEAD OF MYSELF.
You are being recorded.
Express, please!!
宮崎中央郵
Miyazaki Central Post Office
Post Office
CLENCH
WELL DONE, AKIKO...
YOU REALLY DID IT, AKIKO...
YOU'RE THE BEST, AKIKO!
THANK GOODNESS... SOON I'LL BE ABLE TO QUIT THIS JOB!
MY PARENTS WON'T MIND! HOW COULD THEY IF THEIR DAUGHTER'S WORKING SO HARD FOR HER DREAMS?
I'LL JUST WORK PART-TIME AT HIDAKA-SENSEI'S PLACE AND DRAW MANGA.
Started working hard for her dreams waaay too late.
Phew!
LET'S BE REALISTIC, THOUGH!!
SURE, I WAS A DUMBASS WITH A SUPER-INFLATED SENSE OF SELF-WORTH!!
BUT AS A LONG-TIME READER OF BOUQUET, I KNEW HOW AMAZING IT REALLY WAS!!
AND EVERY MONTH, I STARED AT THE "MANGA SCHOOL" SECTION HARD ENOUGH TO BURN A HOLE THROUGH THE PAGES!
It might be hard to believe, but at the time, they printed the winning entries vertically.
MONTHLY AWARD WINNER
ALWAYS
UNLUCKY
They printed two pages of manga vertically on each page...

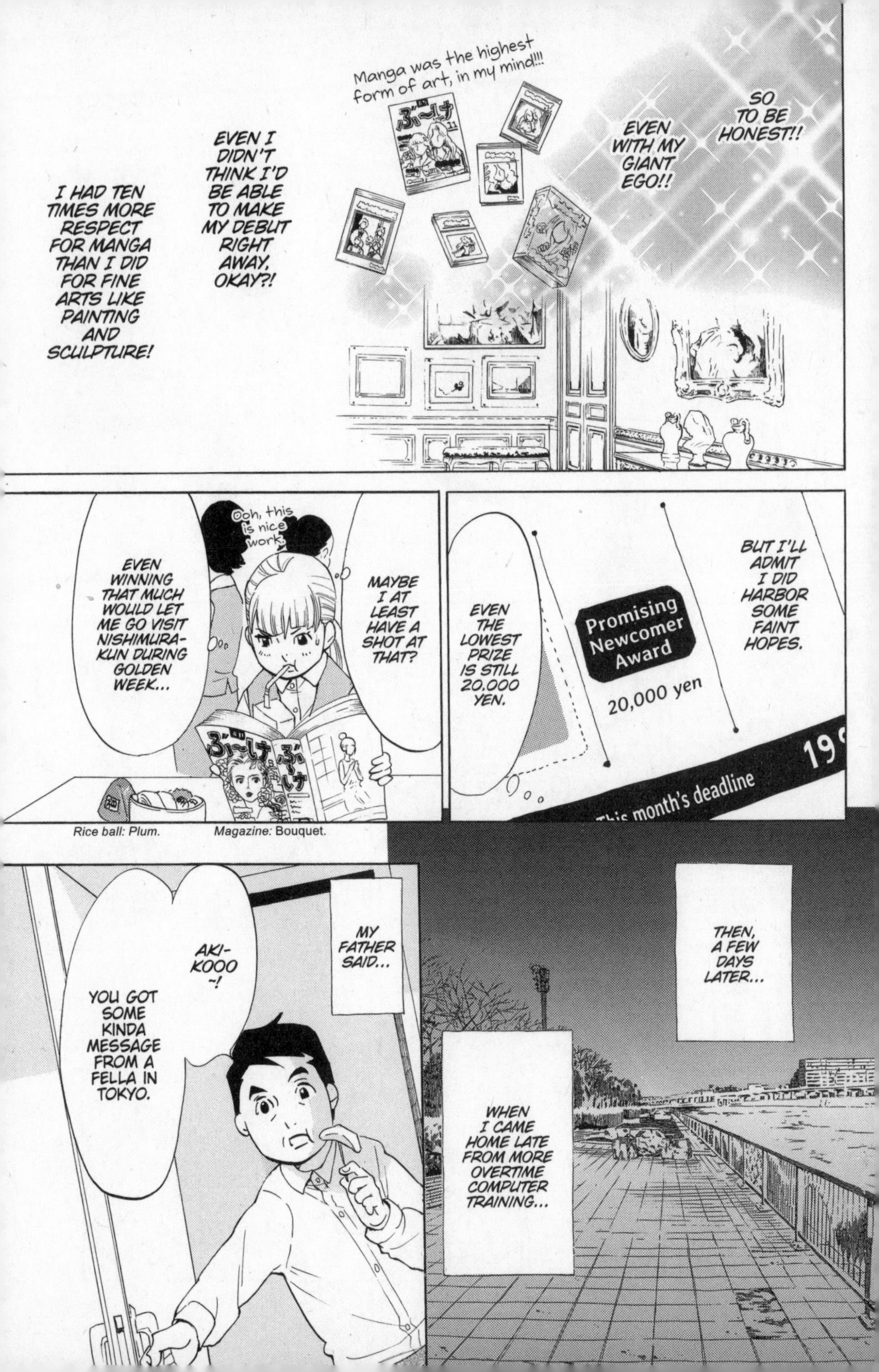
SO TO BE HONEST!!
EVEN WITH MY GIANT EGO!!
Manga was the highest form of art, in my mind!!!
EVEN I DIDN'T THINK I'D BE ABLE TO MAKE MY DEBUT RIGHT AWAY, OKAY?!
I HAD TEN TIMES MORE RESPECT FOR MANGA THAN I DID FOR FINE ARTS LIKE PAINTING AND SCULPTURE!
BUT I'LL ADMIT I DID HARBOR SOME FAINT HOPES.
Promising Newcomer Award
20,000 yen
This month's deadline
EVEN THE LOWEST PRIZE IS STILL 20,000 YEN.
MAYBE I AT LEAST HAVE A SHOT AT THAT?
Ooh, this is nice work.
EVEN WINNING THAT MUCH WOULD LET ME GO VISIT NISHIMURA-KUN DURING GOLDEN WEEK...
THEN, A FEW DAYS LATER...
WHEN I CAME HOME LATE FROM MORE OVERTIME COMPUTER TRAINING...
MY FATHER SAID...
AKI-KOOO~!
YOU GOT SOME KINDA MESSAGE FROM A FELLA IN TOKYO.

Rice ball: Plum. *Magazine:* Bouquet.

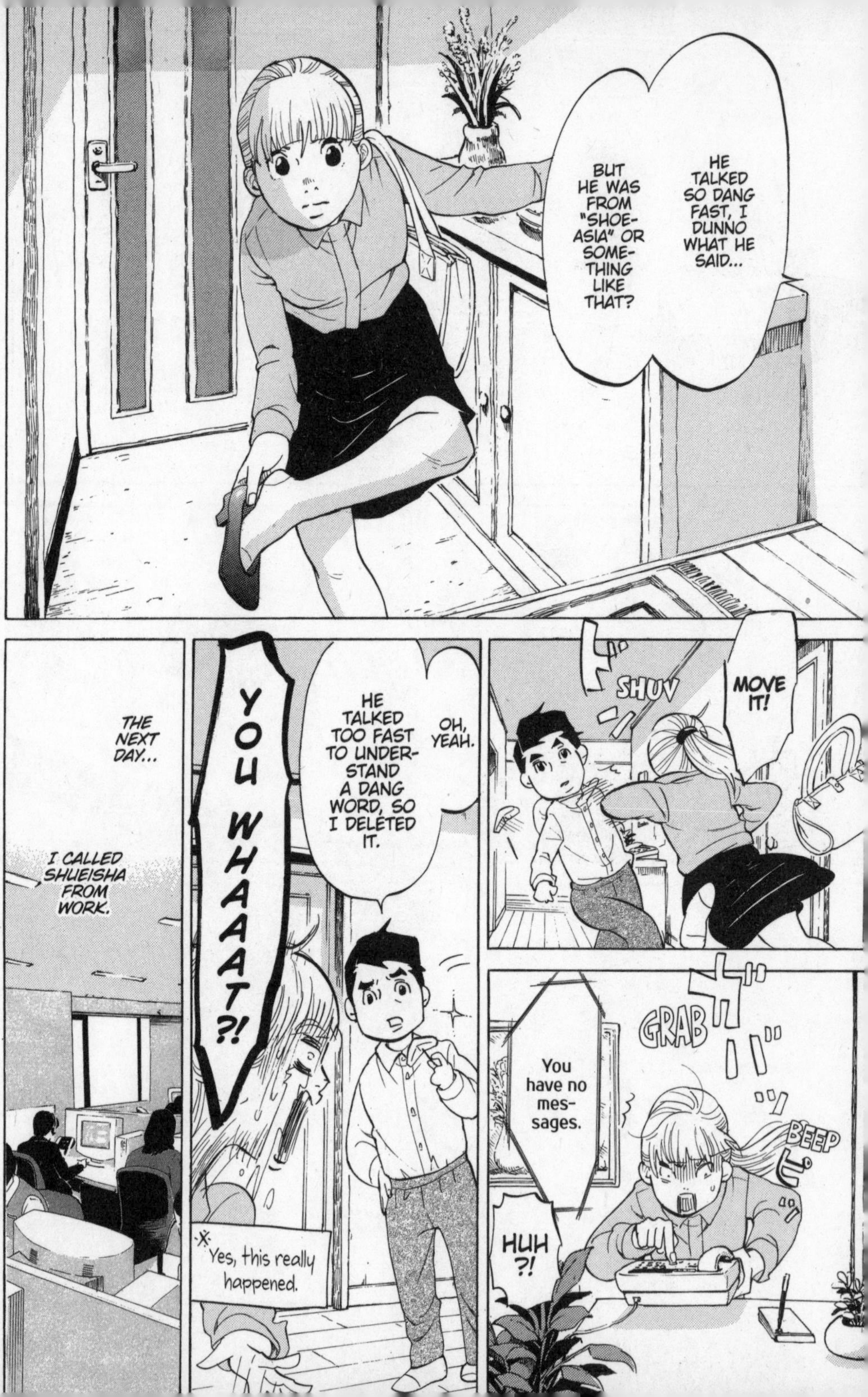
HE TALKED SO DANG FAST, I DUNNO WHAT HE SAID...
BUT HE WAS FROM "SHOE-ASIA" OR SOMETHING LIKE THAT?
MOVE IT!
SHUV
GRAB
You have no messages.
BEEP
HUH ?!
OH, YEAH.
HE TALKED TOO FAST TO UNDERSTAND A DANG WORD, SO I DELETED IT.
YOU WHAAAAT?!
※Yes, this really happened.
THE NEXT DAY...
I CALLED SHUEISHA FROM WORK.

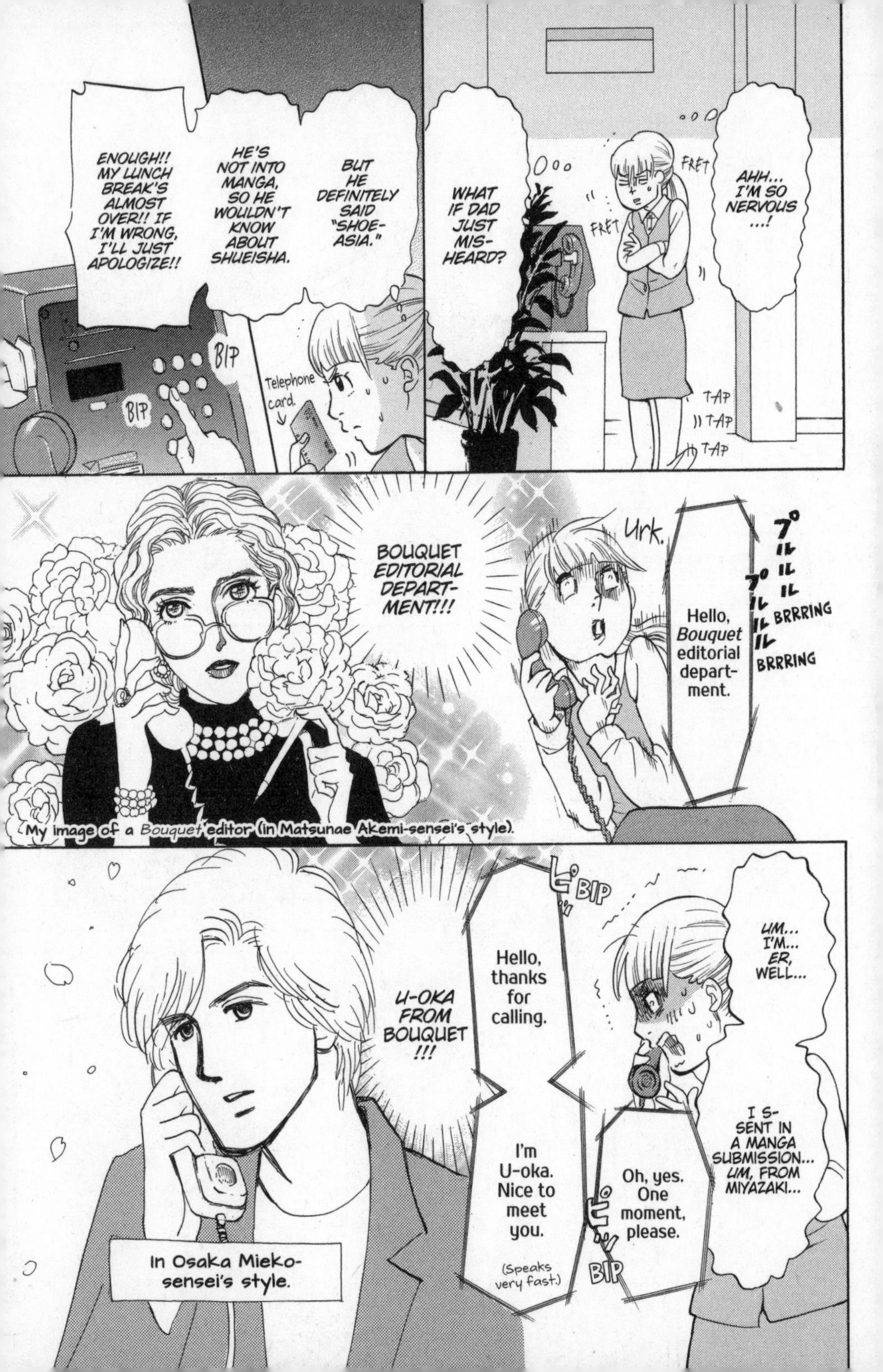
AHH... I'M SO NERVOUS ...!
FRET
FRET
WHAT IF DAD JUST MIS-HEARD?
TAP
TAP
TAP
BUT HE DEFINITELY SAID "SHOE-ASIA."
HE'S NOT INTO MANGA, SO HE WOULDN'T KNOW ABOUT SHUEISHA.
ENOUGH!! MY LUNCH BREAK'S ALMOST OVER!! IF I'M WRONG, I'LL JUST APOLOGIZE!!
BIP
BIP
Telephone card.
BRRRING
BRRRING
Hello, *Bouquet* editorial depart-ment.
Urk.
BOUQUET EDITORIAL DEPART-MENT!!!
My image of a *Bouquet* editor (in Matsunae Akemi-sensei's style).
UM... I'M... ER, WELL...
I S-SENT IN A MANGA SUBMISSION... UM, FROM MIYAZAKI...
Oh, yes. One moment, please.
BIP
BIP
Hello, thanks for calling.
I'm U-oka. Nice to meet you.
(Speaks very fast.)
U-OKA FROM BOUQUET!!!
In Osaka Mieko-sensei's style.

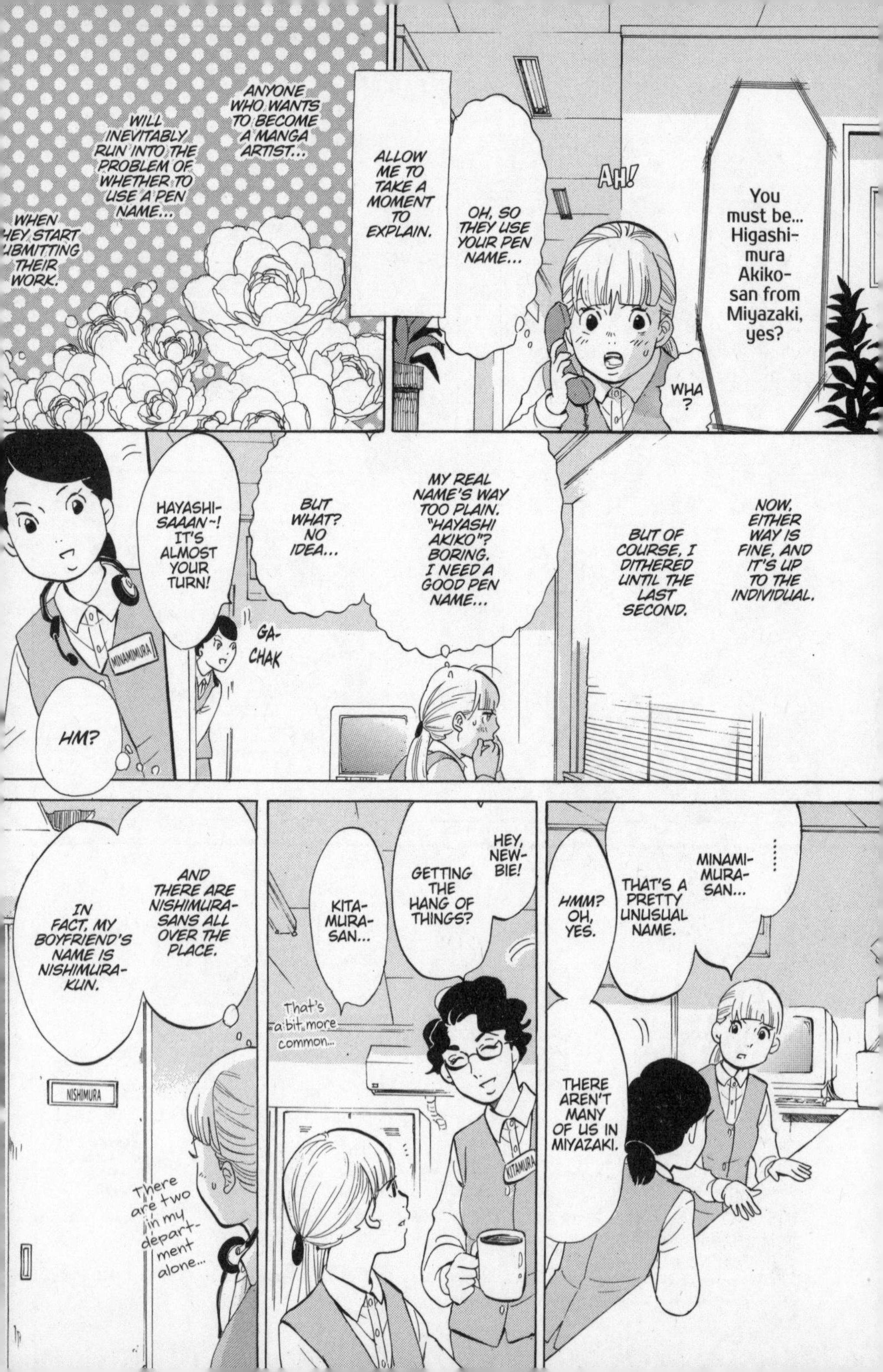
You must be... Higashimura Akiko-san from Miyazaki, yes?
AH!
WHA?
OH, SO THEY USE YOUR PEN NAME...
ALLOW ME TO TAKE A MOMENT TO EXPLAIN.
ANYONE WHO WANTS TO BECOME A MANGA ARTIST...
WILL INEVITABLY RUN INTO THE PROBLEM OF WHETHER TO USE A PEN NAME...
WHEN HEY START UBMITTING THEIR WORK.
NOW, EITHER WAY IS FINE, AND IT'S UP TO THE INDIVIDUAL.
BUT OF COURSE, I DITHERED UNTIL THE LAST SECOND.
MY REAL NAME'S WAY TOO PLAIN. "HAYASHI AKIKO"? BORING. I NEED A GOOD PEN NAME...
BUT WHAT? NO IDEA...
GA-CHAK
HAYASHI-SAAAN~! IT'S ALMOST YOUR TURN!
MINAMIMURA
HM?
......
MINAMI-MURA-SAN...
THAT'S A PRETTY UNUSUAL NAME.
HMM? OH, YES.
THERE AREN'T MANY OF US IN MIYAZAKI.
HEY, NEW-BIE!
GETTING THE HANG OF THINGS?
KITA-MURA-SAN...
That's a bit more common...
KITAMURA
AND THERE ARE NISHIMURA-SANS ALL OVER THE PLACE.
IN FACT, MY BOYFRIEND'S NAME IS NISHIMURA-KUN.
NISHIMURA
There are two in my department alone...

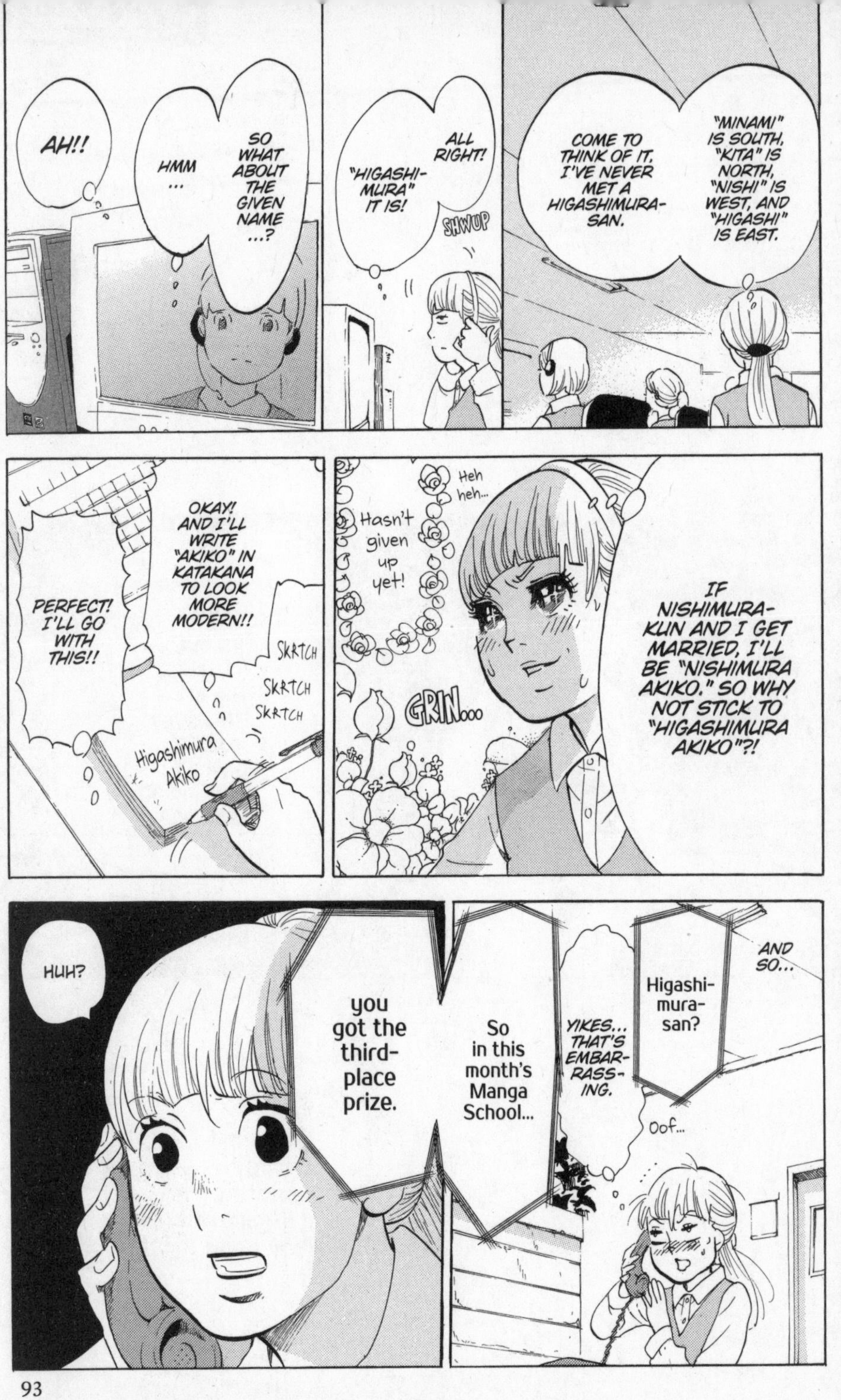
"MINAMI" IS SOUTH, "KITA" IS NORTH, "NISHI" IS WEST, AND "HIGASHI" IS EAST.
COME TO THINK OF IT, I'VE NEVER MET A HIGASHIMURA-SAN.
ALL RIGHT!
"HIGASHI-MURA" IT IS!
SHWUP
SO WHAT ABOUT THE GIVEN NAME ...?
HMM ...
AH!!
IF NISHIMURA-KUN AND I GET MARRIED, I'LL BE "NISHIMURA AKIKO." SO WHY NOT STICK TO "HIGASHIMURA AKIKO"?!
Heh heh...
Hasn't given up yet!
GRIN...
OKAY! AND I'LL WRITE "AKIKO" IN KATAKANA TO LOOK MORE MODERN!!
PERFECT! I'LL GO WITH THIS!!
SKRTCH
SKRTCH
SKRTCH
Higashimura Akiko
AND SO...
Higashi-mura-san?
YIKES... THAT'S EMBARR-ASSING.
Oof...
So in this month's Manga School...
you got the third-place prize.
HUH?

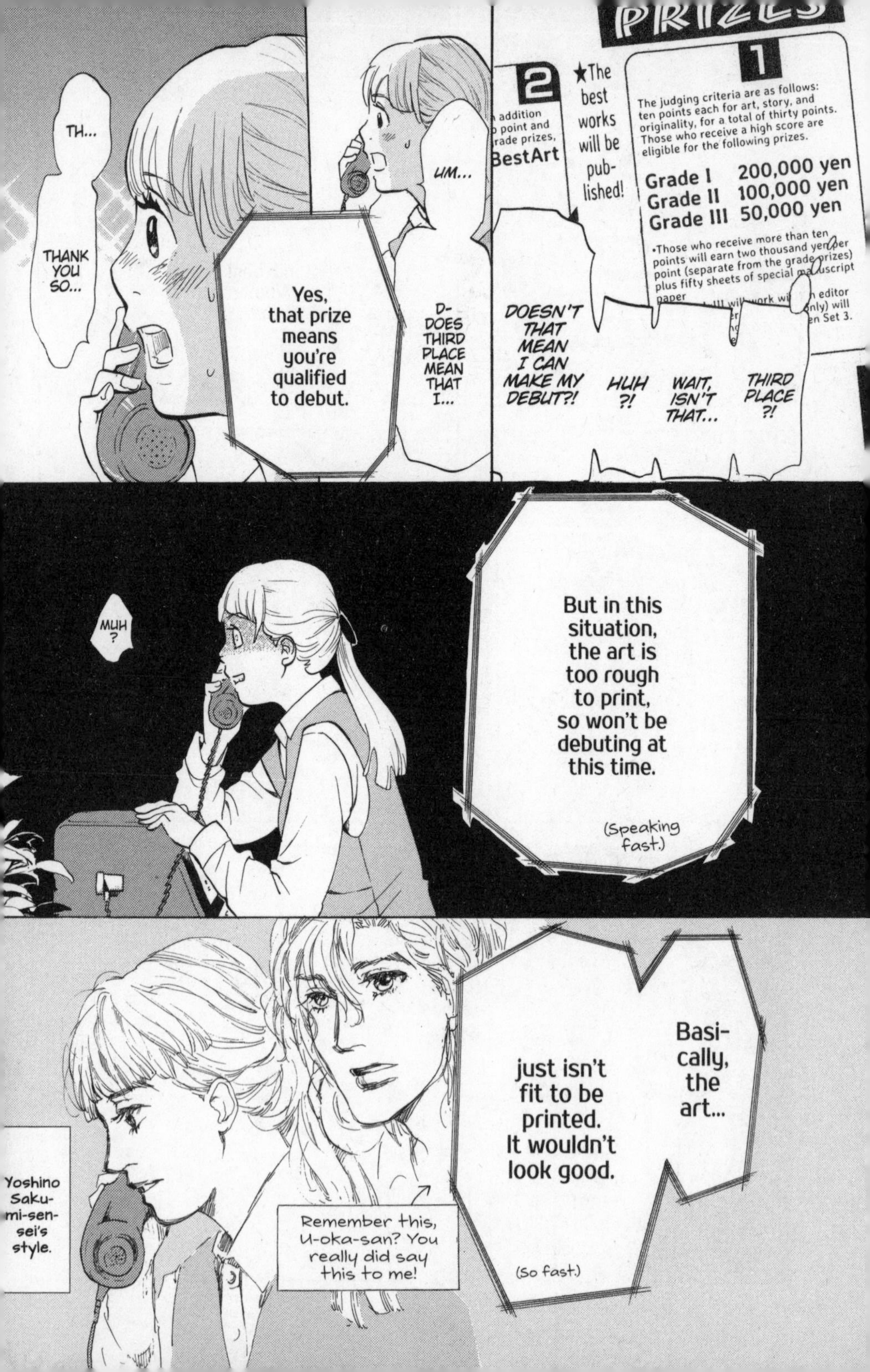
PRIZES
1
The judging criteria are as follows: ten points each for art, story, and originality, for a total of thirty points. Those who receive a high score are eligible for the following prizes.
Grade I 200,000 yen
Grade II 100,000 yen
Grade III 50,000 yen
2
BestArt
★The best works will be published!
THIRD PLACE?!
WAIT, ISN'T THAT...
HUH?!
DOESN'T THAT MEAN I CAN MAKE MY DEBUT?!
UM...
D-DOES THIRD PLACE MEAN THAT I...
Yes, that prize means you're qualified to debut.
TH...
THANK YOU SO...
But in this situation, the art is too rough to print, so won't be debuting at this time.
(Speaking fast.)
MUH?
Basically, the art...
just isn't fit to be printed. It wouldn't look good.
(So fast.)
Remember this, U-oka-san? You really did say this to me!
Yoshino Sakumi-sensei's style.

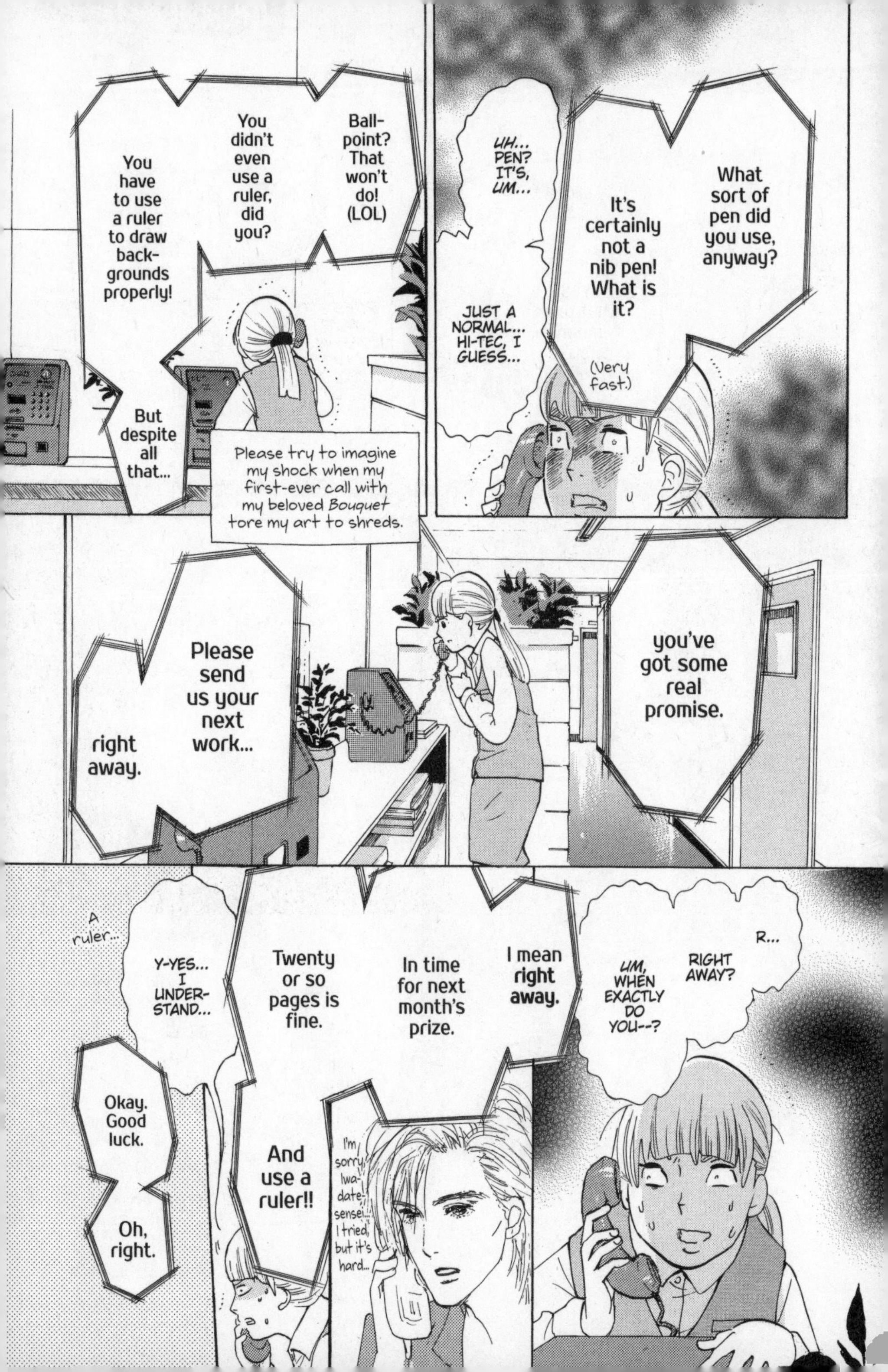
What sort of pen did you use, anyway?
It's certainly not a nib pen! What is it?
(Very fast.)
UH... PEN? IT'S, UM...
JUST A NORMAL... HI-TEC, I GUESS...
Ball-point? That won't do! (LOL)
You didn't even use a ruler, did you?
You have to use a ruler to draw back-grounds properly!
But despite all that...
Please try to imagine my shock when my first-ever call with my beloved *Bouquet* tore my art to shreds.
you've got some real promise.
Please send us your next work...
right away.
R...
RIGHT AWAY?
UM, WHEN EXACTLY DO YOU--?
I mean **right away.**
In time for next month's prize.
Twenty or so pages is fine.
Y-YES... I UNDER-STAND...
A ruler...
And use a ruler!!
I'm sorry, Iwa-date-sensei... I tried, but it's hard...
Okay. Good luck.
Oh, right.

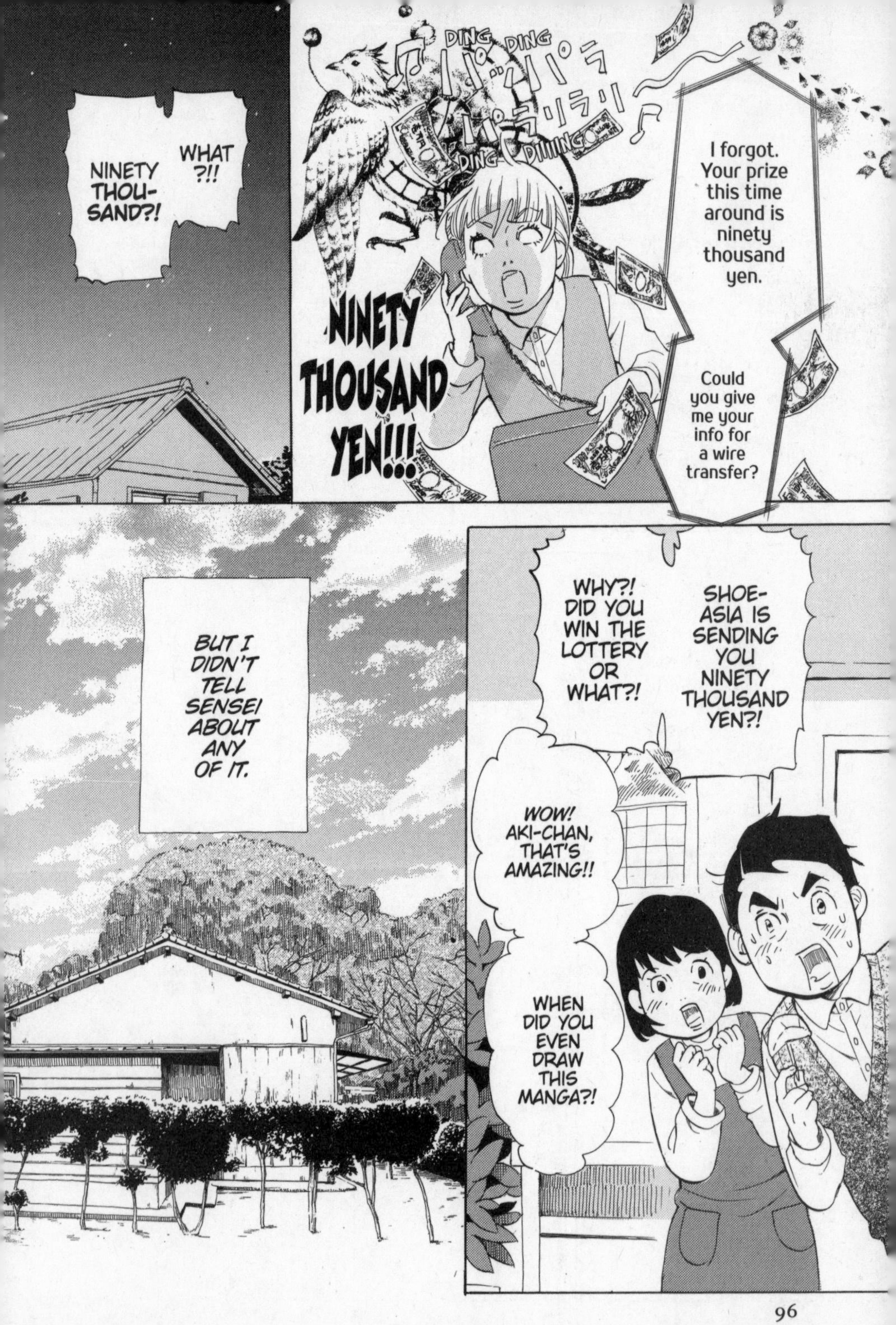
DING DING
DING DIIIING
I forgot. Your prize this time around is ninety thousand yen.
Could you give me your info for a wire transfer?
NINETY THOUSAND YEN!!!
WHAT?!!
NINETY THOUSAND?!
SHOE-ASIA IS SENDING YOU NINETY THOUSAND YEN?!
WHY?! DID YOU WIN THE LOTTERY OR WHAT?!
WOW! AKI-CHAN, THAT'S AMAZING!!
WHEN DID YOU EVEN DRAW THIS MANGA?!
BUT I DIDN'T TELL SENSEI ABOUT ANY OF IT.

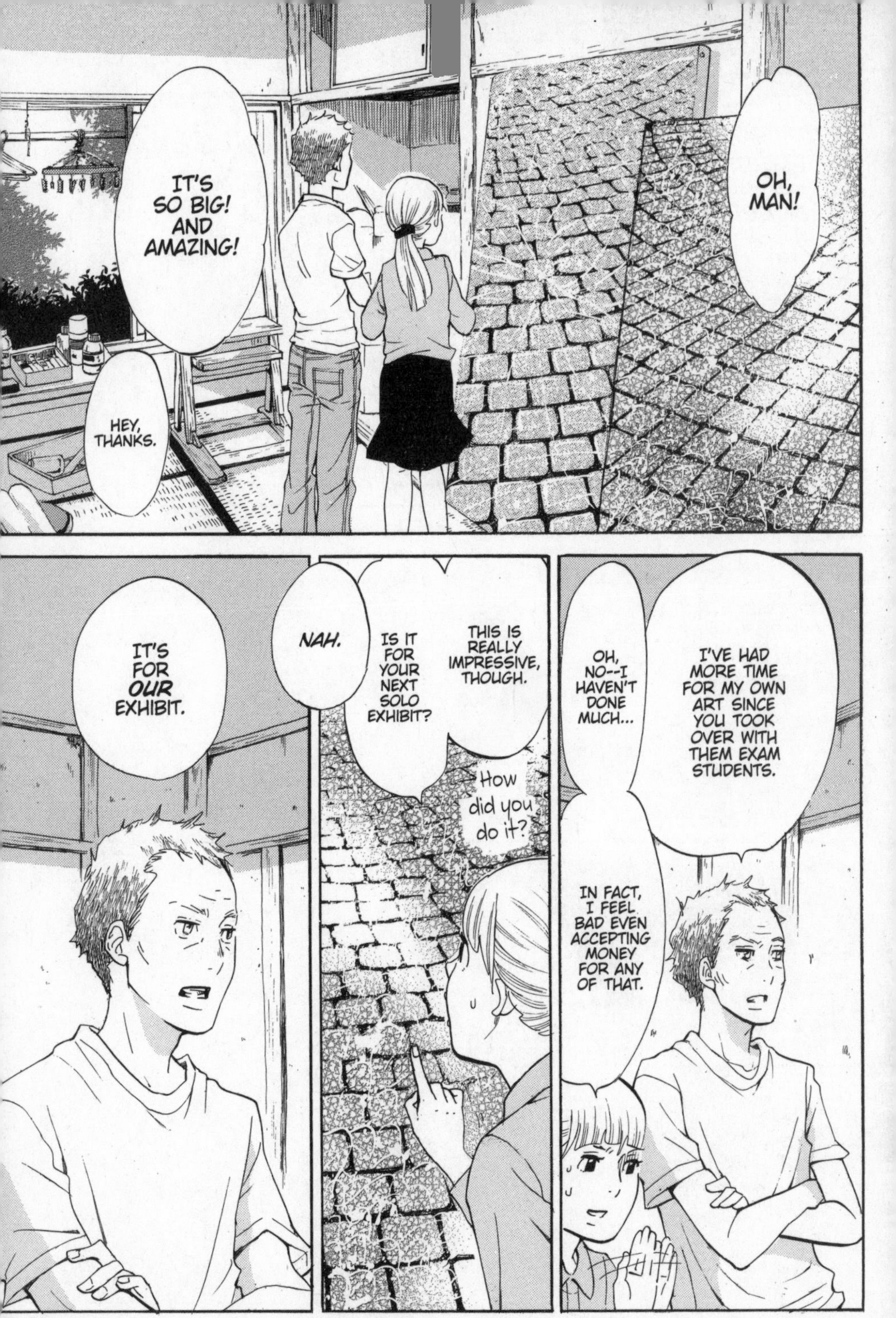
OH, MAN!
IT'S SO BIG! AND AMAZING!
HEY, THANKS.
I'VE HAD MORE TIME FOR MY OWN ART SINCE YOU TOOK OVER WITH THEM EXAM STUDENTS.
OH, NO--I HAVEN'T DONE MUCH...
IN FACT, I FEEL BAD EVEN ACCEPTING MONEY FOR ANY OF THAT.
THIS IS REALLY IMPRESSIVE, THOUGH.
IS IT FOR YOUR NEXT SOLO EXHIBIT?
NAH.
How did you do it?
IT'S FOR **OUR** EXHIBIT.

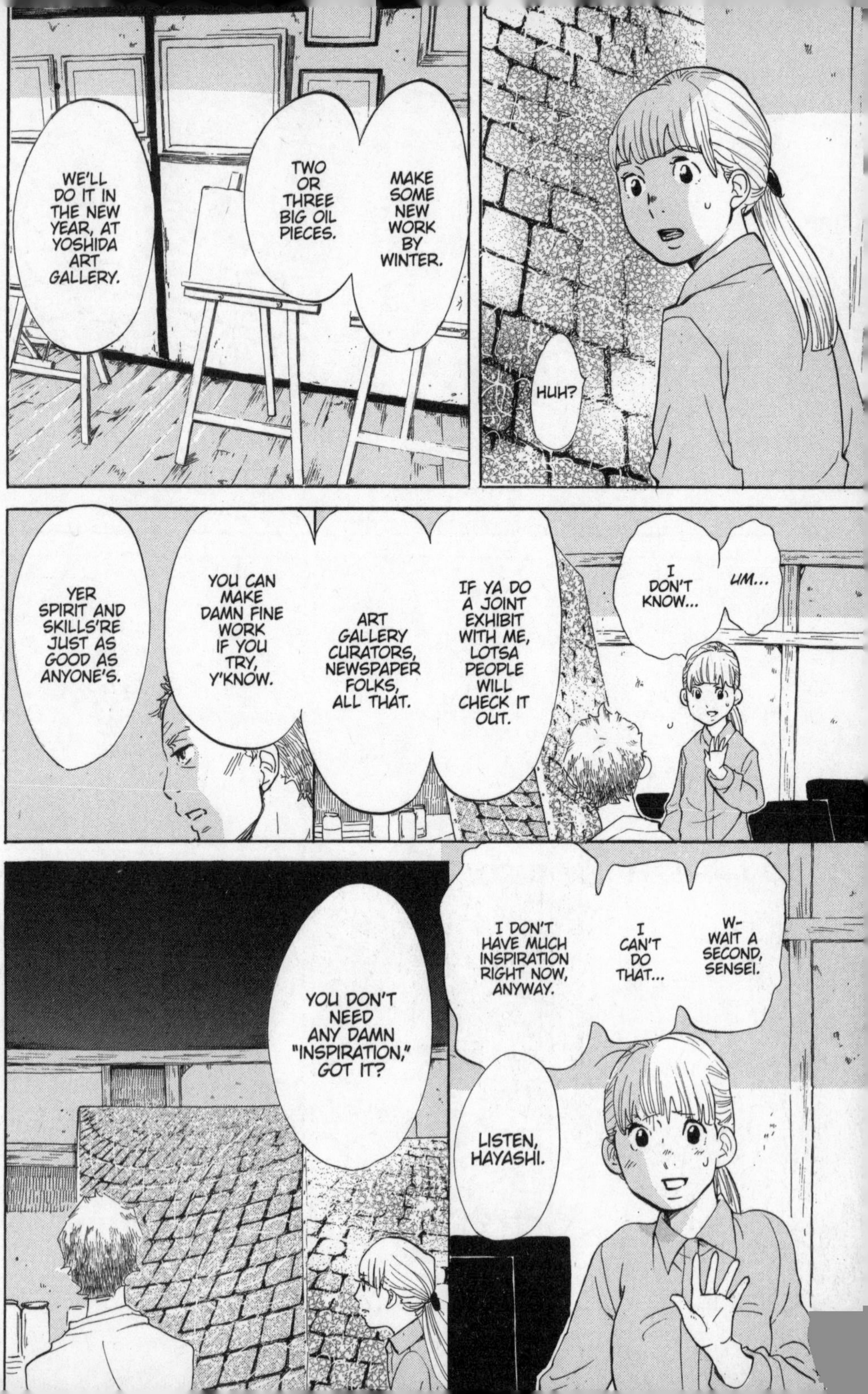
HUH?
MAKE SOME NEW WORK BY WINTER.
TWO OR THREE BIG OIL PIECES.
WE'LL DO IT IN THE NEW YEAR, AT YOSHIDA ART GALLERY.
UM...
I DON'T KNOW...
IF YA DO A JOINT EXHIBIT WITH ME, LOTSA PEOPLE WILL CHECK IT OUT.
ART GALLERY CURATORS, NEWSPAPER FOLKS, ALL THAT.
YOU CAN MAKE DAMN FINE WORK IF YOU TRY, Y'KNOW.
YER SPIRIT AND SKILLS'RE JUST AS GOOD AS ANYONE'S.
W-WAIT A SECOND, SENSEI.
I CAN'T DO THAT...
I DON'T HAVE MUCH INSPIRATION RIGHT NOW, ANYWAY.
LISTEN, HAYASHI.
YOU DON'T NEED ANY DAMN "INSPIRATION," GOT IT?

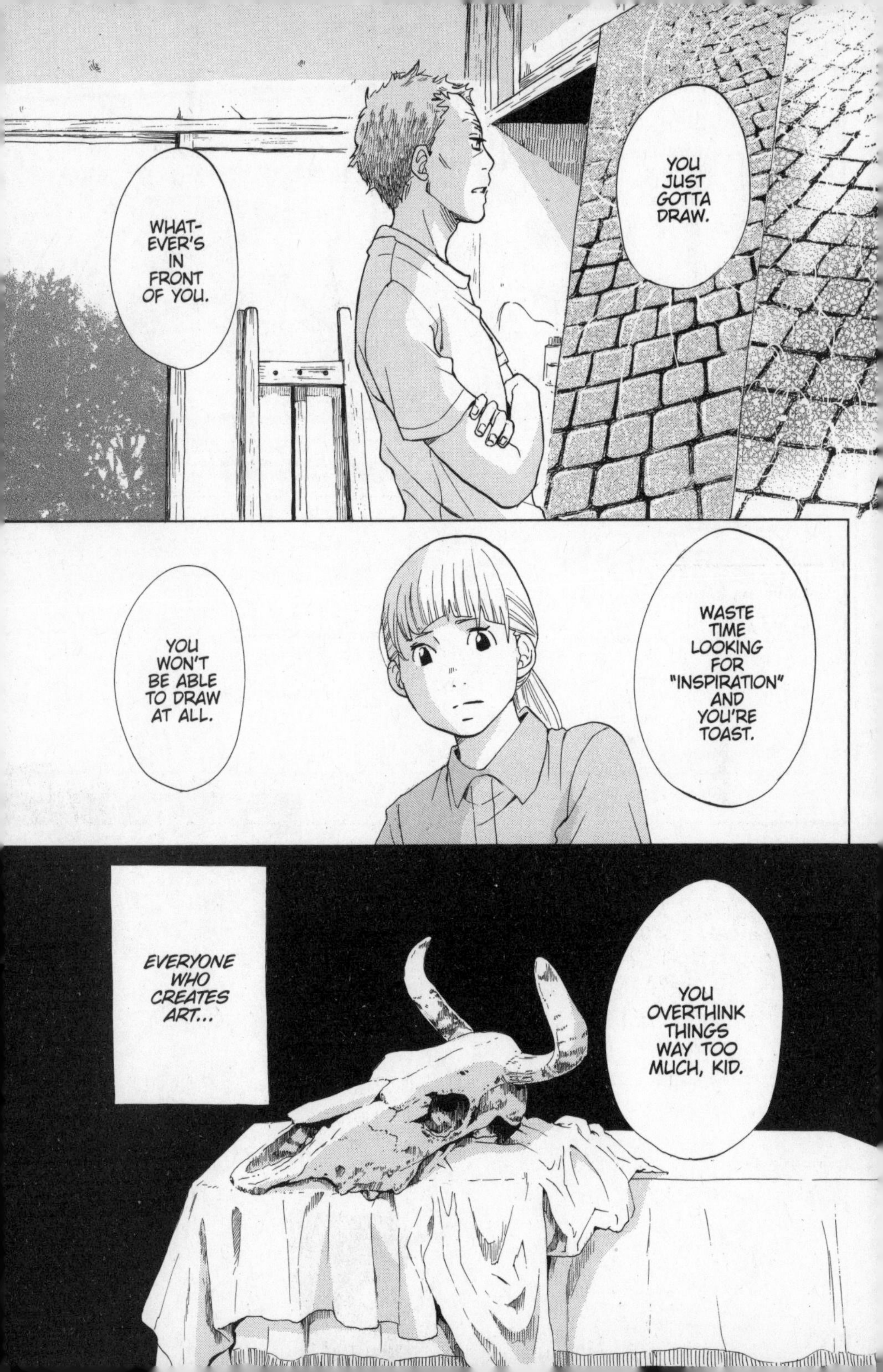
YOU JUST GOTTA DRAW.
WHAT-EVER'S IN FRONT OF YOU.
WASTE TIME LOOKING FOR "INSPIRATION" AND YOU'RE TOAST.
YOU WON'T BE ABLE TO DRAW AT ALL.
YOU OVERTHINK THINGS WAY TOO MUCH, KID.
EVERYONE WHO CREATES ART...

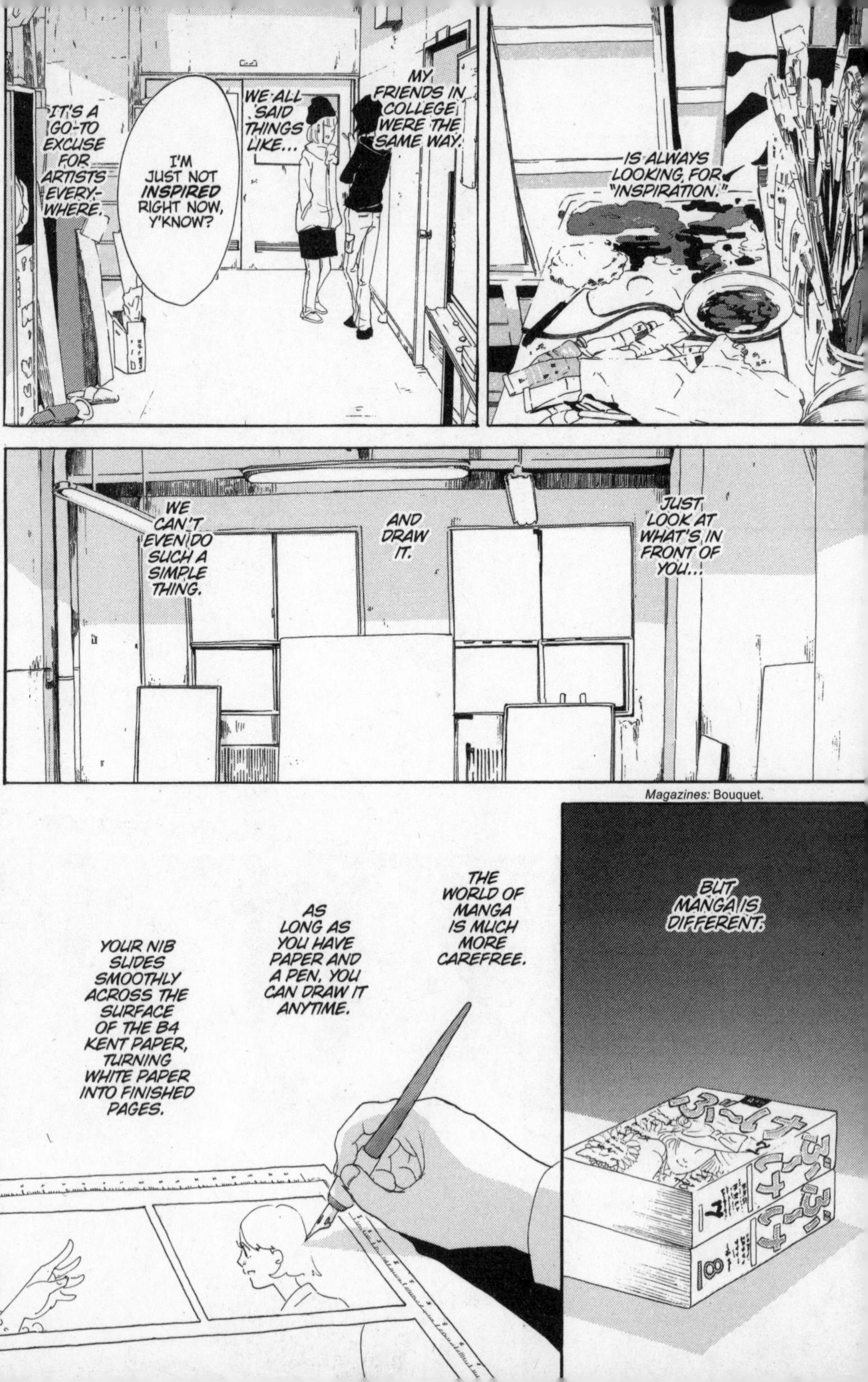
IS ALWAYS LOOKING, FOR "INSPIRATION."
MY FRIENDS IN COLLEGE WERE THE SAME WAY.
WE ALL SAID THINGS LIKE...
I'M JUST NOT INSPIRED RIGHT NOW, Y'KNOW?
IT'S A GO-TO EXCUSE FOR ARTISTS EVERY-WHERE.
JUST LOOK AT WHAT'S IN FRONT OF YOU...
AND DRAW IT.
WE CAN'T EVEN DO SUCH A SIMPLE THING.
Magazines: Bouquet.
BUT MANGA IS DIFFERENT.
THE WORLD OF MANGA IS MUCH MORE CAREFREE.
AS LONG AS YOU HAVE PAPER AND A PEN, YOU CAN DRAW IT ANYTIME.
YOUR NIB SLIDES SMOOTHLY ACROSS THE SURFACE OF THE B4 KENT PAPER, TURNING WHITE PAPER INTO FINISHED PAGES.

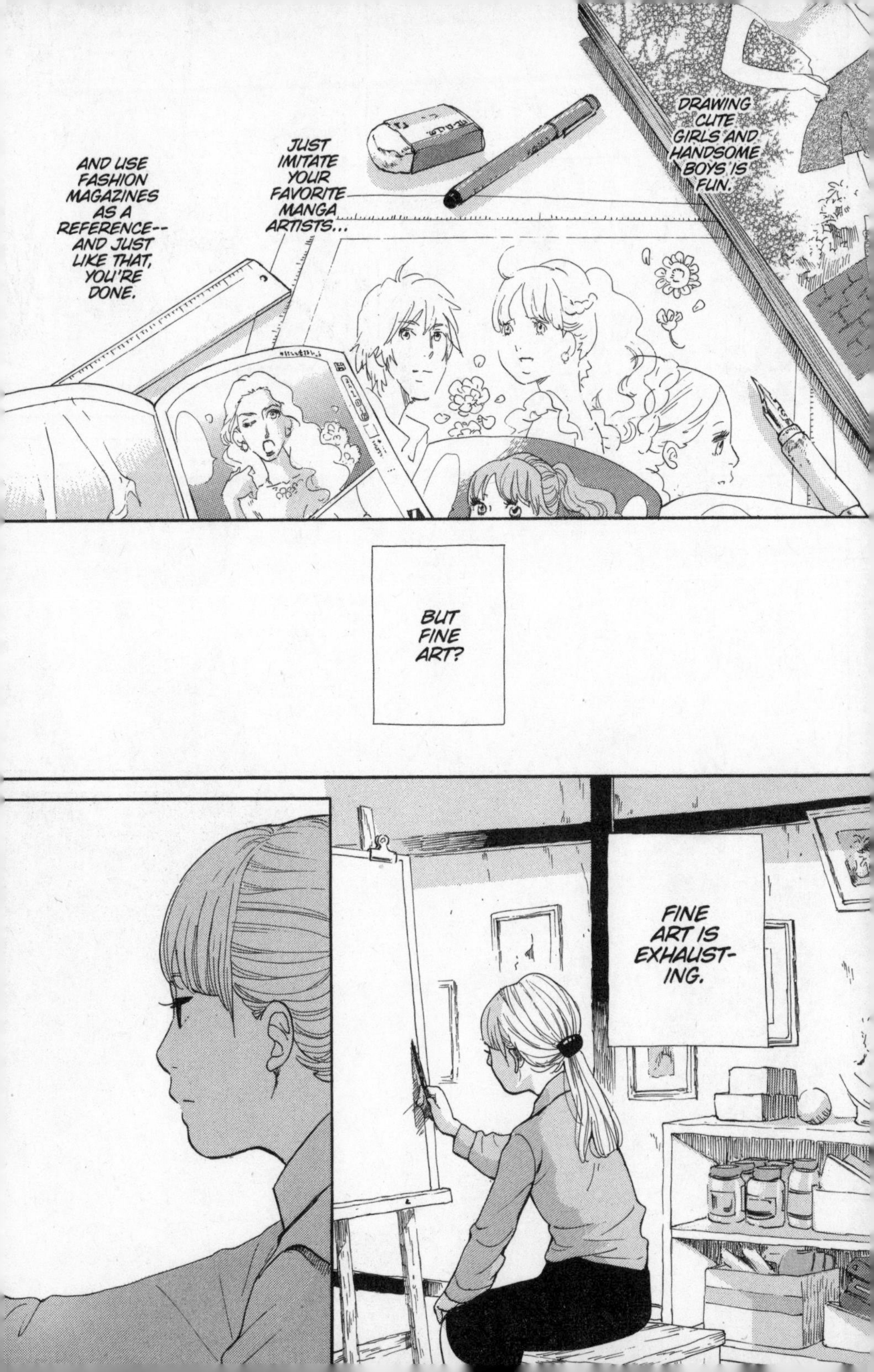
DRAWING CUTE GIRLS AND HANDSOME BOYS IS FUN.
JUST IMITATE YOUR FAVORITE MANGA ARTISTS...
AND USE FASHION MAGAZINES AS A REFERENCE--AND JUST LIKE THAT, YOU'RE DONE.
BUT FINE ART?
FINE ART IS EXHAUST-ING.

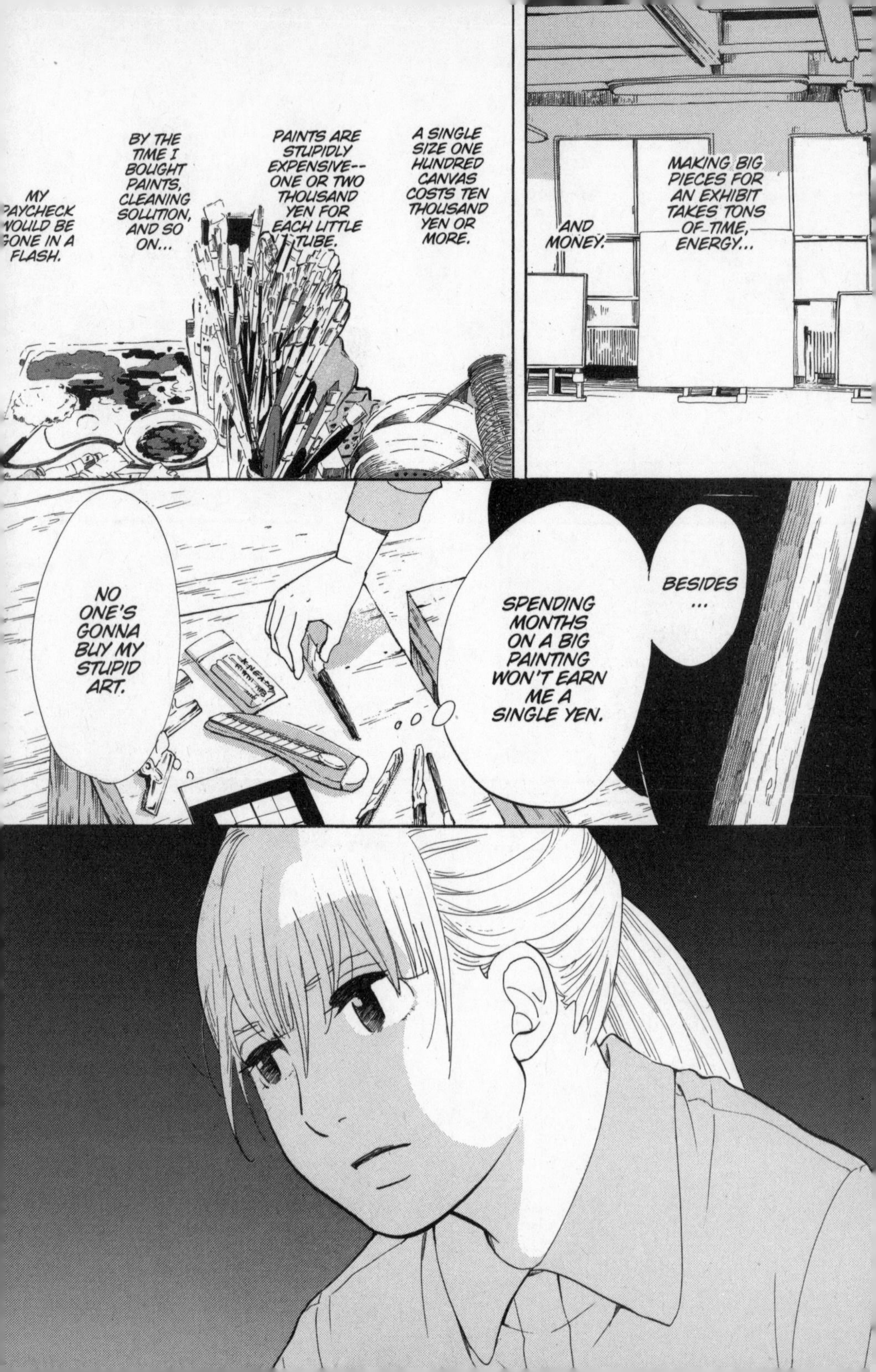
MAKING BIG PIECES FOR AN EXHIBIT TAKES TONS OF TIME, ENERGY...
AND MONEY.
A SINGLE SIZE ONE HUNDRED CANVAS COSTS TEN THOUSAND YEN OR MORE.
PAINTS ARE STUPIDLY EXPENSIVE--ONE OR TWO THOUSAND YEN FOR EACH LITTLE TUBE.
BY THE TIME I BOUGHT PAINTS, CLEANING SOLUTION, AND SO ON...
MY PAYCHECK WOULD BE GONE IN A FLASH.
BESIDES...
SPENDING MONTHS ON A BIG PAINTING WON'T EARN ME A SINGLE YEN.
NO ONE'S GONNA BUY MY STUPID ART.

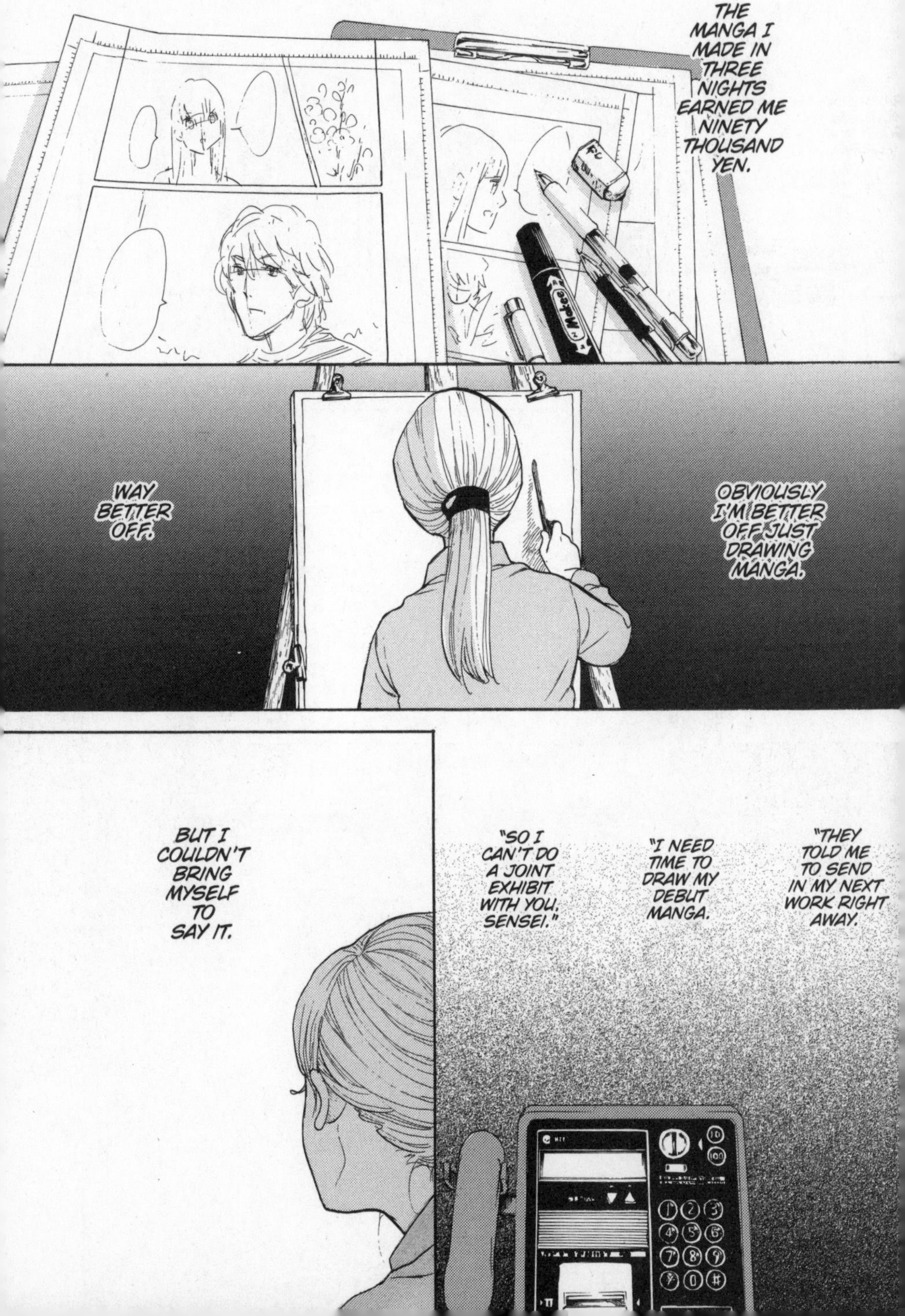
THE MANGA I MADE IN THREE NIGHTS EARNED ME NINETY THOUSAND YEN.
OBVIOUSLY I'M BETTER OFF JUST DRAWING MANGA.
WAY BETTER OFF.
"THEY TOLD ME TO SEND IN MY NEXT WORK RIGHT AWAY.
"I NEED TIME TO DRAW MY DEBUT MANGA.
"SO I CAN'T DO A JOINT EXHIBIT WITH YOU, SENSEI."
BUT I COULDN'T BRING MYSELF TO SAY IT.

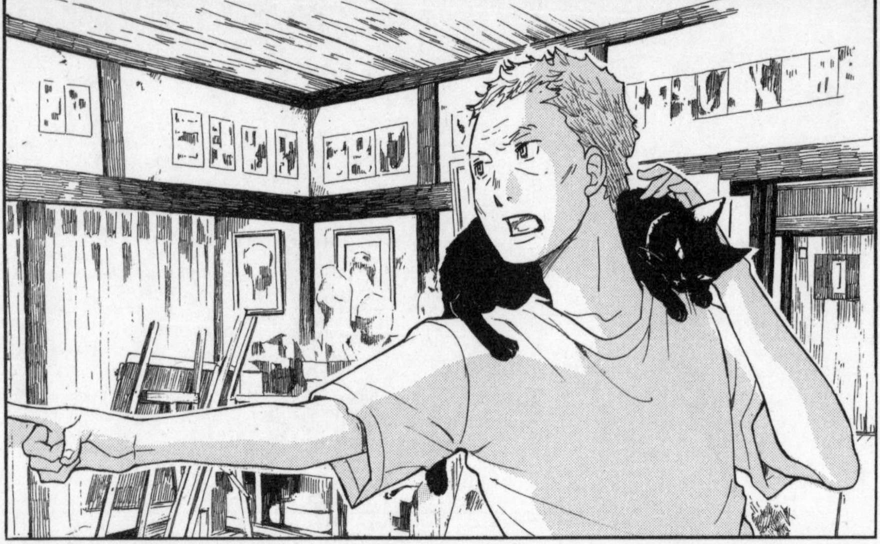

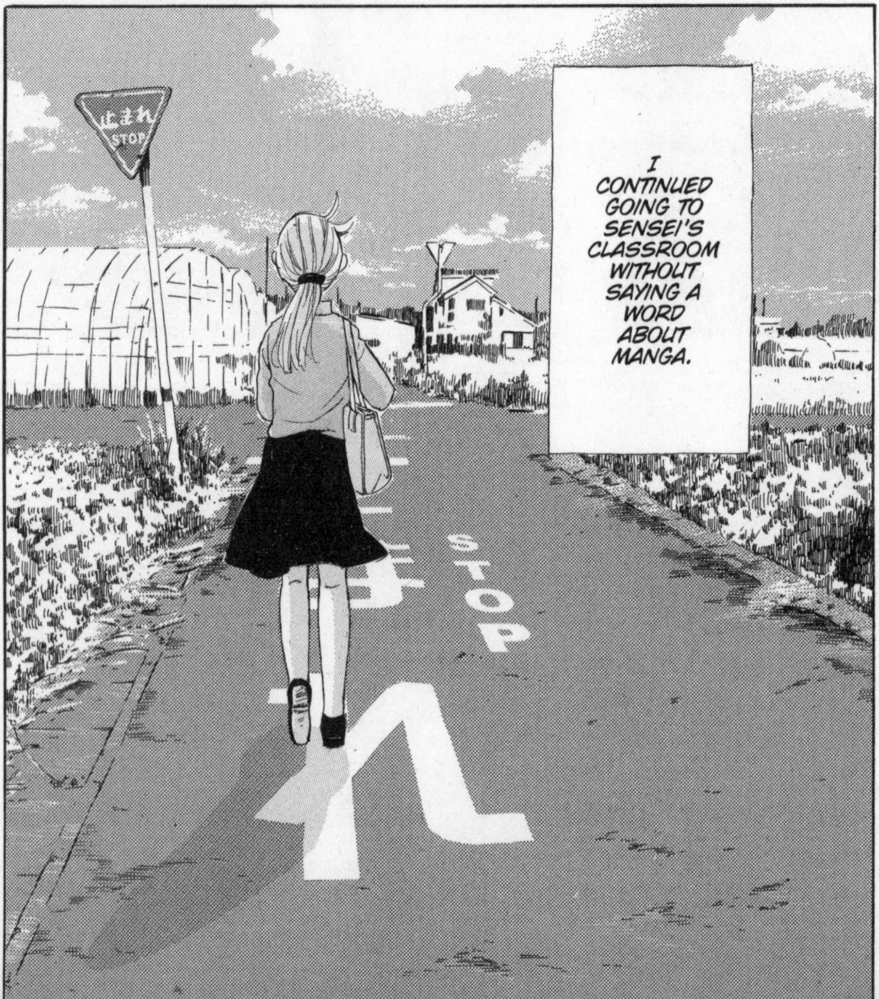
止まれ
STOP
I CONTINUED GOING TO SENSEI'S CLASSROOM WITHOUT SAYING A WORD ABOUT MANGA.
STOP

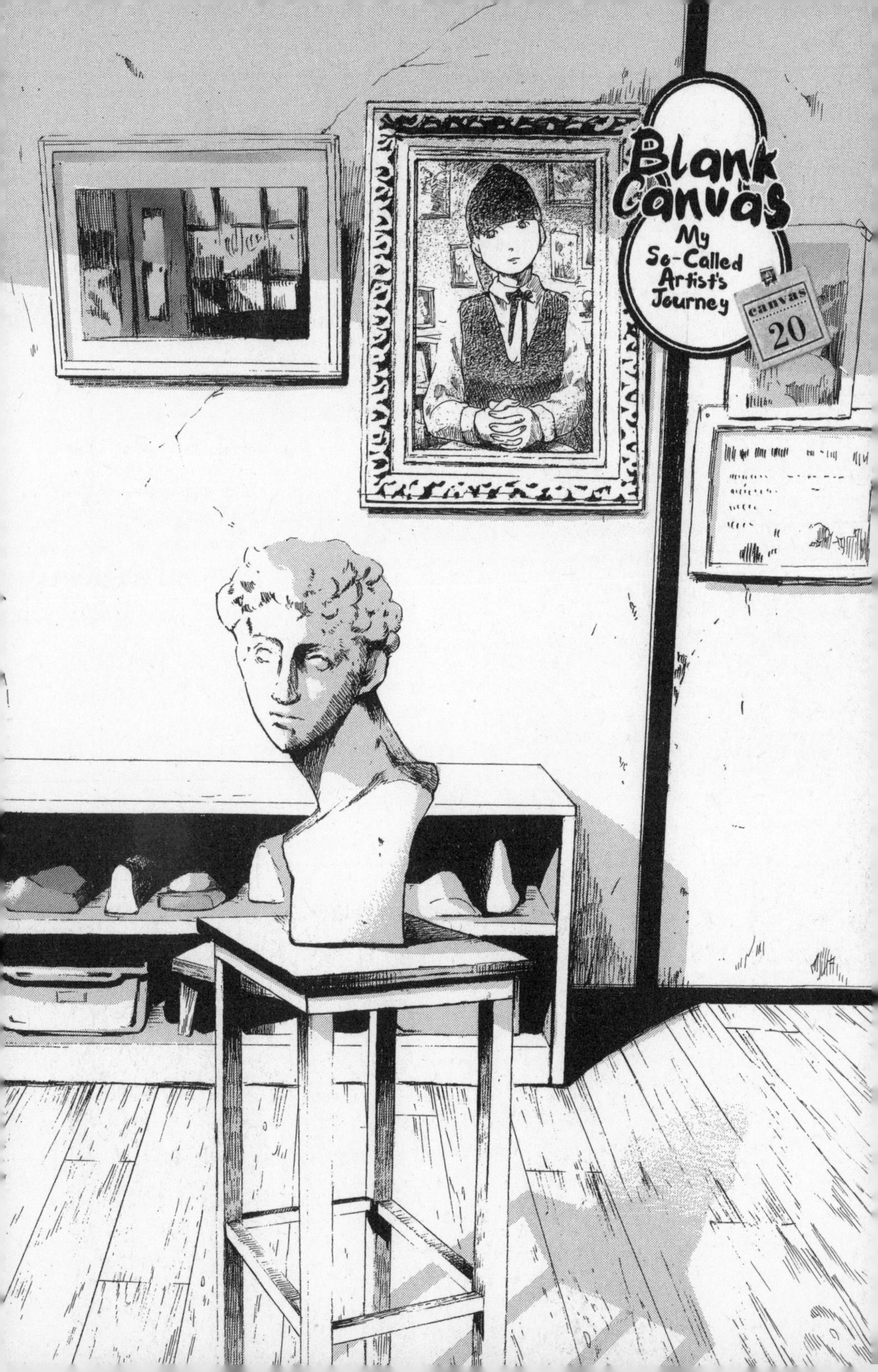
Blank Canvas
My So-Called Artist's Journey
canvas 20

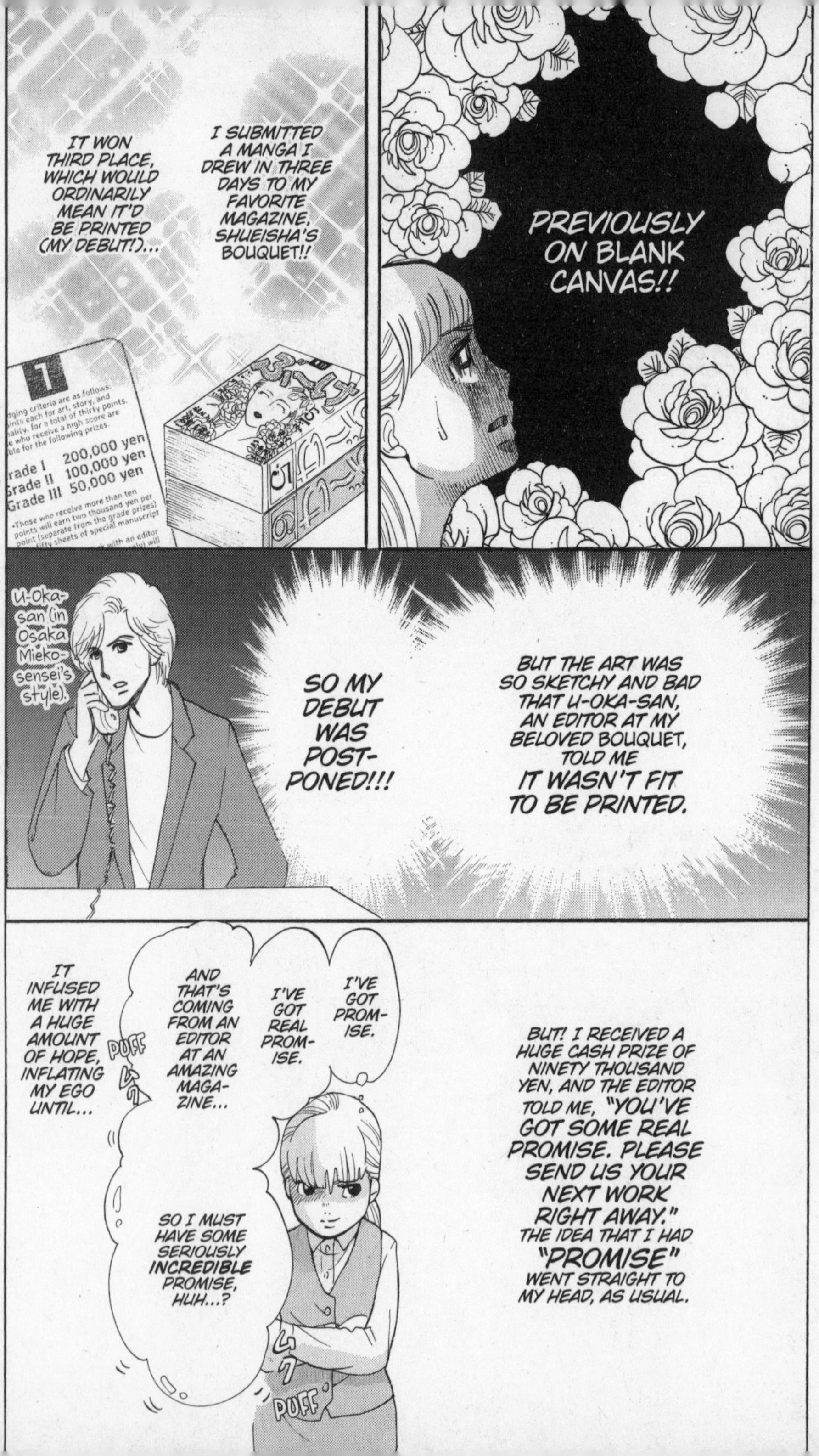
PREVIOUSLY ON BLANK CANVAS!!
I SUBMITTED A MANGA I DREW IN THREE DAYS TO MY FAVORITE MAGAZINE, SHUEISHA'S BOUQUET!!
IT WON THIRD PLACE, WHICH WOULD ORDINARILY MEAN IT'D BE PRINTED (MY DEBUT!)...
Grade I 200,000 yen
Grade II 100,000 yen
Grade III 50,000 yen
BUT THE ART WAS SO SKETCHY AND BAD THAT U-OKA-SAN, AN EDITOR AT MY BELOVED BOUQUET, TOLD ME IT WASN'T FIT TO BE PRINTED.
SO MY DEBUT WAS POST-PONED!!!
U-Oka-san (in Osaka Mieko-sensei's style).
BUT! I RECEIVED A HUGE CASH PRIZE OF NINETY THOUSAND YEN, AND THE EDITOR TOLD ME, "YOU'VE GOT SOME REAL PROMISE. PLEASE SEND US YOUR NEXT WORK RIGHT AWAY." THE IDEA THAT I HAD "PROMISE" WENT STRAIGHT TO MY HEAD, AS USUAL.
I'VE GOT PROM-ISE.
I'VE GOT REAL PROM-ISE.
AND THAT'S COMING FROM AN EDITOR AT AN AMAZING MAGA-ZINE...
IT INFUSED ME WITH A HUGE AMOUNT OF HOPE, INFLATING MY EGO UNTIL...
PUFF
SO I MUST HAVE SOME SERIOUSLY INCREDIBLE PROMISE, HUH...?
PUFF

Magazines: Bouquet.

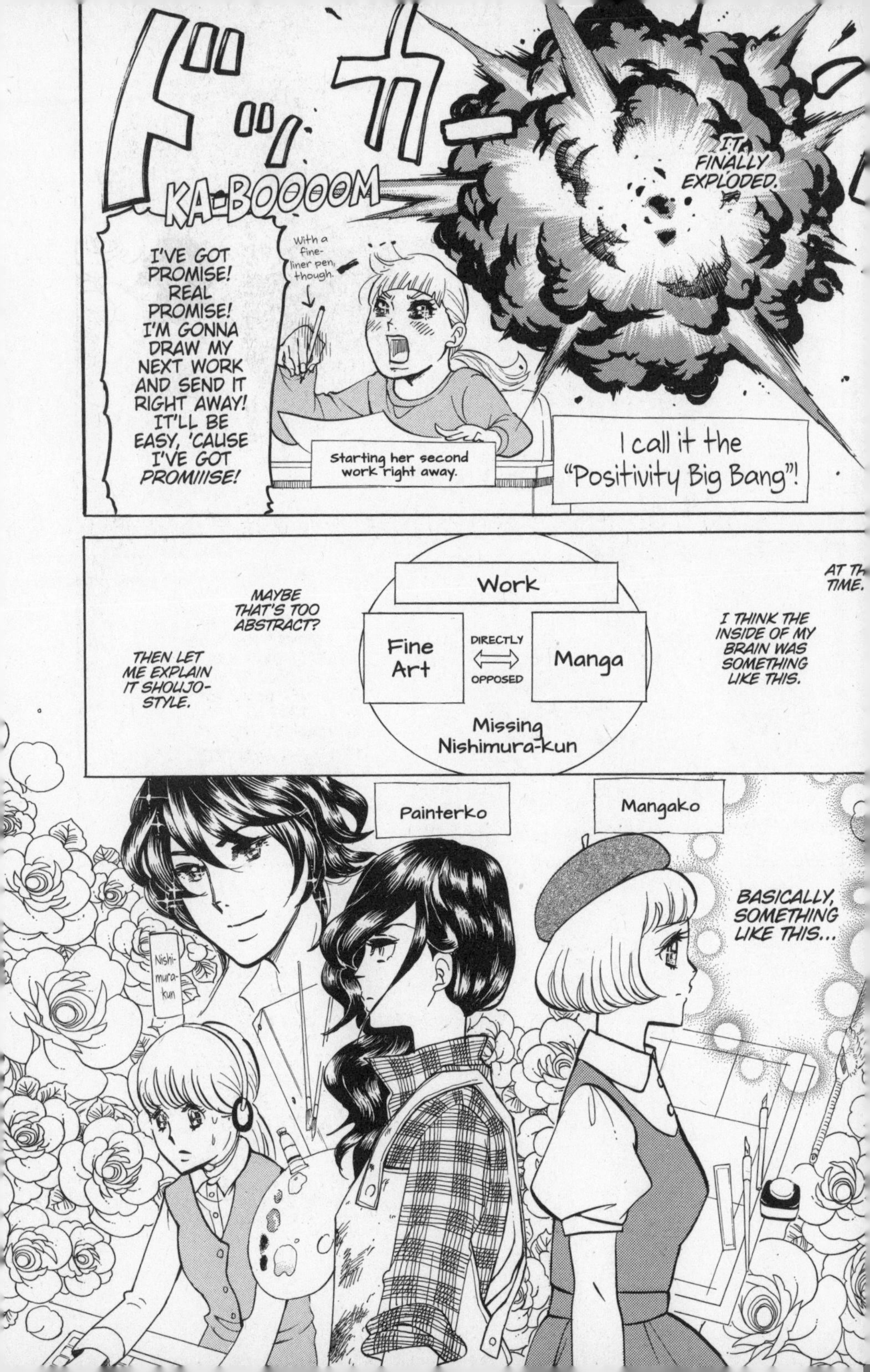
IT FINALLY EXPLODED.
KA-BOOOOM
I call it the "Positivity Big Bang"!
Starting her second work right away.
With a fine-liner pen, though.
I'VE GOT PROMISE! REAL PROMISE! I'M GONNA DRAW MY NEXT WORK AND SEND IT RIGHT AWAY! IT'LL BE EASY, 'CAUSE I'VE GOT PROMIIISE!
AT THE TIME.
I THINK THE INSIDE OF MY BRAIN WAS SOMETHING LIKE THIS.
Work
Manga
DIRECTLY OPPOSED
Fine Art
Missing Nishimura-kun
MAYBE THAT'S TOO ABSTRACT?
THEN LET ME EXPLAIN IT SHOUJO-STYLE.
BASICALLY, SOMETHING LIKE THIS...
Mangako
Painterko
Nishimura-kun

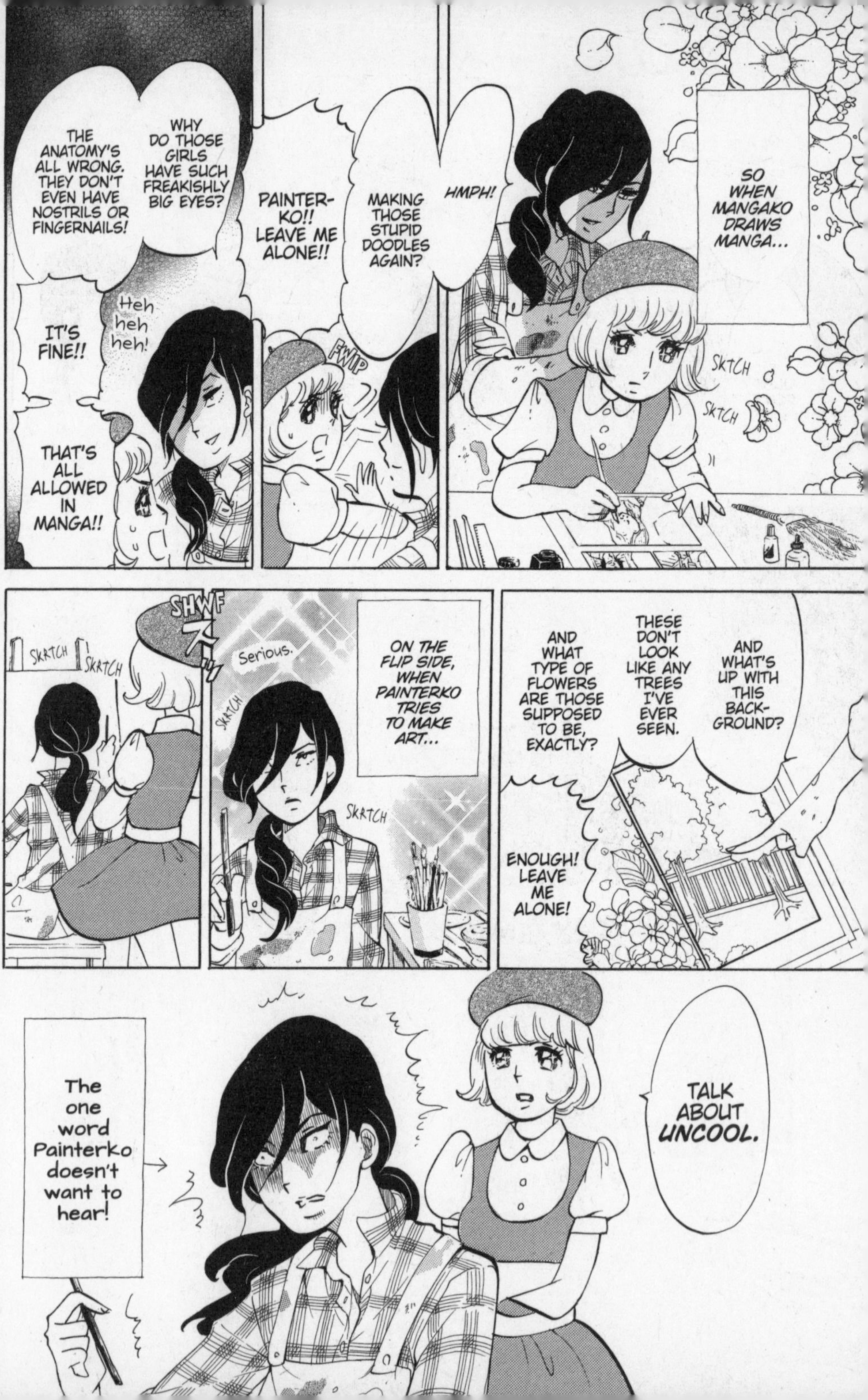

SO WHEN MANGAKO DRAWS MANGA...
SKTCH
SKTCH
HMPH!
MAKING THOSE STUPID DOODLES AGAIN?
PAINTER-KO!! LEAVE ME ALONE!!
FWIP
WHY DO THOSE GIRLS HAVE SUCH FREAKISHLY BIG EYES?
THE ANATOMY'S ALL WRONG. THEY DON'T EVEN HAVE NOSTRILS OR FINGERNAILS!
Heh heh heh!
IT'S FINE!!
THAT'S ALL ALLOWED IN MANGA!!
AND WHAT'S UP WITH THIS BACK-GROUND?
THESE DON'T LOOK LIKE ANY TREES I'VE EVER SEEN.
AND WHAT TYPE OF FLOWERS ARE THOSE SUPPOSED TO BE, EXACTLY?
ENOUGH! LEAVE ME ALONE!
ON THE FLIP SIDE, WHEN PAINTERKO TRIES TO MAKE ART...
Serious.
SKRTCH
SKRTCH
SHWF
SKRTCH
SKRTCH
TALK ABOUT UNCOOL.
The one word Painterko doesn't want to hear!

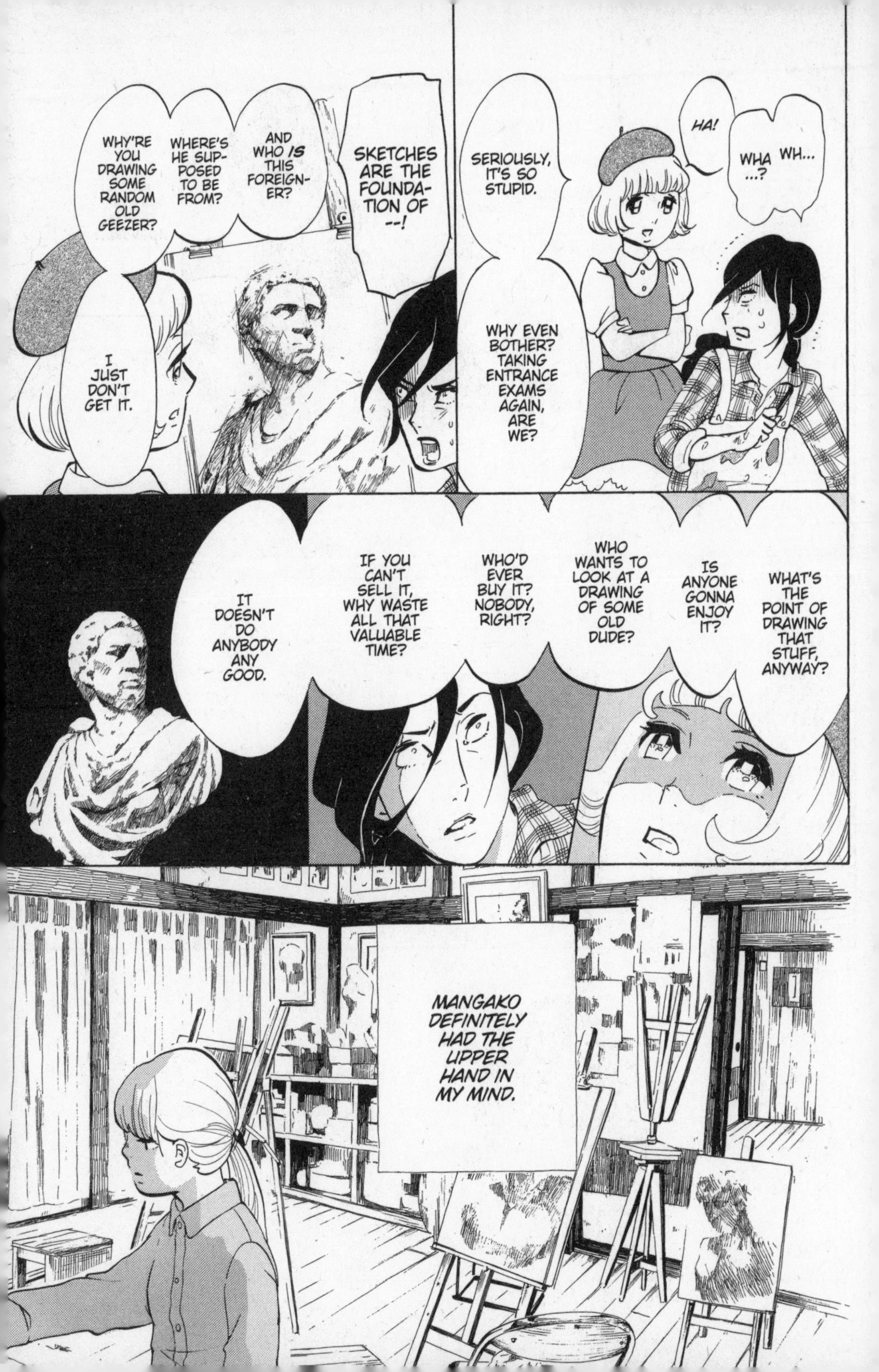
WH...
WHA ...?
HA!
SERIOUSLY, IT'S SO STUPID.
WHY EVEN BOTHER? TAKING ENTRANCE EXAMS AGAIN, ARE WE?
SKETCHES ARE THE FOUNDATION OF --!
AND WHO *IS* THIS FOREIGNER?
WHERE'S HE SUPPOSED TO BE FROM?
WHY'RE YOU DRAWING SOME RANDOM OLD GEEZER?
I JUST DON'T GET IT.
WHAT'S THE POINT OF DRAWING THAT STUFF, ANYWAY?
IS ANYONE GONNA ENJOY IT?
WHO WANTS TO LOOK AT A DRAWING OF SOME OLD DUDE?
WHO'D EVER BUY IT? NOBODY, RIGHT?
IF YOU CAN'T SELL IT, WHY WASTE ALL THAT VALUABLE TIME?
IT DOESN'T DO ANYBODY ANY GOOD.
MANGAKO DEFINITELY HAD THE UPPER HAND IN MY MIND.

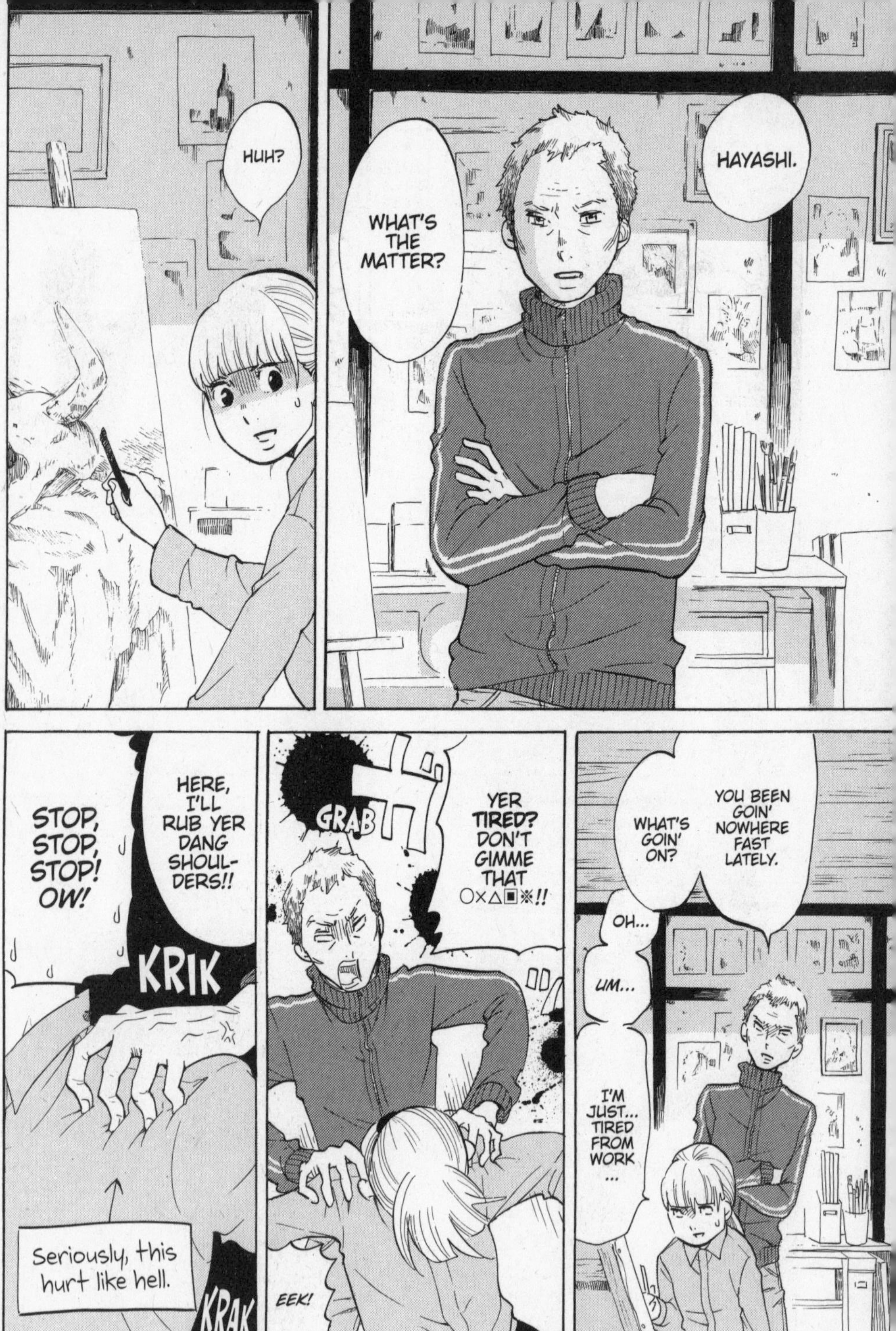
HAYASHI.
WHAT'S THE MATTER?
HUH?
YOU BEEN GOIN' NOWHERE FAST LATELY.
WHAT'S GOIN' ON?
OH...
UM...
I'M JUST... TIRED FROM WORK ...
YER TIRED? DON'T GIMME THAT ○×△▣※!!
GRAB
EEK!
HERE, I'LL RUB YER DANG SHOUL-DERS!!
STOP, STOP, STOP! OW!
KRIK
KRAK
Seriously, this hurt like hell.

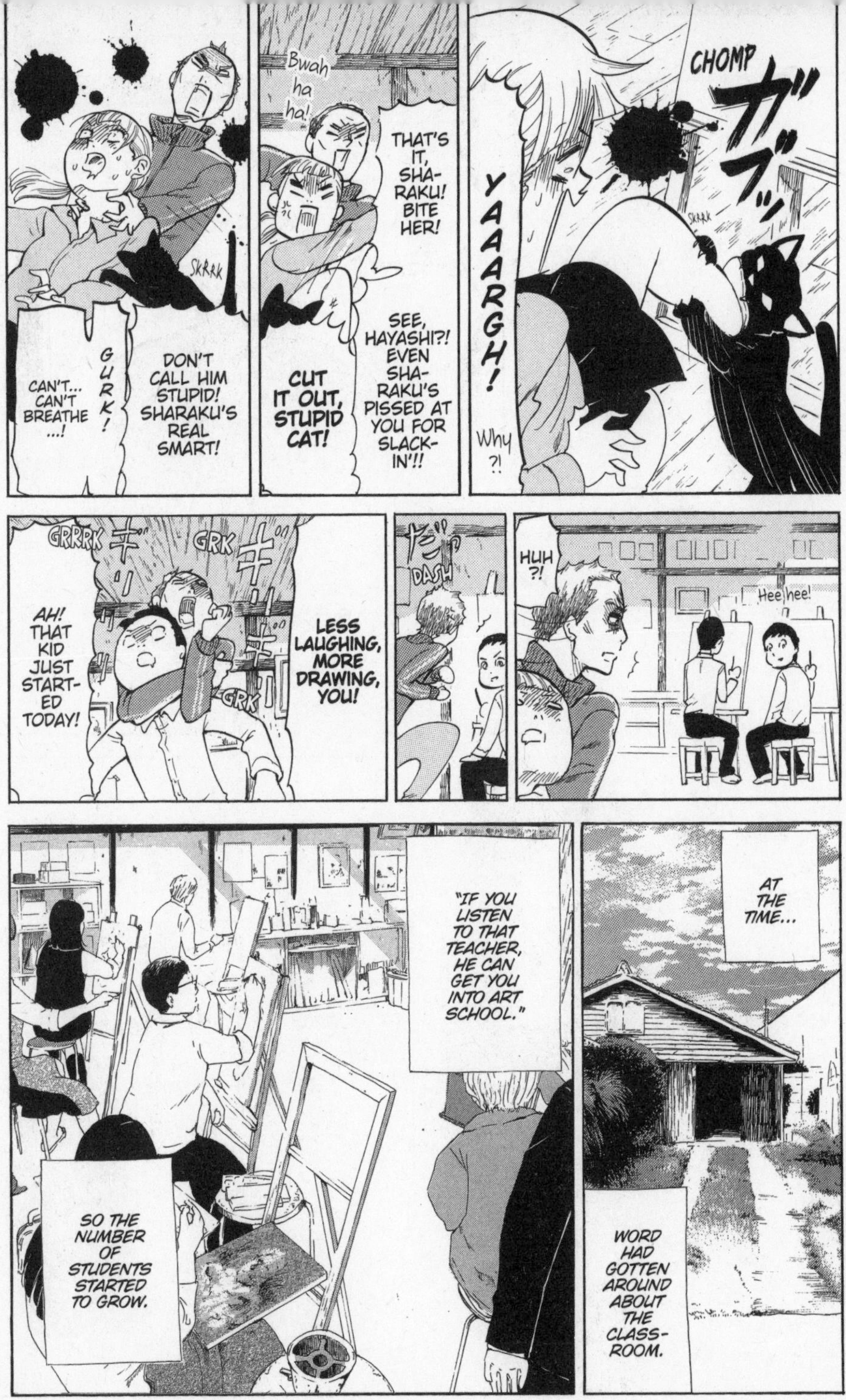
CHOMP
YAAARGH!
SKRRK
Why?!
THAT'S IT, SHARAKU! BITE HER!
Bwah ha ha!
SEE, HAYASHI?! EVEN SHARAKU'S PISSED AT YOU FOR SLACKIN'!!
CUT IT OUT, STUPID CAT!
SKRRK
DON'T CALL HIM STUPID! SHARAKU'S REAL SMART!
GURK!
CAN'T... CAN'T BREATHE...!
HUH?!
Hee hee!
DASH
LESS LAUGHING, MORE DRAWING, YOU!
GRRRK
GRK
AH! THAT KID JUST STARTED TODAY!
GRK
AT THE TIME...
WORD HAD GOTTEN AROUND ABOUT THE CLASSROOM.
"IF YOU LISTEN TO THAT TEACHER, HE CAN GET YOU INTO ART SCHOOL."
SO THE NUMBER OF STUDENTS STARTED TO GROW.

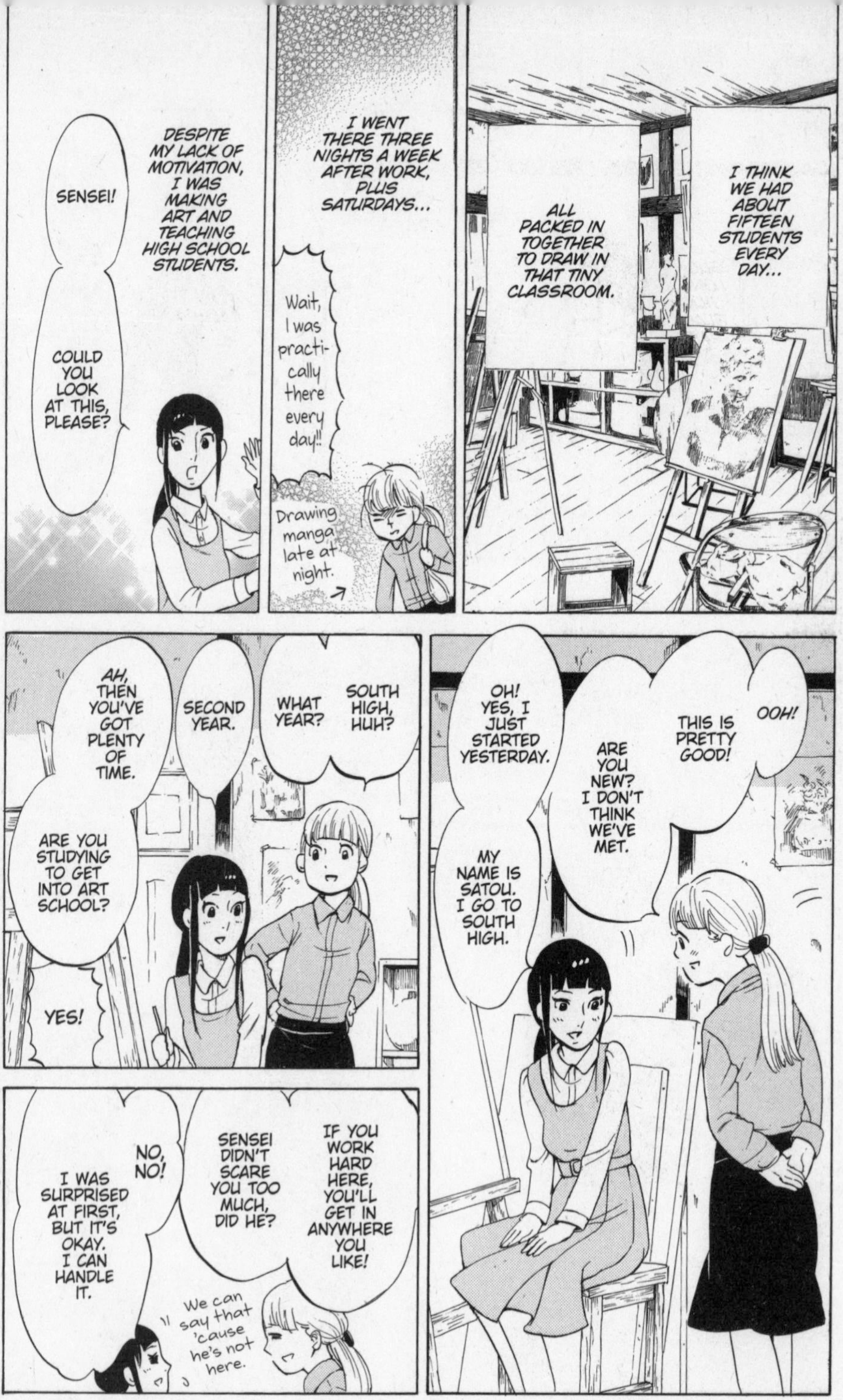
I THINK WE HAD ABOUT FIFTEEN STUDENTS EVERY DAY...
ALL PACKED IN TOGETHER TO DRAW IN THAT TINY CLASSROOM.
I WENT THERE THREE NIGHTS A WEEK AFTER WORK, PLUS SATURDAYS...
Wait, I was practically there every day!!
Drawing manga late at night.
DESPITE MY LACK OF MOTIVATION, I WAS MAKING ART AND TEACHING HIGH SCHOOL STUDENTS.
SENSEI!
COULD YOU LOOK AT THIS, PLEASE?
OOH!
THIS IS PRETTY GOOD!
ARE YOU NEW? I DON'T THINK WE'VE MET.
OH! YES, I JUST STARTED YESTERDAY.
MY NAME IS SATOU. I GO TO SOUTH HIGH.
SOUTH HIGH, HUH?
WHAT YEAR?
SECOND YEAR.
AH, THEN YOU'VE GOT PLENTY OF TIME.
ARE YOU STUDYING TO GET INTO ART SCHOOL?
YES!
IF YOU WORK HARD HERE, YOU'LL GET IN ANYWHERE YOU LIKE!
SENSEI DIDN'T SCARE YOU TOO MUCH, DID HE?
NO, NO!
I WAS SURPRISED AT FIRST, BUT IT'S OKAY. I CAN HANDLE IT.
We can say that 'cause he's not here.

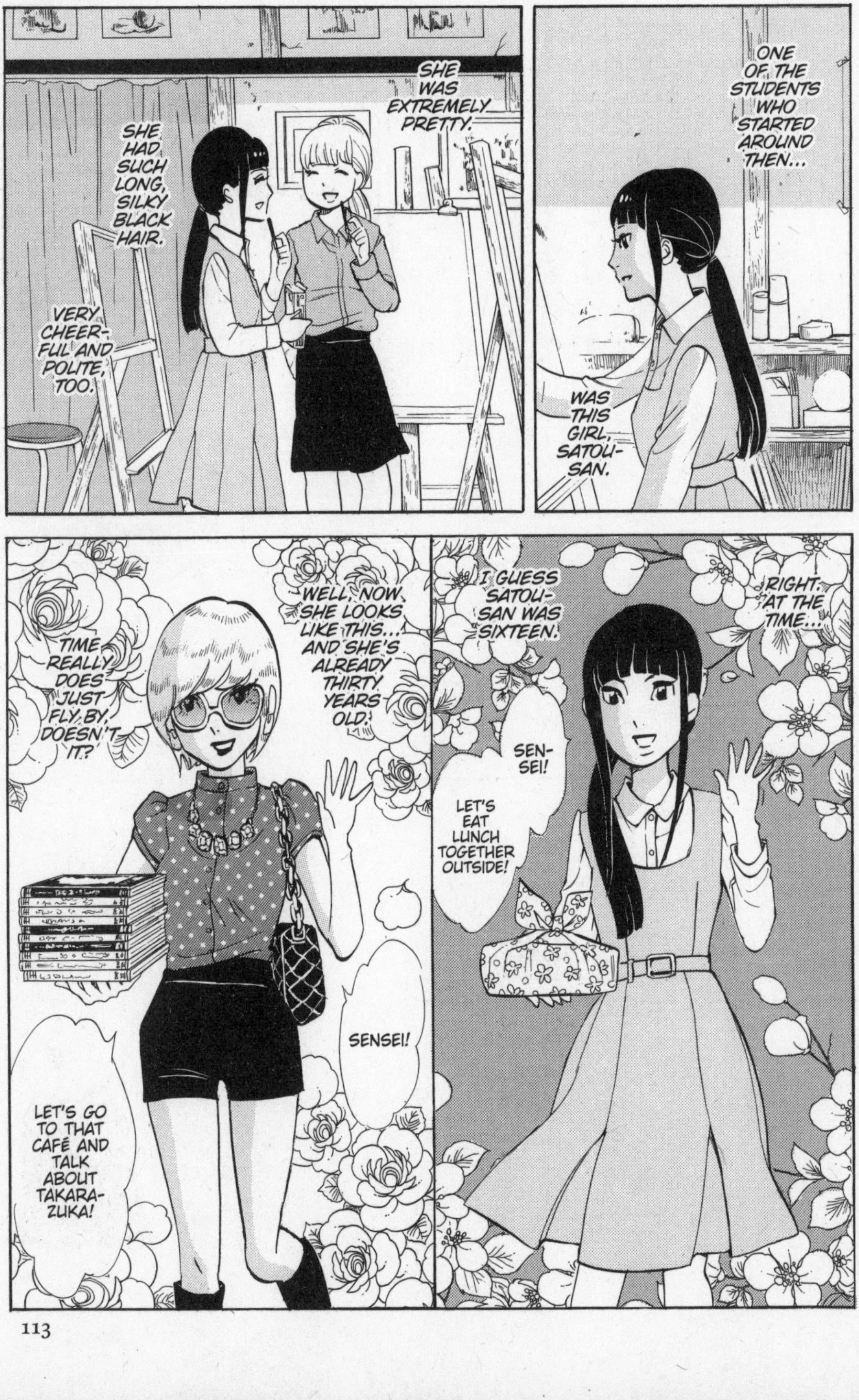
ONE OF THE STUDENTS WHO STARTED AROUND THEN...
WAS THIS GIRL, SATOU-SAN.
SHE WAS EXTREMELY PRETTY.
SHE HAD SUCH LONG, SILKY BLACK HAIR.
VERY CHEERFUL AND POLITE, TOO.
RIGHT AT THE TIME...
I GUESS SATOU-SAN WAS SIXTEEN.
SEN-SEI!
LET'S EAT LUNCH TOGETHER OUTSIDE!
WELL, NOW SHE LOOKS LIKE THIS... AND SHE'S ALREADY THIRTY YEARS OLD.
TIME REALLY DOES JUST FLY BY, DOESN'T IT?
SENSEI!
LET'S GO TO THAT CAFÉ AND TALK ABOUT TAKARAZUKA!

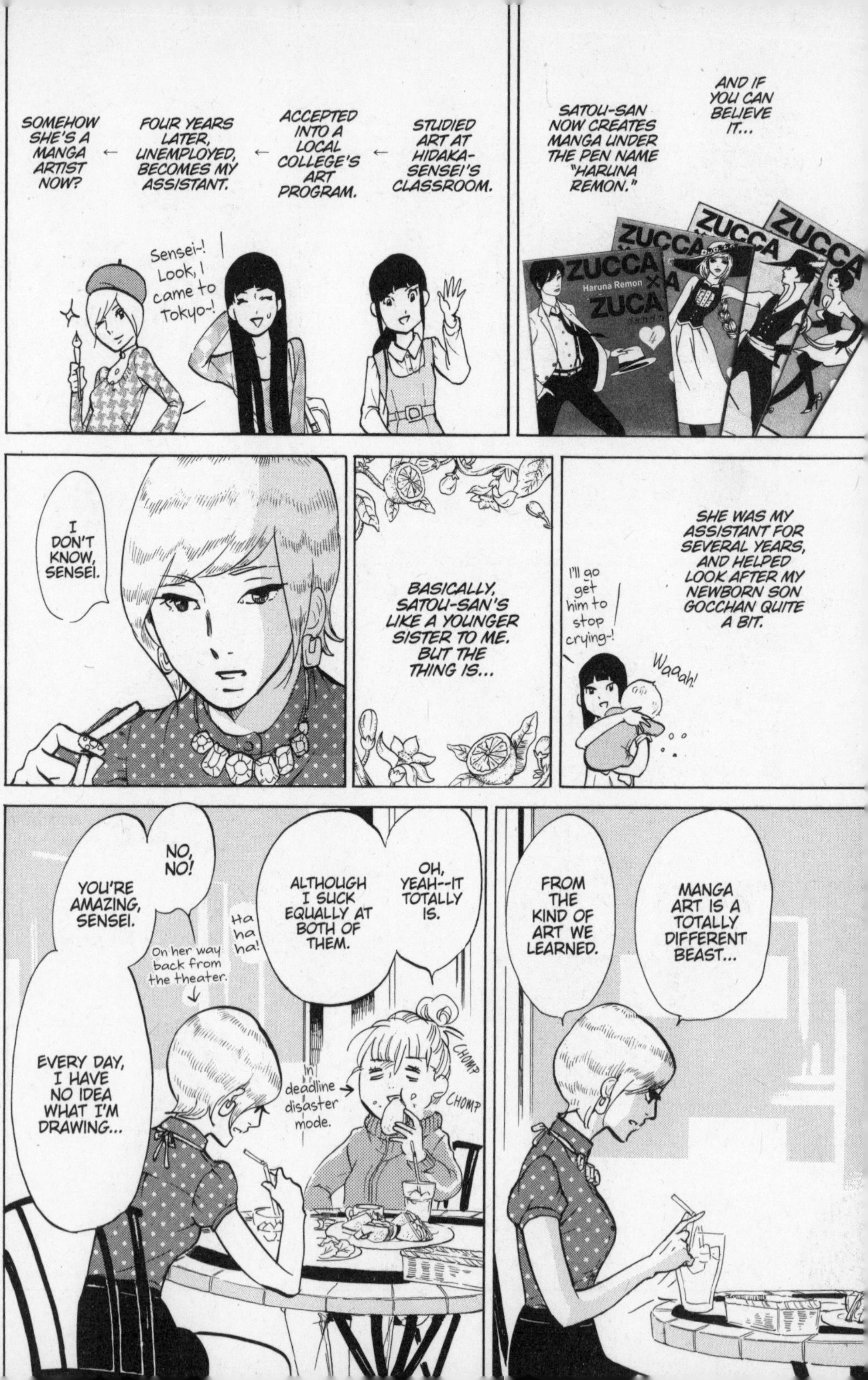
AND IF YOU CAN BELIEVE IT...
SATOU-SAN NOW CREATES MANGA UNDER THE PEN NAME "HARUNA REMON."
ZUCCA
ZUCCA
ZUCCA
ZUCCA
Haruna Remon
ZUCA
STUDIED ART AT HIDAKA-SENSEI'S CLASSROOM.
ACCEPTED INTO A LOCAL COLLEGE'S ART PROGRAM.
FOUR YEARS LATER, UNEMPLOYED, BECOMES MY ASSISTANT.
SOMEHOW SHE'S A MANGA ARTIST NOW?
Sensei~! Look, I came to Tokyo~!
SHE WAS MY ASSISTANT FOR SEVERAL YEARS, AND HELPED LOOK AFTER MY NEWBORN SON GOCCHAN QUITE A BIT.
I'll go get him to stop crying~!
Waaah!
BASICALLY, SATOU-SAN'S LIKE A YOUNGER SISTER TO ME. BUT THE THING IS...
I DON'T KNOW, SENSEI.
MANGA ART IS A TOTALLY DIFFERENT BEAST...
FROM THE KIND OF ART WE LEARNED.
OH, YEAH--IT TOTALLY IS.
ALTHOUGH I SUCK EQUALLY AT BOTH OF THEM.
Ha ha ha!
NO, NO!
YOU'RE AMAZING, SENSEI.
On her way back from the theater.
CHOMP
CHOMP
In deadline disaster mode.
EVERY DAY, I HAVE NO IDEA WHAT I'M DRAWING...

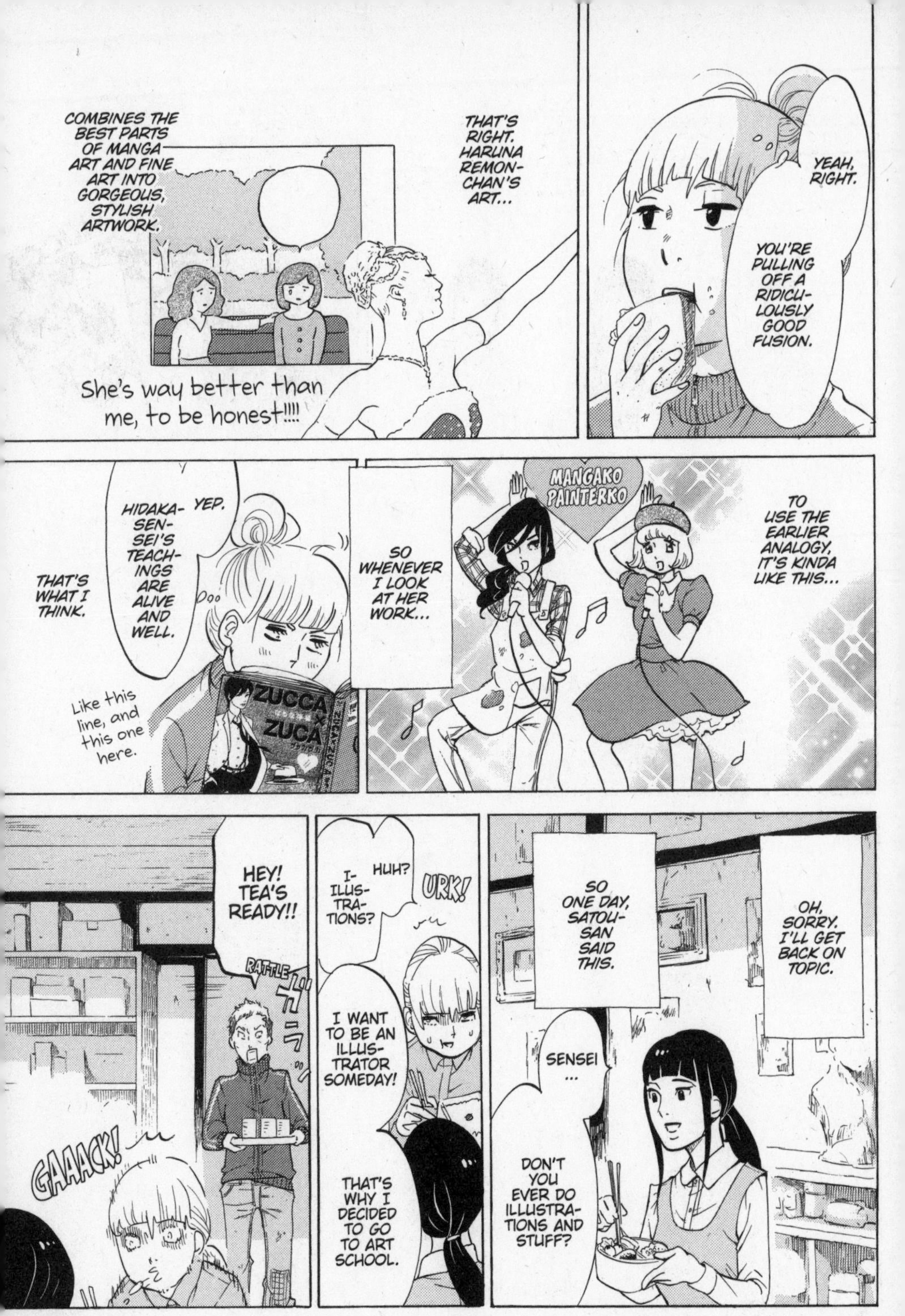
YEAH, RIGHT.
YOU'RE PULLING OFF A RIDICU-LOUSLY GOOD FUSION.
THAT'S RIGHT. HARUNA REMON-CHAN'S ART...
COMBINES THE BEST PARTS OF MANGA ART AND FINE ART INTO GORGEOUS, STYLISH ARTWORK.
She's way better than me, to be honest!!!!
TO USE THE EARLIER ANALOGY, IT'S KINDA LIKE THIS...
MANGAKO PAINTERKO
SO WHENEVER I LOOK AT HER WORK...
YEP.
HIDAKA-SEN-SEI'S TEACH-INGS ARE ALIVE AND WELL.
THAT'S WHAT I THINK.
ZUCCA × ZUCA
Like this line, and this one here.
OH, SORRY. I'LL GET BACK ON TOPIC.
SO ONE DAY, SATOU-SAN SAID THIS.
SENSEI...
DON'T YOU EVER DO ILLUSTRA-TIONS AND STUFF?
HUH?
URK!
I-ILLUS-TRA-TIONS?
I WANT TO BE AN ILLUS-TRATOR SOMEDAY!
THAT'S WHY I DECIDED TO GO TO ART SCHOOL.
HEY! TEA'S READY!!
RATTLE
GAAACK!

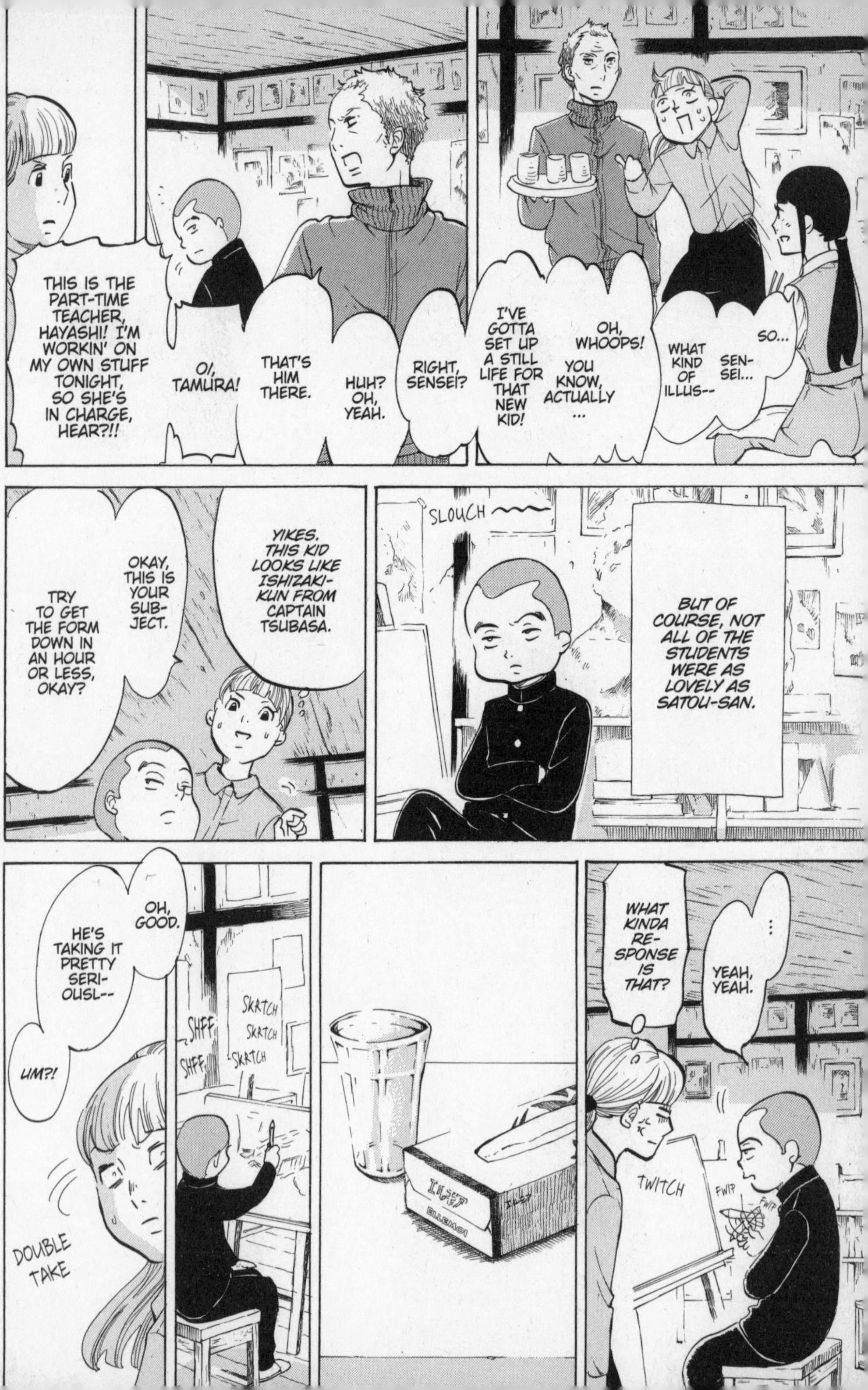
SO... SEN-SEI...
WHAT KIND OF ILLUS--
OH, WHOOPS! YOU KNOW, ACTUALLY ...
I'VE GOTTA SET UP A STILL LIFE FOR THAT NEW KID!
RIGHT, SENSEI?
HUH? OH, YEAH.
THAT'S HIM THERE.
OI, TAMURA!
THIS IS THE PART-TIME TEACHER, HAYASHI! I'M WORKIN' ON MY OWN STUFF TONIGHT, SO SHE'S IN CHARGE, HEAR?!!
BUT OF COURSE, NOT ALL OF THE STUDENTS WERE AS LOVELY AS SATOU-SAN.
SLOUCH
YIKES. THIS KID LOOKS LIKE ISHIZAKI-KUN FROM CAPTAIN TSUBASA.
OKAY, THIS IS YOUR SUB-JECT.
TRY TO GET THE FORM DOWN IN AN HOUR OR LESS, OKAY?
...
YEAH, YEAH.
WHAT KINDA RE-SPONSE IS THAT?
TWITCH
FWIP FWIP
エルモア
ELLEMOI
OH, GOOD.
HE'S TAKING IT PRETTY SERI-OUSL--
SKRTCH SKRTCH SKRTCH
SHFF SHFF
UM?!
DOUBLE TAKE

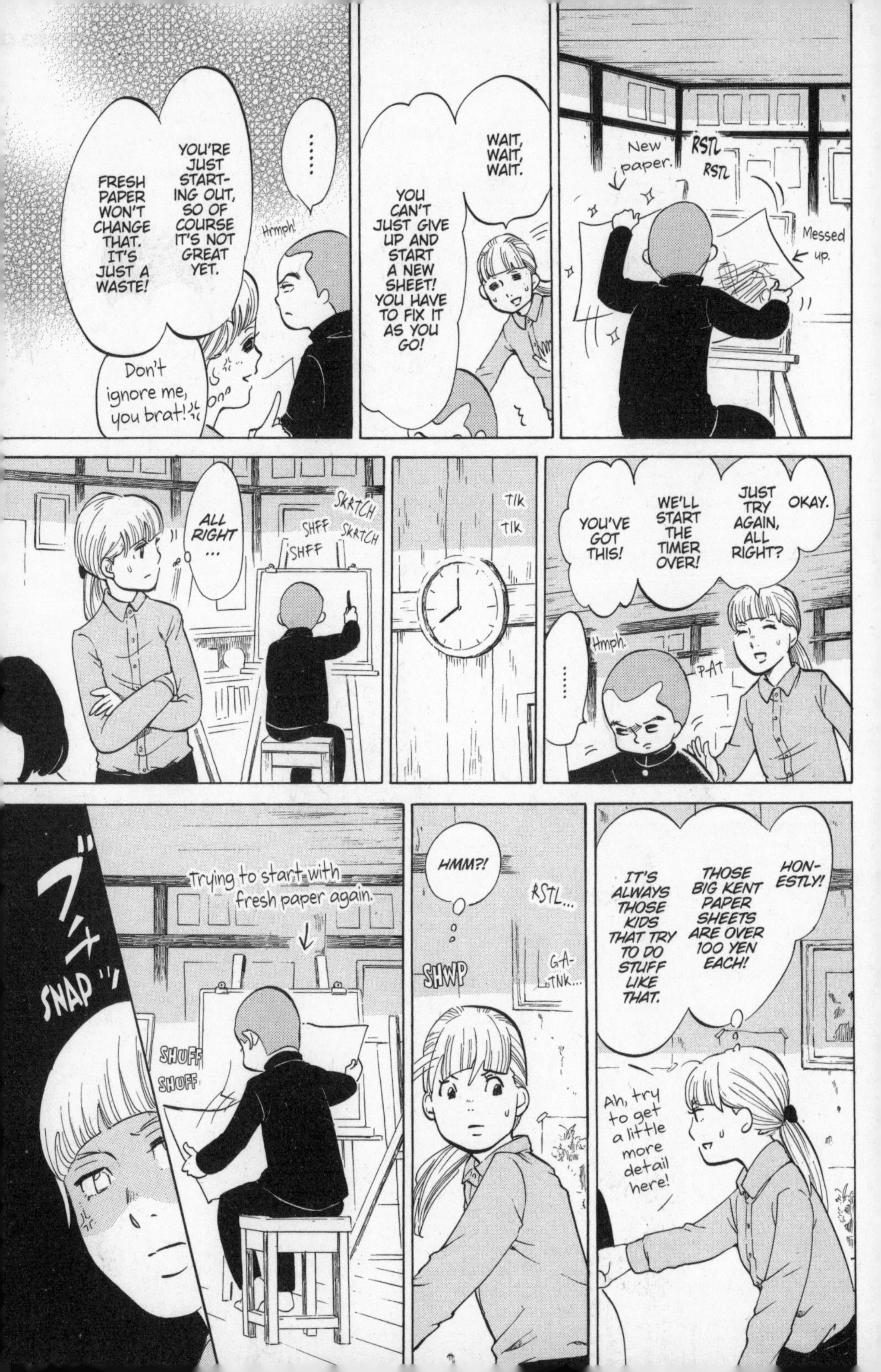
New paper.
RSTL
RSTL
Messed up.
WAIT, WAIT, WAIT.
YOU CAN'T JUST GIVE UP AND START A NEW SHEET! YOU HAVE TO FIX IT AS YOU GO!
......
Hrmph!
YOU'RE JUST STARTING OUT, SO OF COURSE IT'S NOT GREAT YET.
FRESH PAPER WON'T CHANGE THAT. IT'S JUST A WASTE!
Don't ignore me, you brat!
OKAY.
JUST TRY AGAIN, ALL RIGHT?
WE'LL START THE TIMER OVER!
YOU'VE GOT THIS!
PAT
Hmph.
......
TIK
TIK
SKRTCH
SKRTCH
SHFF
SHFF
ALL RIGHT ...
HON-ESTLY!
THOSE BIG KENT PAPER SHEETS ARE OVER 100 YEN EACH!
IT'S ALWAYS THOSE KIDS THAT TRY TO DO STUFF LIKE THAT.
Ah, try to get a little more detail here!
HMM?!
RSTL...
GA-TNK...
SHWP
SNAP
Trying to start with fresh paper again.
SHUFF
SHUFF

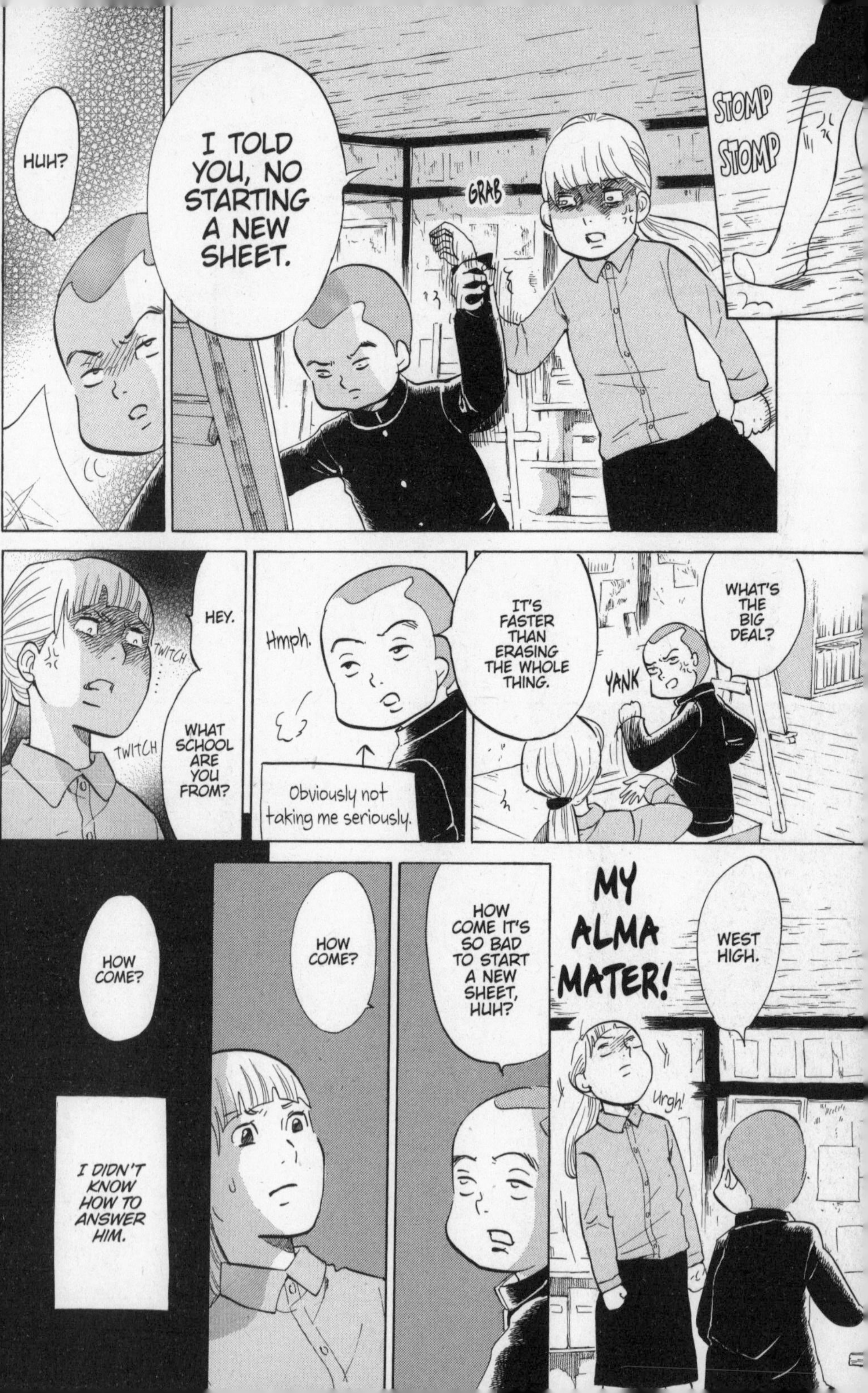
STOMP
STOMP
GRAB
I TOLD YOU, NO STARTING A NEW SHEET.
HUH?
WHAT'S THE BIG DEAL?
YANK
IT'S FASTER THAN ERASING THE WHOLE THING.
Hmph.
Obviously not taking me seriously.
HEY.
TWITCH
TWITCH
WHAT SCHOOL ARE YOU FROM?
WEST HIGH.
MY ALMA MATER!
Urgh!
HOW COME IT'S SO BAD TO START A NEW SHEET, HUH?
HOW COME?
HOW COME?
I DIDN'T KNOW HOW TO ANSWER HIM.

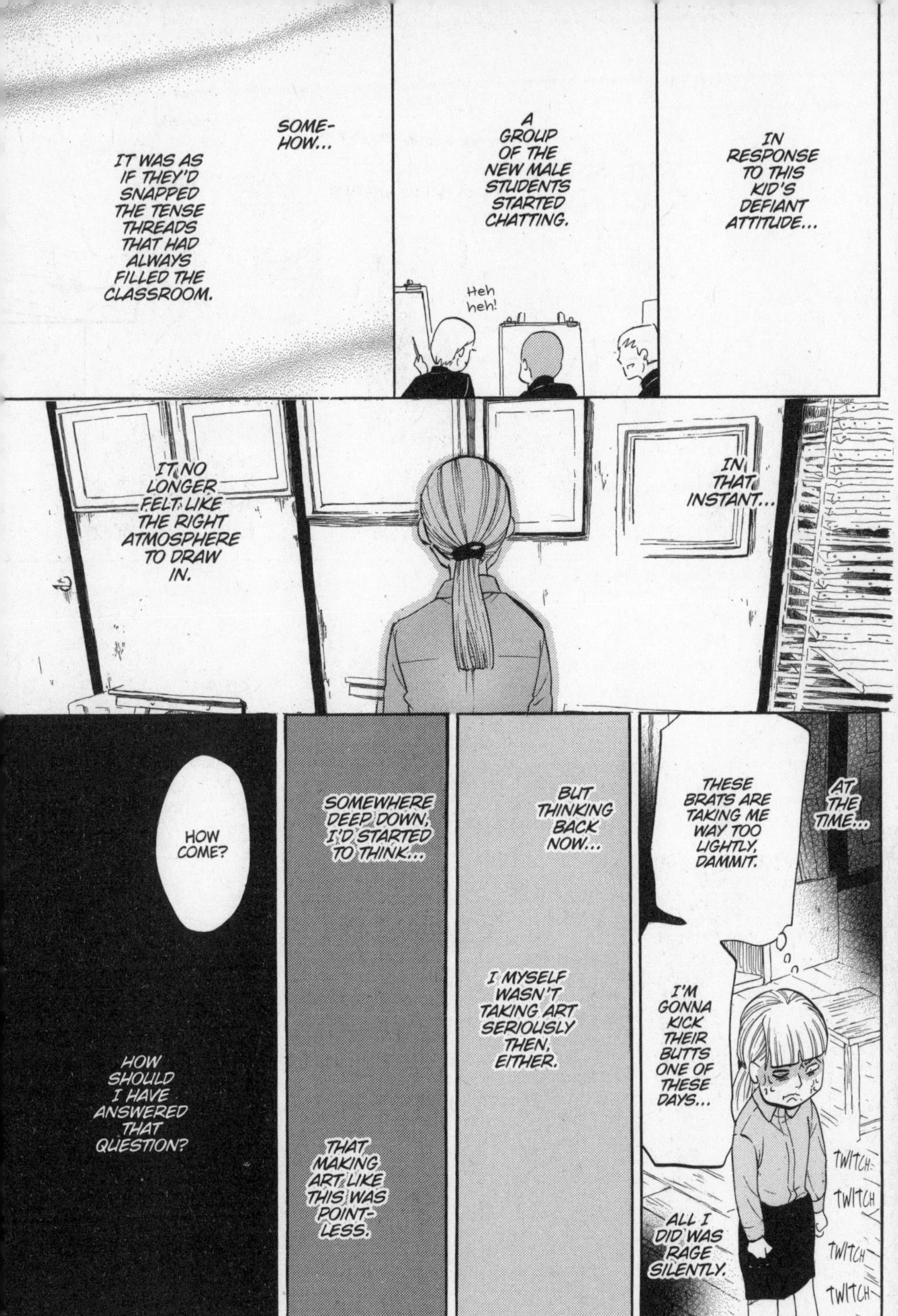
IN RESPONSE TO THIS KID'S DEFIANT ATTITUDE...
A GROUP OF THE NEW MALE STUDENTS STARTED CHATTING.
Heh heh!
SOME-HOW...
IT WAS AS IF THEY'D SNAPPED THE TENSE THREADS THAT HAD ALWAYS FILLED THE CLASSROOM.
IN THAT INSTANT...
IT NO LONGER FELT LIKE THE RIGHT ATMOSPHERE TO DRAW IN.
AT THE TIME...
THESE BRATS ARE TAKING ME WAY TOO LIGHTLY, DAMMIT.
I'M GONNA KICK THEIR BUTTS ONE OF THESE DAYS...
TWITCH
TWITCH
TWITCH
TWITCH
ALL I DID WAS RAGE SILENTLY.
BUT THINKING BACK NOW...
I MYSELF WASN'T TAKING ART SERIOUSLY THEN, EITHER.
SOMEWHERE DEEP DOWN, I'D STARTED TO THINK...
THAT MAKING ART LIKE THIS WAS POINTLESS.
HOW COME?
HOW SHOULD I HAVE ANSWERED THAT QUESTION?

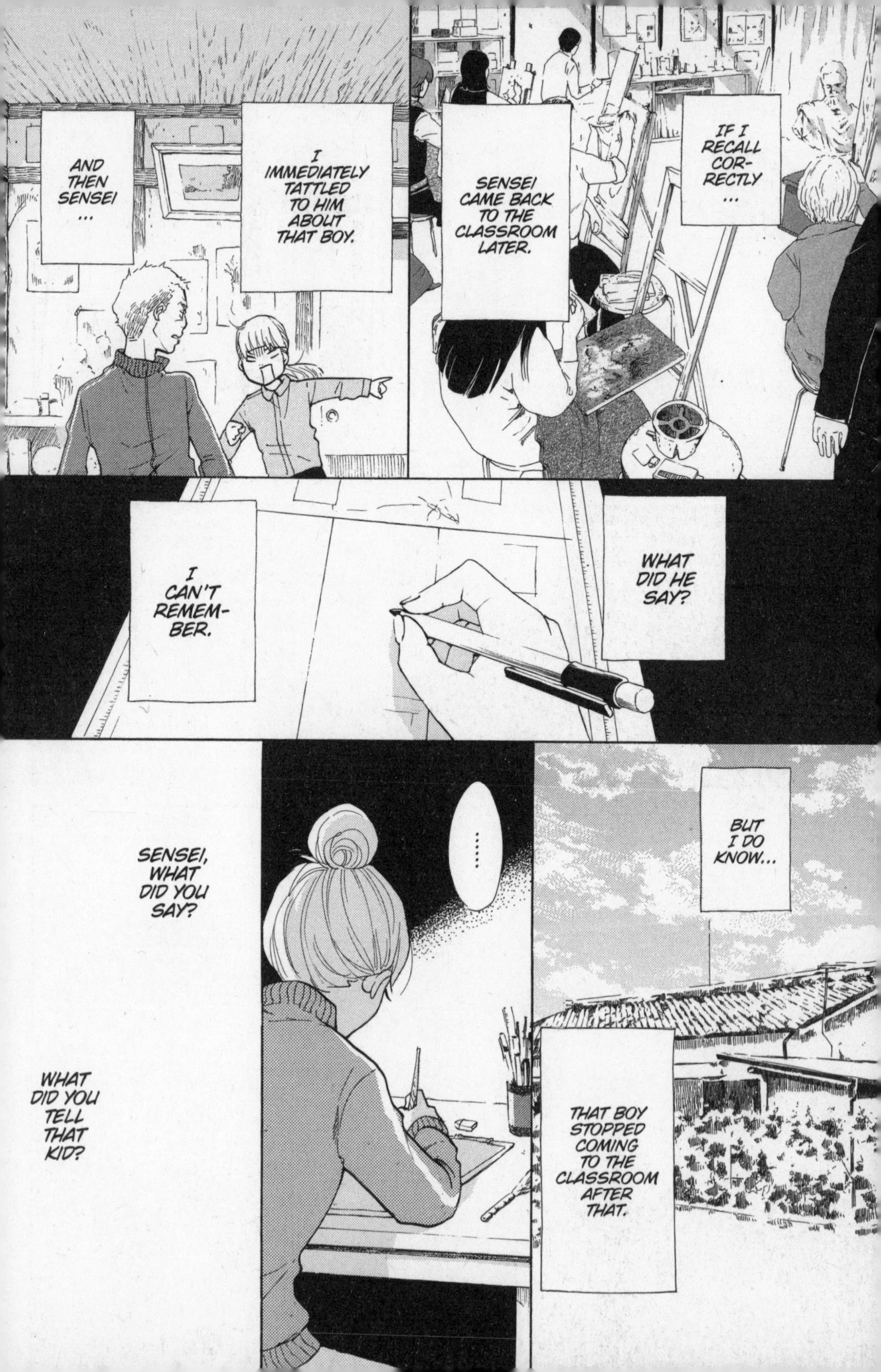
IF I RECALL COR-RECTLY ...
SENSEI CAME BACK TO THE CLASSROOM LATER.
I IMMEDIATELY TATTLED TO HIM ABOUT THAT BOY.
AND THEN SENSEI ...
WHAT DID HE SAY?
I CAN'T REMEM-BER.
BUT I DO KNOW...
THAT BOY STOPPED COMING TO THE CLASSROOM AFTER THAT.
......
SENSEI, WHAT DID YOU SAY?
WHAT DID YOU TELL THAT KID?

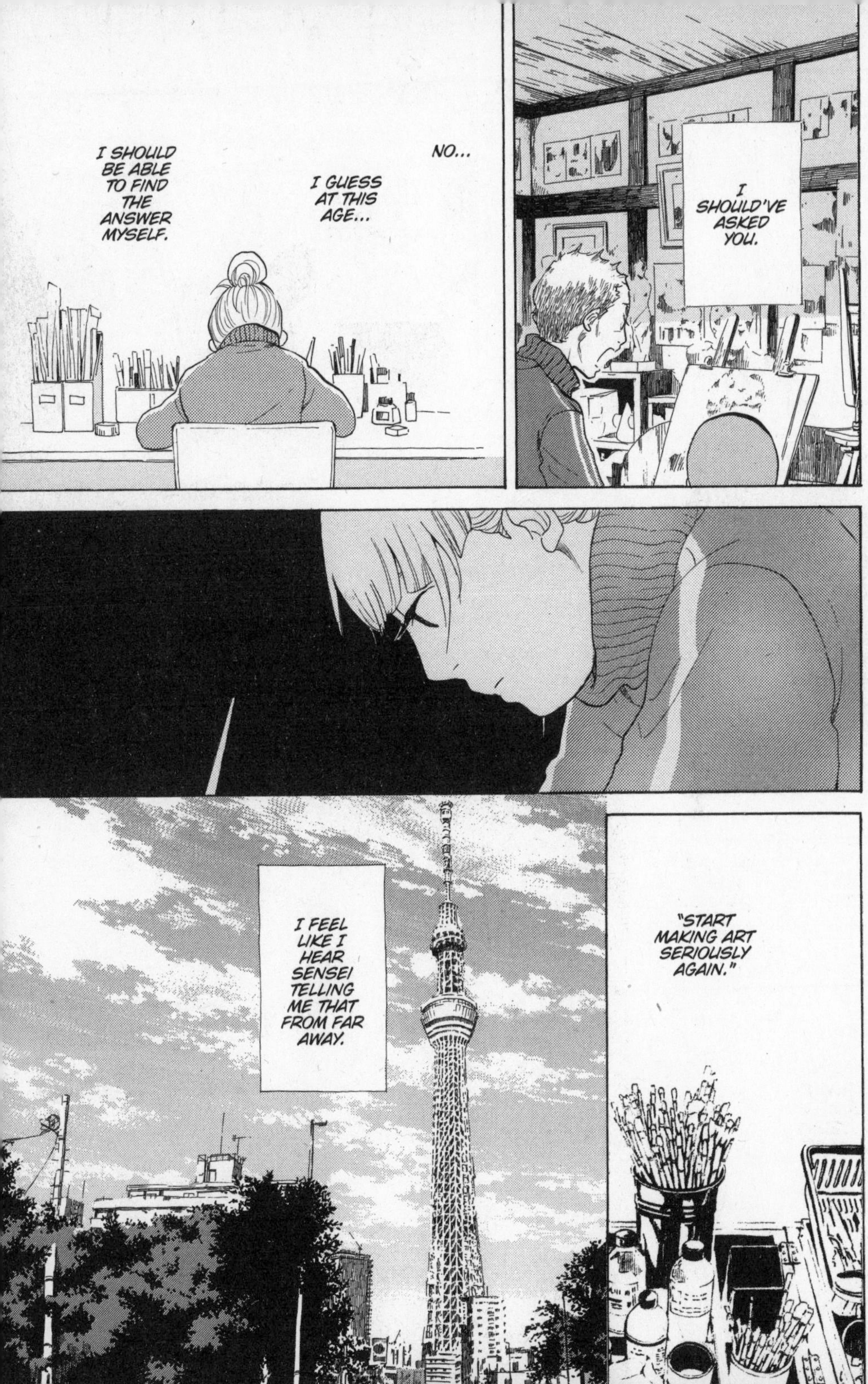
I SHOULD'VE ASKED YOU.
NO...
I GUESS AT THIS AGE...
I SHOULD BE ABLE TO FIND THE ANSWER MYSELF.
"START MAKING ART SERIOUSLY AGAIN."
I FEEL LIKE I HEAR SENSEI TELLING ME THAT FROM FAR AWAY.

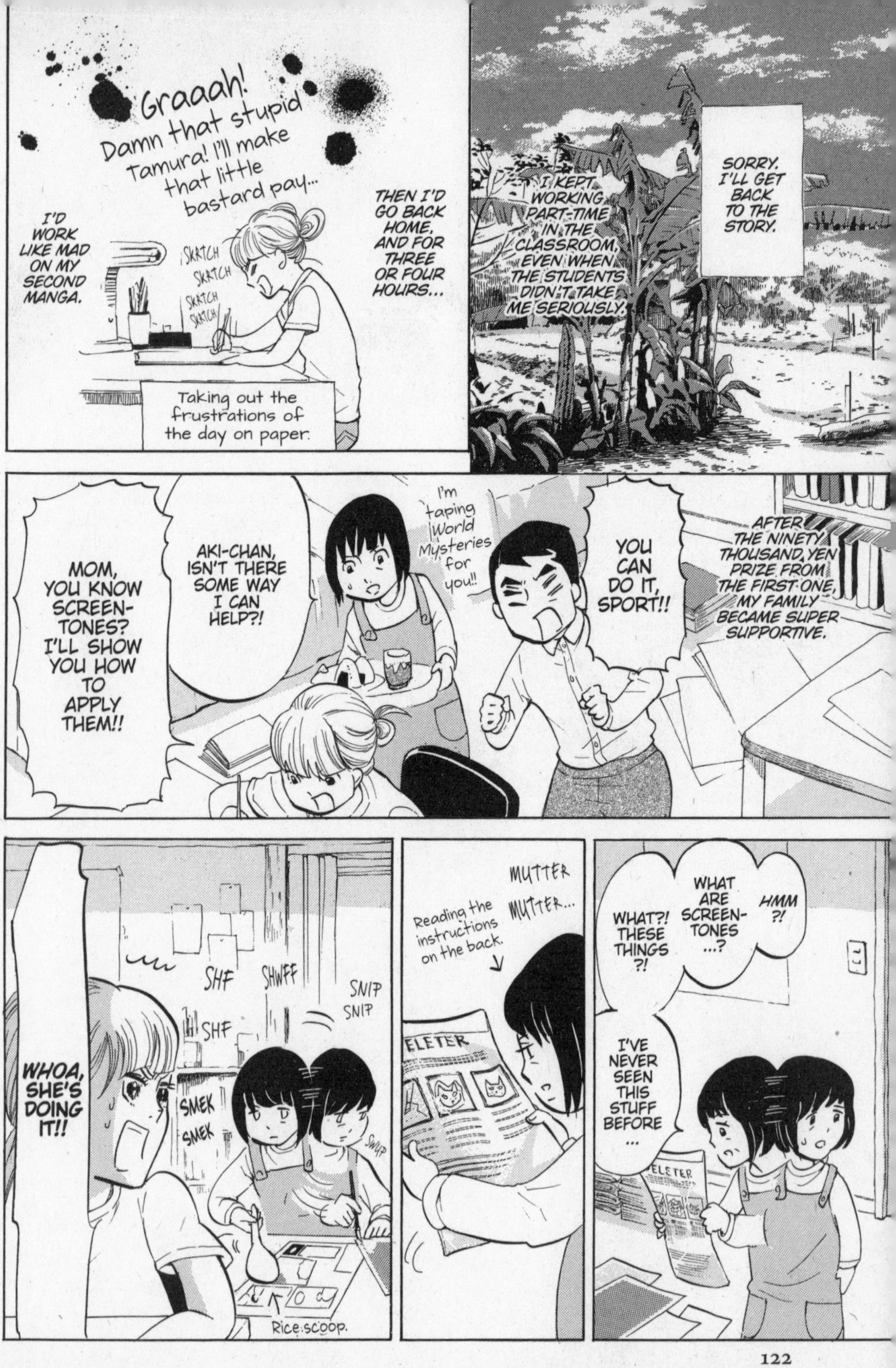
SORRY. I'LL GET BACK TO THE STORY.
I KEPT WORKING PART-TIME IN THE CLASSROOM, EVEN WHEN THE STUDENTS DIDN'T TAKE ME SERIOUSLY.
THEN I'D GO BACK HOME, AND FOR THREE OR FOUR HOURS...
Graaah! Damn that stupid Tamura! I'll make that little bastard pay...
I'D WORK LIKE MAD ON MY SECOND MANGA.
SKRTCH SKRTCH SKRTCH SKRTCH
Taking out the frustrations of the day on paper.
AFTER THE NINETY THOUSAND YEN PRIZE FROM THE FIRST ONE, MY FAMILY BECAME SUPER SUPPORTIVE.
YOU CAN DO IT, SPORT!!
I'm taping World Mysteries for you!!
AKI-CHAN, ISN'T THERE SOME WAY I CAN HELP?!
MOM, YOU KNOW SCREEN-TONES? I'LL SHOW YOU HOW TO APPLY THEM!!
HMM ?!
WHAT ARE SCREEN-TONES ...?
WHAT?! THESE THINGS ?!
I'VE NEVER SEEN THIS STUFF BEFORE ...
ELETER
MUTTER MUTTER...
Reading the instructions on the back.
ELETER
SNIP SNIP
SHWFF
SHF
SHF
WHOA, SHE'S DOING IT!!
SMEK SMEK
SWUP
Rice scoop.

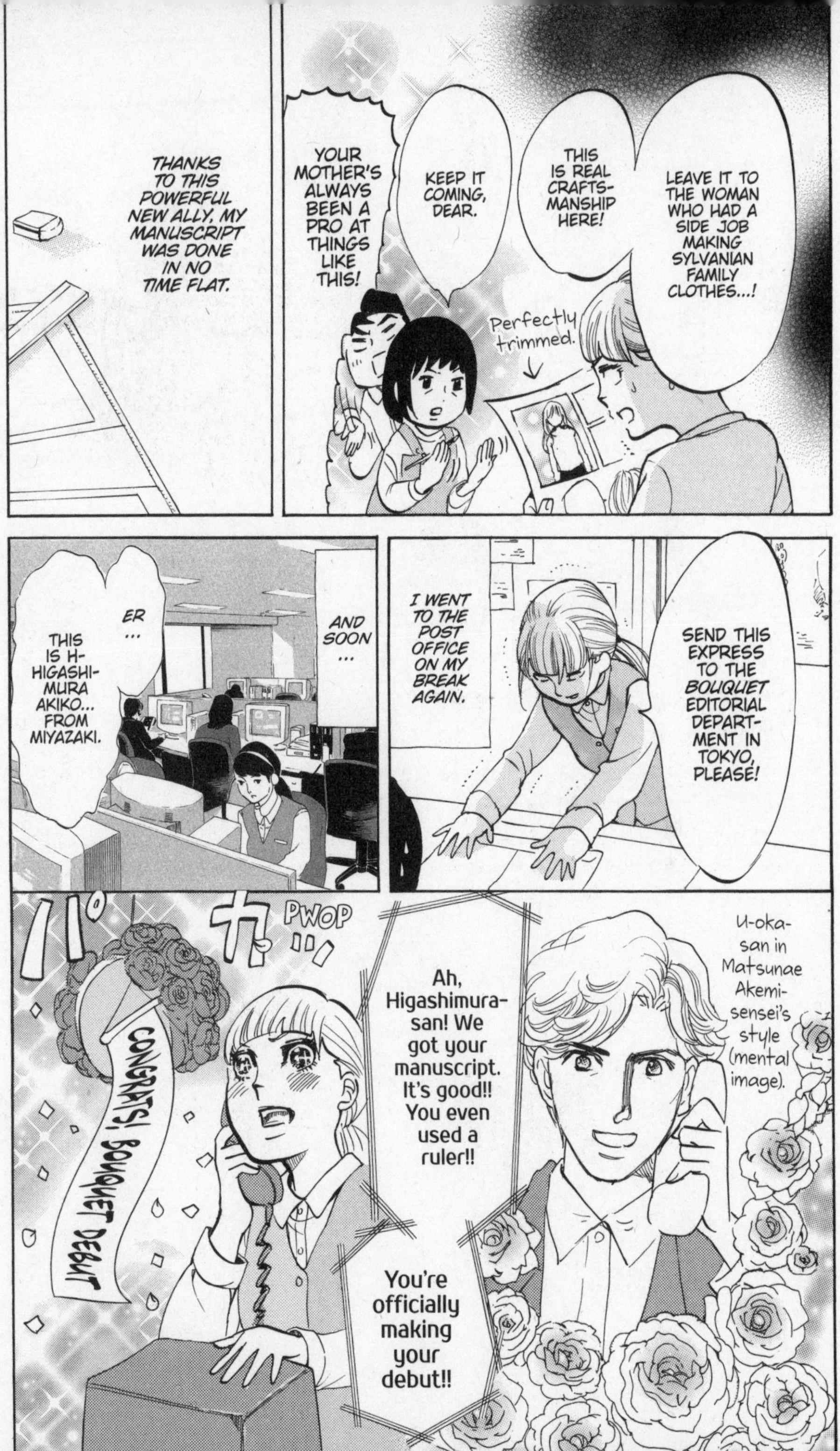
LEAVE IT TO THE WOMAN WHO HAD A SIDE JOB MAKING SYLVANIAN FAMILY CLOTHES...!
THIS IS REAL CRAFTS-MANSHIP HERE!
KEEP IT COMING, DEAR.
YOUR MOTHER'S ALWAYS BEEN A PRO AT THINGS LIKE THIS!
Perfectly trimmed.
THANKS TO THIS POWERFUL NEW ALLY, MY MANUSCRIPT WAS DONE IN NO TIME FLAT.
SEND THIS EXPRESS TO THE *BOUQUET* EDITORIAL DEPART-MENT IN TOKYO, PLEASE!
I WENT TO THE POST OFFICE ON MY BREAK AGAIN.
AND SOON...
ER...
THIS IS H-HIGASHI-MURA AKIKO... FROM MIYAZAKI.
U-oka-san in Matsunae Akemi-sensei's style (mental image).
PWOP
パカ
Ah, Higashimura-san! We got your manuscript. It's good!! You even used a ruler!!
CONGRATS!, BOUQUET DEBUT
You're officially making your debut!!

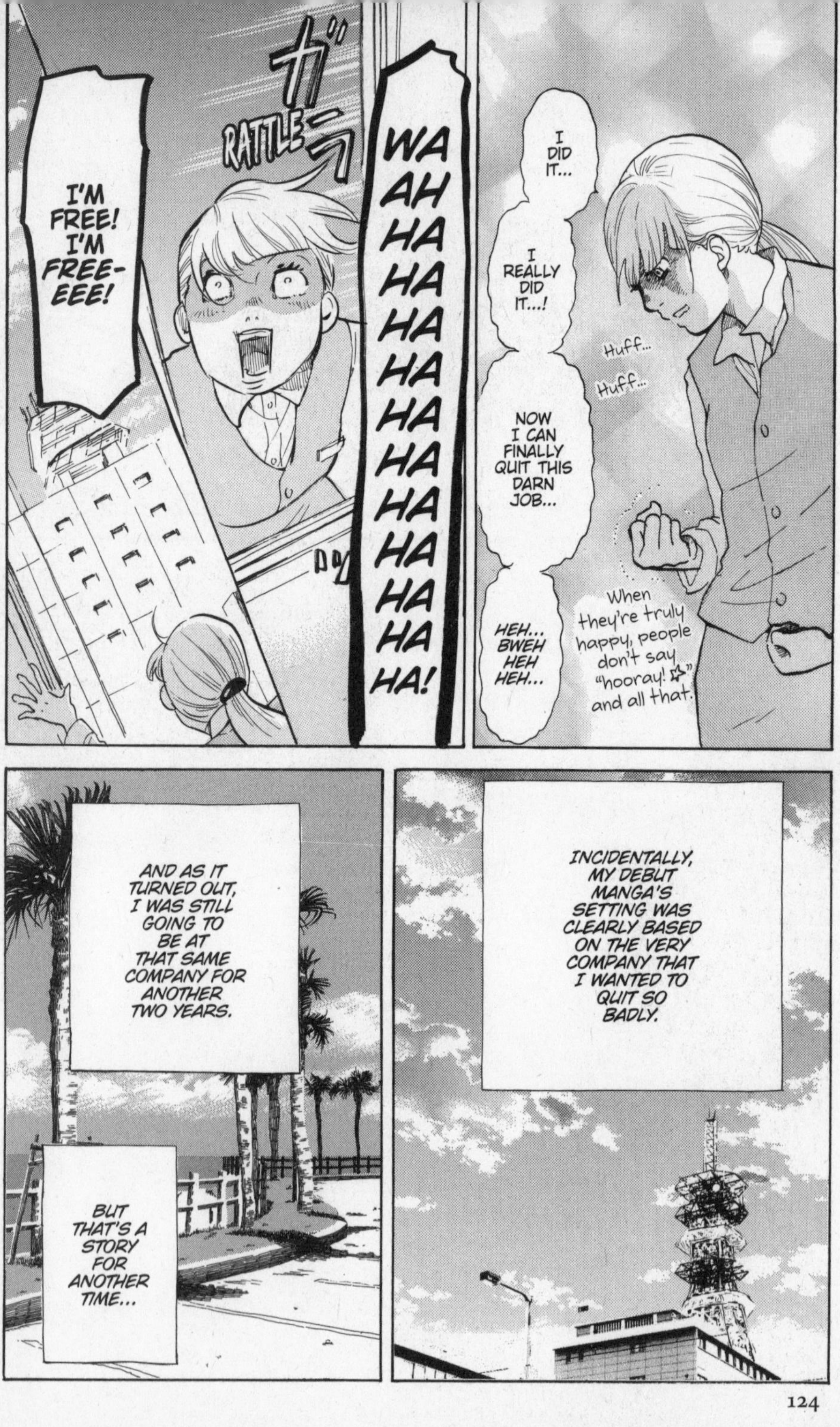
I DID IT...
I REALLY DID IT...!
Huff... Huff...
NOW I CAN FINALLY QUIT THIS DARN JOB...
HEH... BWEH HEH HEH...
When they're truly happy, people don't say "hooray! ☆" and all that.
RATTLE
WA AH HA HA HA HA HA HA HA HA HA HA HA HA!
I'M FREE! I'M FREE-EEE!
INCIDENTALLY, MY DEBUT MANGA'S SETTING WAS CLEARLY BASED ON THE VERY COMPANY THAT I WANTED TO QUIT SO BADLY.
AND AS IT TURNED OUT, I WAS STILL GOING TO BE AT THAT SAME COMPANY FOR ANOTHER TWO YEARS.
BUT THAT'S A STORY FOR ANOTHER TIME...

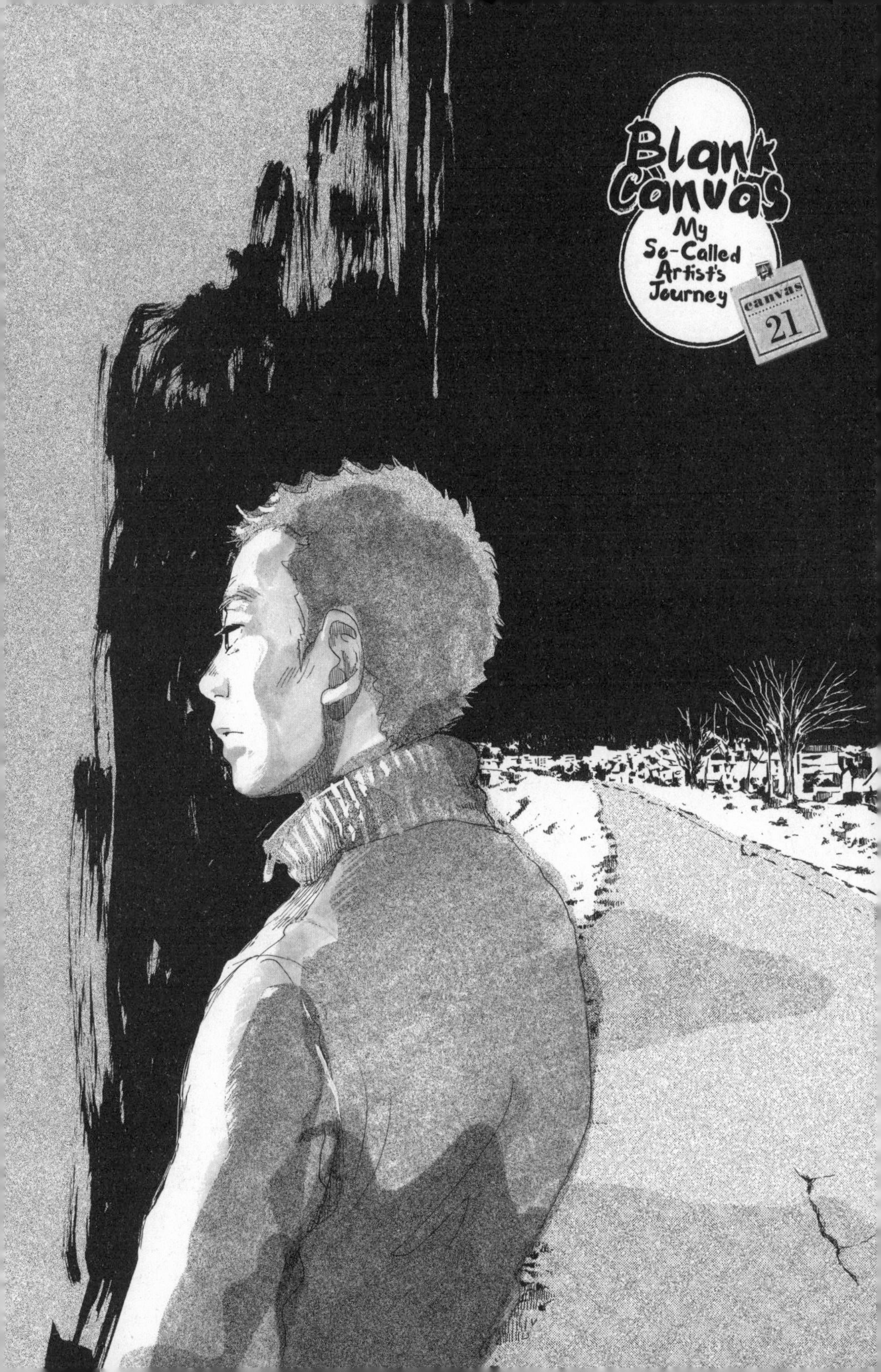
Blank Canvas
My So-Called Artist's Journey
canvas
21

田中書店
一番街店

Tanaka Bookstore
1st Street

ザザ
ZAA

BOOKS
本

ハーーン
DA-
DAAN

DELUXE 100 鈴野比佐子

ド
DUUN

フルーツ
こうもり

Did you know that a bat's cry can echo in a woman's broken heart?

Fruit Bat

Higashimura Akiko
東村アキコ

Bouquet Monthly NEW Manga Course

3		2		1
Excellence Award ¥100,000	Best Art ¥20,000		Grade I ¥200,000	
Best Effort Award ¥50,000	Best Story ¥20,000		Grade II ¥100,000	
	Promising Newcomer ¥20,000		Grade III ¥50,000	

Bouquet NEW Manga Course Submission Information Form

578

Covers: Bessatsu Margaret, From Me to You, Movie Cast Photos; Bouquet Deluxe, All stories self-contained!! Summer of 1999! 90 pp. Mori Hinoto, 100 pp. Suzuno Hisako; Bessatsu Friend.

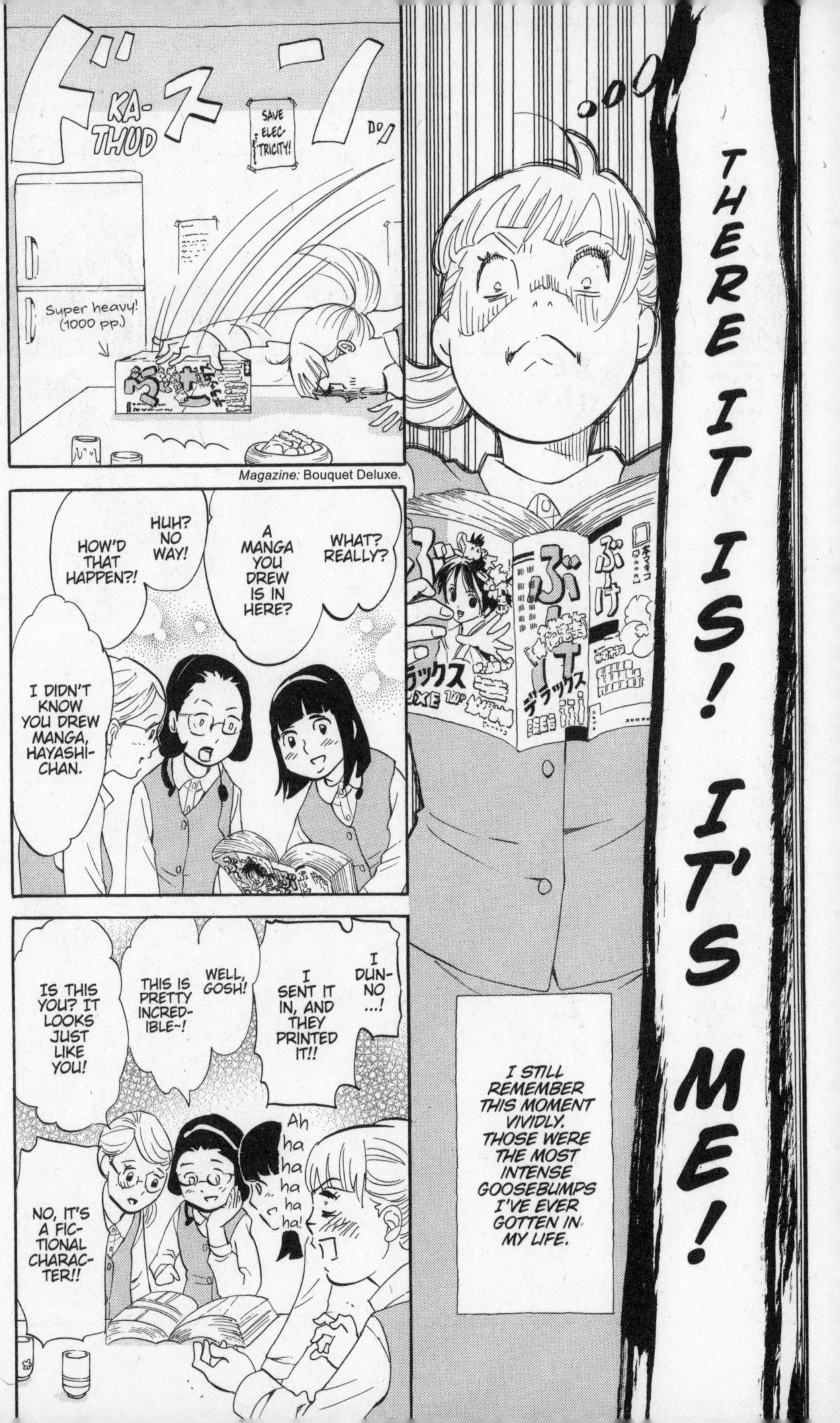
THERE IT IS! IT'S ME!
I STILL REMEMBER THIS MOMENT VIVIDLY. THOSE WERE THE MOST INTENSE GOOSEBUMPS I'VE EVER GOTTEN IN MY LIFE.
KA-THUD
SAVE ELEC-TRICITY!
Super heavy! (1000 pp.)
WHAT? REALLY?
A MANGA YOU DREW IS IN HERE?
HUH? NO WAY!
HOW'D THAT HAPPEN?!
I DIDN'T KNOW YOU DREW MANGA, HAYASHI-CHAN.
I DUN-NO ...!
I SENT IT IN, AND THEY PRINTED IT!!
WELL, GOSH!
THIS IS PRETTY INCREDIBLE~!
IS THIS YOU? IT LOOKS JUST LIKE YOU!
Ah ha ha ha ha ha!
NO, IT'S A FICTIONAL CHARACTER!!

Magazine: Bouquet Deluxe.

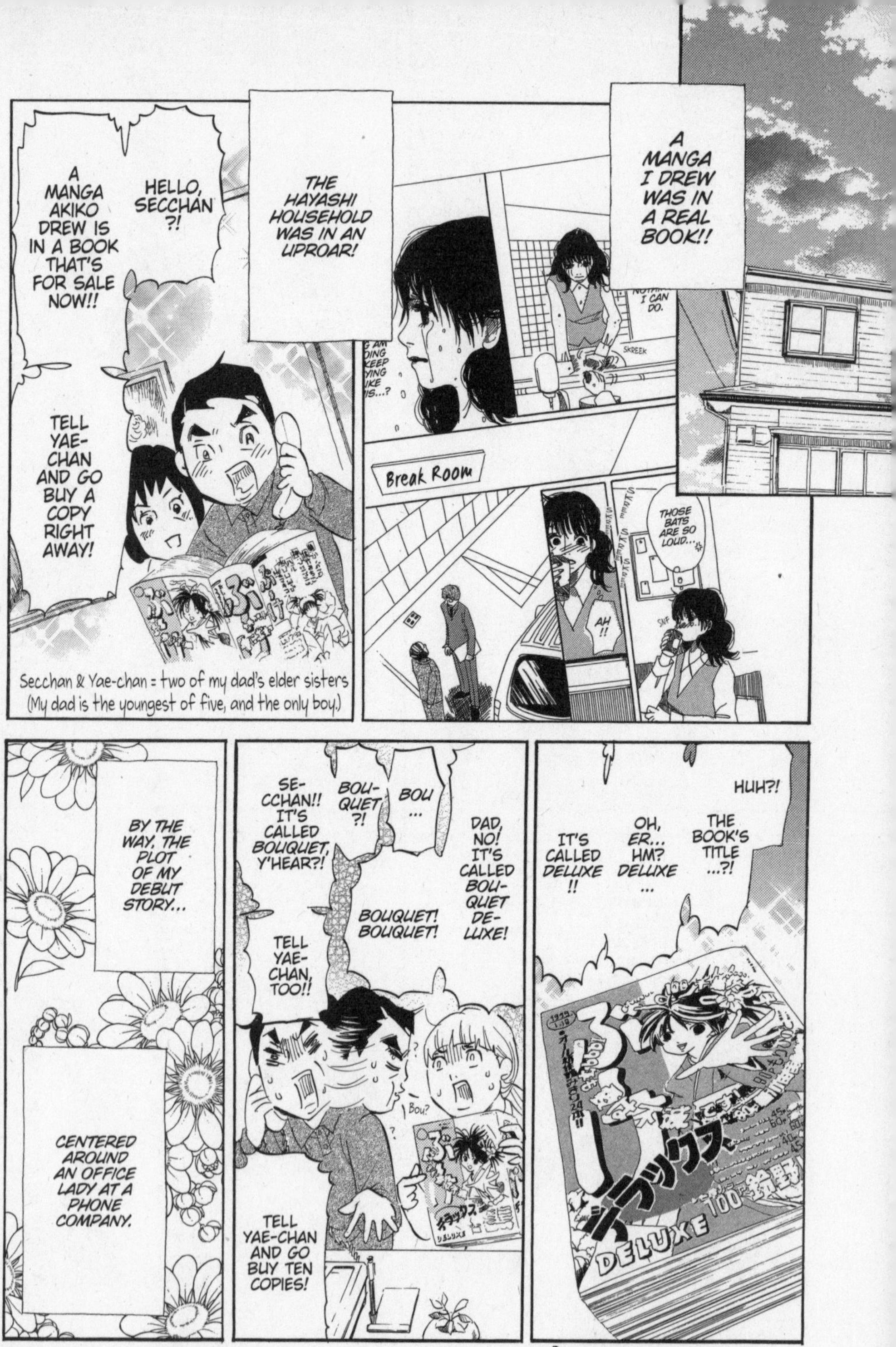
A MANGA I DREW WAS IN A REAL BOOK!!
THE HAYASHI HOUSEHOLD WAS IN AN UPROAR!
SKREEK
Break Room
THOSE BATS ARE SO LOUD...
AH!!
HELLO, SECCHAN?!
A MANGA AKIKO DREW IS IN A BOOK THAT'S FOR SALE NOW!!
TELL YAE-CHAN AND GO BUY A COPY RIGHT AWAY!
Secchan & Yae-chan = two of my dad's elder sisters
(My dad is the youngest of five, and the only boy.)
HUH?!
THE BOOK'S TITLE ...?!
OH, ER... HM? DELUXE...
IT'S CALLED DELUXE!!
DELUXE
DAD, NO! IT'S CALLED BOUQUET DELUXE!
BOU...
BOUQUET?!
SE-CCHAN!! IT'S CALLED BOUQUET, Y'HEAR?!
BOUQUET! BOUQUET!
TELL YAE-CHAN, TOO!!
Bou?
TELL YAE-CHAN AND GO BUY TEN COPIES!
BY THE WAY, THE PLOT OF MY DEBUT STORY...
CENTERED AROUND AN OFFICE LADY AT A PHONE COMPANY.

↑ There was too much information, so all he saw was "Deluxe."

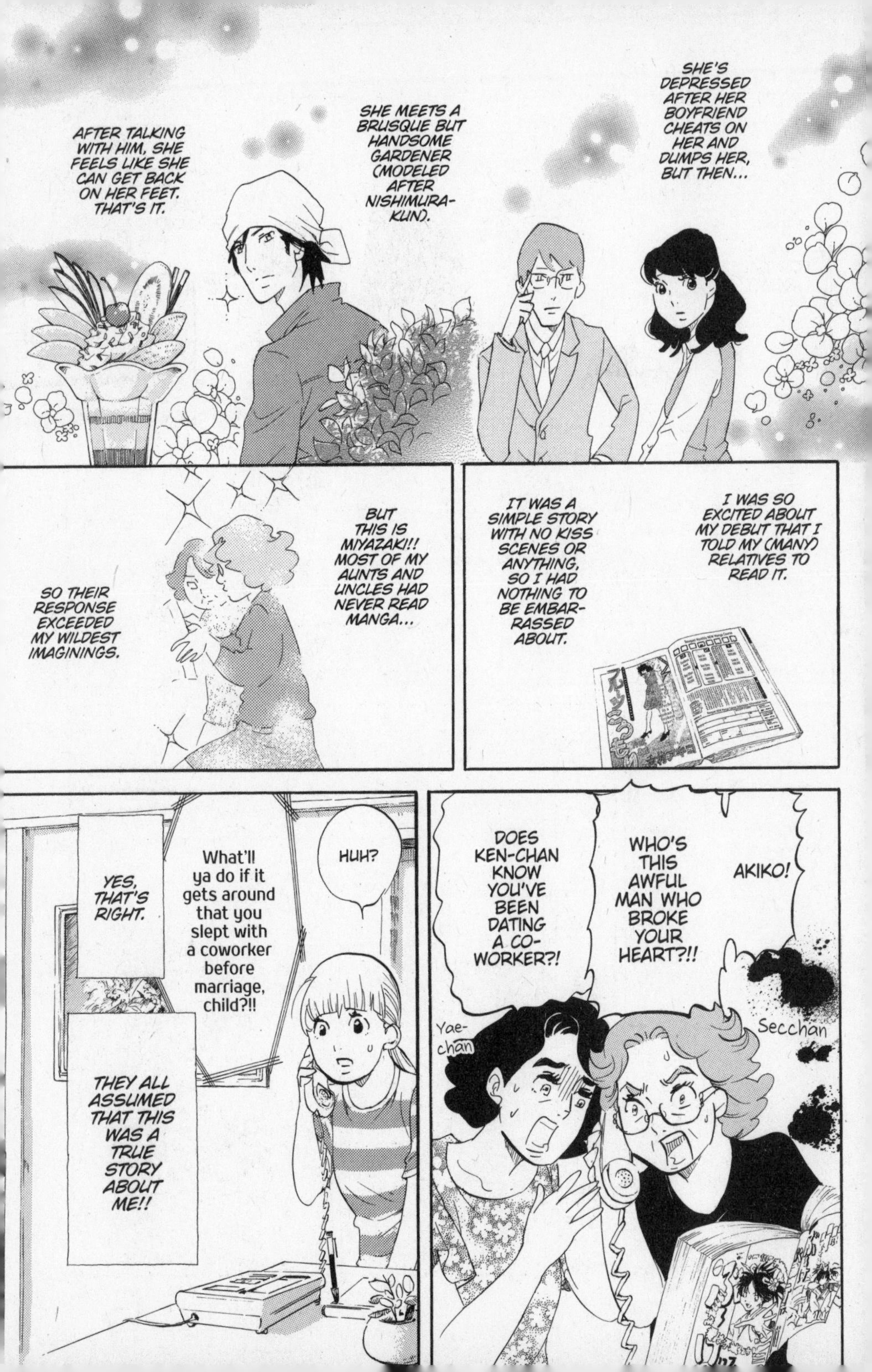
SHE'S DEPRESSED AFTER HER BOYFRIEND CHEATS ON HER AND DUMPS HER, BUT THEN...
SHE MEETS A BRUSQUE BUT HANDSOME GARDENER (MODELED AFTER NISHIMURA-KUN).
AFTER TALKING WITH HIM, SHE FEELS LIKE SHE CAN GET BACK ON HER FEET. THAT'S IT.
I WAS SO EXCITED ABOUT MY DEBUT THAT I TOLD MY (MANY) RELATIVES TO READ IT.
IT WAS A SIMPLE STORY WITH NO KISS SCENES OR ANYTHING, SO I HAD NOTHING TO BE EMBARRASSED ABOUT.
BUT THIS IS MIYAZAKI!! MOST OF MY AUNTS AND UNCLES HAD NEVER READ MANGA...
SO THEIR RESPONSE EXCEEDED MY WILDEST IMAGININGS.
AKIKO!
WHO'S THIS AWFUL MAN WHO BROKE YOUR HEART?!!
DOES KEN-CHAN KNOW YOU'VE BEEN DATING A CO-WORKER?!
Secchan
Yae-chan
HUH?
What'll ya do if it gets around that you slept with a coworker before marriage, child?!!
YES, THAT'S RIGHT.
THEY ALL ASSUMED THAT THIS WAS A TRUE STORY ABOUT ME!!

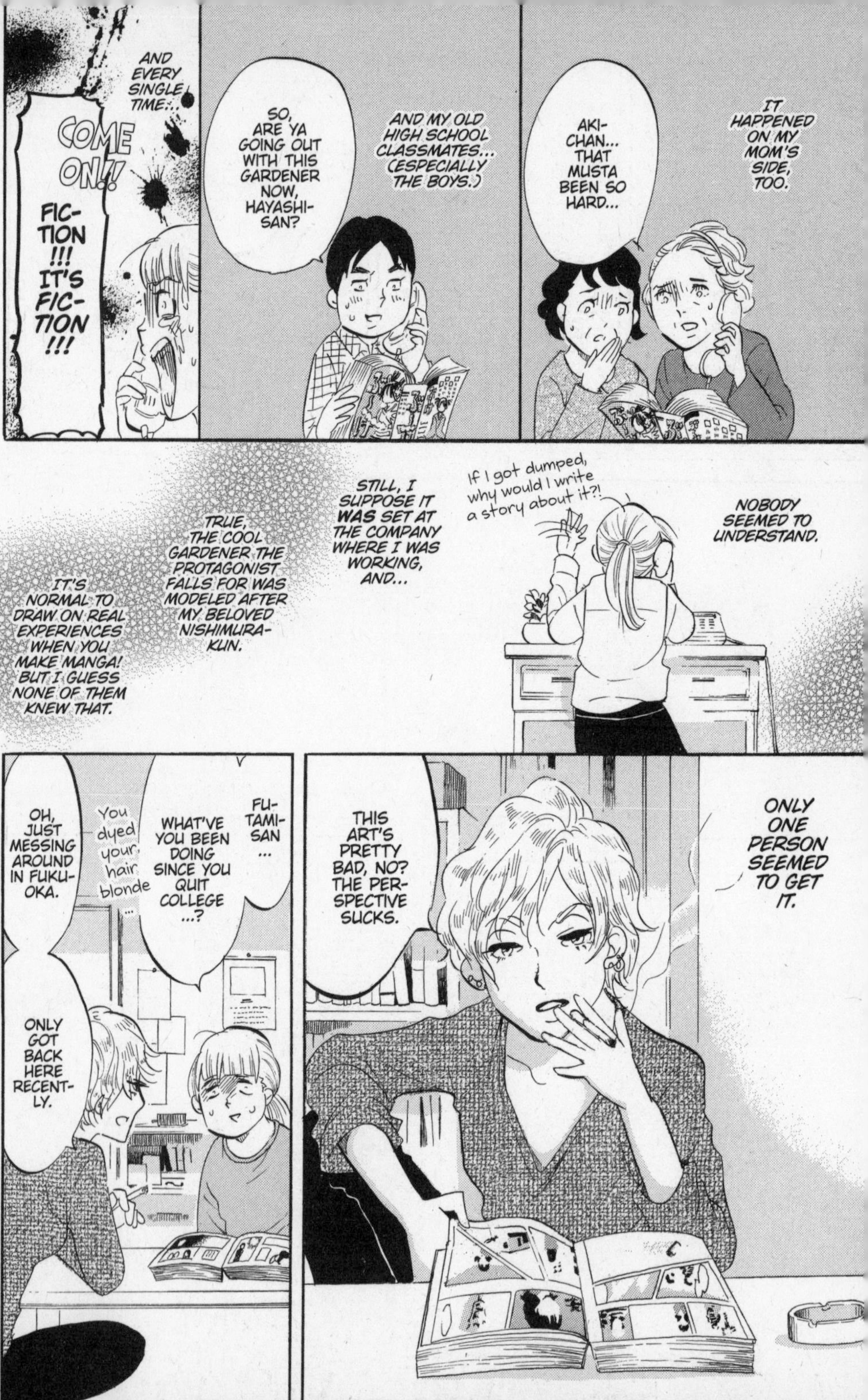
IT HAPPENED ON MY MOM'S SIDE, TOO.
AKI-CHAN... THAT MUSTA BEEN SO HARD...
AND MY OLD HIGH SCHOOL CLASSMATES... (ESPECIALLY THE BOYS.)
SO, ARE YA GOING OUT WITH THIS GARDENER NOW, HAYASHI-SAN?
AND EVERY SINGLE TIME...
COME ON!?!
FICTION!!! IT'S FICTION!!!
NOBODY SEEMED TO UNDERSTAND.
If I got dumped, why would I write a story about it?!
STILL, I SUPPOSE IT WAS SET AT THE COMPANY WHERE I WAS WORKING, AND...
TRUE, THE COOL GARDENER THE PROTAGONIST FALLS FOR WAS MODELED AFTER MY BELOVED NISHIMURA-KUN.
IT'S NORMAL TO DRAW ON REAL EXPERIENCES WHEN YOU MAKE MANGA! BUT I GUESS NONE OF THEM KNEW THAT.
ONLY ONE PERSON SEEMED TO GET IT.
THIS ART'S PRETTY BAD, NO? THE PERSPECTIVE SUCKS.
FUTAMI-SAN...
WHAT'VE YOU BEEN DOING SINCE YOU QUIT COLLEGE...?
You dyed your hair blonde...
OH, JUST MESSING AROUND IN FUKUOKA.
ONLY GOT BACK HERE RECENTLY.

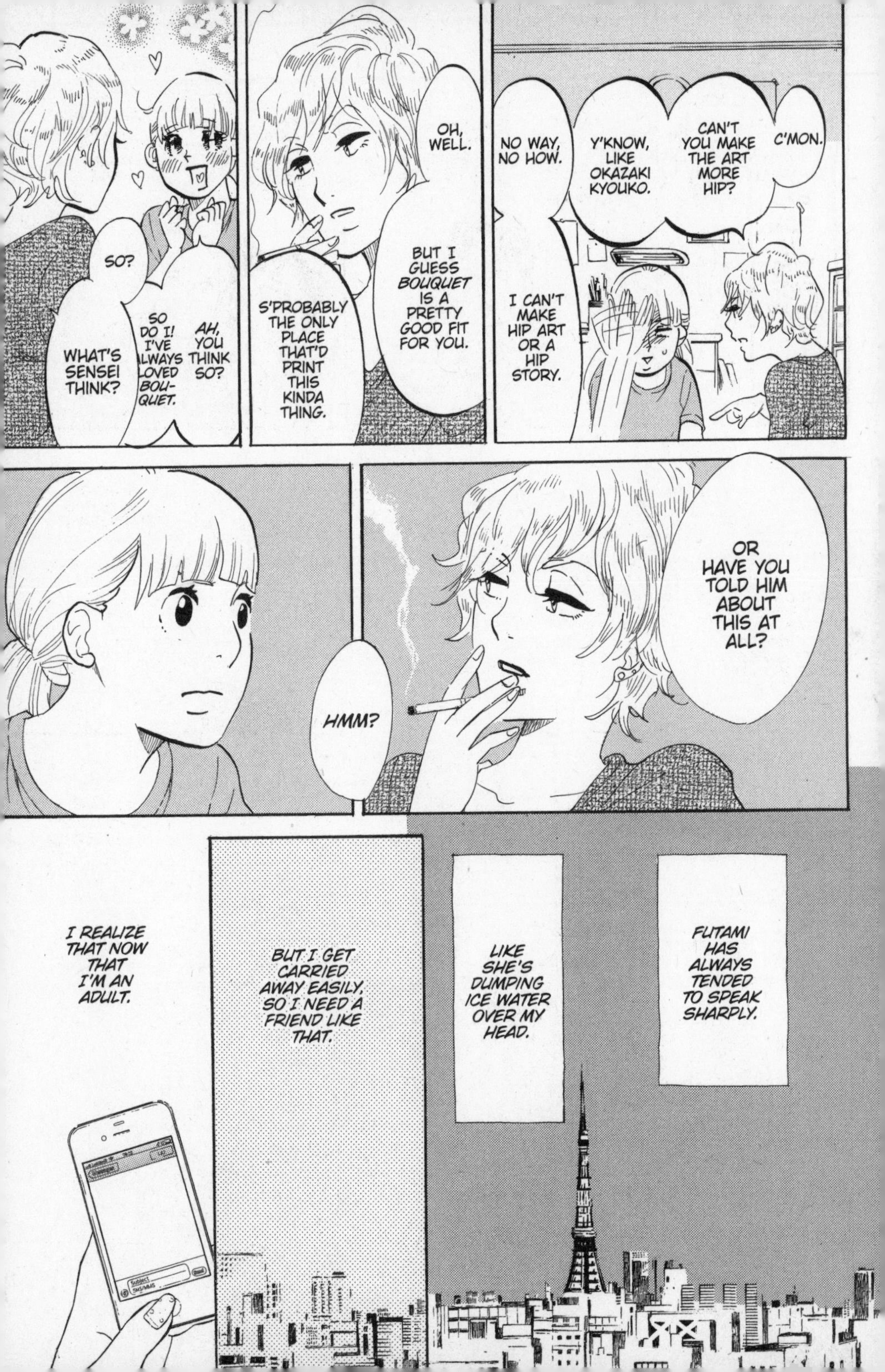
C'MON.
CAN'T YOU MAKE THE ART MORE HIP?
Y'KNOW, LIKE OKAZAKI KYOUKO.
NO WAY, NO HOW.
I CAN'T MAKE HIP ART OR A HIP STORY.
OH, WELL.
BUT I GUESS BOUQUET IS A PRETTY GOOD FIT FOR YOU.
S'PROBABLY THE ONLY PLACE THAT'D PRINT THIS KINDA THING.
SO?
AH, YOU THINK SO?
SO DO I! I'VE ALWAYS LOVED BOUQUET.
WHAT'S SENSEI THINK?
OR HAVE YOU TOLD HIM ABOUT THIS AT ALL?
HMM?
FUTAMI HAS ALWAYS TENDED TO SPEAK SHARPLY.
LIKE SHE'S DUMPING ICE WATER OVER MY HEAD.
BUT I GET CARRIED AWAY EASILY, SO I NEED A FRIEND LIKE THAT.
I REALIZE THAT NOW THAT I'M AN ADULT.

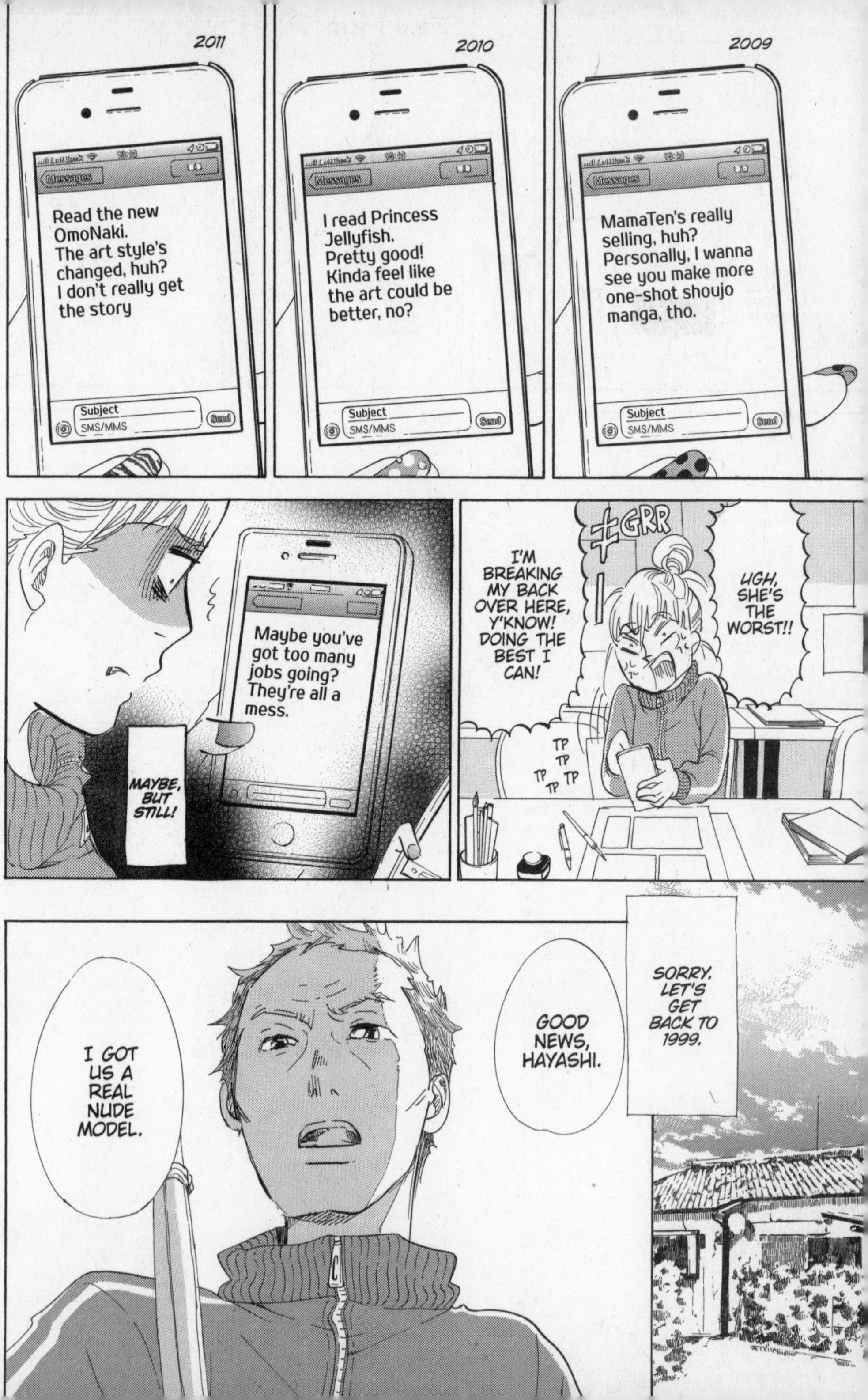
2009
Messages
MamaTen's really selling, huh? Personally, I wanna see you make more one-shot shoujo manga, tho.
Subject
SMS/MMS
Send
2010
Messages
I read Princess Jellyfish. Pretty good! Kinda feel like the art could be better, no?
Subject
SMS/MMS
Send
2011
Messages
Read the new OmoNaki. The art style's changed, huh? I don't really get the story
Subject
SMS/MMS
Send
UGH, SHE'S THE WORST!!
GRR
I'M BREAKING MY BACK OVER HERE, Y'KNOW! DOING THE BEST I CAN!
TP TP TP TP TP
Maybe you've got too many jobs going? They're all a mess.
MAYBE, BUT STILL!
SORRY. LET'S GET BACK TO 1999.
GOOD NEWS, HAYASHI.
I GOT US A REAL NUDE MODEL.

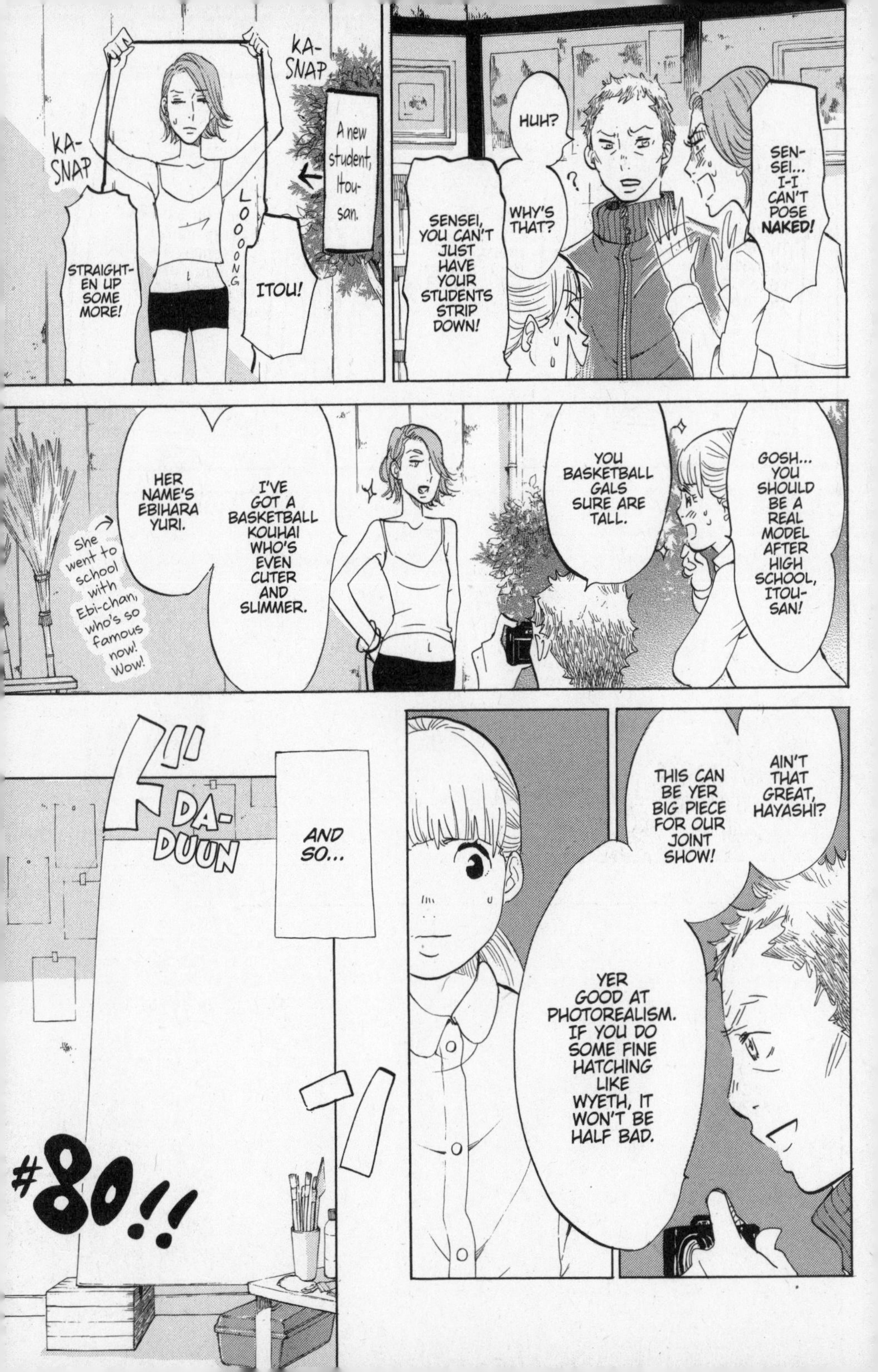
SEN-SEI... I-I CAN'T POSE **NAKED!**
HUH?
WHY'S THAT?
?
SENSEI, YOU CAN'T JUST HAVE YOUR STUDENTS STRIP DOWN!
KA-SNAP
A new student, Itou-san.
LOOOOONG
ITOU!
KA-SNAP
STRAIGHTEN UP SOME MORE!
GOSH... YOU SHOULD BE A REAL MODEL AFTER HIGH SCHOOL, ITOU-SAN!
YOU BASKETBALL GALS SURE ARE TALL.
I'VE GOT A BASKETBALL KOUHAI WHO'S EVEN CUTER AND SLIMMER.
HER NAME'S EBIHARA YURI.
She went to school with Ebi-chan, who's so famous now! Wow!
AIN'T THAT GREAT, HAYASHI?
THIS CAN BE YER BIG PIECE FOR OUR JOINT SHOW!
YER GOOD AT PHOTOREALISM. IF YOU DO SOME FINE HATCHING LIKE WYETH, IT WON'T BE HALF BAD.
JI
AND SO...
DA-DUUN
#80!!

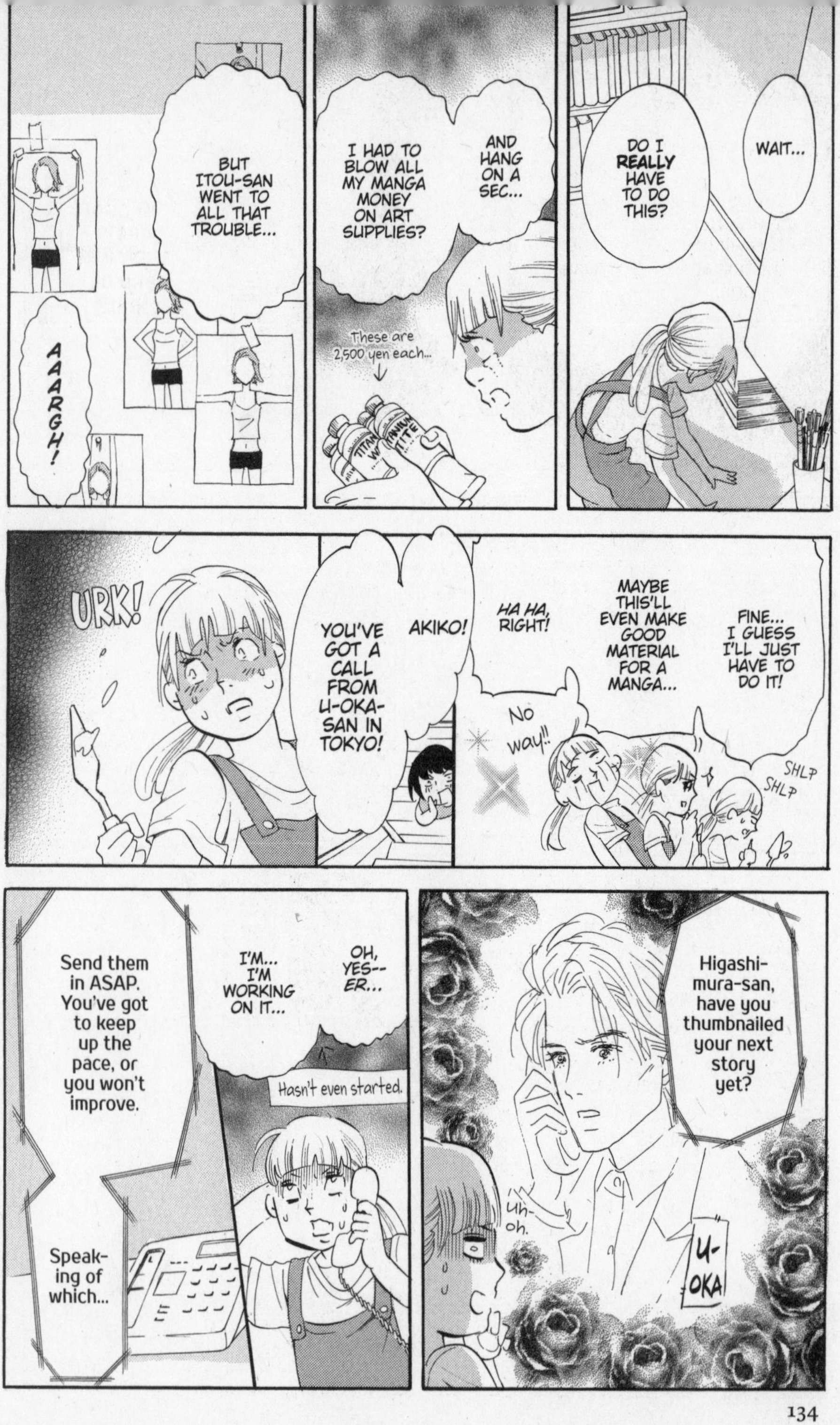
WAIT...
DO I REALLY HAVE TO DO THIS?
AND HANG ON A SEC...
I HAD TO BLOW ALL MY MANGA MONEY ON ART SUPPLIES?
These are 2,500 yen each...
BUT ITOU-SAN WENT TO ALL THAT TROUBLE...
AAAARGH!
FINE... I GUESS I'LL JUST HAVE TO DO IT!
MAYBE THIS'LL EVEN MAKE GOOD MATERIAL FOR A MANGA...
HA HA, RIGHT!
No way!!
SHLP
SHLP
AKIKO!
YOU'VE GOT A CALL FROM U-OKA-SAN IN TOKYO!
URK!
Higashi-mura-san, have you thumbnailed your next story yet?
Uh-oh.
U-OKA
OH, YES-- ER...
I'M... I'M WORKING ON IT...
Hasn't even started.
Send them in ASAP. You've got to keep up the pace, or you won't improve.
Speak-ing of which...

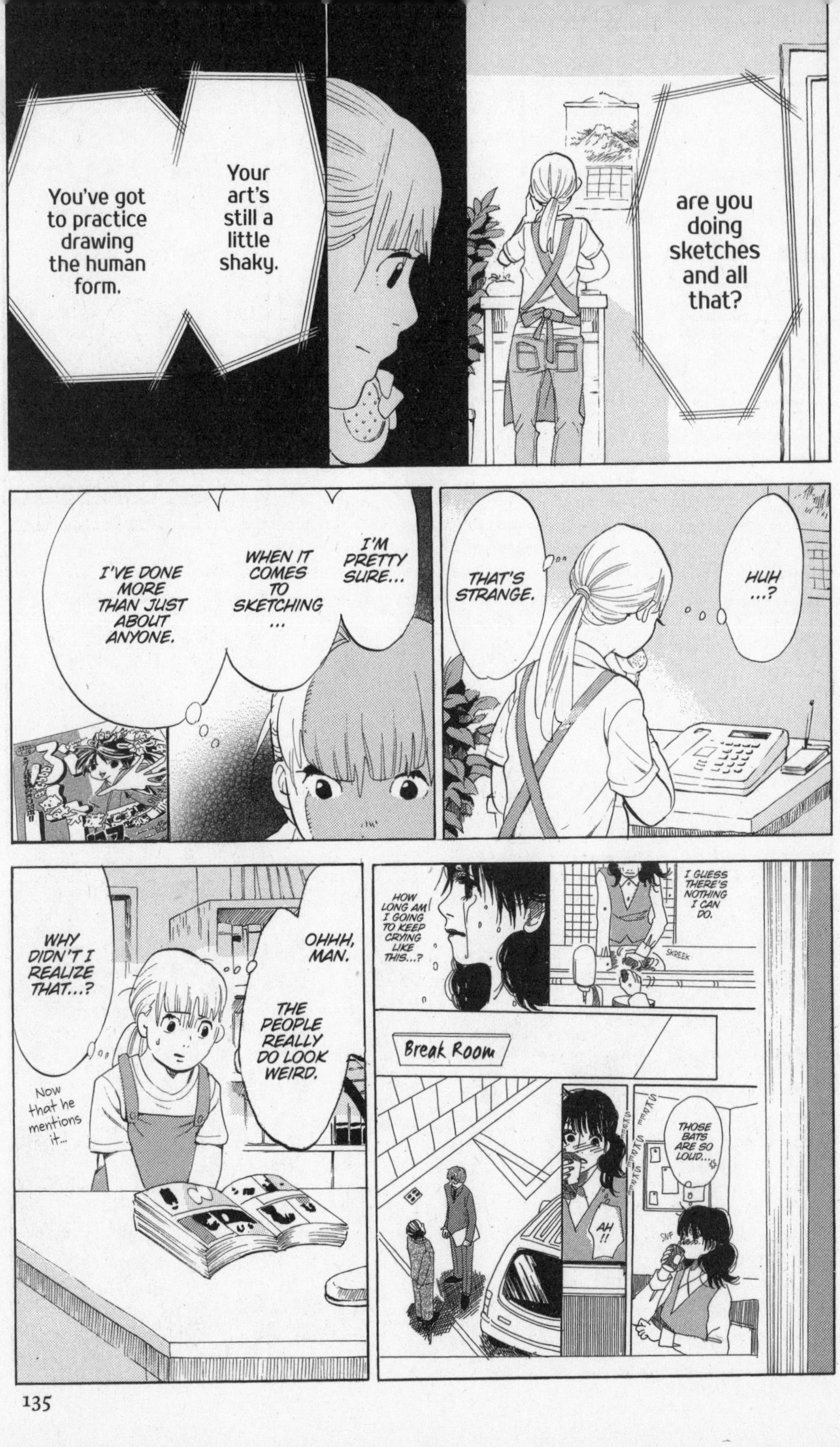
are you doing sketches and all that?
Your art's still a little shaky.
You've got to practice drawing the human form.
HUH ...?
THAT'S STRANGE.
I'M PRETTY SURE...
WHEN IT COMES TO SKETCHING ...
I'VE DONE MORE THAN JUST ABOUT ANYONE.
I GUESS THERE'S NOTHING I CAN DO.
SKREEK
HOW LONG AM I GOING TO KEEP CRYING LIKE THIS...?
Break Room
THOSE BATS ARE SO LOUD...
AH !!
OHHH, MAN.
THE PEOPLE REALLY DO LOOK WEIRD.
WHY DIDN'T I REALIZE THAT...?
Now that he mentions it...

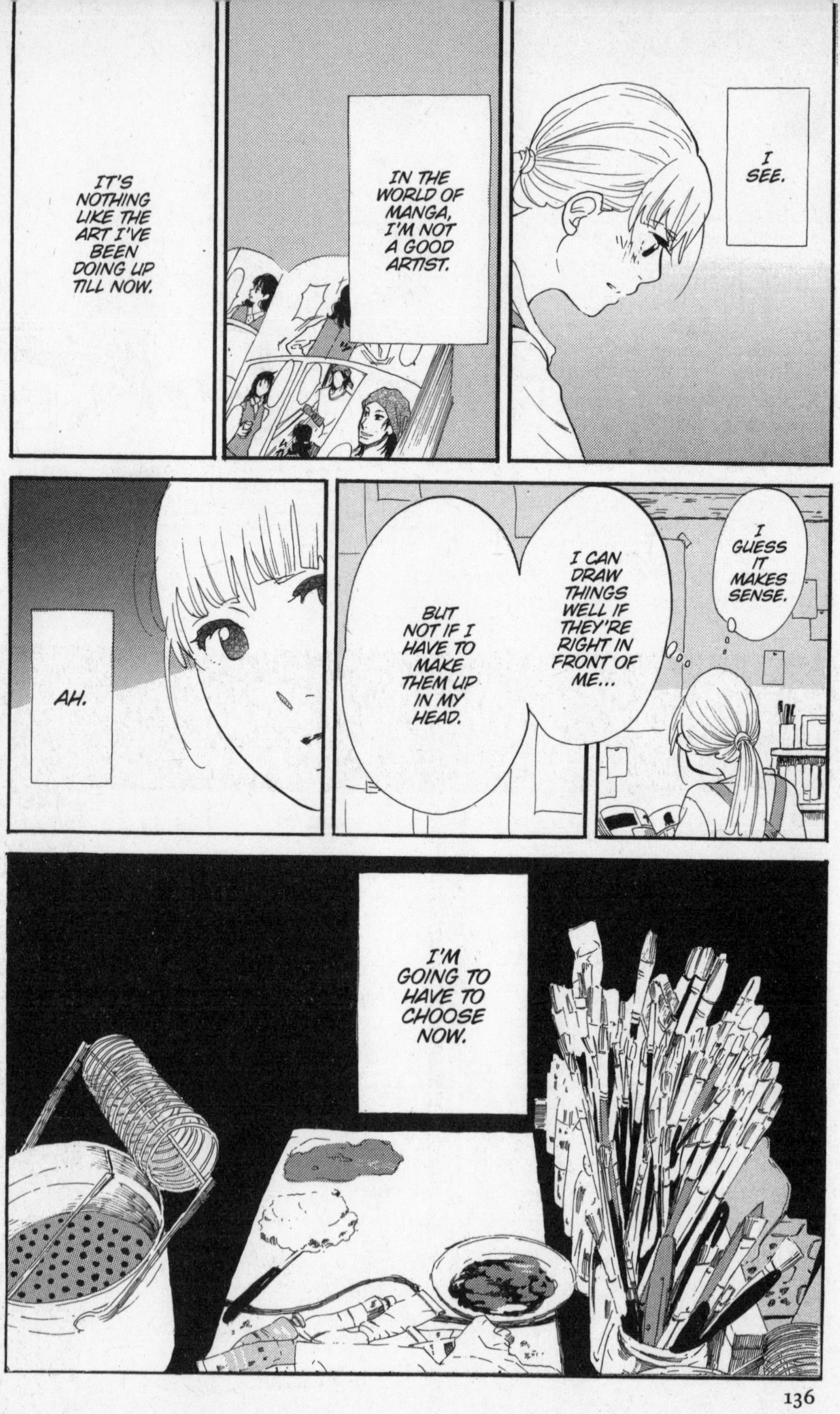
I SEE.
IN THE WORLD OF MANGA, I'M NOT A GOOD ARTIST.
IT'S NOTHING LIKE THE ART I'VE BEEN DOING UP TILL NOW.
I GUESS IT MAKES SENSE.
I CAN DRAW THINGS WELL IF THEY'RE RIGHT IN FRONT OF ME...
BUT NOT IF I HAVE TO MAKE THEM UP IN MY HEAD.
AH.
I'M GOING TO HAVE TO CHOOSE NOW.

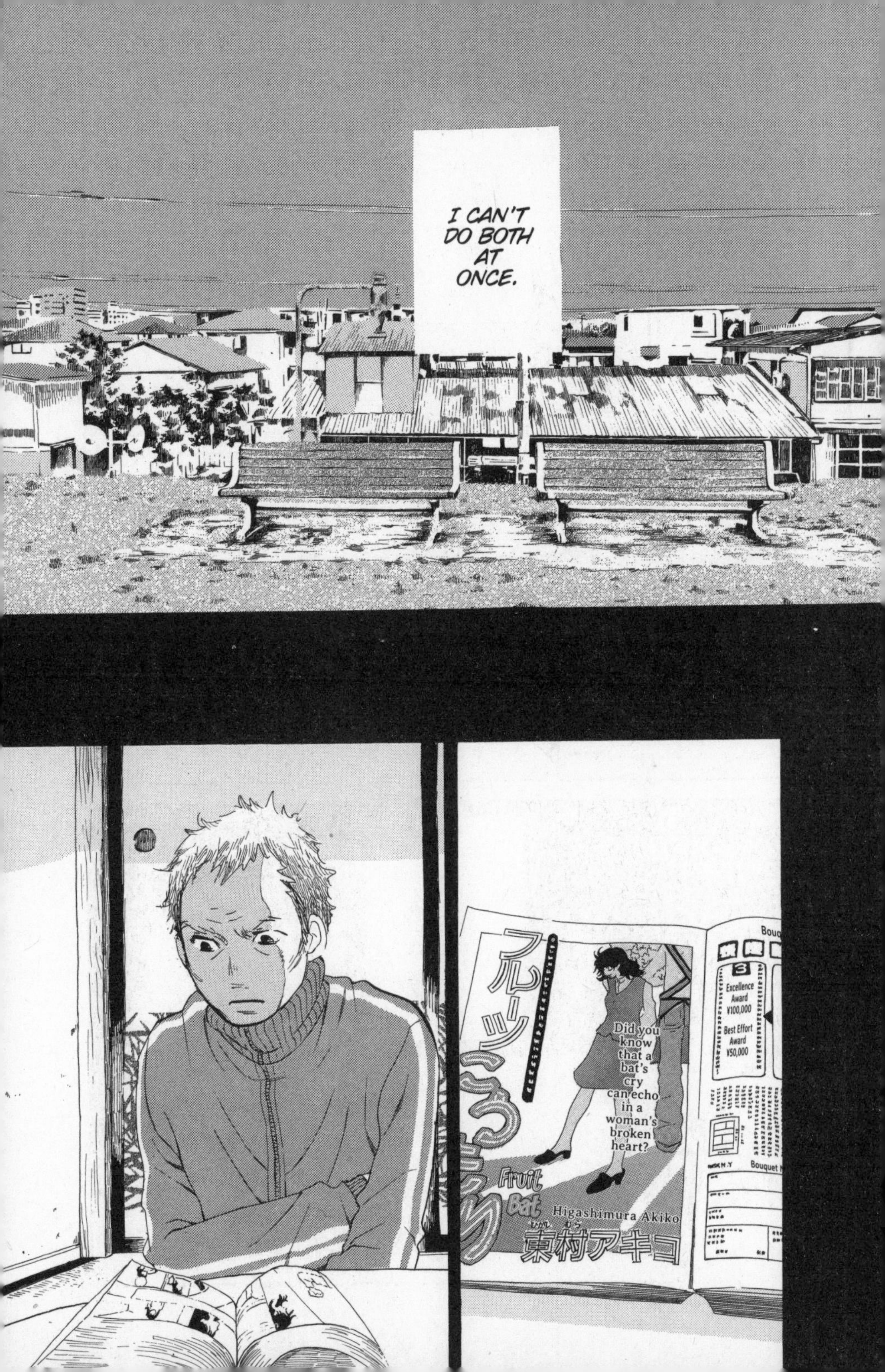
I CAN'T DO BOTH AT ONCE.
フルーツこうもり
Fruit Bat
Higashimura Akiko
東村アキコ
Did you know that a bat's cry can echo in a woman's broken heart?
3
Excellence Award ¥100,000
Best Effort Award ¥50,000
Bouquet

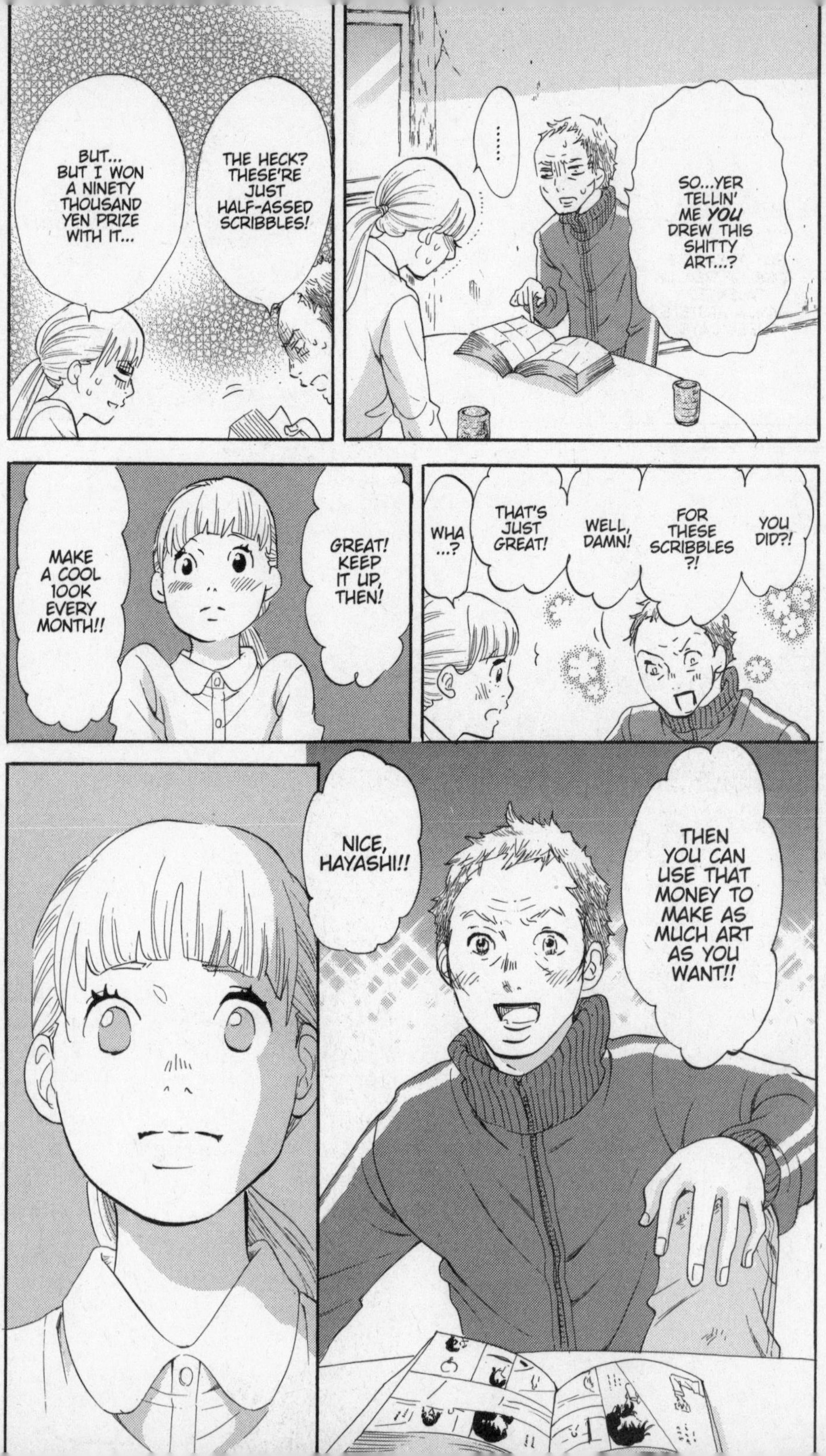
SO...YER TELLIN' ME *YOU* DREW THIS SHITTY ART...?
......
THE HECK? THESE'RE JUST HALF-ASSED SCRIBBLES!
BUT... BUT I WON A NINETY THOUSAND YEN PRIZE WITH IT...
YOU DID?!
FOR THESE SCRIBBLES?!
WELL, DAMN!
THAT'S JUST GREAT!
WHA ...?
GREAT! KEEP IT UP, THEN!
MAKE A COOL 100K EVERY MONTH!!
THEN YOU CAN USE THAT MONEY TO MAKE AS MUCH ART AS YOU WANT!!
NICE, HAYASHI!!

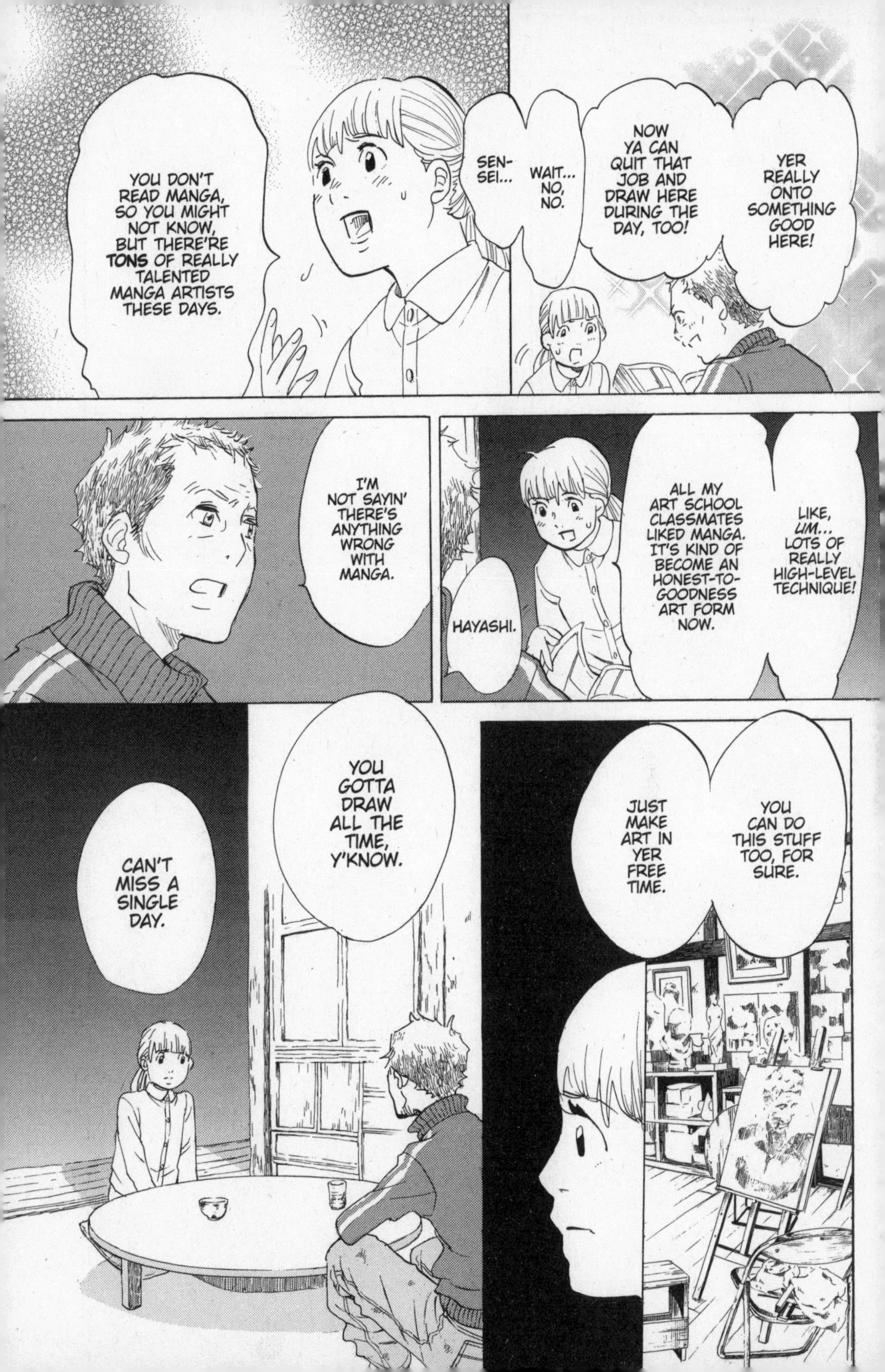
YER REALLY ONTO SOMETHING GOOD HERE!
NOW YA CAN QUIT THAT JOB AND DRAW HERE DURING THE DAY, TOO!
WAIT... NO, NO.
SEN-SEI...
YOU DON'T READ MANGA, SO YOU MIGHT NOT KNOW, BUT THERE'RE **TONS** OF REALLY TALENTED MANGA ARTISTS THESE DAYS.
LIKE, UM... LOTS OF REALLY HIGH-LEVEL TECHNIQUE!
ALL MY ART SCHOOL CLASSMATES LIKED MANGA. IT'S KIND OF BECOME AN HONEST-TO-GOODNESS ART FORM NOW.
HAYASHI.
I'M NOT SAYIN' THERE'S ANYTHING WRONG WITH MANGA.
YOU CAN DO THIS STUFF TOO, FOR SURE.
JUST MAKE ART IN YER FREE TIME.
YOU GOTTA DRAW ALL THE TIME, Y'KNOW.
CAN'T MISS A SINGLE DAY.

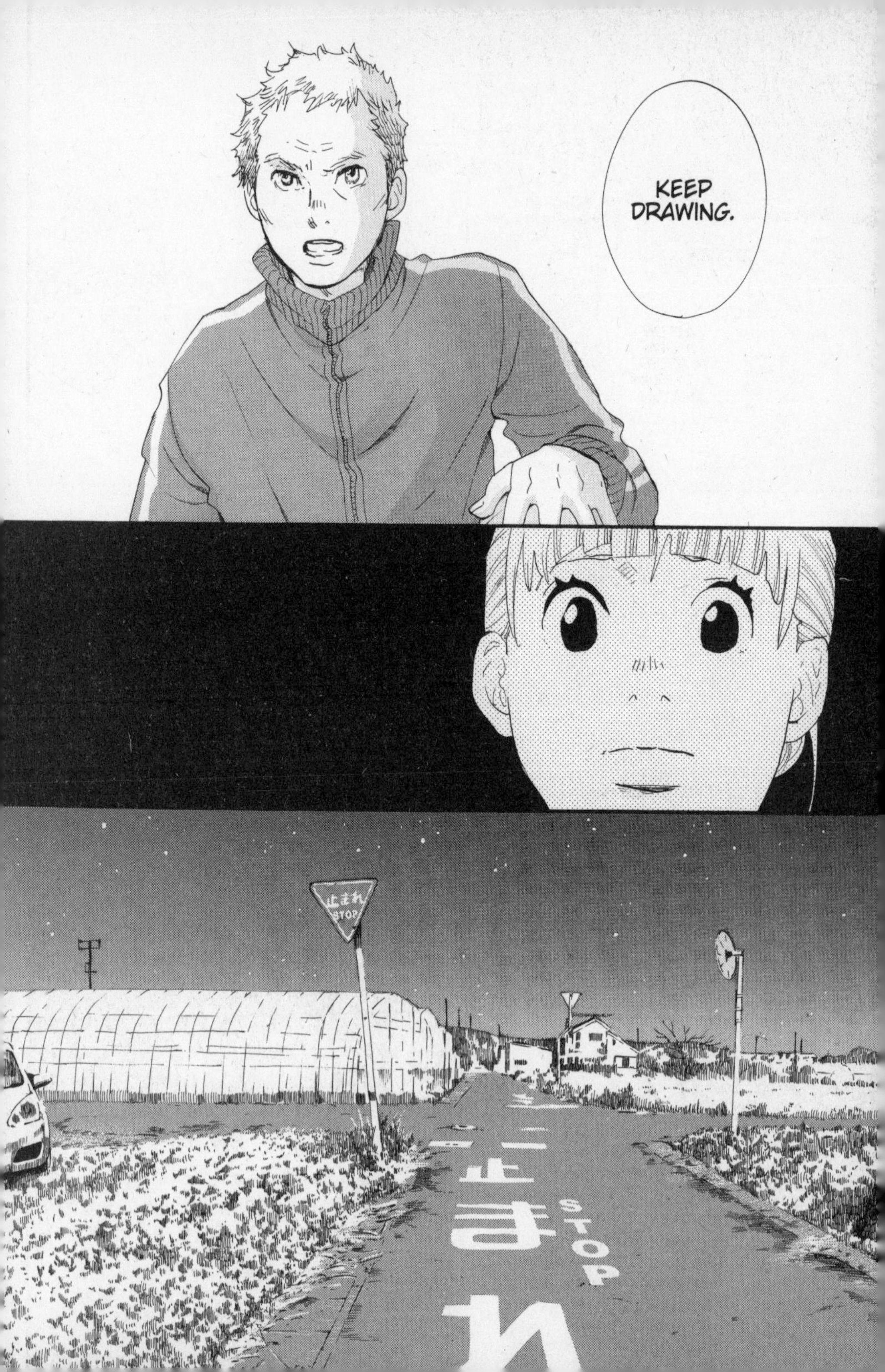
KEEP DRAWING.
止まれ
STOP
止まれ
STOP

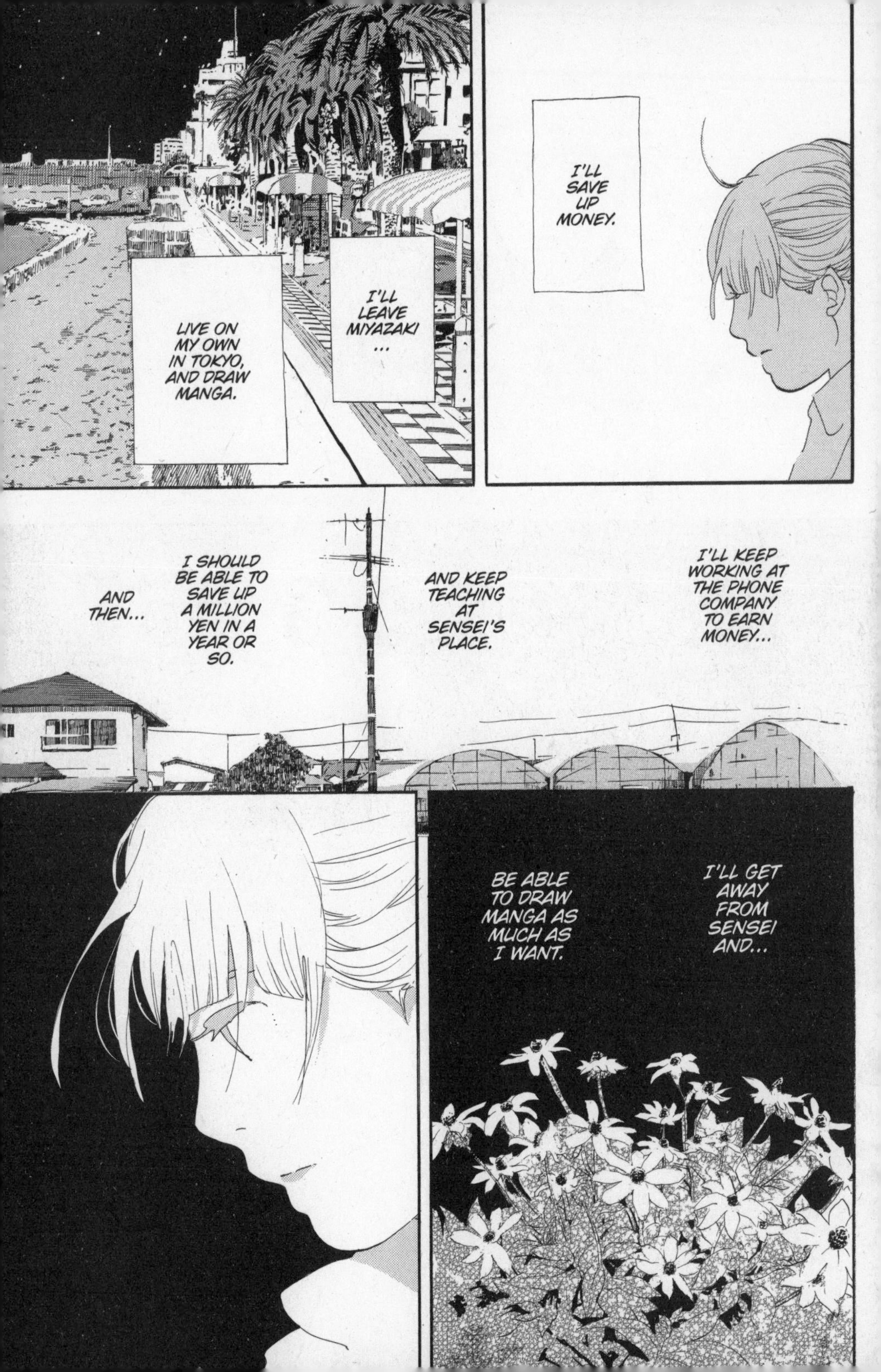
I'LL SAVE UP MONEY.
I'LL LEAVE MIYAZAKI ...
LIVE ON MY OWN IN TOKYO, AND DRAW MANGA.
I'LL KEEP WORKING AT THE PHONE COMPANY TO EARN MONEY...
AND KEEP TEACHING AT SENSEI'S PLACE.
I SHOULD BE ABLE TO SAVE UP A MILLION YEN IN A YEAR OR SO.
AND THEN...
I'LL GET AWAY FROM SENSEI AND...
BE ABLE TO DRAW MANGA AS MUCH AS I WANT.

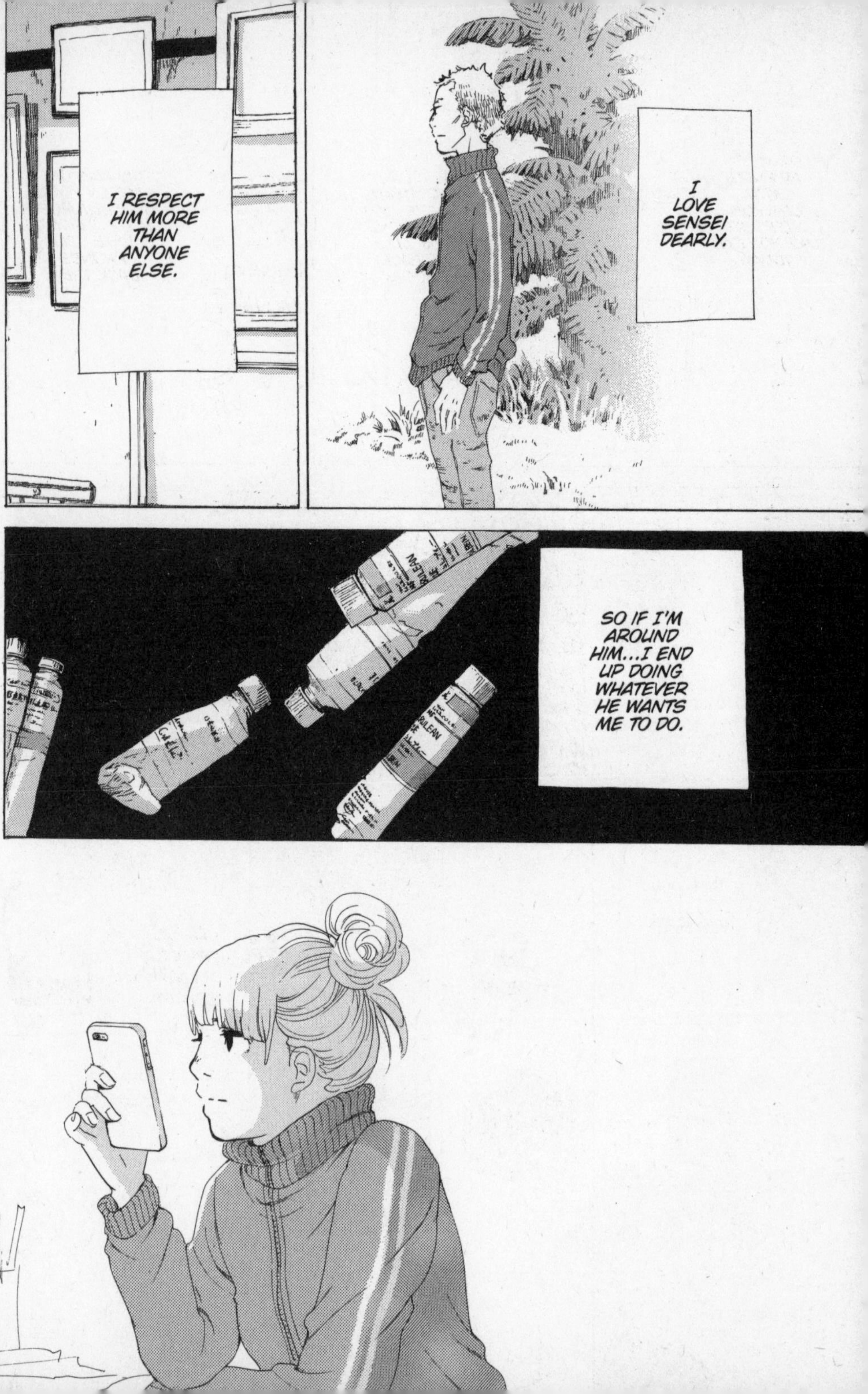
I LOVE SENSEI DEARLY.
I RESPECT HIM MORE THAN ANYONE ELSE.
SO IF I'M AROUND HIM...I END UP DOING WHATEVER HE WANTS ME TO DO.

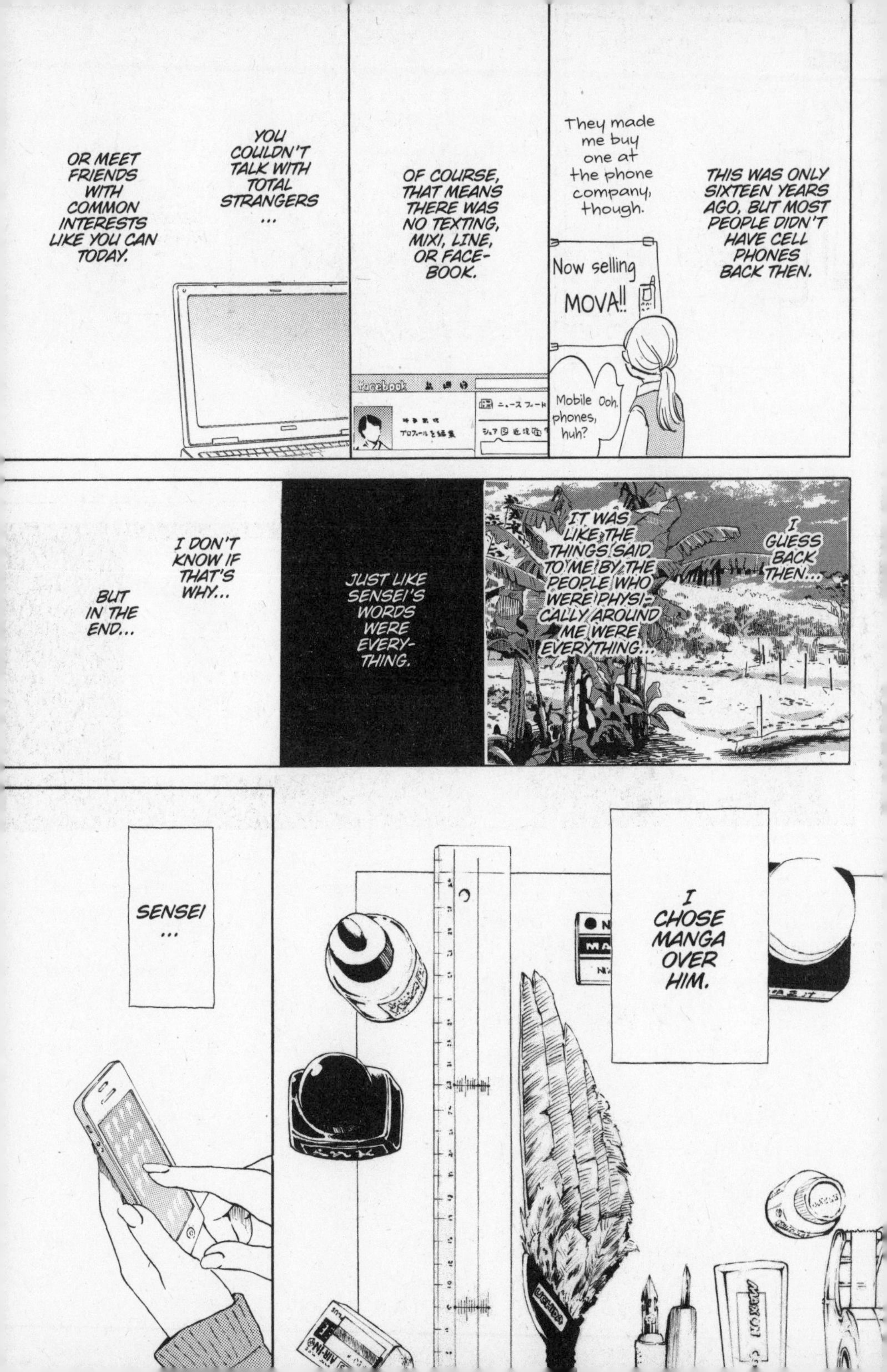
THIS WAS ONLY SIXTEEN YEARS AGO, BUT MOST PEOPLE DIDN'T HAVE CELL PHONES BACK THEN.
They made me buy one at the phone company, though.
Now selling MOVA!!
Ooh.
Mobile phones, huh?
OF COURSE, THAT MEANS THERE WAS NO TEXTING, MIXI, LINE, OR FACE-BOOK.
facebook
YOU COULDN'T TALK WITH TOTAL STRANGERS...
OR MEET FRIENDS WITH COMMON INTERESTS LIKE YOU CAN TODAY.
I GUESS BACK THEN...
IT WAS LIKE THE THINGS SAID TO ME BY THE PEOPLE WHO WERE PHYSI-CALLY AROUND ME WERE EVERYTHING...
JUST LIKE SENSEI'S WORDS WERE EVERY-THING.
I DON'T KNOW IF THAT'S WHY...
BUT IN THE END...
I CHOSE MANGA OVER HIM.
SENSEI...

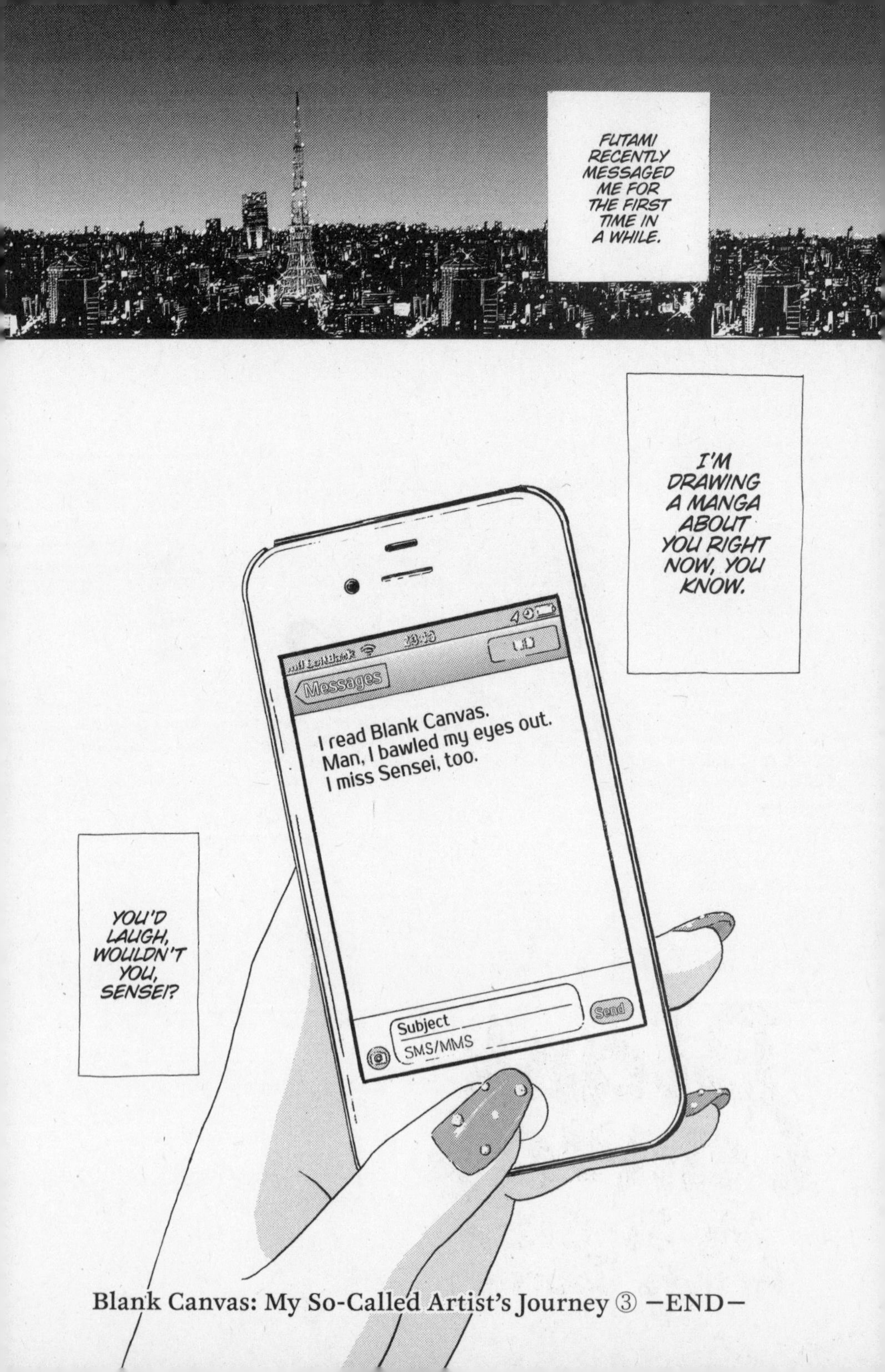
FUTAMI RECENTLY MESSAGED ME FOR THE FIRST TIME IN A WHILE.
I'M DRAWING A MANGA ABOUT YOU RIGHT NOW, YOU KNOW.
Messages
I read Blank Canvas.
Man, I bawled my eyes out.
I miss Sensei, too.
Subject
SMS/MMS
Send
YOU'D LAUGH, WOULDN'T YOU, SENSEI?

Blank Canvas: My So-Called Artist's Journey ③ —END—

Blank
Canvas
My So-Called
Artist's Journey

Blank Canvas

My So-Called Artist's Journey

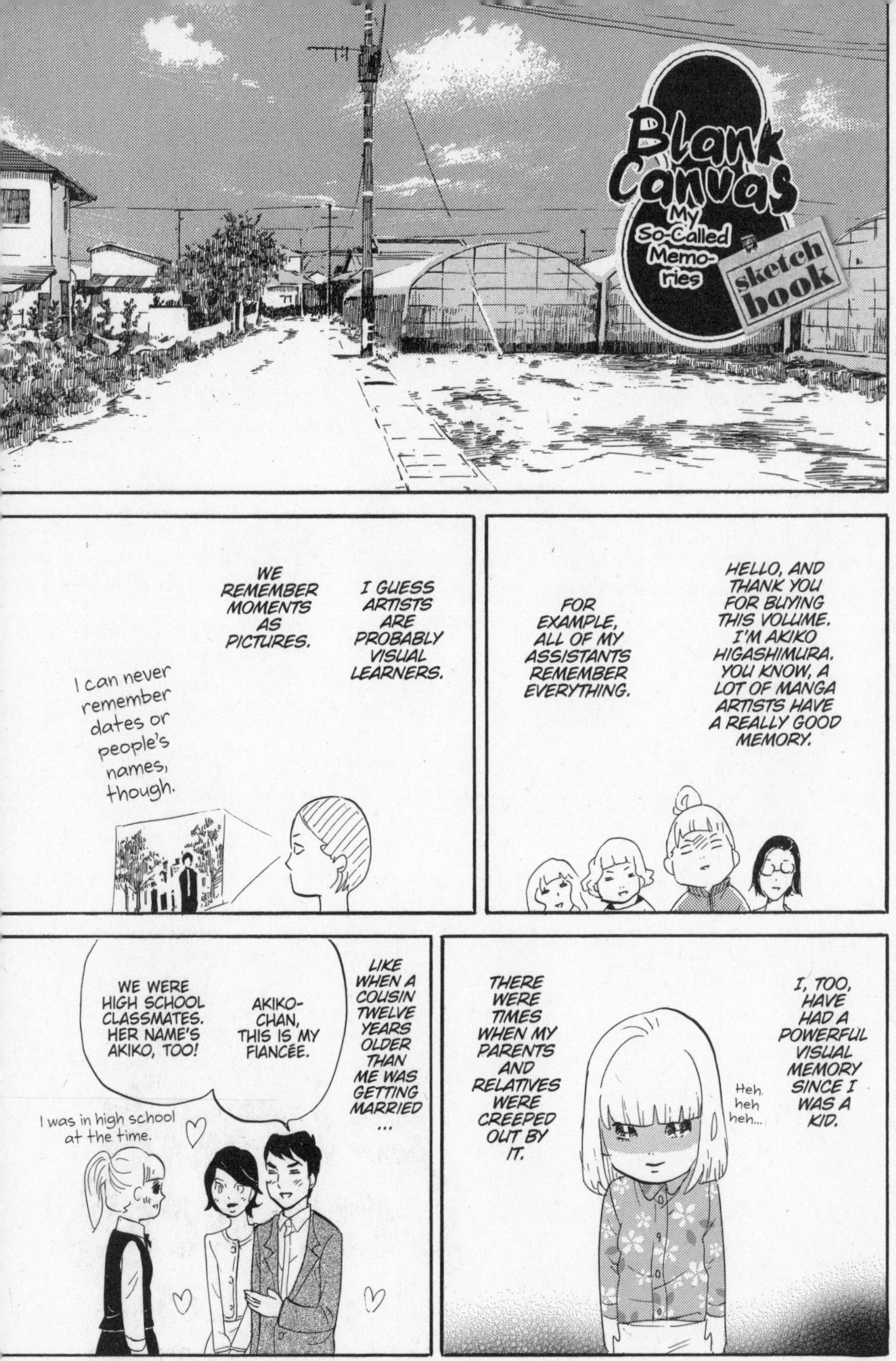
Blank Canvas
My So-Called Memories
sketch book
HELLO, AND THANK YOU FOR BUYING THIS VOLUME. I'M AKIKO HIGASHIMURA. YOU KNOW, A LOT OF MANGA ARTISTS HAVE A REALLY GOOD MEMORY.
FOR EXAMPLE, ALL OF MY ASSISTANTS REMEMBER EVERYTHING.
I GUESS ARTISTS ARE PROBABLY VISUAL LEARNERS.
WE REMEMBER MOMENTS AS PICTURES.
I can never remember dates or people's names, though.
I, TOO, HAVE HAD A POWERFUL VISUAL MEMORY SINCE I WAS A KID.
Heh heh heh...
THERE WERE TIMES WHEN MY PARENTS AND RELATIVES WERE CREEPED OUT BY IT.
LIKE WHEN A COUSIN TWELVE YEARS OLDER THAN ME WAS GETTING MARRIED...
AKIKO-CHAN, THIS IS MY FIANCÉE.
WE WERE HIGH SCHOOL CLASSMATES. HER NAME'S AKIKO, TOO!
I was in high school at the time.

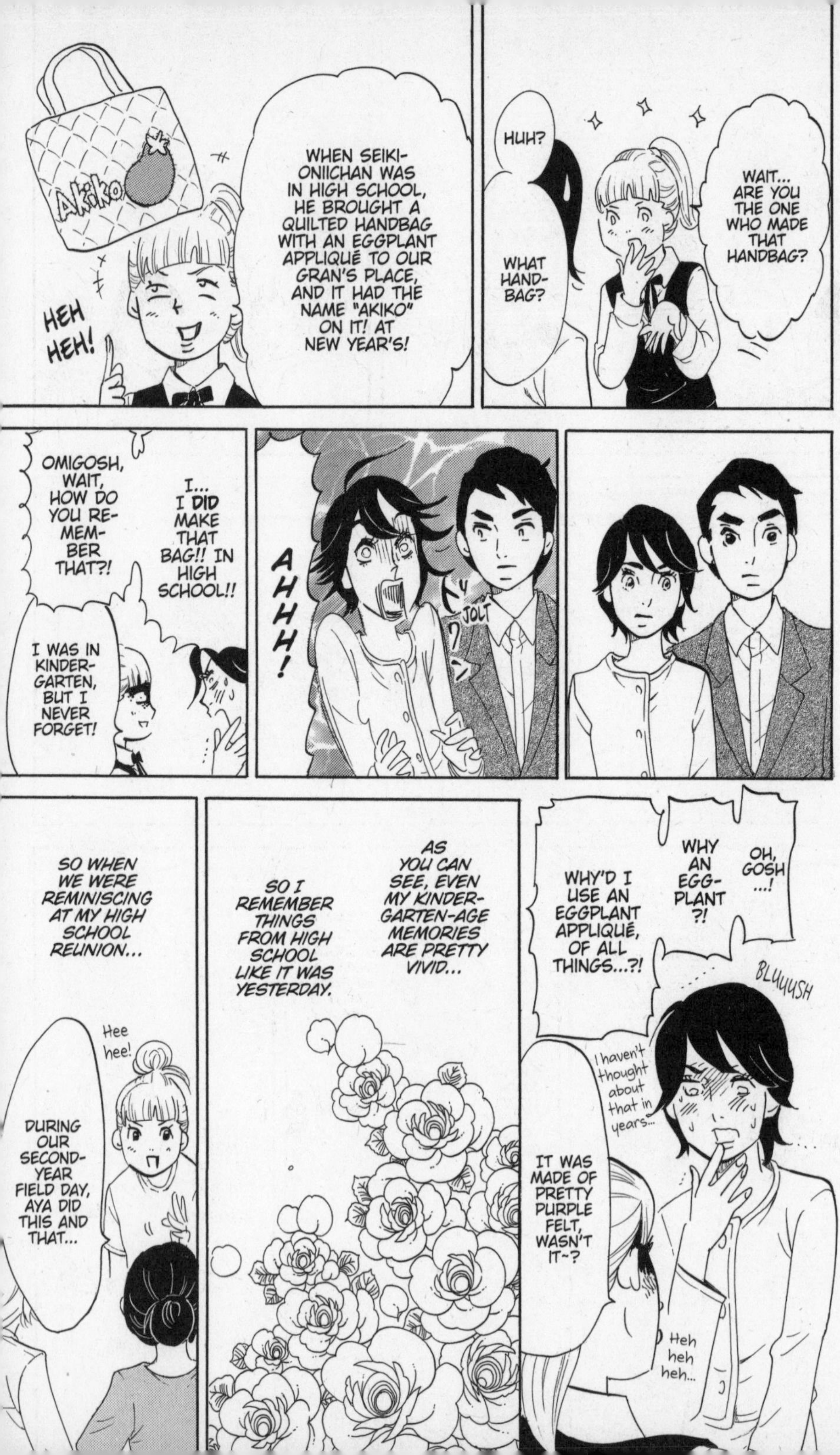
WAIT... ARE YOU THE ONE WHO MADE THAT HANDBAG?
HUH?
WHAT HANDBAG?
WHEN SEIKI-ONIICHAN WAS IN HIGH SCHOOL, HE BROUGHT A QUILTED HANDBAG WITH AN EGGPLANT APPLIQUÉ TO OUR GRAN'S PLACE, AND IT HAD THE NAME "AKIKO" ON IT! AT NEW YEAR'S!
Akiko
HEH HEH!
AHHHH!
JOLT
I... I DID MAKE THAT BAG!! IN HIGH SCHOOL!!
OMIGOSH, WAIT, HOW DO YOU REMEMBER THAT?!
I WAS IN KINDERGARTEN, BUT I NEVER FORGET!
OH, GOSH...!
WHY AN EGGPLANT?!
WHY'D I USE AN EGGPLANT APPLIQUÉ, OF ALL THINGS...?!
BLUUUSH
I haven't thought about that in years...
IT WAS MADE OF PRETTY PURPLE FELT, WASN'T IT~?
Heh heh heh...
AS YOU CAN SEE, EVEN MY KINDERGARTEN-AGE MEMORIES ARE PRETTY VIVID...
SO I REMEMBER THINGS FROM HIGH SCHOOL LIKE IT WAS YESTERDAY.
SO WHEN WE WERE REMINISCING AT MY HIGH SCHOOL REUNION...
Hee hee!
DURING OUR SECOND-YEAR FIELD DAY, AYA DID THIS AND THAT...

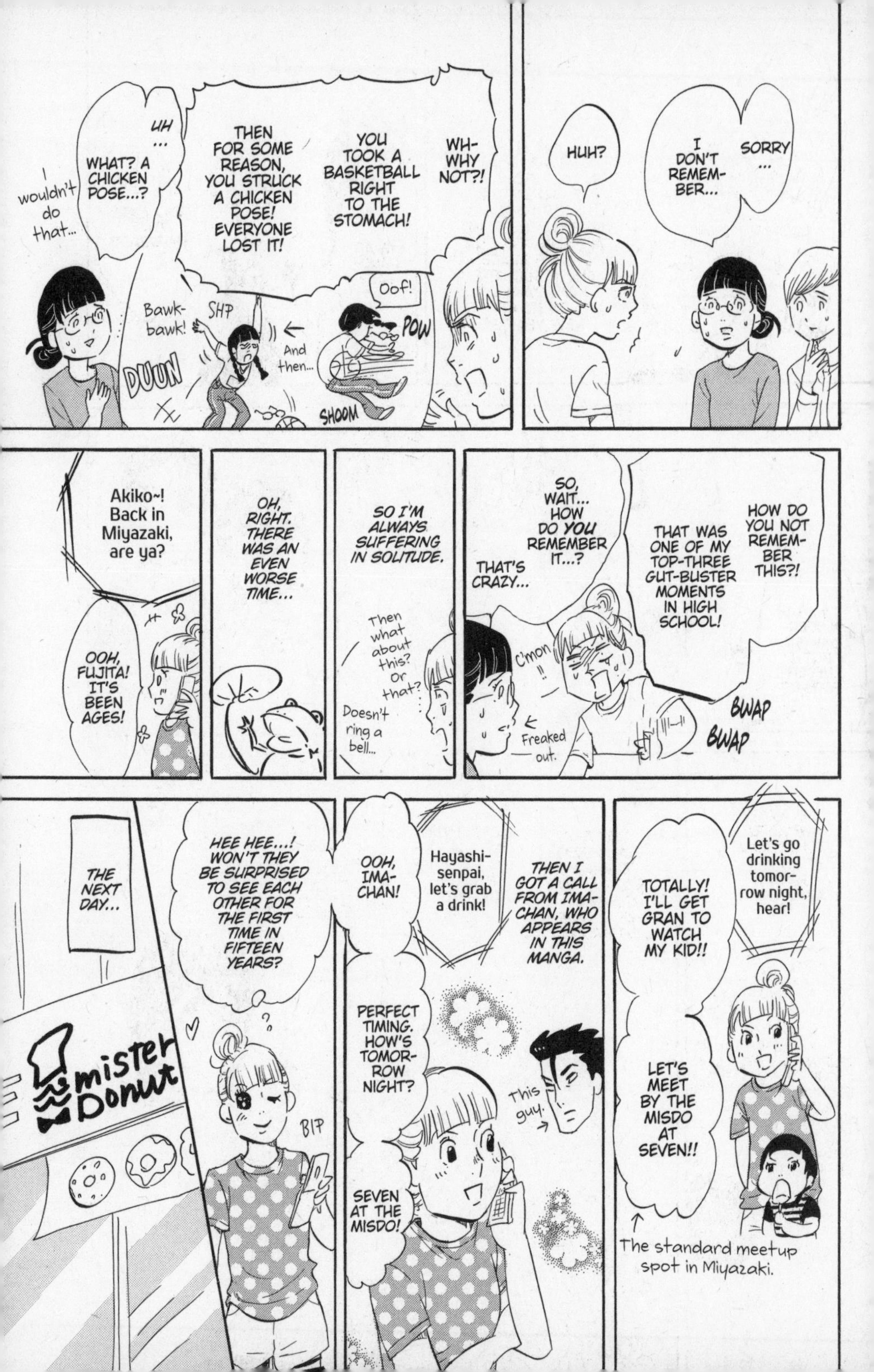

SORRY...
I DON'T REMEMBER...
HUH?
WH-WHY NOT?!
YOU TOOK A BASKETBALL RIGHT TO THE STOMACH!
THEN FOR SOME REASON, YOU STRUCK A CHICKEN POSE! EVERYONE LOST IT!
UH...
WHAT? A CHICKEN POSE...?
I wouldn't do that...
Oof!
POW
And then...
SHOOM
SHP
Bawk-bawk!
DUUN
HOW DO YOU NOT REMEMBER THIS?!
THAT WAS ONE OF MY TOP-THREE GUT-BUSTER MOMENTS IN HIGH SCHOOL!
SO, WAIT... HOW DO YOU REMEMBER IT...?
THAT'S CRAZY...
BWAP
BWAP
C'mon!!
Freaked out.
SO I'M ALWAYS SUFFERING IN SOLITUDE.
Then what about this? Or that?
Doesn't ring a bell...
OH, RIGHT. THERE WAS AN EVEN WORSE TIME...
Akiko~! Back in Miyazaki, are ya?
OOH, FUJITA! IT'S BEEN AGES!
Let's go drinking tomorrow night, hear!
TOTALLY! I'LL GET GRAN TO WATCH MY KID!!
LET'S MEET BY THE MISDO AT SEVEN!!
The standard meetup spot in Miyazaki.
THEN I GOT A CALL FROM IMA-CHAN, WHO APPEARS IN THIS MANGA.
Hayashi-senpai, let's grab a drink!
OOH, IMA-CHAN!
PERFECT TIMING. HOW'S TOMORROW NIGHT?
This guy.
SEVEN AT THE MISDO!
HEE HEE...! WON'T THEY BE SURPRISED TO SEE EACH OTHER FOR THE FIRST TIME IN FIFTEEN YEARS?
BIP
THE NEXT DAY...
mister Donut

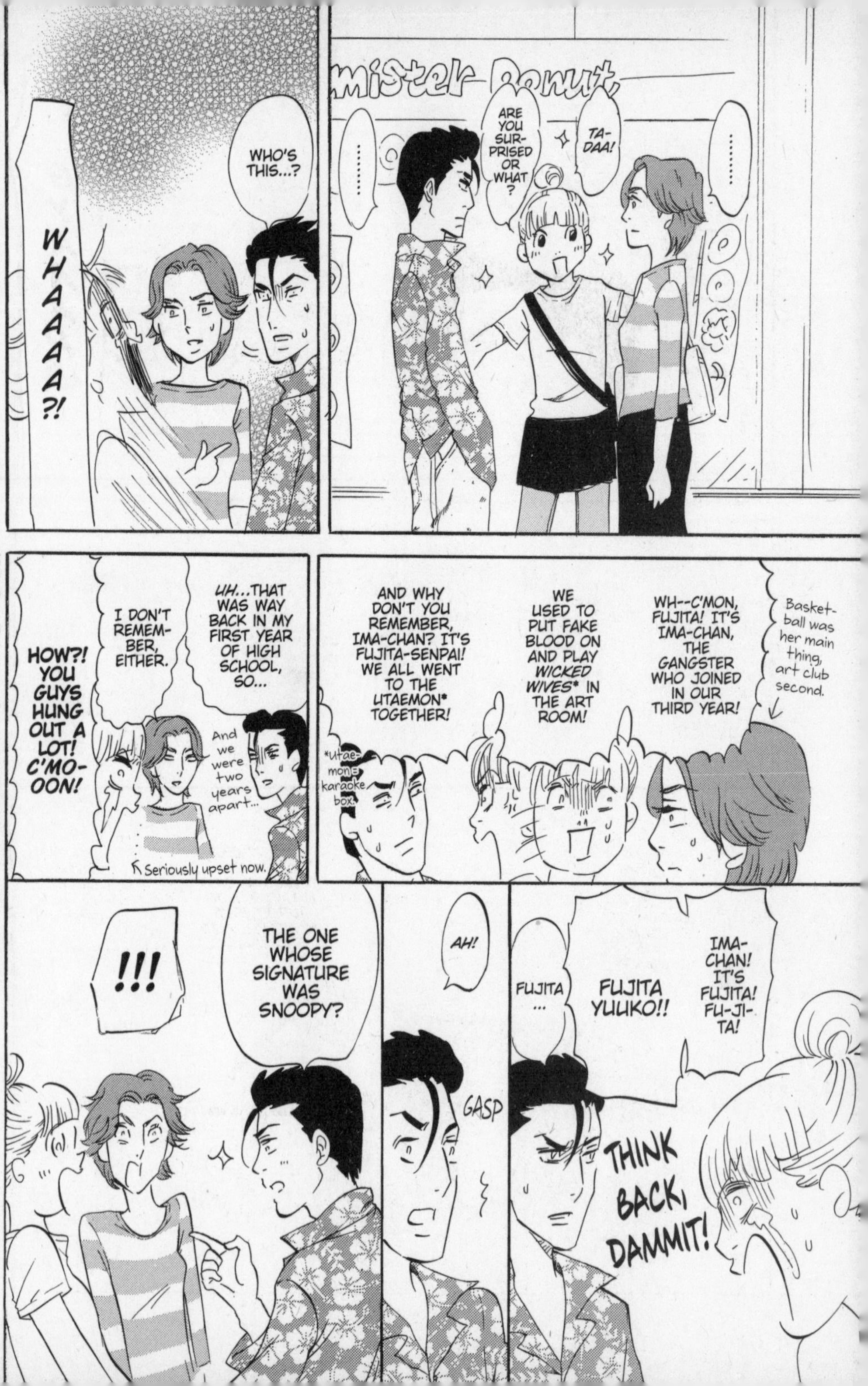
mister Donut
TA-DAA!
ARE YOU SURPRISED OR WHAT?
......
......
WHO'S THIS...?
WHAAAAA?!
......
Basketball was her main thing, art club second.
WH--C'MON, FUJITA! IT'S IMA-CHAN, THE GANGSTER WHO JOINED IN OUR THIRD YEAR!
WE USED TO PUT FAKE BLOOD ON AND PLAY *WICKED WIVES** IN THE ART ROOM!
AND WHY DON'T YOU REMEMBER, IMA-CHAN? IT'S FUJITA-SENPAI! WE ALL WENT TO THE UTAEMON* TOGETHER!
*utaemon = karaoke box.
UH...THAT WAS WAY BACK IN MY FIRST YEAR OF HIGH SCHOOL, SO...
And we were two years apart...
I DON'T REMEMBER, EITHER.
HOW?! YOU GUYS HUNG OUT A LOT! C'MOOON!
Seriously upset now.
IMA-CHAN! IT'S FUJITA! FU-JI-TA!
FUJITA YUUKO!!
FUJITA ...
THINK BACK, DAMMIT!
AH!
GASP
THE ONE WHOSE SIGNATURE WAS SNOOPY?
!!!

*GokuOnna/Gokudou no Onnatachi (Wicked Wives) is a 1986 yakuza movie.

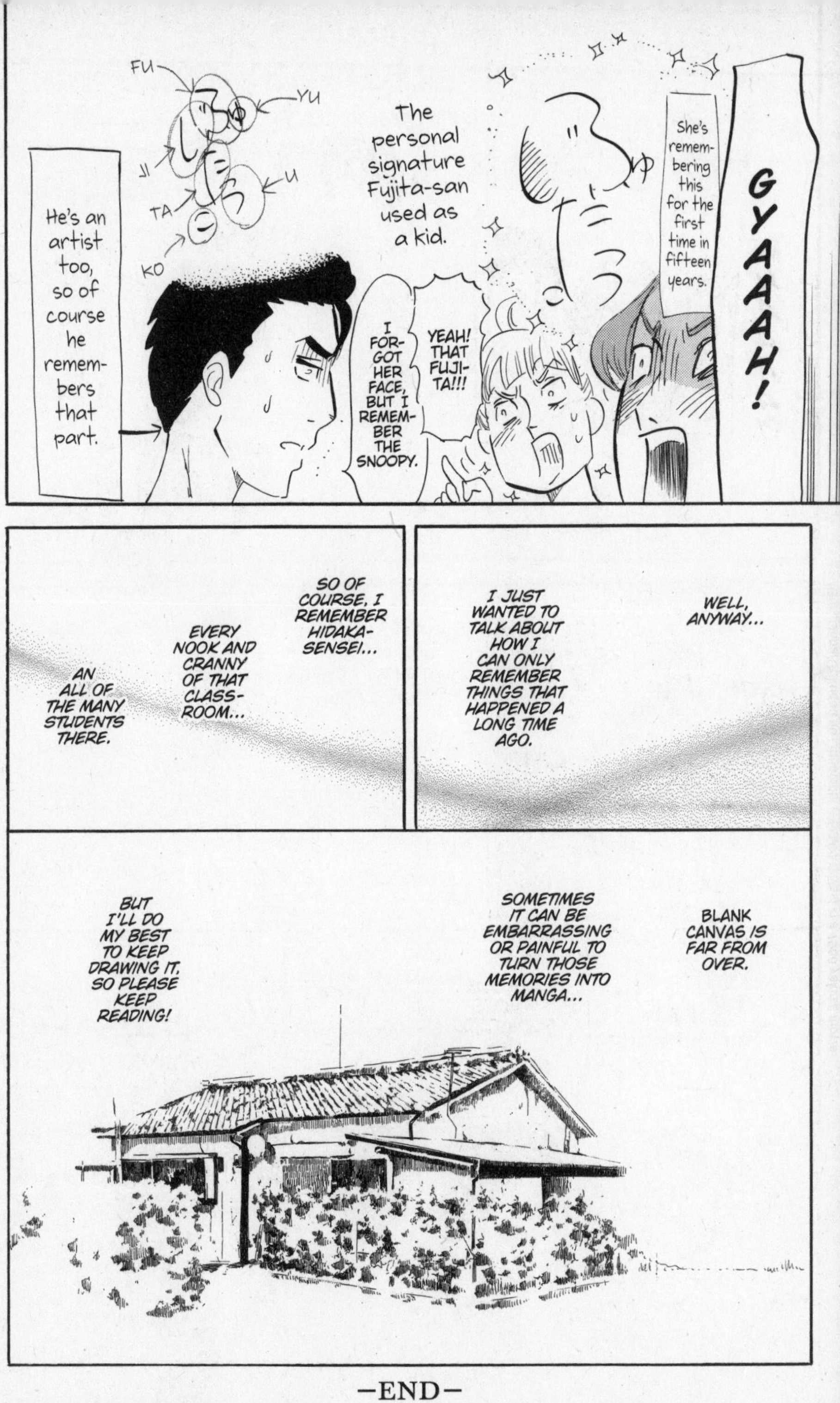
She's remembering this for the first time in fifteen years.
GYAAAH!
YEAH! THAT FUJITA!!!
The personal signature Fujita-san used as a kid.
FU
YU
JI
U
TA
KO
I FORGOT HER FACE, BUT I REMEMBER THE SNOOPY.
He's an artist too, so of course he remembers that part.
WELL, ANYWAY...
I JUST WANTED TO TALK ABOUT HOW I CAN ONLY REMEMBER THINGS THAT HAPPENED A LONG TIME AGO.
SO OF COURSE, I REMEMBER HIDAKA-SENSEI...
EVERY NOOK AND CRANNY OF THAT CLASSROOM...
AN ALL OF THE MANY STUDENTS THERE.
BLANK CANVAS IS FAR FROM OVER.
SOMETIMES IT CAN BE EMBARRASSING OR PAINFUL TO TURN THOSE MEMORIES INTO MANGA...
BUT I'LL DO MY BEST TO KEEP DRAWING IT, SO PLEASE KEEP READING!

—END—

SEVEN SEAS ENTERTAINMENT PRESENTS

Blank Canvas
My So-Called Artist's Journey

story and art by AKIKO HIGASHIMURA VOLUME 3

TRANSLATION
Jenny McKeon

ADAPTATION
Ysabet MacFarlane

LETTERING AND LAYOUT
Lys Blakeslee
Katie Blakeslee

COVER DESIGN
KC Fabellon

PROOFREADER
Kurestin Armada
Danielle King

EDITOR
Jenn Grunigen

PRODUCTION MANAGER
Lissa Pattillo

MANAGING EDITOR
Julie Davis

EDITOR-IN-CHIEF
Adam Arnold

PUBLISHER
Jason DeAngelis

First published in Japan in 2011 by SHUEISHA Inc., Tokyo.
English translation rights arranged by SHUEISHA Inc.
through TOHAN CORPORATION, Tokyo.

Seven Seas press and purchase enquiries can be sent to Marketing Manager Lianne Sentar at press@gomanga.com. Information regarding the distribution and purchase of digital editions is available from Digital Manager CK Russell at digital@gomanga.com.

ISBN: 978-1-64275-071-3

Printed in Canada

First Printing: November 2019

10 9 8 7 6 5 4 3 2 1

FOLLOW US ONLINE: *www.sevenseasentertainment.com*

READING DIRECTIONS

This book reads from ***right to left***, Japanese style. If this is your first time reading manga, you start reading from the top right panel on each page and take it from there. If you get lost, just follow the numbered diagram here. It may seem backwards at first, but you'll get the hang of it! Have fun!!

1
2
3
4
5
6
7
8
9

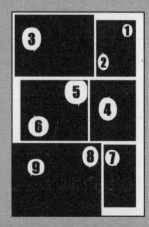

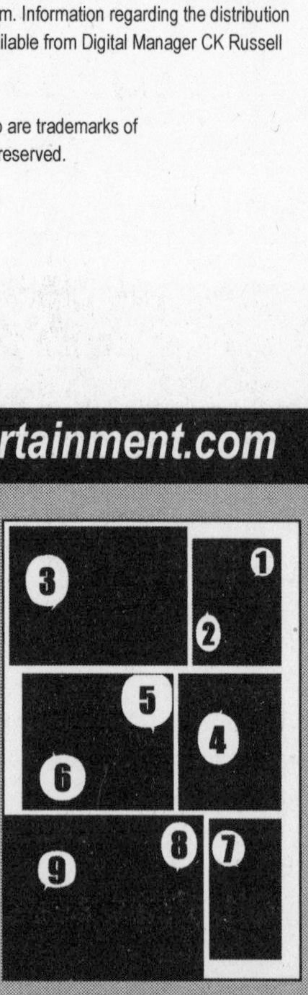